Women in the Middle East

Women in the Middle East

PAST AND PRESENT

Nikki R. Keddie

PRINCETON UNIVERSITY PRESS

PRINCETON AND OXFORD

Library of Congress Cataloging-in-Publication Data

Keddie, Nikki R.
Women in the Middle East : past and present / Nikki R. Keddie.
p. cm.
Includes bibliographical references and index.
ISBN-13: 978-0-691-11610-5 (clothbound : alk. paper)
ISBN-10: 0-691-11610-5 (clothbound : alk. paper)
ISBN-13 978-0-691-12863-4 (pbk. : alk. paper)
ISBN-10 0-691-12863-4 (pbk.)
1. Women—Middle East—History. 2. Feminism—Middle East—History. I. Title.
HQ1726.5.K43   2007
305.40956—dc22——2006008911

British Library Cataloging-in-Publication Data is available

This book has been composed in Sabon

Printed on acid-free paper. ∞

pup.princeton.edu

Printed in the United States of America

10 9 8 7 6 5 4

FOR PARVIN PAIDAR 1949–2005

who illuminated our minds and our lives all too briefly

Contents

Contents of Book One

WOMEN IN THE MIDDLE EAST: A HISTORY

Illustrations

All photos (except 6a and b) were taken by Nikki Keddie 1973–88; Iran photos but one are pre-1979 revolution. Those printed from Kodachrome slides are so labeled. The others are from black-and-white prints. All photos are subject to copyright rules regarding reprinting.

Preface

THIS BOOK, like several of my previous volumes, developed differently from what I had originally imagined. It started as a collection of my articles about women, and was accepted as such by Princeton University Press. When I looked over what was to be the lead item, the fifty-four-page "Women in the Middle East since the Rise of Islam," in *Women's History in Global Perspective*, ed. Bonnie G. Smith (Urbana: University of Illinois Press, 2005), I realized it would be far better and more useful if I lengthened it. Not quite two years later, after much new reading and writing, I finished a section that had more than quadrupled in length and become a book of its own. It is now Book One of this volume, "Middle Eastern Women: A History." This book takes advantage of the ever-expanding explosion since the 1970s of research and writing on Middle Eastern women, and for the first time in a single historical work gives some coverage to all the countries of the Middle East and North Africa. Reflecting the state of research and public interest, it gives the most emphasis and space to the past century, but tries to see contemporary events against a long historical background.

After writing this book, I decided to omit two of the proposed already-published articles and chapters and only include those that covered broad ideas and issues that shed further light on questions discussed in Book One. The much-regretted death of Parvin Paidar, whose work has been of huge help and inspiration to me and to many of us, reminded me that we had coauthored an article covering one such broad issue, and I added this article to my singly authored chapters.

The final, autobiographical section consists of previously published interviews and a current addition, and shows that questions of gender discrimination, protest, and repression are not limited to women in the Global South.

After finishing this volume, I decided to put in the effort needed to include high-quality reproductions of photographs I had taken in the Middle East in the 1970s and 1980s (all photos in the book, except the last two—of me—are mine). I first became a photographer as part of my research. In 1973–74 I had a year's sabbatical in Iran, and after arriving there I narrowed my research topic to a social history approach to handicrafts and carpets. This never resulted in a book, but did give me contact with, and some understanding of, ordinary women and men throughout Iran and later in other parts of the Middle East. For this project I saw I would need photos, and, having come without a camera, I had to delegate my parents to buy one and give it to Jerome Clinton, who was taking a trip to the United States. After a very brief lesson from a professional photographer, I included photography in my research, which involved travel to every province of Iran and among every major ethnic group and several nomadic tribes—contacts I extended or renewed during subsequent summer stays in Iran. Some of the photos included in this volume date from those stays and some from a joint project with Lois Beck among the Qashqai people of Iran, which became an exhibit and illustrated catalog. All the Iran photos but one predate the 1979 Iranian revolution. In the 1970s and 1980s I traveled to most of the major countries of the Middle East as part of a study of religion and politics, and some of the photos date from that travel. In 1983 Jonathan Friedlander commissioned me to take color slides in Yemen, and my photos along with those of several other photographers were included in a major exhibit and book about Yemenis in Yemen and the United States. I have always taken more color slides than black-and-white photos, but most of the photos I chose for this book were from black-and-white originals. My early background in painting no doubt helped me in photography, and I have had various smaller exhibits and sales in addition to those mentioned here. Readers are advised that the photos are copyright and subject to permission for reproduction.

I note that certain kinds of dress in the photos should not be called "traditional." Dress, like other social and cultural practices, is in constant flux. For example, the *jallaba*s and transparent partial face veils on the photo "Women on the road to Marrakesh," widely worn by Moroccan women, were formerly only a men's garment, while women wore a simple rectangular covering outdoors. Their adoption dates from pre–World War II nationalists, who found them more convenient and liberating. The face veil on the book's cover on the woman of Jebel Raima, Yemen, was a recent adoption, when the local religious leader said that women, until then unveiled, should veil after the new modern road brought many strangers to town. It is one sign of the spread of veiling in the countryside in many parts of the Middle East, even before the rise of Islamism, which I already noted in the introduction to *Women in the Muslim World* (1978).

In getting excellent copies of my slides and black-and-white prints to the Press, I am most grateful to my dear brother David Ragozin, who spent a week at my condo installing and perfecting the copying procedures of the latest HP all-in-one, and also to Research Assistant Michael Benson, who, in consultation with me, spent many hours and displayed outstanding talent in producing the final versions of the photos sent to Princeton University Press. There is no manipulation in the photos beyond occasional cropping and adjusting of the contrast.

My debt to others over the many years I studied relevant topics is immense, and for my twentieth-century work is noted in previous books. I am especially grateful to Beth Baron for reading and commenting on the whole of Book One in draft, and to the following persons for reading parts of the manuscript and making useful comments: Leslie Peirce, Homa Hoodfar, Nancy Gallagher, Elizabeth Thompson, and Ehud Toledano. Help in answering questions and getting me needed materials came from Janet Afary, Haleh Esfandiari, Judith Tucker, Ziba Mir-Hosseini, Sherifa Zuhur, Julia Clancy-Smith, Dror Ze'evi, Mounira Charrad, Rudi Matthee, Houchang Chehabi, and Jasamin Rostam-Kolayi. Azita Karim-khany Fatheree, another Research Assistant, provided much aid, including putting together the Book One bibliography. The two Keddie-Balzan fellows for 2005–6, Nayereh Tohidi and Holly Shissler, gave tremendous help in reading parts of the manuscript and doing some research to answer remaining questions. Money from my 2004 Balzan Prize was useful in getting the equipment that facilitated this project. Special thanks are due to Tom Mertes, who continues to give me crucial voluntary help in obtaining needed materials, often at very short notice.

My relations with Brigitta van Rheinberg, history editor at Princeton University Press, were unusually pleasant and productive, and I am especially grateful to her for her sound advice and patience during the time-consuming changes in plan for this book. Others at Princeton Press, notably my copyeditor, Lauren Lepow, have been uniformly intelligent and helpful.

In a work using so many languages and different systems for well-known names I decided to simplify transliteration, to omit initial and terminal 'ains and hamzas, and sometimes to follow unscientific name spellings that are well known in the West. For Turkish I use standard modern Turkish spellings. I made very minor changes in some of the re-printed articles in the interest of fact, style, and consistency of transliteration throughout the volume.

I am aware that there is much more that could and should be done on the topics I have covered, but hope that bringing together basic facts and thoughts regarding what is now known may be useful to a wide public. The current salience of topics like the few female suicide bombers, or the special problems of women in countries suffering war or occupation, should encourage people to learn more about the women involved and the forces that have created their current situation.

Santa Monica, California
March 2006

Most essays in Books Two and Three of this volume were previously published. In Book Two, Part 1, "Shifting Boundaries in Sex and Gender," appeared as "Introduction: Deciphering Middle Eastern Women's History," in *Women in Middle Eastern History: Shifting Boundaries in Sex and Gender*, ed. Nikki R. Keddie and Beth Baron (New Haven: Yale University Press, 1991), 1–22. Part 2, "Scholarship, Relativism, and Universalism," appeared as "The Study of Muslim Women in the Middle East: Achievements and Remaining Problems," in *Harvard Middle Eastern and Islamic Review* 6 (2000–2001): 26–52. Part 3, "Women in the Limelight: Recent Books on Middle Eastern Women's History since 1800," appeared as "Women in the Limelight: Some Recent Books on Middle Eastern Women's History," in the *International Journal of Middle East Studies* 34 (2002): 553–73. Part 4, "Problems in the Study of Middle Eastern Women," appeared under the same title in the *International Journal of Middle East Studies* 10 (1979): 225–40. Part 5, "Sexuality and Shi'i Social Protest in Iran" (coauthored with Parvin Paidar [Nahid Yeganeh]), appeared under the same title with Paidar's pseudonym, Nahid Yeganeh, in *Shi'ism and Social Protest*, ed. Juan R. I. Cole and Nikki R. Keddie (New Haven: Yale University Press, 1986), 108–36. In Book Three, Part 1, "Autobiographical Interview," appeared as "Nikki Keddie," in *Approaches to the History of the Middle East: Interviews with Leading Middle East Historians*, ed. Nancy Elizabeth Gallagher (Reading, UK: Ithaca Press, 1994), 129–49. Thanks to the above copyright holders for permission to republish.

Women in the Middle East

Introduction

THE STUDY of Middle Eastern women, past and present, has developed so rapidly in the past few decades that periodic overviews of the topic are needed to present syntheses of what is currently known and indicate the bases of that knowledge. This book tries to meet some of those needs and features a book-length history of Middle Eastern women. It also includes several essays that elucidate the current state of writing on these women, suggest what is needed to further their study, and analyze what has been accomplished in this field and what remains to be done. In a field of study that is quite new and developing rapidly, it is useful to bring together a summary, based on current knowledge, of the lives, problems, and accomplishments of Middle Eastern women as they have evolved to the present, one that also suggests what approaches might best be utilized to guide future research and writing.

In writing the book-length history, I was struck both by the excellence of many of the monographs and surveys on the subject, and by the difficulty of trying to bring together their results, along with the results of my own primary research and experience, into a narrative history. Middle Eastern women's history has been pursued seriously for only about thirty years, and most of the existing work necessarily deals with limited subjects, so that there are major gaps when one is trying to put together a comprehensive narrative. Also, there are areas for which there appears thus far to be little primary evidence, and areas where authors are very influenced by intellectual or ideological commitments of different kinds. Nonetheless, it appeared worthwhile to try to construct a narrative reflecting what is known today, based largely on the past thirty years of extensive scholarly work in many disciplines, which may be useful for students, scholars, and a broader public.

Apart from the book-length history, the volume includes a selected group of my articles, comprising those that I considered most relevant to the study and analysis of Middle Eastern women. I have not included all the articles and introductions I have authored or coauthored regarding Middle Eastern women, but only those that seemed of most general interest and most relevant to the current book. At the suggestion of my Princeton University Press editor I have retitled some articles to clarify their place in this book, but give the original titles in full references. The region defined as the Middle East in this book goes from Morocco in the West to Afghanistan in the East, comprising lands in which the predominant languages are Arabic, Persian, Turkish, and Pushtu, although not all regions are equally covered in all essays. I do not attempt to cover central Asia to the north or African countries to the south of Morocco or Egypt except when they constitute parts of larger Middle Eastern empires.

Book One consists of the book-length "Women in the Middle East: A History," which utilizes many studies about women past and present that have appeared in recent decades to synthesize an analytic history of the subject from pre-Islamic times to the present. Among its special features is individual coverage of women in most of the many Middle Eastern countries that have come into existence since 1945, most of which have not been the subject of individual narrative historical books or articles. Such individual coverage, however problematic some of the sources still are, is needed, as individual governments differ in laws, in educational, health, and labor policies, and in many cultural and political characteristics. This history also tries to incorporate the best-documented conclusions that result from the many recent studies on a variety of relevant subjects, including analyses of views regarding women in the early Islamic period, assessments of the role of Turks and Mongols, analyses of Ottoman court records, studies of women's rights movements, and works that analyze both favorable factors and obstacles to women's achievement of equality. It also recognizes the scarcity of sources for many periods or questions, and discusses some of the different interpretations of the same materials. The chapter divisions are chronological and, like all chronological divisions, are in some ways arbitrary and do not mean that there was always a major change in all regions of the Middle East after the date of the chapter break. Such factors as the creation of a new religion, massive invasions, and important wars, which mark most of the chapter breaks, do often initiate changes in society, including the position of women, however.

Book Two, "Approaches to the Study of Middle Eastern Women," consists of five parts that provide some of the background, context, and scholarly basis for Book One. They discuss some of the writings on which Book One is based and also present in greater detail the theoretical and historiographical ideas and controversies that underlie it.

Part 1 provides a brief historical overview of women in Middle Eastern society. This overview, "Shifting Boundaries in Sex and Gender," emphasizes the changing social position of women from pre-Islamic times to the present, stressing large trends more than individual cases. It also includes brief critical analyses of some of the views about Middle Eastern women that have been expressed in both the West and the Muslim world. It provides an overall analytic approach to the longer and more detailed history that precedes it. The essay was previously published in 1991, and a few of its statements about the current situation reflect that date.

Part 2, "Scholarship, Relativism, and Universalism," summarizes some of the major trends and works regarding Middle Eastern women, emphasizing their different approaches to women's history and current status. It discusses problems of exaggerated attitudes toward the position of these women, hostile on one side and apologetic on the other, and analyzes the opposite relativist and universalist approaches now found in discussions of the subject. It suggests that there may be a dialectical way that would contextualize historically evolved features now considered positive or negative without appearing to play down or defend practices that are, in today's context, generally seen as unfavorable to women.

Part 3, "Women in the Limelight: Recent Books on Middle Eastern Women's History since 1800," covers a large number of books written on modern Middle Eastern women in the period since 1990, when books on Middle Eastern women's history and society began to be written in significant numbers. The approach is country by country, and reflects the fact that Iran and Egypt have seen the largest number of significant works, with only Iran having an overall narrative history, by Parvin Paidar. The essay emphasizes those fields that have had extensive serious treatment, including the history of women's movements and intellectual activities, and historical works informed by social science considerations and methods. Among them are demography used effectively by Alan Duben and Cem Behar for Istanbul, and sociological consideration of the important conservative influence of tribal and lineage power, by Mounira Charrad and Suad Joseph. The essay also gives brief consideration to social science works not explicitly tied to history, which nonetheless have important information and implications for historians.

Although this essay was written too soon to mention some major book prizes in the field, it is worthy of note that, although Middle Eastern women's studies is a field that has developed only recently, it has now been recognized in other fields as having created books of outstanding quality. Two of the books featured in Part 3 have each won major multiple "best book of the year" prizes not limited to Middle East or women's studies: Elizabeth Thompson's *Colonial Citizens: Republican Rights, Paternal Privilege, and Gender in French Syria and Lebanon* and Mounira Charrad's *States and Women's Rights*. Other works featured in the essay are equally outstanding. There have also been outstanding works written since this essay was published, several of which are cited in Book One.

Part 4, "Problems in the Study of Middle Eastern Women," was first published in 1979. I decided to publish it unchanged after rereading it and seeing, on the one hand, to what a surprising extent the problems it discusses remain problems, and, on the other hand, how some of its

evaluations of the scholarly situation are so changed as to provide a re-
minder of how much important work has been done in the past quarter
century. As this essay requires updating to indicate its current relevance,
I give here more detailed treatment than I do for any other section. The
most obvious current change would be to its statement that "almost no
serious scholarly historical work has been done" on Middle Eastern
women. Regarding the following five suggestions for historians—more
use of anthropology, archaeology, traditional written sources, the arts,
and sources on slaves—some important work has been done, but scholars
could do more with such sources and approaches. This is especially true
of what might be called comparative anthropology—including the suggestion that when similar practices are found among nomads, agriculturalists, or urban dwellers over a huge area from North Africa to Iran, it is
reasonable to assume that these practices go back in time (except for those
that are clearly tied to modernization). It would be important for scholars
to integrate the results of scholarly sociological and anthropological studies into more general books and articles, which could shed analytic light
on popular-class urban, rural, and tribal women who are most often absent from historical sources.

My next point, that scholars have preferred "ideal" sources, is still partially valid, but scholarship has also become more complex and sophisticated. In recent years scholars have made increasing use of material, literary, and statistical evidence about economic and social life. Certain
scholars since this essay was written have emphasized the impossibility
of knowing reality from any written or oral sources. While this view is a
corrective to the literal acceptance of what is recorded in ideal sources, it
can be exaggerated. In all fields of history it is the job of the historian,
based on a weighing of different sources and knowledge of human history,
to judge the probable relation of sources to reality. We certainly know
that the historically documented great wars and battles occurred, and we
know much of what happened; we are on less certain ground in women's
history, but increased documentary evidence means increased certitude or
high probability. This point is relevant to Book One, where scant documentary evidence means that we are unsure about points that come
largely from relatively few and usually "ideal" documents. With time,
however, far more evidence, revision of our views, and greater certainty
regarding some points will emerge.

The growth of interest in women's and gender history has already
brought a substantial increase in documentation and convincing analysis
of documents, as well as contemporary social science studies that are
themselves documents for historians. This can be seen in the recent accel-
eration of publication in an area named in Part 4, "Problems in the Study
of Middle Eastern Women," as "sex," which would today be called "sexu-

ality." Enough research has recently been done for me to include some points about sexuality in my book-length history, although the limited historical research and documentation thus far deal mainly with men and with restricted elites and their male and female slaves. There are, however, implications for women's history in recent studies showing that at least these groups did not respect a number of Quranic and legal rules concerning gender and sexuality, including condemnations of homosexuality and of gender cross-dressing. Scholars have recently undertaken research about past female sexuality, and also studies covering contemporary female sexuality, based largely on interviews of numbers of women or on personal experiences.

Part 4's point about the inadequacy of census figures regarding women, especially with regard to women employed, unemployed, and in the labor force, remains, unfortunately, valid, although several censuses have improved their mode of collection. The main result is that all three of these categories are still understated for women, and it remains questionable, for example, whether the high figures the Turkish census gives for women working in agriculture really mean that many more women are doing such work in Turkey than elsewhere, though the number who are paid wages may be greater. There have been more sample studies and individual projects, most of which show up the inadequacy of census categories and give more credible results.

Part 5, "Sexuality and Shi'i Social Protest in Iran," was coauthored with the late and profoundly missed scholar of Iranian women Parvin Paidar, who was then using the pseudonym Nahid Yeganeh. The sections written by each author are clearly noted. The article presents some of the special history of Shi'i law and practice regarding women, and analyzes the relations of contemporary Iranian Shi'ism to women and sexuality.

The final Book, "Autobiographical Recollections," includes previously published interviews by Nancy Gallagher and Farzaneh Milani, edited in a book by Nancy Gallagher, supplemented by a brief personal essay noting some dramatic incidents involving my political and gendered past. My recollections tell of my changing attitudes toward, and involvement in, women's studies, and also give some details about my scholarly, political, and personal life that those who have heard or read them have found interesting and relevant. It is, among other things, an indication that certain problems for women are not unique to women in the Muslim world. At the end is a bibliography of my works since I last published one in 1995.

While it is unusual to combine a book-length manuscript with surrounding articles, I hope that the interconnections of these items, which shed additional light on one another, make it a worthwhile endeavor.

BOOK ONE

Women in the Middle East: A History

Issues in Studying Middle Eastern Women's History

THE HISTORY OF WOMEN in the Middle East has been intensively studied for only about two decades. While the 1930s and 1940s saw a flurry of works about early Islamic women's history, followed by a few more general works, years passed before the revival of women's studies on the Middle East in recent decades, a revival due in part to the rebirth of women's movements. Books and articles from Western and Middle Eastern authors have appeared in a growing stream, reflecting an intensive interest in Middle Eastern women in all areas of social science and the humanities. The Middle East is here taken to cover the area of the predominantly Arabic-speaking countries of Asia and North Africa, predominantly Persian-speaking Iran, mixed-language Afghanistan, and predominantly Turkish-speaking Turkey, with some coverage of neighboring areas. As past states and empires did not conform to modern borders, some of the discussion will be of larger or smaller territories.

Historians must face problems of sources that are more difficult for the past than for the present, especially for nonelite groups, including women. There is scarce documentation concerning women from pre-Islamic times until about the fourteenth century C.E., which, along with the controversial nature of much documentation, means that what is written about these periods is often more speculative than are writings about recent times. Few extant texts about the Middle East were written before the third Islamic century, and until recently texts overwhelmingly reflect views of elite men about women, rather than direct material about how women lived and thought. Regarding interpretation of texts, besides arguments among scholars, many Muslims have an approach to the Quran not shared by non-Muslims. Believing Muslims regard the Quran as the literal word of God, and many attribute inerrancy to what they consider strongly documented sayings of the Prophet Muhammad, known as Traditions (*hadith*s). Only since the late nineteenth century have a significant number of modernizing Muslims distinguished between the inerrancy of the Quran and the possible fallibility of some Traditions previously judged as sound. A number of such Traditions are hostile to women, as are several sayings attributed to the first Shi'i imam, Ali. This distinction and new interpretations of the Quran have led many Muslims and non-Muslims to point out that most premodern interpretations of the Quran were significantly more patriarchal than is the literal Quranic text, which contains none of the misogyny of some Traditions.

Interpretations of early Middle Eastern women's history must deal with a ubiquitous emphasis on Arabia and the initial decades of Islam, even though evidence is mounting of the importance of other regions and factors. As in other religions, the meaning of scripture has been rendered differently in different times and places. Over the centuries the words of the Quran and hadiths have been interpreted in ways that are in accord with the beliefs and mores of the time of interpretation. Today Muslims who believe in gender equality often interpret the Quran as supporting such equality. In past centuries the opposite trend—to interpret the Quran as far more male supremacist than its text supports and to emphasize gender-inegalitarian Traditions—was often dominant, and still is among many conservative Muslims. Today new interpretations of the Quran are widely accepted as an important means to further gender-egalitarian laws and programs in Muslim states and communities. Hence scholars who see the Quran as reflecting a reforming but not egalitarian view toward women, and as influenced by its times, may encounter arguments from believers who say the Quran is infallible and interpret it according to their values, ranging from a belief that the Quran is gender-egalitarian to one that it is highly inegalitarian.

In addition to this difference, most Westerners who are not scholars of the region exaggerate the negative side of gender relations in the Muslim world, and tend to present Muslim women primarily as victims. The ideals of women's seclusion and the separation of genders were misinterpreted to mean that most women lived lives without meaning or satisfactions. Today there is a countertendency among many scholars of the Middle East, both Muslim and non-Muslim, to stress the positive aspects of women's lives, which is understandable as a reaction to the predominant highly negative view. In writing about women in Muslim countries, as elsewhere, one finds documentation of both positive and negative features, and there is no ideal or "correct" solution regarding how much to emphasize each. Even though most historians now recognize that interpretations of Islam were changeable, and that many factors other than religion profoundly affected the status of women, it is impossible to escape an emphasis on early Islam and the Quran, as these have been central themes of local discourse about women over the centuries and to a degree remain so today.

Documents about events surrounding the rise of Islam and about the nature of the pre-Islamic society in Arabia from which it arose were first preserved orally and were written down long after the events they recorded. Islam arose in the early seventh century, C.E., and the earliest substantial remaining writings date from the ninth century. These writings reflect not only the faults of memory but also society's rapid change, including changes regarding the position of women and attitudes about them, after the Muslim conquest of most of the pre-Islamic empires of the Middle East. The problem of reading later beliefs and practices into earlier events deeply affects basic cultural attitudes and practices. We should interpret the documentation that remains in light of the socioeconomic and cultural situation in the entire Middle East before, during, and after the rise of Islam. Within the limits of space and knowledge, this work attempts to do that.

The closer we come to the present the greater is the contemporary documentation available, so that the problem for a brief general work becomes what points to include and what to exclude. Beginning about the fourteenth century, with the Mamluks in Egypt and especially with the centuries-long and extensive Ottoman Empire, there is a relative wealth of documents, especially legal documents, that is now being mined by historians. An important point regarding women is that in these two empires the social and sexual lives of women were often much freer than a literal reading of Islamic law and writings might leave us to think, and this might also be true for some periods and areas for which we do not have as much documentation.

As we approach recent times, the wealth and reliability of documentation, the amount of monographic scholarship available, and the proliferation of Arab countries with distinct policies and histories regarding women led me to give more space to recent events than to earlier ones and to expand my narrative to give some coverage to each country (omitting a few African countries with very large non-Arab populations that are frequently excluded in definitions of the Middle East). What can be presented in a brief history is a very small part of what has been well studied or documented. For recent times this work concentrates on legal and societal changes, women's movements, and on often conservative Islamist, tribal, and other forces. Regarding this and earlier periods, readers are encouraged to go further in the works cited within and others. This is a general work aimed largely at nonspecialists; it does not try to cite every source, and often groups together citations at the end of a paragraph.

In writing of modern times, I have been struck and no doubt hindered by the absence of overall narrative histories of women in any Middle Eastern country other than Iran, a phenomenon that reflects a period in scholarly writing when such general narratives were often shunned and both monographic and theoretical approaches were favored.[1] While works like the present one and other narratives are bound to make some errors because of their scope and differences in the sources, they are also important for giving a general overview of the past, which can be of great help in enhancing understanding of the present.[2]

This book covers a huge topic and has had to observe limits of space and research time; hence it concentrates on some questions and limits discussion of others. It does not deal extensively with women's literature, arts, and popular culture, which have a large literature of their own and merit more general overviews than they have thus far received. Nor does it cover Middle Eastern women in diasporas, who are having an important global influence. It deals more extensively with Muslim and ethnic majorities than with minorities, and more with those classes that are well documented than with others. These choices do not mean that I consider some women more important than others; rather, they reflect what was feasible for this short work. It makes no attempt to cover that great majority of Muslim women who live outside the Middle East, whose conditions, especially in areas where Islam spread late and peacefully like Southeast Asia and much of Africa, are often quite different from those of Middle Eastern women. In all these and no doubt other fields there remains a great deal to be written that can, like this work, be based on monographic studies but meet the needs of those who want a general analytic overview.

Regional Background and the Beginnings of Islam

HISTORICAL MIDDLE EASTERN SOCIETIES AND GENDER RELATIONS

The societies of the Middle East from pre-Islamic times onward had particular gender relations, which varied by region and by socioeconomic and political structures. Some works on Islamic history concentrate on pre-Islamic Arabian society, but today it is widely recognized that many crucial phenomena regarding women in Islamic times arose not from Arabia but from the pre-Islamic civilizations of southwest Asia, early conquered by Muslim armies. Also, the changeover (partly accomplished under the Prophet Muhammad) from a tribally organized society to one with a state and some set laws altered the position of women. The roles of women in the Middle East after the seventh-century Islamic conquests reflected amalgams of pre-Islamic Arab and Near Eastern cultures, modified to meet the circumstances of new Islamic states, and also reflecting a variety of local circumstances and ideas. The interaction of the cultures and practices of ancient Near Eastern empires with those of largely nomadic but partly mercantile Arab tribes affected gender attitudes and relations. The Arabs who influenced the regions they conquered were mainly those in the center, east, and north of the peninsula, rather than the more settled southern Yemen region.

Ancient Near Eastern civilizations had bordered on these Arabs for centuries. Like other historical civilizations, Near Eastern civilizations were all male-dominant, though ancient Egypt, before Greek and Roman control, was closer than any other ancient civilization to being gender-egalitarian. Some scholars have found similarities regarding gender attitudes among all Mediterranean cultures, while others have emphasized similar gender and family structures and attitudes in a large block of cultures stretching from the Mediterranean to East Asia, with northern Europe and Africa having different patterns.[1] A recent trend among scholars is to emphasize common features among civilizations and to put far less stress than before on the role of Islam in setting gender attitudes and practices. There were, however, features arising from the interaction of Arab tribal and mercantile and Near Eastern imperial traditions that made the Islamic Middle East somewhat different in gender attitudes and practices from both the European Mediterranean and societies further to the east, although it shared some features with each. Islam was often not the overwhelming variable, but evolving Islamic laws and beliefs both reflected and helped to shape ideas and practices regarding women.

Many features commonly called Islamic existed in ancient civilizations of the eastern Mediterranean, including Iranian states and empires, ancient Greece, and the Byzantine Empire. Agriculture and the domestication of animals began in the Middle East many millennia B.C.E., and these produced enough economic surplus to support the specialized occupations characteristic of cities and, later, states and empires. The creation of partly separate female and male spheres and occupations everywhere predated the formation of cities and states, with women in occupations in or near the home owing chiefly to the requirements of frequent childbearing. The rise of cities and states increased the separation of the genders and of gender roles, as it also increased the distinctions among classes and occupations. Men monopolized politics and most powerful religious and economic positions, while women were increasingly specialized in the domestic sphere, which included bearing and raising children and a variety of vital occupations carried out in or near the home. Especially in the heavily tribal Near and Middle East, men's concern about the assured paternity of their offspring and the purity of their lineage led to increasing control over women's public actions and movements and to seclusion of at least upper-class women. States and patriarchically organized families were mutually reinforcing. States, which lacked today's means of entering people's lives, supported patriarchal laws and customs and left the details to male heads of households, who were expected to keep order and assure production and reproduction at home.

The pre-Islamic Middle East and the East European Mediterranean had various forms of veiling and seclusion, especially of elite women. Assyrian law of the late second millennium B.C.E. gave men proprietary rights over women, exclusive divorce rights, and specified rules on veiling. High-status women had to veil, while harlots and slaves were forbidden to, showing a differentiation by class and division of respectability that was to continue later. (Veiling here means covering the hair and much of the face and body.) Large harems for the powerful, including female slaves, eunuchs, and concubines, were found in various ancient Near Eastern empires, including those in Iran.

Most pre-Islamic religions of the area, both polytheistic ones and the scriptural religions—Judaism, Zoroastrianism, and Christianity—supported male-dominant attitudes and practices. Judaism and Christianity saw woman, in the form of Eve, as introducing evil into the world, and Judaism allowed polygamy and strong male privilege in divorce. (Christianity is the only world religion that early disallowed polygamy, which it first did as part of its preference for restricting sexual activity.) Pre-Islamic religions and their gender attitudes influenced Islam, both in its early ideas and in its doctrinal and legal evolution, while other influences came from the practices of pre-Islamic Near Eastern states and empires and from the Arabs.

Some Near Eastern male-dominant elements were similar to those found throughout the premodern world. Male control in the family and society was seen as functional when infant and child mortality was high, frequent pregnancy and childbirth were necessary to ensure reproducing the population, and family households were the central productive and reproductive units. In most premodern societies, women's primary role was seen as childbearing and rearing, and men were concerned to guarantee the legitimacy of the family line by restricting women's accessibility. These common features led to practices and beliefs supporting male dominance in all premodern states and societies. It is only the bare beginning of understanding to call all such historical societies "patriarchal," as this lumps all civilizations together and does not tell us anything about their varying specifics. Gender-inegalitarian ideologies, including female inferiority, were characteristic of all premodern civilizations, as were male dominance in the family, household, tribe, and state, but differences in ideology and practice over time and space are the stuff of history.

Women in pre-Islamic tribal society in Arabia and in the earliest days of Islam had a far more public role than did elite women of the conquered imperial territories or than women came to have in Islamic societies, though their roles in tribal societies varied and most tribes were strongly male-dominant. The social and gender stratification of the conquered Islamic territories and the wealth that came to the Islamic conquerors favored the development of elite harems, domestic slavery, veiling and seclusion of women, and other features characteristic of both the pre-Islamic and Islamic Middle East. The egalitarianism of tribal societies should not be exaggerated, and many Middle Eastern gender attitudes and practices resulted from the interactions of the patriarchal practices of nomadic tribal pastoralists or recently settled tribes with those of settled states.

The scarce documentation on pre-Islamic and early Islamic gender relations may be supplemented by later studies, primarily by anthropologists, on societies in the Middle Eastern and Mediterranean regions. When practices are found widely and deeply embedded in the past and present of geographically separate areas of the Middle East, it is reasonable to believe that they go back in time, especially when ecology and social structures were similar to those investigated later. Such widespread practices and ideas among early Arabs and many later Muslims include the salience of tribal-nomadic organization and structures, the importance of patrilineal kinship and the preference for marriages between paternal cousins, and strong concepts of honor centering on female virginity and chastity, all of which have been found in the past and present in much of the Middle

East. When there are such widespread practices and ideas, it is reasonable to conclude that they had similarities in a past for which we have less documentation than we do for recent times.

The Middle East has long been characterized by an arid, semiarid, or mountainous landscape with limited rainfall, and a few river valleys that could be made very fertile via irrigation. These fertile valleys and the usable grains and animals found in the region made the Middle East the ideal spot for agriculture to originate, before it was developed anywhere else. However, thousands of years of agricultural settlement later led to deforestation, a rising level of salt in the soils, soil erosion, and long-term limits on agricultural productivity, so that the early economically pioneering role of the Middle East suffered a relative, and in some cases absolute, decline over the centuries, including the later Islamic centuries.[2]

Three basic economic structures were found in the Middle East: settled agriculture, nomadic pastoralism, and urban settlement. All were interdependent, and nomadism did not precede agriculture but both developed out of a mixed agricultural-pastoral productive mode. Aridity or mountainous terrain favored the expansion of nomadic pastoralists, people whose main product was herded animals and who were organized into kin-based clans and tribes, often without a state. States had more control over agricultural settlements than they did over armed and mounted nomads, part of whose income came from raids and warfare. States arose once an agricultural surplus made possible urban settlements, social stratification, and urban control of the countryside. Nomadic tribes tended to live on the margins of state-controlled territories and were harder to control, and even settled tribes had and have an internal solidarity and leadership that often contest those of the state.

The organization and culture of agriculturalists, urban dwellers, and nomadic tribes involved specific features in the treatment of, and attitudes toward, women on the part of dominant males. All three groups, like all historical societies, were patriarchal and male-dominant, but they were so in somewhat different ways. The pre-Islamic Middle Eastern empires saw, among their rulers and urban elites, the rise of harems, female slavery, and elite women's veiling, partial seclusion, and separation from the hard physical labor that most women and men had to do. Nomadic tribes had far less economic surplus and hence less social and gender stratification, as everyone had to do various physical tasks. Nomad women were not veiled or secluded, nomad men did not have harems, and women had a role in warfare and in public arenas. On the other hand, in the Arabian Peninsula, the home of the Arabic-speakers who later spread their language via conquest, most nomads tended to be very concerned about genealogical purity and family control over women's sexuality, expressed in part in their preference for marriage of paternal cousins, which also preserved family property. Such marriages were one component of patriarchal extended families, in which the male (agnatic) line was more important than was the marital relationship, although when both parties were from the same line, there was less conflict between the two. Male control of female relatives was strong in most tribes, although pre-Islamic poetry shows that there were other tribes where women were far more independent, husbands went to live with their wives' families, divorce was easy for women, and even polyandry (multiple husbands) may have occurred.

In the Middle East and the northern Mediterranean there has long been a stress on female virginity and chastity as central to male honor. It has been argued that this is connected with the difficult terrain and mixed settlement of areas near the Mediterranean and the prevalence and position of nomadic or transhumant tribes and clans. These tribes' beliefs and practices, along with the struggle of differently organized groups for scarce economic resources, put special value on the cohesion of the patriarchal family and its strong reaction to any felt attacks, which affected the position of women. Male honor included qualities like strength and hospitality, but also dominance over women, crucially including control of their sexuality. Many of these conditions continued through the centuries.[3] The practice of "honor killing," usually by males in the natal family, of some girls and women suspected of transgressing rules of sexual behavior, is a tribal custom not limited to Islam and not found in the Quran or Islamic law, and has continued, however small the absolute numbers, in some areas with large tribal populations.

Among pastoral tribes, even more than in settled areas, the kin group was the most important economic and political unit. These tribes and clans, as they had to move through large unbounded territories, often used raids and warfare to protect themselves, accumulate land and goods, and increase their power, and the size and strength of kin groups were crucial. Even more than elsewhere, women were valued for the number of sons they produced, and purity of lineage was a special concern. Most Arab tribes favored endogamous marriages of sons with fathers' brothers' daughters or, failing that, more distant paternal cousins. The importance of lineage purity to both tribal and settled groups involved an emphasis on female virginity at marriage and fidelity during marriage, and a belief that men's honor depended on women's chastity and fidelity. Some similar beliefs were and are found elsewhere in Asia and in non-Islamic tribal Mediterranean regions.

Settled tribes made up a large part of the population in Arabian cities before Islam, nomadic tribes predominated in the early Islamic armies that conquered the Middle East, and many Arab tribespeople remained in the conquered areas. In some Islamic periods tribal peoples were both powerful and respected, so that their customs entered Middle Eastern culture in degrees superior to their numbers. The influence of the settled conquered peoples was also strong, including especially their economic, legal, and political ideologies and practices, and the Islamic synthesis that developed reflected both tribal-nomadic and settled cultures, often in uneasy symbiosis and with major internal contradictions. This synthesis in time meant less of a public role for women than had existed in pre-Islamic Arabia, and an emphasis on partly tribal ideas of honor and protection of the lineage via control of women.

Pre-Islamic Arabia and the Rise of Islam

Existing documentation regarding pre-Islamic Arabia indicates that many tribes were patrilineal, with brides going to live with their husbands' families, but there were some groups with matrilineal systems that counted descent and inheritance in the female line and had husbands going to live with the wife's family. As noted, there was variety in other customs, with some tribal groups reportedly allowing polyandry and some allowing women freely and easily to divorce their husbands. In patriarchal and patrilineal tribes, men reacted strongly to threats to their wives, daughters, and sisters (among nomads such threats included abduction of women and girls). Preference for marriage between paternal cousins existed in pre-Islamic times and increased after the rise of Islam. The position of women in pre-Islamic Arabia, for which sources are scarce, remains controversial, with some stressing the reformist role of the Prophet Muhammad regarding women; they argue that women before Islam had a low status, that they were essentially bought, sold, and stolen, and that female infanticide (denounced in the Quran) was prevalent. Such scholars say the position of women was dramatically improved by the Quran's rules and admonitions.[4] Other scholars assert that women had more varied rights and status and were more independent and more active in the public sphere in pre-Islamic Arabia than they became after the rise of Islam.[5] It is possible that most women were less secluded and more publicly active in pre-Islamic and early Islamic times than they later became, but that they lacked rights accorded them in the Quran, including having the male dower go directly to them, not to their male guardian, and the right to inherit in legally fixed shares. It seems, from the poetic and other sources that remain, that there was a variety of customs, with patriarchal ways becoming more dominant as tribes settled into urban life.

The Prophet Muhammad (ca. 570–632 c.e.) and his revelations, as later reported in the Quran, had a great role in world history and in founding a major world religion. More controversial is the role of the Quran in changing the position of women. The idea that Muhammad and the Quran brought a great favorable change in the position of women is endorsed by a number of scholars but has been challenged by others. Many now believe original Islam improved the position of women, and note that several revelations include identical moral admonitions addressed to men and women, while the later legalistic revelations contain more regulations that distinguish male and female behavior, some of which were directed only at Muhammad's wives but came to be applied to women generally. Those who stress the gender-reformism of the Quran note that it condemns the practice of female infanticide, says the male dowry should go to the wife, not to her male relative, and endorses women's ownership and control of property, saying that women should inherit (half of what men got). Others, however, believe that pre-Islamic Arab women already controlled property, though they may not have had defined inheritance rights, and that women had a larger role in the public sphere, including helping men in warfare, than they did later. In pre-Islamic times many women could operate without guardians' having to make every basic decision, and widows could apparently remarry without any guardian's approval.[6]

Those who stress the gender-reformist view of the Quran say that the decline of women's position after the earliest Islamic period was due to foreign and local patriarchal accretions, not to what was in the Quran, which one modern group of Islamic reformists sees as implicitly gender-egalitarian and interprets in ways that support this view. Emphasis on the words of the Quran as a major determinant in the position of women, overstating its objective role in determining this position, is reflected in the propensity of later Muslims to appeal to interpretations of the Quran as the basis of their views on this question. Some see the gender-inegalitarian interpretation of Islam, based largely on Traditions (hadiths) that were believed to recount the words and deeds of the Prophet but were written down only from the ninth century C.E., as the crucial intellectual element in the forms that male supremacy took in the premodern Muslim world. This, too, may overstate the role of words in determining social practices.

According to many scholars, the rise of Islam in an area already acquainted with Jewish and Christian scriptural monotheism was in part a response to the influence of such monotheisms and also to problems in the Arabian towns of Mecca and Medina. Both cities were experiencing conflicts that could not be managed in a situation where tribal structures were breaking down but state structures did yet not exist. Although the nature of the social and religious situation that formed the background to the rise of Islam is disputed, we can reasonably posit a role for the socioeconomic circumstances accompanying the transition from tribally ruled societies to a state-ruled one with common laws and beliefs.

Some scholars doubt that we can even be sure of the basic later account of events during and soon after the life of Muhammad, but there is no doubt that this account and the emphasis on the Prophet's revelations and Traditions have greatly influenced generations of Muslims. In this account, the Prophet Muhammad was an orphan in a minor branch of the dominant Quraish tribe; he became a trader of Mecca who at age twenty-five married a well-off merchant for whom he worked, Khadija, who was then in her early forties. Until she died, he remained monogamous, and Khadija was the mother of all his four daughters and two of his three sons, who died in infancy. At age forty he had his first revelation, followed by several others. Khadija became the first of a group of believers in the religion that became known as Islam (meaning submission, i.e., to God). The message of the early revelations was strict monotheism, fear of the Day of Judgment when humans would go either to paradise or to hell, and a call for moral behavior, including good treatment of orphans, widows, and the unfortunate.

Most Meccans, who had a vested interest in the old ways, including a major Meccan shrine to three goddesses, did not accept Islam, and in 622 Muhammad moved to the contentious town of Medina, called there as an arbiter among tribal groups, which included Jewish tribes. He soon became the real ruler of a newly formed state centering in Medina. Several of his revelations in Medina were legalistic and later became a key element in Islamic law. The Muslims conquered Mecca in 630, and most of Arabia expressed allegiance to Muhammad before his death in 632, after which there were revolts in Arabia that were suppressed, with women prominent in some revolts. After Khadija's death Muhammad married several more girls and women, many of them apparently in order to promote tribal and other alliances. His most prominent and apparently favorite wife was A'isha, daughter of Abu Bakr, who became the first Muslim caliph. They were married when she was still a small girl, but the marriage was not at first consummated. She was eighteen when Muhammad died.

Those concerned with women's rights often divide the revelations in the Quran into two groups besides the widely recognized and related division into Meccan revelations, which stress general principles, and the legalistic ones from Medina, where Muhammad was legislating. Regarding women, one sizable group of revelations, often specifically addressing both men and women, deals equally with both as believers, who are enjoined to act identically regarding morality, modesty, and so forth. The other group contains rules for women that are separate and unequal, though generally less unequal than what later became Islamic law and practice. Some revelations reformed pre-Islamic tribal customs in ways beneficial to women. Among these was one concerning the (substantial) dower (*mahr*) that all grooms had to give upon marriage. The Quran says that the wife and not her male relatives (as was the custom) should receive the dower: "And give the women their dower as a free gift" (verse 4:4). In Islamic law, the male dower was seen as an indispensable payment for exclusive sexual rights to the wife.

In most customary laws of the Arab tribes inheritance was based only on the agnatic (male) line, while Quranic rules included fixed inheritance shares for certain close female relatives not in the agnatic line. In general, females got half of what similarly related males did. On the other hand, the Quran sanctified superior rights for men, including the right of a husband to punish, and as a final sanction to beat, a wife who persists in disobedience; the right of men but not women to divorce simply by a thrice-stated declaration; the right of men but not women to have several spouses; the idea that women should be obedient to their male kin and husbands and agree to sex whenever the husband wanted it; and women's inheritance as half that of men. On the last point, it is often noted in compensation that women control their own property and that husbands must support their wives, but not vice versa, so that women often control significant property (though studies show that rural and tribal women do not inherit as much property as the Quran says they should and rarely inherit land or animals).

The verse allowing men to have more than one wife (two, three, or four, which was interpreted as a limit), appears in the context of verses on protecting widows and orphans, who must have been numerous in the time of battles to extend the domains of Islam in Arabia. It is also followed by a limiting verse (4:3, and 4:129):

> Marry women of your choice, two, three or four. But if you fear that you shall not be able to deal justly [with them] then only one. . . .
>   You are never able to be fair and just as between women, even if that were your ardent desire.

In modern times, the circumstances of this revelation are often interpreted as meaning that polygamy was to be encouraged only in conditions of male shortage or female barrenness, and that the Prophet favored monogamy. Proponents reinforce this view of a preference for monogamy by citing the verse telling men to marry only one wife if they fear they cannot be just to all, followed by a statement that they cannot be just, even if they try. These are not traditional interpretations. Overwhelmingly, justice to all wives was interpreted as meaning equal material treatment for each and equally shared nocturnal visits. Even this was not enforceable but depended on predominant custom.

Some interpreters say that the Quran's limits on polygamy reformed a pre-Islamic situation of unlimited polygamy. Some modern researchers, however, suggest that there is little evidence of unlimited polygamy for

Mecca and Medina, that what plural marriages existed in Arabia likely involved ties to other tribal groups without the bride's joining the groom's household, and that lists of several wives for a man, like lists found of several husbands for a woman in pre-Islamic times, may well involve a series of marriages and divorces.[7]

The revelations that were later interpreted as meaning that all women should veil do not say this, and it seems that women did not veil in early Islamic times. The verse that directly mentions *hijab*, which then meant a curtain but later came to mean the head and body covering of a woman, is verse 33:55, which concerns the Prophet's wives. The relevant part says:

> Oh, believers, do not enter the Prophet's houses except that permission is given you for a meal. . . . And if you ask them [the women] for a thing, then ask them from behind a *hijab*. That is purer for your hearts and their hearts.[8]

By some Muslim interpreters, this revelation "is seen mainly as the legislation of a means to provide domestic comfort and privacy for the female elite of Islam. This notion, in turn, connotes an element of 'privilege.' And, indeed, the medieval Hadith informs that the *hijab* was imposed upon the Prophet's wives as criterion of their elite status."[9] The word *hijab* in time came to mean women's seclusion and also the garments used to ensure it.

Soon after the revelation of the above verse came that of Quran 33:59–60, which states that women should draw their cloaks close about them when they go out, so that they will be known and not molested, with no indication that a face veil was involved. This verse relates to all women. A temporally later revelation, verse 24:30, directed at Muslim men, tells them to restrain their eyes and guard their private parts, and the immediately following 24:31, says:

> Tell the female believers that they restrain their eyes and guard their private parts, and not display of their adornment except for what is apparent, and draw their kerchiefs over their bosoms. . . . And that they not stamp their feet to give knowledge of the adornment which they hide.

This verse was later interpreted as meaning covering the whole body, including hair, and most of the face. This interpretation is illogical. If the whole body and face were meant, there would be no reason to tell women to veil their bosoms specifically, while the later interpretation of "adornment" to mean everything but the hands, feet, and (possibly) the face is a forced one. The reference to not revealing the presence of hidden ornaments through stamping the feet indicates that "adornment" (often rendered "ornament") had at the time of this revelation its obvious meaning of jewelry, bangles, and the like. The above verses, which call for wearing a cloak outside and hiding ornaments and bosoms, were later taken to enjoin veiling on all women at least from puberty to menopause. As summarized by Leila Ahmed:

> Veiling was apparently not introduced into Arabia by Muhammad but already existed among some classes, particularly in the towns, though it was probably more prevalent in the countries that the Arabs had contact with, such as Syria and Palestine. In those areas, as in Arabia, it was connected with social status, as was its use among Greeks, Romans, Jews, and Assyrians, all of whom practiced veiling to some degree. . . .
>
> Throughout Muhammad's lifetime veiling, like seclusion, was observed only by his wives. Moreover, that the phrase "[she] took the veil]" is used in the hadith to mean that a woman became a wife of Muhammad's suggests that for some time after Muhammad's death . . . veiling and seclusion were still considered peculiar to Muhammad's wives. . . . The Muslim conquests of areas in which veiling was commonplace among the upper classes, the influx of wealth, the resultant raised status of Arabs, and Muhammad's wives being taken as models probably combined to bring about their general adoption.[10]

Regarding spatial seclusion, a late Quranic revelation came after some crisis in Muhammad's relations with his wives, and again a verse that originally applied only to Muhammad's wives was extended by medieval jurists and theologians to all women. This verse was 33:33:

> And stay in your houses . . . and do not strut about in the manner of the former Jahiliyya, and perform the prayer and give the alms, and obey God and His Prophet. God wishes but to put all filthiness away from you, People of the House.

Strutting about, *tabarruj*, was interpreted very broadly by medieval jurists (and conservatives today use it for hair, makeup, and Western or revealing clothing). A verse explicitly directed to Muhammad's wives was extended to all women, and contrary behavior was said to be un-Islamic, and characteristic of the pre-Islamic age of ignorance, the *jahiliyya*, and a threat to Islamic society. The direction to Muhammad's wives to stay in their houses was later applied to all women, though only women who did not have to go out to do work and errands could observe it. This verse was also used to legitimate Muslim women's exclusion from participation in public affairs; "women's secluded space, concealing clothing, and unfitness for public activity emerged as three powerful determinants in the medieval Islamic paradigm on women's societal role."[11]

These extensions of late admonitions to Muhammad's wives to all women did not occur immediately, but there was a diminution in women's public role as some of the elite customs in the conquered empires spread and combined with Arab tribal and familial concerns. Beginning with the mid-eighth-century Abbasid state, there grew up a religious establishment entrusted with the formulation of Islamic law and morality. They interpreted Quranic rules on women's dress and seclusion in an increasingly absolute fashion, which reflected the practices and cultural assumptions of their own era more than those of Quranic times.[12]

Regarding the effect of Quranic rulings and early Islamic practice on the position of the Arabian women to whom they first applied, Leila Ahmed says that the situation of women varied in Arabia, and that jahiliyya marriage practices suggest greater sexual autonomy and participation in public life for women than existed after the rise of Islam and its single model of patriarchal marriage.[13] Ahmed notes that Khadija was a wealthy widow who before marrying Muhammad employed him to oversee her caravans, and apparently proposed marriage to him. Her wealth freed him from economic needs and allowed him to lead a life of contemplation, and her support was crucial to him after his early revelations. As she was already in her fifties when Muhammad got these revelations, it was pre-Islamic society and customs that shaped her way of life. Her economic and personal independence and her monogamy with Muhammad may reflect pre-Islamic practices. No similar autonomy from male control or monogamy characterized Muhammad's later wives. A'isha, Ahmed says, lived during a transition between pre-Islamic and Islamic ways, and her brief political leadership role in the struggles that followed Muhammad's death had roots in earlier customs.

Several authors emphasize, regarding the change in political and public roles for women, developments after Muhammad's death and the conquest of Middle Eastern empires. Women apparently remained publicly active in the earliest Islamic period, as they had been before, even supporting men in various ways in the warfare that remained frequent during and after Muhammad's life. This support included loud cries of encouragement near the battlefield, nursing, and occasional combat roles. Women's public role decreased, however, after the period of conquest that followed Muhammad's death.

Regarding changes in marriage patterns following the rise of Islam, Ahmed says: "Islam selectively sanctioned customs already found among some Arabian tribal societies while prohibiting others. Of central importance to the institution it established were the preeminence given to paternity and the vesting in the male of proprietary rights to female sexuality and its issue. Accordant customs, such as polygamy, were incorporated while discordant or opposing customs were prohibited."[14] Ahmed, however, distinguishes the ethical gender-egalitarianism of some Quranic verses as a major strain in the Quran that implicitly conflicted with its inegalitarian rules. Men and women, for example, were given the same admonitions regarding charity, chastity, truthfulness, patience, and piety. Ahmed maintains that these two visions of Islam characterized much of later Islamic history. One could argue that the two were not contradictory except in a modern view; that in premodern societies everyone could be asked to adhere to certain ethical and religious standards without an implication that everyone had equal qualities of reason and judgment that entitled them to equal rights. Such views were not exclusive to Islam, but were found in many traditional societies and religions. In Islam as in other religions, there were minority movements that stressed greater equality between men and women, and some who did not accept the Quranic rules regarding women. They did not, however, in premodern times, speak of an internal split in the Quranic attitudes to women between the ethical and the formal.

From the Pious Caliphs through the Dynastic Caliphates

THE AGE OF PIOUS CALIPHS AND MAJOR CONQUESTS

After the Prophet's death, the first four leaders of the new community, known subsequently as the "pious caliphs," were chosen by a small group of the Muslim elite. The first of these, Abu Bakr (632–34), crushed the Arabian revolts that occurred after Muhammad's death, when many tribal and other leaders apparently believed that their adhesion to Islam ended with the Prophet's death, while some, continuing a trend of prophetic religious claims that had begun before Muhammad, declared themselves prophets of new religions. One armed rebellion was led by a woman, Salma bint Malik, and one of the "false prophets" who led a revolt was also a woman, Sajah bint 'Aws. In Haudramaut in Yemen six women led a large group of women who spoke out against Muhammad and encouraged another resistance.[1] These movements, as well as several male-led revolts, were defeated by Abu Bakr. He also began successful raids into the territories of the Byzantine and Sasanian Empires, which had been weakened by recent wars against one another.

The second caliph, Umar, 634–44, led the major Islamic conquests and added to state controls and laws, including more stringent laws involving punishments for women and restrictions on their movements. Umar's strict rules regarding women are reported in various oral accounts that entered the literature and practices of medieval Islam. Under Umar's caliphate many of the practices of Islam were instituted. Regarding adultery, the Quran requires four eyewitnesses to the physical act or a confession for it to be punished, by a hundred lashes for both male and female adulterers, and includes high penalties for false accusations. These conditions were so difficult to meet that in several periods we know that adultery was almost never punished under Islamic law. Umar began the practice of stoning adulterers to death, and this punishment was at some point put in the form of a Tradition of the Prophet, despite its contradiction of the Quran. Most scholars believe stoning to death for adulterers came into Islam from Jewish law, where it was decreed, and indeed one key hadith has the Prophet asking an accused Jewish couple what punishment was prescribed in their law and then prescribing stoning. On the basis of such hadiths, stoning for married adulterers entered later Islamic law.

Studies of various court records in different places and periods indicate the death penalty was very rarely practiced, however.[2] Umar tried to prevent women from going to mosques, a prohibition that was ended only briefly by the next caliph, Uthman, 644–56, who also, but only temporarily, reversed others among Umar's restrictive rulings. With the growth in the size and wealth of the state and imitation of the practices of the conquered peoples and their imperial elites, the tide was turning toward more restrictions on women.

By 656 the caliphs' armies had conquered all of the Sasanian Empire, which centered on Iran, and much of the Byzantine Near East, including greater Syria, Egypt, and much of North Africa. In these Byzantine provinces most people belonged to different Christian sects from those professed by the Byzantine rulers, and some were glad to escape Byzantine persecution by agreeing to give up their cities peacefully to the Muslim forces in return for freedom to follow their religion. These promises were generally kept, as Islam included tolerance for "People of the Book"— Christians, Jews, Sabeans, and (in most cases) Zoroastrians. Conversion in these areas occurred later and was overwhelmingly voluntary, and the minority religions remained, though much reduced in size. Followers of these religions had to pay a special tax, and were sometimes discriminated against by special decrees and practices—facts that encouraged conversion—but overall Islamic states and their subjects had a far better record of tolerance of religious minorities than did premodern Christianity.

Religious and political dissension in the Muslim community led to oppositional groups and the murder of the third caliph, Uthman, followed by civil war. One group, who became the Shi'a, believed that Muhammad's closest male relative, his son-in-law and cousin, Ali, should have inherited the caliphate after Muhammad's death, and that Ali and his male descendants were the legitimate leaders of the Muslim community. Another group of Muslims favored a successor from the Umayyad family of the third caliph, Uthman.

The last woman to play a major public role in the first centuries of Islam was A'isha, Muhammad's favorite wife. When Uthman was murdered and Ali became caliph, A'isha took a leading role among Ali's opponents, becoming a highly visible rallying point and standard-bearer for those favoring Uthman's family. She called for vengeance against Uthman's killers and also against Ali during what became known as the first civil war. She gathered one faction opposed to Ali's caliphate around her and directed much of the fighting from a camel above the battlefield. After A'isha and her allies were defeated in the key Battle of the Camel, her failed leadership was utilized as a warning against allowing women to take roles in politics or even to appear or speak in public.

Traditions on this and other matters were collected beginning soon after the Prophet's death and were, after selection, gathered into authoritative compendia of Traditions in the ninth century C.E. The criterion of selection of "sound" traditions was chiefly the believed reliability of the chain of hadith reporters who had handed them down, and the canonical hadiths often reflected restrictive and negative attitudes about women that had become current.

Under the first four "pious caliphs" (632–61) doctrinal disagreements grew. The most important dissenters were those who said that leadership should pass by birth to Ali and his male descendants. These became known as the party of Ali (the Shi'at-Ali, or Shi'a). In the first period Shi'ism was essentially a political movement, but in later decades it developed into a religiopolitical one, in which Ali and his descendants were considered infallible imams, second in theory to the Prophet Muhammad, but with Ali and his son Husain often more popularly venerated than Muhammad by Shi'is. After Ali's defeat by the first Umayyad caliphate in 661, Shi'ism came to be seen as a separate branch of Islam, whose followers often rebelled against caliphal rulers they considered illegitimate in the name of their legitimate imams. The five holiest people in Shi'ism are Muhammad, Ali, his two sons Hasan and Husain, and their mother Fatima. Fatima's holy powers appeared in religious literature and folklore, which, as she was the Prophet's daughter, spread into mainstream Sunni Islam and even into Christianity. (A Shi'i dynasty, the Fatimids, who began in North Africa in 909 and spread to Egypt and Syria until 1171, took their name from her, claiming descent from her and Ali.)

Some Shi'i laws differed from Sunni laws. Temporary marriage (*mut'a*, literally pleasure), in which the marriage is for a set time, was known before Islam and continued to be practiced in Islam's first years. Umar forbade it, and it remains forbidden among Sunni Muslims. Among Shi'is it has its own legal rules, including a different marriage contract and a shorter time before remarriage is permitted. More favorable to women is Shi'i inheritance law, which gives more rights than does Sunni law to certain female relations, especially daughters, and to relations on the female as well as the male side. This may be in part because the imams' descent from the Prophet passed through the female line, and also because early Sunni law embodied a recrudescence of tribal customs favoring relatives on the male side (agnates).

Another dissenting group, the Kharijis, said that anyone who merited it could be elected caliph. They also rejected concubinage and child marriage, saying that God gave the Prophet privileges not shared by other men. They said that women had to participate in holy war, and women did take part in their early warfare.[3] Although important in the early period of Islam, they later had few adherents except in Oman.

The main event in this period was the rapid conquest of a huge territory, from Spain in the West to northwest India (Pakistan) in the East. This was facilitated by the decline of the Sasanian and Byzantine Empires and the constant warfare between them, which weakened both. The Arabs (like the later Turks and Mongols) had the advantage of steppe and desert armies who had mastered warfare on camel- and horseback. The Muslim Arabs were also able to sign treaties with several towns and cities allowing them to take over peacefully in return for a promise of free exercise of religion. At first the conquering armies lived separately in what became new cities, but soon many conquered people came to offer goods and services, and were absorbed as clients (*mawali*) of the tribes. These clients began to convert to Islam, which gave them tax and other benefits, and gradually a more widespread trend to conversion grew, although Christian, Jewish, Zoroastrian, and Sabean "People of the Book" remained tolerated minorities. One sign that the position of women was not simply a by-product of Islamic doctrine is that their position and practices in such minority communities was quite similar until modern times to that among Muslims.

By the time collections of Traditions and other writings concerning women began, the image of women like A'isha had been denigrated, but enough remains regarding earlier times to show that many women were important and respected in the first decades of Islam. Despite the negative portrayal of A'isha as a leader, her positive role in other aspects of Tradition remained. Other women among Muhammad's wives and followers were significant as transmitters of Tradition and, to a degree, in public life. One such woman was Zainab, the daughter of Ali and Fatima and sister of the third Shi'i imam, Husain, who challenged the Umayyad caliph and, along with most of his followers, was killed in battle. Husain's martyrdom at Karbala in 680 C.E. became the occasion for Shi'i mourning ceremonies over the centuries. Zainab is remembered as a heroine, having protected Husain's last living son from death, and having shown courage when brought as a prisoner before the Umayyad caliph Yazid in Damascus, where she has a major shrine. She has become a role model for women, particularly but not exclusively in Shi'i communities in recent decades, where she is seen as an exemplary Muslim woman who fought heroically for her family and her religion.

WOMEN IN MEDIEVAL MUSLIM SOCIETY

Some surviving documents draw on reports from the period of the first dynastic caliphate, the (Syrian) Umayyads (661–749), but direct surviving documentation comes from the period of the Abbasid caliphate (749–

1258) centering in Baghdad, Iraq. This caliphate was centralized only in its early centuries, called the "golden age" of Islam, when economic and intellectual life flourished, although it was not a golden age for women, slaves, or the poor. Local rulers later took increasing power, and the caliphs mostly became religious symbols. There were numerous Shi'i revolts, and a Shi'i countercaliphate, the Fatimids, ruled first North Africa and then Egypt and Syria from 906 to 1117. The period also saw the Crusades and the anticrusading leader Saladin, who ended the Fatimid caliphate and set up the Ayyubid dynasty, which ruled Syria and Egypt until they were overthrown by a new type of "slave" dynasty, the Mamluks. The thirteenth-century rise of the Mamluks and the Mongol conquest of much of the Middle East, including the Baghdad Abbasids, are here taken to mark the end of the early medieval period. What we know about women in this period comes mainly from legal and hadith documents, with little that tells us much about the lives of most women, although a few outstanding figures are better known.

While the increased seclusion of women limited the documentary record, scholars are beginning to unearth more material about women than a reading of the secondary literature would suggest, in hadiths, in various forms of literature, and in biographical dictionaries.[4] Important for the history of women were presentations and exegeses of Traditions and law, which helped to set views about gender and reflected the times in which they were written. After the first Islamic generation, women were increasingly excluded from participation in public life, and upper-class and many middle-class urban women were secluded. There was a rise in negative views of women, reflected in theological and legal interpretations of the Quran, in Traditions, in law, and in other writings.

Medieval Islamic society was more patriarchal in practice and male supremacist in written ideas than early Islamic Mecca and Medina. Much influence on the inegalitarian status of women came from conquered areas, especially the Sasanian and Byzantine Empires. This influence came both from ruling-class practices and from religious and other ideas among the conquered peoples. Islam did not begin as the most male-supremacist of the Middle Eastern religions, but Jewish and Christian Bible-related traditions, and Greek and southwest Asian ideas more hostile to women than were the Quran or original Islam came to be integrated into Islam once Islamic society adopted many features of Middle Eastern empires. Dominant Islamic Traditions stressed the supposed emotionality and inferior rationality of women, and saw women and their sexuality as evil threats to males and to the social order. These themes were read into Islamic scripture, though in many cases one can trace a biblical influence on their formulation. This view of women prevailed even when other biblical themes were rejected, suggesting that a negative view of women filled social needs. In recent centuries modernists began to reject these Traditions and called for a return to a reinterpreted Quran and the rejection of medieval accretions, but many of these gender images still survive in conservative views of the Quran and Traditions.

The early centuries of Islam saw contradictory developments regarding gender that continued into later periods. For example, on the one hand, the writings of the strict *ulama* (men with Islamic education and functions) stressed the importance of clear definition and separation of male and female, with no cross-dressing or homosexuality permitted.[5] On the other hand, in court and elite circles male and female cross-dressing, especially but not exclusively by slave entertainers, and homosexuality and homoerotic poetry, including a few references to female homosexuality, were common. In both early and later periods, beardless adolescent boys were often seen as at least as attractive and dangerous as women, as well as being more accessible, and the "active" role in sex was equally masculine whether the object was a woman or a boy.[6]

From the eighth century caliphs began to seclude their wives and create large harems of wives and slaves, practices increasingly followed by others among the rich and powerful. The later Umayyads emulated Sasanian court practices, including seclusion, veiling, and large harems. These practices were carried further by the Abbasids. Under the late Umayyads and the Abbasids many conquering Arabs adopted the settled ways of the conquered Sasanian and Byzantine peoples. Although the Arabic language became dominant outside Iran, many of the ways of life changed from Arab nomadic traditions to those of the settled empires, while the patriarchal aspects of tribal traditions continued to be influential.

ISLAMIC LAW (*SHARI'A*) AND TRADITIONS (HADITHS)

The above changes were reflected in the development of Islamic Traditions, beliefs, and law. After Muhammad's death those who wanted more guidance than was found in the Quran increasingly relied on Traditions (hadiths) about his sayings and deeds that passed down from his wives and companions through later pious and learned persons. Given the importance of Traditions, authorities justified many legal and other practices of the conquered areas by giving them the form of Traditions—attributing them to the Prophet and creating a chain of transmitters back to the Prophet. Legal rulings were in the earliest Islamic period largely ad hoc and often followed the laws and customs of the conquered areas. Once the community began to want distinctively Islamic law that went beyond the Quran, many local practices and laws—including Jewish, Roman, and the mixtures that made up provincial law—entered into Islamic law, often in the form of hadiths.[7] The schools of Islamic law developed in the ninth century and reflected the restrictive view of women of the time. Quranic verses were interpreted as meaning strict veiling, and women's subordinate position in marriage and other matters became part of law. Aside from recognized property rights, law and custom treated women in many ways like minors, insofar as they needed male approval to marry, move about, and undertake public activity. Such gender stratification reflected the rise in urban populations; increased gender stratification and segregation were features of urban society, not of the rural or tribal life still lived by most women and men. In the countryside and among nomadic tribes work and other needs made gender segregation impossible, although tribal customs were strongly patriarchal in other ways.

Before this time, legal rulings had been more varied, with jurists allowing the use of reasoned opinions (*ray*) in legal judgments, which produced considerable diversity. The first founder of a durable school of law, Muhammad al-Shafi'i, initiated the limitation of the sources of law to four: the Quran, the Prophet's *sunna* (reported in hadiths), analogical reasoning, and the consensus of the community. The main Quranic verses concerning women are cited above. As to the Prophet's sunna, numerous sayings and practices attributed to the Prophet were circulated, and in the mid-ninth century were sifted, collected, and ranked as to soundness in several books. Judgments about the soundness of hadiths were based on unbroken chains of transmission going back to the Prophet. Some modern scholars, beginning with Ignaz Goldziher and Joseph Schacht, doubt that such chains really show reliability, and suggest that men living in later times when strong chains were valued often invented such chains. There is little doubt that the winnowing process weeded out many hadiths that endorsed practices foreign to most Muslims and endorsed those in accord with that community's dominant standards. The views of women or slaves counted for little.

The third source of Muslim law, *qiyas*, or reasoning by analogy, discovers the reasons for a legal rule. Among the early uses of qiyas was fixing a minimum marriage dower from the groom to the bride demanded by all schools of Muslim law, which analogized the loss of virginity to theft, and set the minimum dower at the highest value that stolen goods could amount to before the penalty of amputation of a hand was applicable.[8] This was one aspect of a Muslim view of marriage as a contract giving the husband exclusive rights to sex with his wife, for which he paid the dower.

The fourth source of law is *ijma*, the consensus of the jurists on an issue. It derives its authority from a hadith in which the Prophet says, "My Community will never agree on error." If there were questions and problems that had no Islamic precedent, jurists applied their own effort of reasoning, *ijtihad*; over time if their conclusion became widely accepted, it entered law.

Three of the four Sunni schools of law developed subsidiary legal methods. Regarding women, the four Sunni schools differ more than is often realized, with the Hanafi school, unlike other Sunni schools, allowing a woman who has reached maturity to conclude her own marriage contract, while other schools put the contract and the first marriage under the control of her father or male guardian. The schools also differ on the ages to which children remain in the custody of divorced wives, after which they go to the husband or his family—in this case the Maliki school has the oldest ages of transfer. Shi'i law differs in allowing temporary marriage, and in giving some women larger inheritance shares and disfavoring agnatic male relatives who are favored in the Sunni schools as heirs. The differences among schools were lessened by interpretations from the late Middle Ages on, and in modern times states have combined elements from different schools in their codified laws in ways that reduced discrimination against women.[9]

According to most scholars, in the tenth century the consensus of legal scholars established that the elaboration of law was complete, and "the door of ijtihad" was closed. Henceforth jurists were to follow the established doctrines, and juristic consensus became a conservative force. Legal handbooks written by the founders of the great law schools and their followers became authoritative for the judges (*qadis*) who applied the law. The basic laws relating to women and the family were set.[10] Some scholars now deny that the door of ijtihad was ever really closed, and most agree that in practice judges continued to produce novel rulings. It remains true that freedom of thought and novel ideas declined after the tenth century, along with some socioeconomic decline, and that law became more rigid than it had been earlier.

One example of attitudes toward women is the changed interpretation in medieval times of the story of Adam and Eve. The Quran speaks of Adam and his wife but neither names her nor says how she was created. It was to Adam that Satan (Iblis) whispered that the tree was forbidden, and when the couple ate of it, they perceived their shame and covered themselves, and Iblis caused the expulsion. Adam and his wife asked God for forgiveness. Quranic narratives regarding this event vary, but the man and woman are treated equally. Later Muslim interpretations depart from this, using biblical and Judeo-Christian stories to greatly change it, especially regarding woman's role. Medieval writings emphasize hadiths that blame Eve, and by implication women, for the weakness and guile that enabled Satan to bring about Adam's downfall. God's curse on woman was the most severe, worsening the nature and intelligence of women for all time to come. Because Eve tempted God's servant and made the Tree bleed when she picked its fruit, she was condemned to bleed once a month, to carry and deliver children against her will, and often to be close to death at delivery. God also made women foolish, though he had created her wise and intelligent.

Women in some Islamic sayings and writings became Satan's tools, cursed by moral, mental, and physical deficiency. Men embodied human conscience, having repented, become free of God's curse, and been forgiven. Variations in Traditions involved special points, like stress on the evil of nudity, which has remained strong. One later hadith attributed to the Prophet said, "If I were to order anyone to prostrate himself before another but God, I would command the woman to prostrate herself before her husband because of the magnitude of his rights over her." Another hadith says that "woman was created from a crooked rib. If you set out to straighten her, you will break her, and if you leave her alone while there is crookedness in her, you will enjoy her." The Eve story in these hadiths was believed to demonstrate women's lower moral, mental, and physical nature, and the consensus of the ulama supported and perpetuated this teaching as part of the faith.[11]

The idea of women as the "rope of Satan" exists among some Muslims down to today. It has strong precursors in Christian, Jewish, and other traditions that influenced Islam, and is not unique to Islam, though it has lasted longer in the Middle East than in most of the West, owing in part to later modernization of the Middle East. Religious doctrine was one among several factors that justified practices of discrimination against women, practices that may originally have stemmed largely from the hierarchical nature of society and desires to assure male control of households, certainty of paternity, and the perceived purity of genealogical lines.

Along with restrictive hadiths and new interpretations of religious stories to denigrate women, there were similar interpretations of historical events, notably A'isha's failed leadership in the first Islamic civil war and her defeat in the Battle of the Camel. This was taken, among both Shi'is and Sunnis, to mean that women should not enter into politics and public life, and that their advice should not be sought on such matters. The first Shi'i imam, Ali, whose election as fourth caliph elicited A'isha's enmity, in the popular book of sayings attributed to him speaks against women, especially in public life. Some Traditions see women as *fitna*, or "source of temptation or chaos," or even as predominant among the inhabitants of hell owing to their lack of reason. Some cite Muhammad as warning against female rule. Not all such Traditions were tied to A'isha, but misogynist interpretations of her role are found as early as the first collections of Traditions in the ninth century, and, like the reinterpretations of the role of Eve, contributed to a negative view of women endorsed in medieval Islamic texts.[12] This view had many parallels elsewhere, including in Judaism and Christianity, and should not be taken to mean that average women were normally treated as if they were evil causes of major trouble. Hadiths on women's inferiority and evil were questioned especially from the eighteenth century on, with reformers stressing the Quranic idea of the full personhood of women. More gender-egalitarian hadiths have recently been emphasized by feminist scholars.

Like many premodern peoples and religions, Islam included concepts of the religious uncleanliness of menstruating women. Menstruating women were exempted from prayer and fasting, and were, like the sick, asked to make up for fast days later. (Muslims must fast from sunrise to sundown for the whole holy month of Ramadan.) The belief in women's inferiority encompassed women's testimony in court having half the value of a man's, the evidence of two women being needed to equal that of one man, and limitations on women's travel and work and conditions on their pilgrimage to the holy Arabian cities. While learned discussions of sex, like those of other matters, varied over time, most followed Aristotle in seeing women's bodies as defective male bodies, and active penetration as superior to sexual reception.

MARRIAGE, DIVORCE, CHILD CUSTODY

Although detailed information is not available for the early centuries, what we do know is congruent with later widespread patterns, and may be reconstructed with fair certainty. As in many historical civilizations, a first marriage was the most important set event in the lifetime of women, and it often involved time-consuming efforts by whole families, and especially the father and mother of the bride. A major job for them, and especially the mother, was to find a suitable match, in family, status, and economic prospects, for their offspring and to bargain with their prospective in-laws over the marriage conditions and contract. Sometimes female matchmakers or go-betweens were employed. Bridegrooms had to provide a major dower, which, from early times until now, has meant that many men married late. The bride also brought a substantial trousseau to the marriage, even though she usually went to live in her husband's parents' home. Unlike the situation in the Christian West, which valorized celibacy, in the Muslim Middle East marriage has been virtually universal for women, and as far as we can tell, premenopausal divorced women could often find new husbands. There was probably a surplus of men, owing mainly to polygamy among some of the elite. The favoring of paternal cousin marriage meant that some boys and girls had met their future spouses when they were small children and had some protection against the vagaries of marriage with a complete stranger.[13] In premodern times most people lived in villages or towns where people knew one another and distant migrations were infrequent, so it was rare for a bride to move far from her first home, which she normally visited.

Marriage in Islam is not a sacrament but is based on a civil contract, whose parties are the bridegroom and the bride's guardian (*wali*), who is normally her closest male relative. The sunna recommends that the bride should consent, but silence is considered agreement by a virgin bride. The widespread Hanafi school of law allows an adult woman to arrange her own marriage, provided it is to a man of her rank with an adequate dower. Fatemeh Etemad Moghadam, in agreement with many scholars of Muslim law, says in summary: "Legally a woman's entitlement in marriage includes her dower (*mahriyeh*) and upkeep (*nafaqeh*). From a legal point of view, a Muslim marriage contract . . . is essentially a sale contract, and the object of sale is female sexuality and reproductive labor."[14] Unlike the situation in much Western law until recently, the wife retains property rights, and she does not have a legal responsibility to contribute financially to the household. The required male dower was usually smaller when a bride married a paternal cousin, remaining in the paternal family group. In many cases the dower was and is divided into an immediate payment and a delayed one, in case of divorce or death of the husband. The status and desirability of the bride helped determine the size of the dower; widows and divorced women commanded lower dowers. In some schools of law, marriage contracts could contain conditions, such as one forbidding a husband to take a second wife without the first wife's permission, but such conditions were rarely added.

Islamic law requires separate living space for each wife, which was one reason why multiple marriages were chiefly the prerogative of the wealthy. Men could have any number of slave concubines. Shi'i men could also have temporary wives. Temporary marriages had a contract, often oral, with a smaller dower, which set the marriage at anywhere from minutes to ninety-nine years. Children of these marriages were legitimate. Though such marriages were often looked down on, and brief ones often considered "legalized prostitution," this institution served other needs, including long-term marriage, easier remarriage for some widows and divorcées, and fictitious marriages that enabled more males and females in a household to see and speak to one another.[15]

Muslim men may marry women "People of the Book" (Jews, Christians, Zoroastrians, and Sabeans), but Muslim women cannot marry non-Muslims. As conversion to Islam is easy, many non-Muslim men, past and present, convert to marry Muslim women. After divorce, a woman must wait three months before remarrying (to avoid uncertain paternity in case of pregnancy). Puberty is a condition of marriage, but there is a difference in legal opinions as to when it occurs, with some schools setting it very low for girls.

Husbands are responsible for providing their wives with shelter, food, and clothing. By law a wife cannot be made to contribute to household work or expenses, although those who could not afford servants certainly had to do heavy domestic labor. The wife retains control of her own property and can freely dispose of it, thus having a far more favorable position regarding property than Western women until quite recently.

Some Traditions and legal interpretations give husbands authority over wives' possessions, particular sexual behaviors toward him, and movements, including leaving the house. These probably reflect widespread customs in some regions. Other Traditions, however, urge men to treat their wives well.

The word zina', often translated "adultery," means any sexual relations outside marriage or slaveholding, thus including fornication, adultery, rape, and homosexuality, which were sometimes given various individual defining terms. Adultery is punishable for both men and women, with the Quran prescribing a hundred lashes. Hadiths with the force of law, attributed to the Prophet, said that both should be stoned to death. Stoning for adultery was part of Jewish law, and there is strong evidence that it, like many other laws, came into Muslim law from Jewish law.[16] Punishment was, however, greatly restricted by the Quranic demand (4:19) that four eyewitnesses to the adulterous act must testify to it, with a fourfold confession later allowed, while an accuser who could not produce four witnesses was lashed for slander. A husband can call on God to witness the truth of his allegation, but his wife can do the same. The strict four-witness limitation followed an incident that caused gossip and attacks on A'isha. Partly because of these conditions, the court records we have from later periods indicate stoning to death was very seldom invoked, and many court records suggest that cases concerning adultery were very rarely brought to court.

More common were familial punishments based on tribal codes of honor, which might punish or, more rarely, kill girls and women suspected of misconduct. The woman's brother or father usually did the deed, though in some areas and cases it was the husband. This is one of many indications of the primacy of the patrilineal family. The patrilineal family also had a positive role for the married woman in providing her with natal family intervention, a place of refuge for a mistreated wife, and a home for a divorced or deserted one. The rarity of stoning and the occurrence of extralegal honor killings are examples of a more general point about Islamic law regarding women—that its prescriptions were sometimes altered or even ignored in most times and places for which we have records, as indicated especially by recent studies on various parts of the Ottoman

Empire. Also, studies of current law courts show that real circumstances were often altered to fit the law—this also happens in Western law.

A marriage could be dissolved by divorce, the most common form of which was *talaq*, repudiation of the wife by the husband. After a man pronounces the formula of repudiation twice, he can still take it back, but after the third time the divorce is valid. If the man desires later to remarry the same woman, she must first have a consummated marriage with another, then a divorce, before she can go back to the first husband. Some men undertake this required intermediary marriage and divorce procedure for a fee.

Women's right to divorce is far more limited, and unlike men's requires the intermediary of a court. *Khul'*, redemption, allows the wife to purchase her freedom from a consenting husband with a sum often equal to her dower. Some men wanting a divorce behave so badly that their wives will be forced to buy one. A number of provisions, varying by law school, such as certain illnesses, long desertion, and severe mistreatment, also allow women to divorce. Some marriage contracts can be written to allow divorce under certain conditions, such as a second marriage or severe beating, but this possibility has not been widely used. After divorce the father or his family get legal guardianship of children, though the mother gets custody of minor children until an age that varies by legal school, with the Maliki school, prevalent in North Africa, having the oldest ages. Then they revert to the father or his family. (Fathers' custody of children was also standard in the West until quite recently.) This has made many mothers reluctant to do anything that might make their husbands divorce them. There were some important obstacles to divorce, mainly the economic and social investment of the families involved in finding a good alliance and their reluctance to undo this arrangement. There was also the divorcing husband's obligation to pay whatever was still owed from the dower. Dower was lower for noninitial marriages, and divorced or widowed women had greater control over their marriage partner and conditions than did virgin brides.

Hadiths indicate that in the first centuries women took advantage of their right to pray in mosques, though separately from men. Other Traditions oppose women's presence in mosques, and in most of the Middle East women stopped going to mosques.

WOMEN'S LIVES AND CODES OF HONOR OVER THE CENTURIES

While there is little documentation about medieval Islamic women's lives other than law, Traditions, and literature, we may infer from such sources and from the spread of certain practices throughout the entire Middle

East that some practices go back far in time even though they are well documented only after the medieval period. The normal or average situation of most women has involved both male dominance and age dominance, in which women continued to have important spheres of autonomy and often power and respect. Evidence mainly from later centuries suggests certain prevalent patterns. Girls had special contact with their mothers, whom they helped with household and other work. Girls usually entered arranged marriages soon after puberty. A bride brought the groom's dower and her own household gifts to the marriage. After marriage she entered the husband's family's household, where she had to work hard and was dominated by her new family, especially her mother-in-law. A bride's status was precarious until she produced sons, but if she did, her position improved and ties to her sons gave her increasing power. Once a son married and she became a powerful mother-in-law in turn and, especially after menopause rendered her no longer a threat to lineage purity, her freedom of speech and movement improved. Most women had satisfactions coming from their social life and visiting with other women and from important roles in their families and productive activities. Women's reaction to oppression, insofar as we hear of it, usually centered on fear of divorce and polygamy and lack of protection from abusive husbands. Partly as a result of negative texts and lore about women, some women were treated as untrustworthy inferiors and women in abusive families might have little protection, though some could find temporary or permanent refuge with their natal families.

Another set of beliefs, with less scriptural foundation, is usually called Honor and Shame, although "shame," as a desired attitude for women, also comprises "modesty." Such beliefs are found in many Mediterranean societies with tribal backgrounds, and have little connection with original Islam, though those who hold these beliefs may consider them Islamic. They occur in societies with extended patriarchal tribal kinship units, which often follow their own customary laws more than Islamic laws. Many people, especially in rural and tribal areas, were only partly governed by Islamic rulers and rules, and followed the rules of their own kin groups. In some tribal areas this is still true. Honor and modesty codes vary from region to region but overall are so similar in large regions of the Middle East that it is likely that they go back far in time.

In this code the honor of the patrilineal family is crucial to that extended family's respect and power. Family honor includes good behavior, strength, and uprightness for men, but depends primarily on the perceived good behavior of its females. This involves modest deportment, no mixing with unrelated males, deference and obedience to males, modest dress, and eschewing all behavior that could cast doubt on the virginity of girls or the fidelity of married women. Not only chastity and fidelity are crucial, but also the avoidance of looks, gestures, or words that could lead others to doubt the chastity of a girl or woman. Boys and girls in traditional surroundings are socialized into this code of behavior, which involves deference for women and superior attitudes and sometimes public aggressiveness by men. If doubt is cast on a girl or woman, it is usually up to the agnatic relatives, especially brothers, to wipe out the stain by punishing, or even killing, the offending females. Though we do not know how many girls and women suffered honor killings, it appears that such killings are far rarer than are the relevant suspicions, and that usually another solution is found. The possibility, especially in some tribal areas and villages, of such a sanction is, however, a strong deterrent to any hint of misbehavior. Honor killings are carried out mainly in poorer areas with tribal connections, and there is much evidence of unpunished nonmarital sexual relations throughout Islamic history.

Family punishment for breaking the honor code is not sanctioned by the Quran, which marked a break with tribal law and practices. Indeed, as noted, the Quran makes conviction on a charge of adultery so difficult as to be almost impossible. Even if proven, adultery was to be punished, according to the Quran, by lashes. Later Islamic law sanctioned stoning to death, but this was very rare, and unknown in several periods. The continuation of honor code punishments or threats of punishment suggests the continued importance of local, especially tribal, customs in many matters, especially where Islamic rule and law courts were distant. The difficulty of enforcing the rigid conditions of Islamic law for proving adultery may also have encouraged honor codes. Through the centuries there have been conflicts between those who enforced Islamic law and those who followed tribal or local rules. Islamic judges sometimes spoke out against local and familial enforcement of customary rules regarding sexual behavior.

The patrilineal extended family was in many ways more important than the marital family. Girls were often close to their brothers and fathers, and might return to their paternal homes in case of divorce or widowhood. There was a widespread custom whereby a wife might show her displeasure with her husband by returning to her paternal family until her husband negotiated a satisfactory solution with her. This may seem surprising in societies where a husband could divorce a wife simply by a thrice-stated declaration, but divorce was often avoided, especially as it might involve returning to the wife part of the substantial male dower.[17] Although a girl left her home to live with her husband's family, her natal family was often her chief protector. It was common in rural and tribal areas for a woman not to get the property due her by Islamic law on her father's death, but there was often an implicit bargain to the effect that she retained a claim for support from her paternal family in case of need.

CLASS AND SLAVERY

The early medieval period saw an increase in status gaps between men and women and among different classes of society. Such stratification reflected the growing economic surplus and urbanization. Seclusion of women was characteristic of urban society rather than of the rural or tribal lives still lived by most Middle Easterners. Prosperity was also a major factor in the increase in male and especially female slavery that characterized the Middle East from this period onward. Slavery and concubinage were recognized in the Quran, which, however, recommends good treatment of slaves and sees the emancipation of slaves as a virtuous act. Muslims were not to be enslaved, and slaves in the early period were mostly war captives or those born as slaves. Later, there was a centuries-long slave trade between Christian and Muslim countries, though the African slave trade and black slaves came to be dominant from later medieval times onward, except for some specialized positions. Slaves sometimes were exploited in large-scale production, but were mostly domestic or employed in commerce. New slaves were in theory, and mostly in practice, taken from among non-Muslims beyond the Islamic borders. Female slaves were largely domestic workers, sexual partners, and entertainers. Slave girls and boys were often trained as singers, dancers, and musical performers. In various periods there was cross-dressing by male, and in some cases by female, entertainers.

In Islamic law men could have sexual relations with female slaves. Males could take their own slave women as concubines, and throughout history some slave wives were important figures. Some slave women who were concubines of rulers or other powerful men became powerful themselves, as was also true of some nonslave wives. Abdelwahab Bouhdiba plausibly argues that concubines, who often had greater training and education in the arts and greater access to the outside world than did wives, and were more freely chosen by their masters, often were more attractive to males than were wives, and rivalries and alliances were not only among wives, but among all women to whom a man had sexual access.[18] Women's influence, whether slave or free, was often constructed by writers as a factor in the decline or disarray of dynasties, from Abbasid down to Ottoman dynasties, an idea that has been revised by recent scholars.

From Abbasid times on, male slaves, especially Turks and Caucasians, were used as soldiers, and some of these slave soldiers came to found slave-ruled dynasties in the Middle East and South Asia. Slaves had certain rights. With their master's consent slaves could marry, with male slaves allowed up to two wives, but a slave owner could also force his slaves to marry. Slaves could not be forced into prostitution. The owner of a female slave who had borne her master a child was not allowed to sell her or transfer her, and she became free on her master's death. Legally the children of concubines had the same status as those of free wives. Certain punishments and postmarital waiting periods for slaves differed from those of free persons.

Islam and its laws are widely considered egalitarian, which is true regarding male believers, but discriminatory laws covered women, slaves, unbelievers, and People of the Book. The medieval Muslim world was more egalitarian than the Christian West regarding the equality of believers, male and female, who did not need a clergy; equal legal treatment of free men; lack of formal aristocratic or clerical privileges; encouraging manumission of slaves; and tolerance of some other religions—although egalitarianism did not obviate distinctions of socioeconomic class and social status. Laws prescribed different legal treatment between men and women, between free and slave, and between believer and unbeliever, with People of the Book favored. While slaves and unbelievers might be emancipated or converted, the male-female distinction was unchangeable. This differentiation of groups regarding legal rights is not unique to Islam and existed in Christianity until recently, with slaves, various ethnic groups, and women on some matters facing more unequal treatment in Christian than in Muslim areas.

Probably related to female slavery is most medieval writers' permission of birth control, either by coitus interruptus or various blocking methods, though most said that free women must agree to it. This indicates, as do many sources, that women's sexual nature and needs were recognized. Leila Ahmed argues, however, that this permission of contraception mainly reflected the legal right of children of slaves to inherit, which was disliked by free wives and by many husbands whose free wives were chosen for appropriate family background.[19] The emphasis on free wives' agreement to birth control, however, shows that they were also considered.

Slaves helped enable the seclusion of their female masters, and some urban middle- to upper-class women scarcely left their homes and were heavily covered when they did. Architecture reflected this seclusion, with buildings built low so as not to overlook courtyards or women's quarters. Aside from the very rich and powerful, however, harems did not house multiple wives, concubines, and slaves. Most marriages were monogamous, with multiple wives reserved to a small elite. Most non-Muslims in Muslim-ruled societies had veiling-seclusion customs somewhat similar to the Muslims', although each religious community had particularities in its family law. Our knowledge of the Jewish community shows that their seclusion rules were less strict than the Muslims', and this may have been true of other communities, as it also was of the rural majority of

Muslims and even those urban Muslim women who had to work. Westerners often thought seclusion deprived women of all status, freedom of action, and satisfactions, but direct evidence shows that this was not so, though it did reinforce some problems and inequalities. Covering the body could afford a useful anonymity in other cases.

Regarding property rights, while local customs varied, according to Islamic law free women had a right to control their property and were not obligated to contribute to household expenses, as one of the husband's duties was to support his wife and family. Women's inheritance rights were rarely recognized in rural and tribal areas, where they would have meant passing flocks or lands out of the patrilineal family's control, although sometimes various means were used to give something to daughters, especially personal property upon marriage. One way to avoid inheritance laws was to create a perpetual endowment, or *waqf*, during one's lifetime, administered by one of the ulama. Waqfs could benefit one's descendants, a charitable endowment, or both. Waqfs for descendants were widely used as a means to exclude female heirs, while far fewer favored them. According to Claude Cahen, "We are certain that from the best-known early times until today the institution [waqf] was in fact used to undermine as far as possible the rulings of Muslim succession law in favor of daughters. . . . There seems to be no doubt that the waqf was utilized right away to reinforce the patriarchal family, beyond, or contrary to, Qur'anic law." Joseph Schacht see the exclusion of female Quranic heirs as a main reason for the early rise and rapid spread of waqfs.[20] Some women, however, endowed waqfs, and there have been studies of women's waqfs, including those that went to building monuments.[21]

In Islamic law, women were owed financial support and sex in marriage, while men were owed obedience and sex on demand. Many less-documented aspects of male-female relations were not included in Islamic law but reflected strong persistent local, and often tribal, customs. Very widespread was extreme concern over female virginity and chastity, which was the main reason given for female seclusion. In a minority of societies—Egypt and East Africa, and some nearby societies—many girls, both Muslim and non-Muslim, experienced what is best called female genital cutting (henceforth FGC), which where it was practiced often came to be considered Islamic, though it is not in the Quran or Islamic law.

The first Islamic centuries saw limits on the public role of women, increasing seclusion, and the development and enforcement of a male-dominant legal system. That system, however, also protected women's rights in several areas, including property ownership; it provided certain divorce rights, some protection against extreme abuse, and rights to support and sex from the husband. For all the inequalities that Muslim women faced, there were important areas for self-expression, economic activity, and cultural life. Minority branches of Islam and popular religion, and especially the mysticism (closeness to the divine) known as Sufism, often had a far larger role for women and their religious expression than did mainline Islam. The first Muslim saint was a woman Sufi and poet, Rabi'a (d. 801). With the development of large Sufi orders from the late Abbasid period, some had parallel women's groups and a few had women as equal members, though a few others barred women. Among non-Sufis women and male relatives instructed women in various Islamic rituals, and in the later Shi'i world such women religious leaders were called mullas, like their male counterparts, and had a good education. Women's religious life included visits to shrines and saints' tombs, which were also a chance for outings and conversation.[22] Some girls were educated at home or in Quran schools or informal public lessons, with a few women achieving very high levels of education. Many women are named in biographical dictionaries, and they were especially known as experts, teachers, and transmitters of hadiths.

On the social level, aside from extensive home visiting and contact with female tradespeople who came to middle-class homes, there was the important, generally weekly, ritual of the public bath where women gathered for hours to be cleaned and groomed and to talk. Urban women, in addition to their home crafts and textiles, were in some professions, like midwives, bathhouse keepers, and home peddlers, while rural women engaged in a variety of productive activities.

In literature, there were some female authors and poets, and much depiction of women. The popular collection *The Thousand and One Nights* features the brilliant Shahrzad, whose tales save the lives of untold young women destined to be killed in vengeance for one wife's infidelity. Many of the stories present women as interesting and clever but unfaithful and driven by sexual passions.[23] Other literary works, including several Persian poems, have a more exalted view of women and of unrequited or difficult loves. It is reasonable to assume that many women composed and recited poetry, but most of these poems have not come down to us.

THE LIVES OF MEDIEVAL WOMEN AS RECORDED IN THE CAIRO GENIZA

Most of the scant documentation about medieval women concerns powerful women rather than ordinary ones. Unique in telling about the lives of both elite and nonelite men and women is the mass of documents of the Jewish community in Cairo from the tenth through the thirteenth centuries known as the Cairo Geniza. These included letters, bills, and other everyday writings; the community did not want to destroy them, as they might include the name of God or holy matters, and so they were saved in storehouses. Studied for decades and analyzed especially by S. D. Goitein, these documents give a picture of everyday social life relevant to the Muslim as well as the Jewish community, as the communities often had similar laws and customs, were not residentially ghettoized, and frequently dealt with, and influenced, one another. Unfortunately, we have no such sources from Muslim communities in this period.

According to Goitein, there was a decline in the position of women in Jewish and other ancient Mediterranean communities when they became Hellenized: "Popular Greek scientific theory combined with ancient Near Eastern prejudices to reduce the stature and activity of women. . . . In Judaism, the exclusion of women from the study of Scripture, which was the main expression of piety, inevitably had a degrading effect."[24] After antiquity, the Jewish community became overwhelmingly urban. In the medieval period, although seclusion of women was stricter in Islam than in Christianity and Judaism, the Iranian and Iraqi Jewish communities insisted on housing seclusion. But Jews who had migrated to Syria, Egypt, and North Africa developed different customs, along with their growing affluence, especially in Egypt, where Muslims, too, were less strict. Visitors to Egypt from stricter Muslim regions "were shocked by the easygoing ways of the Egyptian capital, where wine was publicly sold and women enjoyed much freedom."[25] Some considered the Muslim women of Cairo licentious. Jewish laws regarding women were theoretically the same everywhere, but, as was true in Islam, laws might be modified in practice by local custom.

Many economic conditions recorded in the Geniza were also found among Muslims. The documents contain references to women entering the workforce only beginning in the twelfth century, and by the next century some persons voice concern that women had to work owing to economic need. Few, ill-paid, professions were open to women. Many widowed or divorced women had to deal with men to work or receive community welfare payments. Women held wealth mainly via gifts and inheritance, and owned and managed all forms of immovable property. Middle- and upper-class women bought and sold slaves. Some Jewish women were slaves, and some became concubines. Women often had commercial experience, and were frequently appointed as legal guardians of their children and executors of estates. Nonetheless, women were normally restricted to certain entrepreneurial roles—real estate, moneylending, and buying and selling women's goods. They were not in large-scale production and exchange. Most women were dependent on men economically, and few were literate.

Like Muslim women, Jewish women appeared for themselves in court, though some women and men appointed representatives to appear for them. Few women accompanied their husbands on long business trips, but they traveled to visit relatives, shrines, and Jerusalem. Probably like Muslims, urban Jews generally brought grain to mills to be ground, and bought bread at bakeries. Because fuel was expensive, whole meals were bought outside. Girls cared for younger siblings and were married in their teens, and boys began to work young. Middle-class families usually had a slave maidservant. The most often mentioned women's occupation was embroidery, and women also spun, wove, and sewed. Great pride was taken in a beautiful wardrobe and trousseau. Household errands were done by a servant or husband, but women handled the purchase and sale of textiles.

Women went to the synagogue and they frequented bathhouses about once a week, which was a major social event. (Muslim women early stopped attending mosques, but their visits to bathhouses, relatives, celebrations, and shrines were quite similar to those of Jewish women.) Weddings, childbirth, mourning, and visits to family and friends gave reasons to leave the home. A minority of both Jewish and Muslim women were independent of men.

Christian and Jewish women were required to cover their hair and dress modestly, but were not obliged to veil their faces and could talk to non-family men. The Geniza shows that an unrelated Jewish male could discuss economic matters with a woman without her husband's being present. The churches and synagogues of old Cairo (Fustat) had women's galleries, and men and women mixed in the court. Jewish homes had no separate women's sections.

Jews resembled Muslims in limiting sex to marriage and expecting everyone to marry. Concubinage with slaves was legal but discouraged, and was affordable only to the wealthy. References to adultery and prostitution are rare.[26] Polygamy was legal, but not widespread, and some marriage contracts forbade it. It might occur when a wife had no children in ten years of marriage, or if she was unable to care for her children. An already-married brother had to make the required levirate marriage to his widowed sister-in-law. One group of Egypt's religious authorities ruled against polygamy, asserting that such a brother had to divorce his existing wife. Marital disagreements were often submitted to legal authorities for rulings. There were several legal safeguards for women. Jews, like Muslims, put great emphasis on having sons and grandsons:

> No letter has yet been found in which a father is congratulated on the birth of a girl, or in which God is invoked to look after a man's daughter. At the birth of a girl, the father (or the family) is congratulated on the mother's . . . "deliverance" . . . from death or other harm in childbirth. Only once, in a letter of a sister . . . are good wishes expressed for a newly born niece, and lovely

things are said about the addressee's daughters. But even there, the wish is that God grant the letter's recipient something "to lift up his heart, namely, a manchild."[27]

As among Muslims, daughters had to be endowed with goods upon marriage, when they entered another family and did not perpetuate their natal family line or add to its property. There were thus practical reasons among both Jews and Muslims for preferring boys, and family continuity was seen as passing only through the male line. This does not mean that daughters were not treated with affection among both Jews and Muslims.

From the Geniza we have more information about Jewish widows than about their often similar Muslim neighbors. For women without substantial property or businesses, widowhood could be a calamity. However, widowhood or divorce freed some better-off women to be independent in financial and other matters, and to choose a husband and marriage conditions. Widows often had great difficulty collecting anything from their late husband's estate. Some lived with adult sons, but most persons who needed public welfare were women.[28]

Despite social and religious discouragement of divorce, it was relatively common. In Jewish, like Islamic, law the husband had the right of unilateral repudiation, and by the time of the Geniza only the husband's actions could bring legal divorce. As happened in Islamic khul', some wives got their husbands to repudiate them by renouncing what was due them from dowry and gifts. There were some provisions for child support.

Husbands inherited from wives but not vice versa. For most of the Geniza period daughters and sons usually inherited equal shares, despite Jewish laws favoring sons. In the thirteenth century the Muslim government began to intervene in Jewish matters, and fathers might leave half shares to daughters to accord with Muslim law. Girls and married women had guardians or male relatives who administered their financial affairs. Many women whose husbands died were left destitute, their daughters the poorest of the poor, with few chances for a good marriage though most did marry. People preferred slaves as domestic servants to orphans who might marry and leave.

From the Turkish and Mongol Invasions to 1798

Turks, Mongols, and Mamluks: New Rulers and Gender Attitudes

The northern tribal and steppe peoples who increasingly came to rule and populate the Middle East from the eleventh century on had more egalitarian practices regarding women, at least for the elites that have left documentary records, than did either the pre-Islamic Near Eastern empires or the indigenous tribal peoples. This was part of an overall difference between these two groups of tribes recently analyzed with emphasis on the different ecology and history of the northern invaders and their greater ability to set up long-lived empires.[1] The nomadic Turks, who had earlier spread from eastern China to the northern borders of the Middle East, entered the Middle East first as slave soldiers, a position from which they came to control several local dynasties that arose under the Abbasids. Important migration into the Middle East of Turkish tribal peoples came with the internal decline of the Abbasids and the creation of smaller autonomous states in Iran and elsewhere, which facilitated the invasion and conquest of much of southwest Asia by Turks. These invasions, which included migration into the Middle East of nomadic Turkish peoples, began with the Seljuks from the eleventh century on, and continued for several centuries. Several states with Turkish (and later some Mongol) rulers were created in Iran, Anatolia, Afghanistan, central Asia, and south Asia. Most of them became largely Iranian in high culture and used Persian as the elite or court language, and Iranians provided much of their bureaucracy. Their high culture had both Turkish and Iranian influences, along with Islamic and local ones. Turkish impact on the status of women seems to have been felt mainly among the Turks and some others in the ruling group, the only group for whom we have significant documentation.

Among the Seljuks and later Turkish- and Mongol-ruled dynasties, women often played a powerful public role as relatives of rulers, participated in administration, horseback prowess, and warfare, and sometimes became de facto rulers.[2] This reflected pre-Islamic practices of their ancestors and the continuing consideration of female and male members of tribes and clans as having virtually equal status. The Mongol invasions of the early thirteenth century actually brought in more Turks than Mongols as soldiers, though the Mongols ruled. Like the Turks, the Mongols were a tribal nomadic people among whom women had an important public role, however negative other aspects of the destructive Mongol conquest were.

Among the widespread dynasties that arose from Turkish groups was the Iranian Safavid dynasty (1501–1722), whose military forces were mainly Turkish-tribal and who had two de facto women rulers in the sixteenth century. In the epic stories of these Turkish tribes the "women have great freedom and . . . do not sit passively in their tents. Moreover . . . they control their own finances."[3] As stated by Maria Szuppe, one of several scholars of this phenomenon:

> Turko-Mongol nomadic cultural tradition, as compared with Irano-Islamic customs of settled people, gave a much larger place to women's social and political activities and to family blood ties on both paternal and maternal sides. Among the Mongols and Ilkhans . . . female members of ruling families enjoyed a privileged position. They were entitled to a share of booty and had the right to participate in the *qurıltay*, the all-Mongol assembly. Not only did they become regents of their minor sons, but also under certain circumstances they could themselves lay claim to the throne. Even after Islamization progressed . . . women retained much of their social position.[4]

Guity Nashat adds that "lively participation was especially characteristic of the wives of the great Mongol Ilkhans, whose exploits are recounted in Rashid al-Din's . . . *Universal History.* . . . He justified his departure from the contemporary norms of Islamic society, which left women unmentioned, by explaining that the Mongols accord their women equal treatment."[5]

The Seljuks and later rulers who originated from the steppes and mountains to the north and east of the Islamic Middle East, as did the Egyptian-based Mamluks and the Mongols, converted to Islam either shortly before or after they entered the Middle East, and each group came in time to be, if they settled, practicing Muslims and largely to conform to Middle Eastern settled norms, including those regarding the role and position of women. Scholars say that most of the soldiers and tribespeople who came to the Middle East during and after the thirteenth century Mongol conquest were of Turkish origin, and a number married Iranians, so the customs described affected more than Mongols, although Irano-Islamic culture had a counterinfluence over time. Turkish and Kurdish popular religious groups having special practices, like the Bektashi Sufi order, the Alevis of Anatolia, and the Ahl-e Haqq of Iranian Kurdistan continued until modern times to have largely equal participation of often unveiled women in their activities. Most of the conquered non-Turkic peoples were less affected in their gender relations by Turkish conquest than were some

Turkic or Kurdish groups. Those tribespeople who remained nomadic after entering the Middle East, however, as well as many indigenous tribespeople, often retained powerful public positions for women, who, as is reported of their medieval ancestors, often rode, fought, and did most of the physical labor of the tribe, while leading women often took command in the absence of their husbands.

The famous fourteenth-century Arab traveler Ibn Batuta, starting out from a world where women were veiled, secluded, and kept from public assertiveness, notes with distaste a few Islamic peoples among whom he observed a freer and more assertive role of women. Of the Turks he says:

> A remarkable thing which I saw . . . was the respect shown to women by the Turks, for they hold a more dignified position than the men. [There follows a description of the rich garments and respected treatment of a princess and her retinue.] I also saw the wives of the merchants and commonality. One of them will sit in a wagon which is being drawn by horses, attended by three or four maidens to carry her train, and on her head she wears a conical headdress incrusted with pearls and surmounted by peacock feathers. The windows of the tent are open and her face is visible, for the Turkish women do not veil themselves. Sometimes a woman will be accompanied by her husband and any-one seeing him would take him for one of her servants; he has no garment other than a sheep's wool cloak and a high cap to match.[6]

Other sources tell of the participation of Turkish and Mongol women in battle and in rule, something that was found as late as the early periods of the Turkish-ruled Safavid and Ottoman Empires. As time went on, strong women tended to exert influence from within the harem rather than in public, but in both the Ottoman and Safavid Empires the influence of royal mothers and wives sometimes amounted to de facto rule. We have no reason to assume that the relatively high position of rulers early in these dynasties was reflected in the way that ordinary women lived, however. We cannot say whether ordinary Turkish women were freer than some other tribal women. The Turkic and Arab tribal custom, probably going back to pre-Islamic times, of kidnapping some brides has different meanings: it may be used by a couple to escape an unwanted arranged marriage, but it can also be a real kidnapping, against the bride's wishes and more unfavorable to her than the usual arranged marriage.

Another source of rule by largely Turkic groups was the military slaves, who came into Muslim armies in large numbers from the ninth century on. Most military slaves were of Turkish origin, and were often purchased or captured as boys and trained both militarily and in Islam. Unlike the Egyptian Mamluks, these were not usually freed, although at times manu-mission did take place. In some cases they took over as rulers, as did the

Mamluks, who ruled Egypt, Syria, and western Arabia 1250–1517, and among whom some women had important roles. Although "Mamluk" means slave, it was normally used not for ordinary or domestic slaves but for military and governmental slaves, who had a higher status. As they were freed and their children could not inherit rule, their ranks had to be constantly replenished by slaves from non-Muslim territories, mainly Turks, but also others. The first Mamluks defeated the Crusaders and stopped the advance in the Muslim world of the Mongols, who had taken over much of the Middle East and had ended the Abbasid caliphate in 1258. Mamluk rule was long-lived despite the absence of direct dynastic inheritance.

Some authors stress the founder of the Mamluk dynasty, Queen Shajarat al-Durr, of Turkic slave origin, the widow of the last Ayyubid ruler, who took the title of sultan in 1250 after her husband and stepson were killed in the Crusader invasion under Louis IX of France. She ruled for a few years. Her role is subject to controversy, with earlier male historians suggesting she had little independent power or importance, and recent feminist writers listing her as one of the most important women rulers in the Islamic world.[7] According to Wiebke Walther:

> After her subjects had sworn the oath of allegiance to her, she carried on the business of government, signed the Sultan's decrees, and, as usual for an Islamic ruler, was mentioned in the Friday prayers as the sovereign. For the first time in an Islamic country, coins were minted bearing the name of a woman. . . . But then, when the oath of allegiance to the Sultana was required from the Syrian viceroy, a dispute broke out in the course of which the Mamluk Emirs decided that they could not leave the reins of State in the hands of a woman, and transferred power to Aybak, Supreme Commander of the armed forces. Shajarat ad-Durr afterwards became his wife . . . contemporaries continue to describe her as the real regent who did what she wanted with the realm and issued orders which were obeyed . . . when she heard that Aybak intended to take a . . . co-wife, she had her husband murdered.[8]

Some female historians, on balance, agree with earlier male historians that she was essentially a tool of men's politics, however.[9]

Other Mamluk ruling-class women also played important public roles. The Mamluks' tribal and ethnic background in Turkish and Caucasian populations where women's status was high helped make such roles possible, and constant male warfare also created many widows who were well positioned to take over some of their husbands' or brothers' power. However, as noted in the above discussion of Fatimid times, Egyptian women were known for their freedom in speech and action well before the Mamluks, and they can be seen as a documented example of what was without doubt a wider, though less documented, phenomenon—that many Middle Eastern women did not follow the strictures of behavior and rigid sexual segregation that Muslim ulama who wrote about such subjects said they should.

The Mamluk period is one of the first for which extensive documentation remains, and several studies point up the active role of both ruling-class and ordinary urban women. Several Mamluk women were powerful in government; many more controlled property, and some used it to endow important institutions, of which they often served as trustees.[10] Although women endowed and were trustees of the major educational institutions, the madrasas, they did not attend them. Many girls and women were, however, educated, either by family members or in informal public or private groups, sometimes apparently along with men. Women continued to be prominent as hadith specialists.[11] A prominent conservative *alim* (singular of *ulama*) inveighed against activities he said were common in Cairo. These included women's going out in several ways that allowed their being in contact with men, including shopping, frequent group visits to shrines, participation in Sufi group activities, partying and picnicking with their families in public parks, and even receiving unrelated men in their homes. Women were also told they should not be naked in women's baths, as they commonly were. Women were told not to listen to sermons in mosques, to end laxness in veiling, and to stay at home, not even looking out at male activities outside their houses.[12] Such sources show that in Egypt and probably elsewhere women often did not behave or dress in ways that conservative ulama approved. The greater role of women found in documents from the thirteenth century on was due not only to Turkish influence, but also to a greater variety in actual practice than we can confidently infer from scantier references to women in the limited earlier sources.

Women's main role continued to be marriage and bearing and raising children. Cooking and cleaning were, as in other premodern societies, far more laborious and time-consuming than they are today. There were some women's jobs and professions, including such long-standing ones as midwifery, bath attendance, selling merchandise to women in their homes, small trade, some roles in religion and entertainment for other women, and matchmaking, and much domestic service was carried out by slaves, male and female. Many women property owners played active parts in the management of their property or its donation as waqf. Women worked in textiles and carpets, either in the home or in small workshops. Rural and tribal women had a wide range of nondomestic work, in agriculture, food processing, and spinning and weaving. Rural and nomadic women were less secluded than urban ones, but this does not mean that they had better lives. Rural women often were poorer, worked harder in difficult conditions, and had less access to education. Urban women might have access to education; they were more likely to inherit as Islamic law said they should, and more likely to go to court to protect their rights. Many had more varied leisure activities than did rural women.

OTTOMANS AND SAFAVIDS

The Ottoman and the Safavid dynasties dominated the Middle East in the early modern period. The Ottomans, beginning in the early fourteenth century from a small group in Anatolia, in time conquered much of the Balkans and Anatolia, and, with the 1453 conquest of Constantinople, popularly called Istanbul, took over the remaining Byzantine Empire. In the early sixteenth century they conquered most of the Arab world. Theirs became the best-organized and longest-ruled Middle Eastern empire, ending only after World War I. The Ottomans were Sunni Muslims. The Safavids originated in a Sunni Sufi order in Turkish-speaking Iranian Azerbaijan. Fifteenth-century leaders of this order gained followers in eastern Anatolia among tribes who followed popular Shi'ism, and the Safavids became Shi'is. In the early sixteenth century they conquered Iran and made it a Shi'i state, partly to distinguish it from Sunni rivals in the West and East. Iran's identification with Shi'ism dates from the Safavids; earlier most Iranians were Sunnis. Shi'is continued as an important minority in Arab Asia and non-Arab Afghanistan.

In the first periods of Ottoman and Safavid rule royal women kept some of the publicly displayed power they had in Turkic nomadic societies. In the sixteenth century several Ottoman and Safavid women were openly powerful in central and provincial courts. Later their power was more usually expressed from within imperial harems, but even males like the Ottoman sultan and princes were somewhat similarly hidden from the public. The power of royal women remained important and, in the seventeenth-century Ottoman Empire, often decisive.

Until recently, the predominant view was that the Ottoman Empire, after two centuries of expansion and flourishing under strong rulers, declined and ceased to be well ruled after the death of Sultan Süleyman (1520–66), known in the empire as "the lawgiver" because of his issuing major laws and law codes (*kanuns*). This alleged decline has from Ottoman times onward been tied to the rise in power in the subsequent century of the imperial harem's leading women. Recent historians have challenged the decline thesis, and Leslie Peirce's seminal study of the imperial Ottoman harem shows how that institution was a crucial part of the administration, and not a center of sex, idleness, and harmful intrigue. Until Süleyman's time, royal princes were often warriors and provincial governors, and royal marriages were generally used for political purposes. With the transition to a more bureaucratic state, princes were confined to a newly centralized imperial harem, where the sultan's consorts were concubines, not wives, but no less powerful for that. Queen mothers of princes and of sultans were especially powerful, and had ties to the outside world chiefly via eunuchs and powerful sons-in-law, married to princesses. Princes brought up in the harem were much influenced by the women there, especially their mothers. In cases of underage or incompetent sultans queen mothers became regents and de facto rulers. The belief that "harem rule" in the seventeenth century was disastrous for the empire has been effectively challenged, and Peirce sees imperial women as effectively holding together the centers of power in a time when sultans were less able than in earlier times. The imperial harem was a branch of the state, with many young women brought in who were not in sexual relations with anyone but were educated there and then frequently married, often to powerful persons. The harem had a hierarchical organization, running the full gamut from domestic slaves, who were often manumitted, to the senior queen mother. As in other powerful institutions, there were inner conflicts, especially regarding future rulers. Peirce's study shows that the frequent division of the Muslim world into public (male) and private (female) and the view that women's power was either nonexistent or nefarious are wrong.[13] Simpler but similar structures were found in Ottoman provincial harems and in Safavid central and provincial harems, where leading women were more influential on policy than past historians have realized.[14]

Many recent scholars have utilized extensive legal and other archives found in Istanbul and other Ottoman cities to shed more light on Ottoman history, including that of women and families, than is available for earlier periods. Among useful documents are court records and documents of pious foundations. Research on women was pioneered in articles and chapters by male scholars, and has been greatly extended in books and articles mainly by women.[15]

Archival sources show that women came, or sent representatives, to courts more frequently than was previously imagined, and that qadis tended to protect women's Islamic legal rights to inheritance, property, and legal treatment in marriage and divorce. Neither law nor judgments were gender-egalitarian, but they did tend to uphold women's legal and property rights and were not instruments to increase gender inequalities beyond those in law. Writings based on such documents are crucial to the study of Middle Eastern women, gender, and the family.[16]

Some of these works underline that age hierarchies were as important as gender hierarchies, with older women exercising much control over young males and females, and with young men "often as vulnerable and powerless as young women. With maturity, women, as well as men, acquired positions of greater authority and responsibility. Moreover, short life spans and male mortality sometimes made women de facto heads of households."[17] This was especially true in Egypt, where the manumitted military slaves sometimes called Mamluks continued to be powerful after the Ottomans conquered Egypt in 1516. Their frequent internal conflicts brought early death, leaving much property to their widows. Women in eighteenth-century Egypt were highly involved in trade and agricultural management, and this was reversed with the nineteenth-century centralization and modernization that began with Muhammad Ali.[18]

Some note that despite the value of Ottoman legal records, they fall far short of completely reflecting reality (much like U.S. court records of the causes for divorce when divorce was permitted only for reasons that plaintiffs tried to fit). Annelies Moors writes:

> The relation between the information provided by written sources and the reality of social practice always must be questioned. . . . With respect to court actions, authors have pointed out that women may turn to a court to ask one thing . . . in order to get something else . . . women's turning to the court . . . may have divergent meanings . . . it may . . . point to the lack of any other viable options . . . women's access to property does not necessarily imply gendered power; women may claim their share of an inheritance because they find themselves in a highly problematic situation rather than as an expression of strength.[19]

Judith Tucker notes that in Ottoman Syria and Palestine legal cases seldom dealt with real or suspected sexual transgressions by girls or women, which were, despite discouragement by Muslim jurists, mostly dealt with by families.[20] Sexual transgressions were covered in Muslim law, but some Ottoman rulings explicitly or implicitly left punishments to family members.[21] How often male relatives punished or even killed girls and women accused of transgressions is unknown from past legal records. The picture suggested by recent Ottoman studies is one where women had legal protections if they went to court, but these courts' judgments may have been less important to many women, especially in the popular classes, than were customary practices.

Whether or not their practice was connected to their Turkish background, some Ottoman sultans issued important laws and legal collections that were more favorable to women than was shari'a law. While the sultans recognized most of the shari'a regarding women, and did not explicitly try to change it, several sultans issued laws (kanuns) that changed the legal status of women and continued in force after the sultan's death. Kanuns issued under Sultan Süleyman prescribed punishments for violent sex crimes against women, including abduction and harassment, which were usually ignored in contemporary shari'a compilations. Punishment for fornication, which mostly fell on women, was reduced from execution in some cases to a fine. Indeed, the kanuns favored fines, often higher for higher-status persons, or at most banishment, as punishments, and physical punishments and executions were rare. (Research in other periods indicates that, before recent "Islamic" rules in a few states, death penalties for fornication or adultery were extremely rarely imposed by courts, owing partly to the Quran's virtually impossible conditions for conviction, and that women had more to fear from extralegal "honor killings," even though they, too, were uncommon.) Women were viewed by the kanuns as independent agents, equal to men regarding culpability and financial means. Historians have debated the influence of kanun laws in the administration of justice, but Leslie Peirce shows that in fornication cases in Anatolian towns and villages the kanuns played a significant role, and the same is probably true elsewhere.[22]

Recent work on Ottoman and Safavid times and later shows some conditions regarding sexuality that research suggests also existed in earlier periods. Despite Islam's theoretical strict lines between male and female and prohibition of homosexuality, it was practiced and is documented especially for the elite classes, among whom the "active" role was considered masculine, and young adolescent boys were regarded as sexually similar to girls and women. Female homosexuality is less documented, but has left some Ottoman, Safavid, and earlier evidence.[23] Surprisingly to many, it was only with modern and Western influences that homosexuality came to be widely condemned among classes whose members had formerly, often rather openly, practiced it. Only then did practices change, and pederasty and cross-dressing by boys and women came to be frequently condemned. (These condemnations were bolstered by similar preexisting condemnations in strict Islam.) Both sexual behavior and language came in modern times to be subject to limits that were more Victorian than traditional. Modern women, supported by male reformists, put forth new views of marriage and objected to their husbands' homosexual affairs and preoccupations. Modern limits also reflect the increasing number of women entering the public sphere and the rise in mixed-sex audiences for written and oral forms of expression. Language limits affected the educated classes and mixed-sex audiences more than the common people and single-sex gatherings.[24] Contradictory stereotypes of premodern Middle Eastern society as either having the strictest of gender limits or being almost unqualifiedly tolerant of homosexuality are being revised and refined on the basis of new scholarship on important parts of society.

Mamluk, Safavid, and Ottoman documents show that women, especially upper-class women, held considerable urban land, controlled significant amounts of money, engaged in many kinds of trade, and managed businesses. Secluded women sometimes used agents to conduct business, and women were active in property management and speculation, and in providing capital for trade, business, and construction. Women in the Ottoman imperial harem financed important buildings, many of which were used for social services. Women were also prominent in making waqf endowments, which often had female administrators and beneficiaries.[25] Women went, or sent representatives, to courts, and there in business and financial matters had essentially the same rights as men in presenting and often winning cases. Less information is available about poorer women.

WESTERN VIEWS OF MIDDLE EASTERN MUSLIM WOMEN

Western attitudes toward Islam and the Middle East often emphasized condemnation of the treatment of women, and rarely more sympathetic or nuanced views. Hostility in the Christian West to the Muslim Middle East in both medieval and Ottoman times was largely based on military threats and on seeing Muslims as followers of a false prophet. Much was made of Muhammad's supposed sexual appetites. Polygamy, veiling, seclusion, and harems were attacked through the ages, Muslim women were often seen as little more than slaves, and there were fantasies about imagined hypersexual harems and the prevalence of homosexuality.

There was much projection onto Muslims of Western characteristics, including aggressiveness and religious intolerance, despite the gratuitous slaughter of many peaceful Muslims in the Crusades and Spain's expulsion of Muslims, which have no equivalent involving Muslim perpetrators. Until recent times Christians were far less religiously tolerant than Muslims, who recognized a place in society for monotheists and often for others, and yet Christians saw Muslims as intolerant. Europeans were long convinced that their women had a uniformly higher position than Middle Eastern women, even though this was not true regarding property ownership, involvement in business, inheritance, legal cases, and some possibility for divorce. Westerners assumed that sexual segregation and seclusion meant terrible oppression of women, whereas court documents demonstrate more women's independent activity regarding wealth and property than existed in the contemporary West.[26] Westerners sometimes projected onto Muslim society their own sexual fantasies, based on ignorance of Muslim women.

Some women who wrote about the Ottoman Empire, especially in the eighteenth century—notably Ladies Mary Montagu and Elizabeth

Craven—had a different view. The men who wrote about Middle Eastern women seldom had contact with them, while Lady Mary did and entered into upper-class harem activities. She compared Ottoman women's position favorably to that of Western women, especially in their owning and controlling property, having social lives she saw as free and positive, and even using the head-to-toe outer garment as a means to hide sexual affairs.[27] Elizabeth Craven said, "I think I never saw a country where women enjoy so much liberty, and free from all reproach, as in Turkey. . . . The Turks in their conduct towards our sex are an example to all other nations."[28] These women were reacting to property and other discrimination against women in England, and their enthusiasm, while a better-informed counterweight to dominant views, was not based on the average Ottoman woman. Even in the nineteenth century, however, some women who knew Turkey praised Muslim and criticized Western Christian practices.[29]

The nineteenth century saw the flowering of the Western negative stereotypes about the Muslim Middle East that have come to be known, following Edward Said, as Orientalism.[30] Said's book brilliantly and usefully points up a number of important phenomena, and extensively documents and analyzes long-standing Western prejudices, particularly against Muslims. It has inspired many useful studies. It also has problematic aspects. For one, Said sees Orientalist attitudes as going back to the ancient Greeks, many of whom indeed had negative stereotypes about Iran and the Orient. But attitudes varied and evolved over the centuries, and, beginning with Islam, negative attitudes toward Middle Easterners were more based on their religion than on their Eastern origin.

Moreover, the postmedieval rise in the West of secularism, nation-states, and secular varieties of Eurocentrism was largely due to Western priority in developing modern capitalism and new modes of warfare, which facilitated domination of much of the world. Especially in the nineteenth and early twentieth centuries, there was a rise of "scientific racism," which attributed inferiority to nonwhite peoples (with black peoples seen as inferior to Orientals). Writers mixed language and race, and said that those who spoke Indo-European ("Aryan") languages were superior to those who spoke Semitic languages, including Arabs and Jews. These color-based and language-based attitudes cannot meaningfully be called "Orientalist," and neither stressed the East-West division as crucial.[31] Some professional Orientalists, trained in languages and religious studies, helped spread biased attitudes, but they had a smaller role than did journalists, politicians, missionaries, and popular writers. Those Orientalist scholars who were prejudiced against Islam reflected as much as they caused Western attitudes. Much evidence cited by Said and others comes from nonscholars, including artists and writers, also called "Orientalist" in a separate meaning of the term that does not involve study of the Orient. What is true is that anti-Islamic prejudices have been strong in the West from medieval times until today, and that these are often now called "Orientalist." Racial prejudices put darker peoples on a lower rung than Arabs, Turks, or Iranians.

Although Said says little about gender, his *Orientalism* inspired works analyzing the sexual images of the Orient prevalent in the West. It was not usually scholars, but the so-called Orientalist artists and writers, who perpetuated highly sexualized images of Middle Eastern women. Studies of the role of such images in stereotyping Middle Eastern women and sexuality are useful, although it is sometimes forgotten that Western and other non-Oriental women were often sexualized in somewhat similar ways in Western arts, photographs, and postcards.

Westerners who heeded journalists, travelers, missionaries, and politicians tended to view Middle Eastern Muslim women as totally oppressed, with no independence, and as a symbol of evils found in the nonwhite and non-Christian world. Evangelical Protestant missionaries, who became numerous in the Middle East during the nineteenth and twentieth centuries, were often leading advocates of negative views about Islam. Although they were forbidden to convert Muslims, they could and did create schools and clinics that included some Muslims, and often were among the pioneers in educating Muslim girls. Their writings, the writings of colonial officials, travelers' accounts, and Western art and literature were main sources of Western attitudes. Partly because it was scholars who claimed the credentials to tell the world what Islam really was, Middle Eastern and Western intellectuals often concentrate on scholarly Orientalism in their own recent studies.

Said's critique of Orientalism is more valid for Western and Israeli views of Arabs than it is for views of Iranians or Indians, who often were admired by Orientalists, partly because they spoke Indo-European languages. This negativity toward Arabs persisted not only because of their Semitic language and Islamic religion, but partly because only Arab Middle Eastern countries were colonized by the West, and attacks on Arab treatment of women were part of the colonial strategy of Westerners in the areas they ruled or dominated. The countries colonized either directly or via protectorates or mandates were all primarily Arabic-speaking, while Iran, Afghanistan, and Turkey escaped colonial rule. Colonial rulers wanted to point up bad treatment of women as one part of Arab "backwardness" and incapacity for proper self-government.

Change in the Long Nineteenth Century 1798–1914

An Overview of Change

European contacts with the Middle East became more important with the rise of modern warfare, European expansion, and more extensive trade from the fifteenth century on. Some European diplomats, traders, travelers, and missionaries traveled and lived in the area for extended periods and wrote accounts that, despite their biases, tell something of women. Local Christians, especially Armenians and Greek Orthodox, and also Jews became prominent in economic and other relations with Europeans. They began to have Western-type educations, often sponsored by Western Christian or Jewish groups, which in time included girls. Though many of these schools were later also open to Muslims, a far lower percentage of Muslims attended. Because of contact with the West, minority religious communities saw growing differentiation from the Muslim majority in women's roles and education, whereas previously differences had been less marked. After 1800 there was also increasing cultural differentiation among Muslims, between those middle- and upper-class groups with social, economic, and educational ties to the West and the majority of the population. The latter tended to have gender relations often called "traditional," while the former group increasingly adopted modes influenced by the West.

In the Istanbul area certain Westernizing trends affecting women and the family began in the eighteenth century, but in most other areas such changes came later and at different rates. Cities near the Mediterranean had the most European trade and Western influence, while places like Afghanistan or Arabia were affected less. Influences also differed by class and mode of production, with elites turning to modern education and to Western mores that affected women.

There continue to be controversies and sometimes conflicting research results about how modernization and contact with the West affected women in different classes and regions. Many Western and local writings formerly expressed the view that local and Islamic cultures were extremely negative for women and that Western-influenced innovations were overwhelmingly positive, and such views are still current, particularly in nonscholarly writings. Recently many scholars have reacted against this simplistic view and have stressed the positives for women and men in premodern ways and the negatives brought by the Western impact, such as economic deprivation for many and the loss of much of the support given by same-sex networks and extended families. Overall, one may say that the gradual introduction of modern education and increased public roles for women, and, more dramatically, modern medicine, hygiene, and public health measures, had more positives than negatives, but in other areas results were more mixed and, for some, more negative than positive. The rise of more powerful states, which mobilized or used women for their own purposes, often placed new burdens on women, and the gradual decline in the help and companionship offered by extended families was not immediately offset, except among some of the elite, by any significant decline in arbitrary male power in nuclear families. Western presence and power since 1798 often contributed to a reaction of defense of local customs, including those involving the treatment and dress of women. As time went on, more women became educated and entered the public sphere in various ways, but this was a slow and laborious process; most states have devoted little or no effort to changing attitudes of male dominance via the educational system or other means. Male-dominant attitudes and practices have regained considerable power with the recent rise of Islamist movements, but there is the countervailing trend of women and progressive males interpreting Islam in reformist and even gender-egalitarian ways.

The usual dividing line for major Western influence and control is Napoleon's 1798 invasion of Egypt, although many scholars now give this less importance than formerly. In Cairo Napoleon and his officers introduced unveiling and Western treatment of some women, but there was a backlash against this and against the women involved after Napoleon left. For a time the presence of Western foreigners reinforced veiling and seclusion, as a reaction to the presence of outsiders, much as the coming of strangers to rural localities continues to do.

Napoleon's advance weakened the military rulers of Egypt under Ottoman suzerainty, who have often been considered revivers of the Mamluks, but not by recent scholars.[1] A military officer, Muhammad Ali—or Mehmet Ali—(r. 1805–48) destroyed the remaining ex-rulers and took control of Egypt and then Syria. Muhammad Ali appreciated Western military strength and worked to build a modern army, supported by modern industries, translation bureaus, and medical and technical schools. His policies affected women: some whole families had to contribute forced labor; women whose husbands were conscripted had to work more on the land; and some women worked in the new factories. One new school, for women medical practitioners, at first could not attract free women, and instead educated women of African slave origin, but it soon attracted free women and was the first school to give women a modern education. While there was some new employment for women, overall women were pushed out of many of their roles as active owners and traders of goods and property, and many peasant women had to work harder for less return. Egypt under Muhammad Ali pioneered in trends that reduced the economic status and independence of many women in the nineteenth-century Middle East, owing to the policies both of government centralizers and Westerners. These included a combination of increased male-controlled trade and formal land registration and new household structures where only males were wage-earners and acquired new knowledge, while many women lost their role in trade and landowning and were limited to the home.[2]

Elsewhere women's roles changed more slowly. Modern European economic domination meant that the rest of the world increasingly exported raw materials, with cotton and oil two Middle Eastern examples, and imported factory-made goods. In the early nineteenth century European powers used military victories or crises to make Egypt, Iran, and the Ottomans sign trade treaties guaranteeing free entry of European goods and very low tariffs. These hurt chances for industrialization and hastened the decline of many handicrafts. Resultant economic disruptions affected men and women, though there were some contrary trends regarding handicrafts, notably demand for some textiles and carpets, which employed women and girls in workshops and at home. Women and children worked in textile workshops in Syria, Anatolia, North Africa, Iran, and elsewhere. Women's pay was low and conditions often bad. There were also cultural barriers preventing women, especially Muslim women, from working for wages outside the home, and these were sometimes overcome only by economic necessity.[3] The Western impact seems to have reduced women's independent role in trade, landholding, and other activities, owing to both socioeconomic and cultural interactions.[4] With the import of cheap Western manufactures, there was a decline in family self-sufficiency in spinning and weaving. This was compensated for in some areas by the rise in "putting out" textile and carpet industries, where merchants supplied dyed yarns and sometimes looms to homes or family workshops and paid for the finished product. Dramatic declines in handicraft noted in nineteenth-century cities mainly hurt the guild-based male urban crafts. Several less skilled, lower paid, and largely female crafts had a market and often expanded.

Some scholars stress the negative aspects of modern changes in women's status and roles, while others emphasize the positive. Most major historical changes have contradictory effects, and many affect some groups primarily positively and others mainly negatively. Some recent scholars combat distorted views of Muslim women as horribly oppressed by stressing the positive sides of older mores. They note that earlier women often had a greater role in trade and landholding, and also a more interclass social life than later ones, with the more privileged women socializing with female servants and women of different classes mixing more than today—residentially, in baths, and in visits and trips to shrines. Extended families and households provided some women more protection and socializing than does the recent norm of nuclear families. The economic losses brought to many women by modernization seem more demonstrable than do losses relating to premodern households and extended families. Then, many servants and family clients may have had more support than popular-class women did later, but these premodern women were often locked into poverty and service or slavery, and they had even less recourse than many women do now against arbitrary husbands and in-laws or honor codes. In both East and West, changes that came with capitalism were hard on some women, especially popular-class women, but were also crucial to many developments that favor women— the gradual spread of women's education, public activity, and legal gains, and major advances in hygiene, health, decreased mother and child mortality rates, choice in marriage and other phenomena involving more freedom of choice for many women. If most women have not yet benefited nearly as much as they should, and if many have suffered from economic changes and from local or colonial governments, this does not mean that the past was better. Overstating past virtues while neglecting negatives can play into the hands of those who do not want women to advance.[5]

What was exaggerated was the tendency to see local culture and traditions as so negative that they had to be completely overturned and Western ways completely adopted for men and women to have a positive life. This view was strong among Western and Eastern writers, who typically stressed the position of women. They often blended prejudices against Islam, "scientific racism," and a conviction that countries could advance only if they totally Westernized. The ills of Muslim women and the correctness of Western gender relations were standard themes of colonial ideology.[6] The Westernizing approach of many local intellectuals was reinforced when local nationalisms—Iranian, Turkish, and varieties of nationalism in Arab countries—became prominent among thinkers and rulers in the twentieth century. Many nationalists, including Atatürk and the Pahlavi shahs, constructed national traditions full of Western values and disdained traditional and Islamic practices. Some Arab nationalisms saw Islam as part of Arabism, but still stressed modern Western values read into the Arab-Muslim past.

Many modern changes in women's status and in ideas occurred both in colonies and in independent countries. Current criticism of imitating Western ideas rarely notes that these ideas were not intrinsically Western but developed in Western countries only when changes in social and economic realities made them appropriate. "Western" ideas of women's marital choice, public roles, and, for a time, "scientific" domesticity came only with capitalism, which developed first in the West. They were borrowed only when they were locally appropriate, at least for certain classes. Industrial capitalism involved the separation of production from the home and a restructuring of women's roles in domesticity and child rearing, especially for women who did not have to work. Western ideas of domesticity became appropriate outside the West once capitalism began there, while with more recent developments, women's employment came gradually to be valued. Western power and prestige encouraged the adoption of Western ideas, but they became influential only when local changes made them appropriate.

Western policy was influenced by the interests of capitalist producers and traders, who wanted markets and did not want competition in producing and exporting manufactured goods. This was one reason why most Western powers were hostile to Muhammad Ali's efforts to industrialize, and why they promoted treaties with Iran, Egypt, and the Ottoman Empire limiting their tariffs. Relations with the West affected the position of women. Egypt and the Western regions of the Ottoman Empire saw the earliest modern socioeconomic change, arising largely from trade with Europe. The gendered division of labor grew, with men employed in producing cash crops, and women left more to the domestic sphere plus ill-paid employments and crafts. European demand for raw materials meant a rise in the production for export of such commodities, notably cotton in Egypt, opium and cotton in Iran, and oil in the twentieth century. The area felt increasing market fluctuations and crises, sometimes leading to famine and epidemics. Although new medical methods including quarantines began to be used, parasitic diseases remained rampant and in some areas increased. When women and children produced crafts for export, their pay was low and conditions bad.

We lack the statistics to know whether most popular-class families benefited or suffered from the Western impact. Some families' conditions worsened when men lost craft or other employment, or there were economic crises. However, new crops and employments gave other families income—opium, cotton, and other crops might bring more money, and new textile or cotton employment might mean more family income, however bad the conditions. Some scholars underestimate the difficulty of most people's lives before the Western impact, and it is not clear whether that impact usually made life better or worse for the popular classes. What is clear is the widening socioeconomic and cultural gap between the popular classes and the wealthier classes who benefited from Western contacts. Those benefiting from relations with the West were often cultural Westernizers, while those who did not benefit often sought protection against dubious changes by reasserting traditions.

Family life changed less among the non-Westernized. Dalenda Largueche has uncovered in the Tunisian archives evidence of a kind of jail for disobedient wives, where they were sent until they were found ready to be obedient.[7] To what extent such institutions existed outside Tunisia is unclear, but we know that some husbands could force wives to return home, while some wives were protected from mistreatment by Islamic courts or by taking refuge with their natal families. According to Judith Tucker, as compared to the conditions of elite women "greater flexibility about marriage arrangements, divorce, and women's public activities characterized the lives of lower-class women."[8] Popular- and middle-class women's culture included not only baths, visiting, pilgrimages to saints' tombs, and celebrations, but also performances for other women, though some performers continued to be slaves.

From the late nineteenth century on, new circumstances and ideas led to a decline in large harems, a rise in marriage ages, the beginnings of marital choice, and a decline in large powerful households with their many slaves and clients. Stronger states and provincial governments, whether colonial or indigenous, took over functions formerly performed by households. Istanbul pioneered these changes. Alan Duben and Cem Behar show that in the late nineteenth century most people in Istanbul lived in monogamous households of four to five people, had few children (implying some form of birth control), and married only in their late teens or later. In these features Istanbul was comparable to some western European countries.[9] We have no such studies for other Middle Eastern cities, but probably other western cities of the Ottoman Empire had some resemblance to Istanbul, and similar trends showed up later in many Middle Eastern cities. The Istanbul features are evidence that some parts of the Ottoman Empire began modernizing as early as the eighteenth century. Changes in the family add to our knowledge that parts of Ottoman Turkey had undergone significant change in family structure and the position of women well before Atatürk's reforms.

A crucial aspect of the change toward smaller households and fewer large harems was the decline in slavery, which by the nineteenth century involved mostly black domestic slaves. Slave trading was formally outlawed between the 1850s and the 1890s in the Ottoman Empire, Egypt, and Iran. Abolition came later, but once bans on slave trading were enforced, slavery declined rapidly, as manumission of slaves continued to be widespread; and the children of free men and slave women were free. Large harems, dependent on polygamy, concubines, slaves, and eunuchs, were increasingly seen as unsuited to new conditions.[10] In some areas less touched by the West, like Arabia and Mauritania, slavery continued in the twentieth century.

Egypt is often taken as exemplary of the effects of Western contacts, even though these were as strong in Istanbul and western Anatolia, Lebanon, and perhaps a few other Mediterranean centers as they were in Egypt, since the history of women in modern Egypt has been far more studied, and there were more widely influential writers in Egypt. The leader of Muhammad Ali's educational mission to Paris, Rifa'a al-Tahtawi, in a book on France recommended that girls get the same education as boys, as was done in strong nations. The Egyptian Educational Council recommended public education for girls in the late 1830s, but aside from the 1832 school for women medical practitioners—who treated women and gave vaccinations[11]—nothing was done until the 1870s.

In Egypt and elsewhere, upper-class girls increasingly got Westernized educations at home, while missionary schools pioneered in modern education for both genders. Missionaries in Middle Eastern countries were forbidden to convert Muslims, but increasing numbers of Muslims came to their schools, and local Christian communities, Coptic, Orthodox, and Armenian, set up their own schools. The French-based Alliance Israélite Universelle created schools for Jewish children from Morocco to Iran, and the French government subsidized Catholic missionary schools and clinics throughout the Middle East, particularly in Syria and Lebanon with their large Christian communities. British and American Protestant schools and clinics were not government-subsidized, but often had close relationships with their governments' representatives, and were often resented by Muslims, who feared proselytizing despite missionary agreements not to counter Islamic law by converting Muslims. The role of missionaries was two-sided; they helped spread health and education, including practical education, but were often hostile to local culture and aided Western powers. They were frequently the first to introduce girls' schools and modern medical care covering women, and in some areas were the first to bring in modern schools and medicine for anyone.

As to state schooling, in Egypt Khedive Isma'il (r. 1863–79) created a committee that began modernized schools for boys and girls, and Tahtawi wrote a textbook stating that women should be educated, and advocating equality in marriage. Isma'il established a few primary and secondary schools for girls, but a financial crisis, Isma'il's abdication, and especially the British occupation of 1882 slowed educational expansion. Muslim societies and missionary schools had more girls enrolled than did government schools in the early twentieth century. Some Egyptian women also took the initiative in women's education. Elite women created the Society for the Advancement of Woman and its journal. Liberals founded several groups, some of which innovated in having public lectures for women.

A Women's Section, focusing on lectures, was created at the Egyptian University before women were admitted. It lasted only three years, from 1909 to 1912, and faced threats.[12]

The Ottoman state made more impressive reforms in girls' schooling, concentrated in Istanbul. The Medical School started training midwives in 1842; state girls' secondary schools began in 1858, a girls' vocational school in 1869, and a teacher training college in 1870. Although the reign of Abdulhamid II (1876–1909), who ruled autocratically, is no longer considered a period of pure reaction, women's education advanced little further until the Young Turks took over from him.[13]

MODERNIZING REFORMS AND COLONIAL RULE

The realization that Western education and technology accounted for much of European strength led to modernizing reforms in the nineteenth and twentieth centuries that often impacted women. The Ottoman sultan Selim III (1789–1808) began an abortive program of military reforms in 1789, but a true reform program, like that under Muhammad Ali in Egypt, could begin only when Sultan Mahmud II (1808–39) destroyed the military janissary corps in 1826. Mahmud was followed by ministers who led in various reforms until a constitution was declared in 1876, and even the next, conservative, sultan, Abdülhamid II (1876–1909), did not abandon reform. Reform was slower in Iran, which had less European contact, but in all areas there were beginnings in modern education and in public health measures that began to affect the position of women and gender attitudes, at least among the educated.

Colonization, which began with the French conquest of Algeria from 1830, also affected women. In 1881 Tunisia was made a French protectorate, and in 1882 Egypt became a British one in all but name. Libya became an Italian colony in 1911 and Morocco a French protectorate in 1912. Most of the Middle East remained Ottoman or independent until after World War I, but was subject to huge Western economic and political interference. British and French rulers were highly critical of "Muslim" treatment of women, but did little to advance women's education and explicitly refrained from interfering with Muslim family law. The French, especially in Algeria, identified with unveiling and Westernizing women, which brought on considerable nationalist and Islamist backlash. In the late nineteenth and early twentieth centuries the Ottoman Empire and Egypt introduced several modernized civil, criminal, and commercial law codes, but Islamic laws relating to women, family, and inheritance remained and Islamic law in practice became synonymous with inheritance and family law. Western-influenced criminal and civil laws were also often unfavorable to women. The ease with which Islamic civil, criminal, and commercial law could be abolished, as contrasted with the continued difficulty of reforming laws on gender relations, shows the cultural centrality of gender and family questions. Many men whose lives were disrupted or worsened by the Western impact clung to old ways regarding women and the family, while those open to more egalitarian practices came mainly from the better-off classes, who often profited from Westernization.

In this period women participated in politics in ruling households, as seen in the continued nineteenth-century influence of several Ottoman and Iranian rulers' wives and mothers. Women from various classes were also active in bread and other riots and in rural and urban revolts in Egypt, Algeria, Iran, and elsewhere. In Iran the Babi messianic religious movement that began in the 1840s and adopted a reform program had one outstanding radical woman preacher and poet, Qorrat al-Ain, who sometimes spoke unveiled. In the 1860s most Babis chose to follow a new prophet, who founded the Baha'i religion, which adopted liberal views including women's rights. Women participated in several national revolts and rebellions in Iran between 1891 and 1979. In the 1891 revolt against a British tobacco monopoly, the shah's wives refused to smoke once the leading Shi'i cleric declared a boycott. In the constitutional revolution of 1905–11 women set up revolutionary and nationalist organizations and took several actions in favor of the constitutionalists and against foreign encroachments.[14] Elsewhere middle- and upper-class women participated in nationalist movements aimed at ending European rule and setting up modern national states. In Turkey the writer and public speaker Halide Edib deployed her eloquence in nationalist and reform causes beginning with the successful Young Turk 1908 revolt against Abdülhamid and continuing with the defense of Turkey against dismemberment by the Western allies after World War I, and advocacy of social reform. Other Turkish women were also active.

DEBATING MIDDLE EASTERN WOMEN'S STATUS AND ROLES

The changing position of women led to different views of their proper role. Few girls attended modern schools, but more girls, especially upper-class ones, got a modern education at home with tutors. In Egypt and the Ottoman Empire there were a few mixed-gender salons in which women of the ruling family played a prominent role. From the late nineteenth century there developed a women's press, especially in Egypt and Istanbul, which largely advocated scientific domesticity, including rationalized home management, child rearing, and health and hygiene. There were articles advocating better conditions for women, the pros and cons of veiling, and reports of mistreatment of women.[15] Some women also began to demand reforms in family law and increased access to education and work, as well as political rights.

Many Westerners stressed the seclusion and bad conditions of women as justifications for Western rule or tutelage. Many Middle Eastern advocates of greater equality for women saw no alternative to posing it in Western terms. This Westernizing approach was problematic for classes tied to more traditional parts of the economy, many of whom saw no benefit in becoming like the inhabitants of the very countries that were threatening their ways and sometimes their livelihoods. While a variety of positions were current regarding women, as on other issues, those who advocated imitating Western steps toward gender equality, like Tahtawi, were less controversial before the West became colonial rulers than after. Once the British took over Egypt in 1882, advocating Western ways became problematic among those who stressed national independence, which many tied to a defense of traditions. There was a division among male thinkers and politicians, some of whom advocated various degrees of Western-style reform, based either on modern interpretations of Islam or on liberal nationalism, while others held cultural nationalist positions that stressed the virtues of what they presented as tradition, including the traditional roles of women. As in other cultures, many of these traditions were very recent or invented, though inegalitarian gender relations were not.

While many of the arguments for reforming women's position were stated first by Ottoman women and men who wrote in Turkish, those who wrote in Arabic were more influential in most of the Middle East and have been studied more, and so will be treated first and in greater detail here. Many male thinkers and novelists gave special importance in their work to the position of women.[16] The Egyptian Islamic modernist thinker and educator Muhammad Abduh was the first influential Arab Muslim to argue that Islam was gender-egalitarian, and that unequal treatment of women came from later corruptions of Islam. He was the first important Islamic modernist, and laid the groundwork in methodologies used to reinterpret Islam to harmonize with the modern world on gender and other matters. Abduh stressed the distinction in both Quran and hadiths between religious observances ('*ibadat*) and social transactions (*mu'amalat*), which modernists considered rules specific to their time. He and later modernists said that social transactions (often including most of the Medina legal rulings) should be interpreted in accord with the needs of each age. Laws specific to the time of Muhammad no longer applied literally. Abduh revived the concept of legal interpretation by qualified persons, ijtihad, to support the Islamic concept of "the public welfare." Modernists claim to find the true spirit or values behind the literal meaning of the Quran.[17] They also play down the importance of the hadiths as compared to the Quran, and question whether even hadiths traditionally considered "sound" always accurately represented the sayings and actions of Muhammad. The lesser weight given to hadiths greatly reduces the patriarchal and misogynist texts that had often been considered inerrant, and the separation of Quranic rules into eternal and time-related ones also reduces or eliminates male-dominant rules to be followed. Many liberal men and women held similar positions in the late nineteenth and early twentieth centuries, though not all were concerned to find scriptural justifications.

The late nineteenth and early twentieth centuries saw the beginning of nationalisms—Egyptian, Syrian, Turkish, Iranian, and others, including (Christian) Armenian and Kurdish. Nationalists, who included non-Muslims, often stressed what they considered national traditions more than Islamic ones, which they might find conservative. Many located modern ideas, including more gender-egalitarian ones, in their national pre-Islamic traditions. Islamic modernism and liberal nationalism provided different ways to combine modern values, including more gender-egalitarian ones, and local or regional traditions.

Varieties of Islamic modernism, pioneered by Abduh, continued important among male and female intellectuals in Middle Eastern countries; more recently, however, they have been countered by Islamist trends that became especially popular from the 1970s, although they began earlier. Islamic modernism usually included reform in the position of women, although some modernists—like the international figure who influenced Abduh and other activists, Sayyid Jamal al-Din al-Afghani—were far more concerned with self-strengthening and liberation from outside control than with women's rights. Islamic modernists tended to see restrictions on women as against the true spirit of Islam. In the twentieth century, some Muslim women adopted an explicit feminist identity and did not see this as contrary to Islamic identity. They said that greater gender equality is more truly Islamic than are the views of religious conservatives.

By the late nineteenth and early twentieth centuries, women launched journals and published articles in the general press, often advocating new women's roles. Some families, beginning with the elite, were adopting or adapting European ways. Growing interest in changing the position of women reflected not only Western models, but also the incompatibility of phenomena like extensive harems and domestic slavery with the development of a more modern market capitalist system. There were also advantages in modern methods of health, hygiene, and child rearing, which began to spread. Progressive men and women began to advocate public health measures and cleanliness especially for children. Though such ideas spread slowly, the call for careful housekeeping and hygiene in writings by and for women was a force for healthier families and was in many ways modern, however old-fashioned it may seem in an age when women's careers are given priority.[18]

The most discussed writer on women was the Egyptian Qasim Amin. In his *Liberation of Women* (1899), widely translated from the original Arabic and read throughout the Middle East, Amin advocated Western ways and strongly criticized Egyptian ones, especially the ulama's ideas. Amin used Islamic modernist arguments to oppose patriarchal oppression. He called for ending abuses of divorce and polygamy and said women must be educated. His most controversial recommendation was for ending facial veiling and seclusion, which he said had no connection with Islam. His call for unveiling faces was rejected both by conservatives and by some female advocates of women's rights who felt that other issues were more important and less divisive. Perhaps it was because of his fame or his bold tone and his call for unveiling that his work became so much more widely known and discussed, making him for some an icon for women's liberation, than were a variety of other important and original works regarding women that were written, often by women, at about the same time, or even earlier, in Arabic, Turkish, and Persian.

For over a century veiling has had a central place in debates about Muslim women. Veiling until recently included covering much of the face as well as the body, and was closely tied to seclusion both in reality and in reformist responses to it. Veiling has evolved to dress forms that leave the face uncovered, and no longer implies seclusion. Traditionally many urban women veiled, though most other women covered their hair and bodies in various, often colorful and less concealing, ways. The veil was meant to keep women unseen by unrelated men, and was part of a complex of interconnected practices of gender segregation. Some opponents of veiling exaggerated the importance of dress, but most did not. The veil attacked by Amin and others was not the hijab found on many women today, but was part of a complex that said women should be hidden, should not play public roles, and should have many key decisions taken for them by men. As summarized by Barbara Stowasser:

> Of all scriptural legislation concerning the Prophet's wives, the *hijab* . . . and its medieval . . . extensions have during the last century gained prominence as focus of Muslim paradigmatic self-definition. Attacked by foreigners and indigenous secularists alike and defended by the many voices of conservatism, the *hijab* has come to signify the sum total of traditional institutions governing women's role in Islamic society. Thus, in the ideological struggles surrounding the definition of Islam's nature and role in the modern world, the *hijab* has acquired the status of "cultural symbol." . . .

> Amin . . . understood the *hijab* as an amalgam of institutionalized restrictions on women that consisted of sexual segregation, domestic seclusion, and the face veil. . . . Women's domestic seclusion and the face veil, then, were primary points in Amin's attack on what was wrong with the Egyptian social system of his time. Thereafter, both of these items came to be the focus of the conservative Islamic defense, in Egypt and elsewhere.[19]

Leila Ahmed makes controversial criticisms of Amin that show the complexity of debates over the veil in the history of Western domination of the Middle East and resistance to it:

> Amin's book . . . marks the entry of the colonial narrative of women and Islam—in which the veil and the treatment of women epitomized Islamic inferiority—into mainstream Arabic discourse. And the . . . veil came to symbolize in the resistance narrative, not the inferiority of the culture and the need to cast aside its customs in favor of those of the West, but, on the contrary, the dignity and validity of all native customs, and in particular those customs coming under fiercest colonial attack—the customs relating to women—and the need to tenaciously affirm them as a means of resistance to western domination.[20]

One important discourse said that the veil, and male privileges in marriage, divorce, and elsewhere, were a distortion of true original Islam. As governments increasingly Westernized without becoming democratic or egalitarian, their opponents often stressed values they found in original Islam. Some such opponents were conservatives, but others, like the nineteenth-century constitutionalist Young Ottomans, whose most famous writer was Namik Kamal, were not. As women's role became ideologically contested, all sides claimed women's position was better served by adherence to their ideas. One group stressed the superiority of Western ways. Those who criticize secular reformers' and feminists' imitation of the West may forget that Western ways represented to many industrial and military strength, participation in government, increased citizen and gender equality, and reduced elite privileges. Islam and tradition were often associated with old regimes and ways of life, and only after these regimes were overthrown could new versions of Islam and tradition become politically potent.

The ideological situation became more complex once it was intertwined with colonialism, imperialism, and anti-imperialism. Some nationalists, in Egypt and other countries subject to colonialism, defended traditional ways, including aspects of the treatment of women—among them the Egyptian nationalist Mustafa Kamil. This defense countered exaggerated attacks on local culture and appealed to classes who identified with that culture, especially middle- and popular-class persons with traditional occupations and educations. Nationalists in noncolonized areas like

Iran and those in the Ottoman Empire who called themselves Turkish, however, differentiated themselves from Arabs, and said their pre-Islamic culture contained many modern values, including a freer position for women.

Egyptian debates regarding women were the most influential in the Middle East, but similar debates occurred elsewhere. Works in Persian and Turkish have not been given the attention they deserve. The Young Ottomans Ibrahim Şinasi and Namik Kamal criticized women's subordination.[21] Fatma Aliye, a highly educated and intelligent daughter of Cevdet Pasha, the main author of the Ottoman Civil Code, pioneered in the discussion of women's status and problems in several novels, in a popular book titled *Muslim Women* in 1891, and in a polemic against a conservative cleric's defense of polygamy, where she wrote that the Quran did not support polygamy and that women had an exalted position in the time of the Prophet. Her usual approach was to present herself as a moderate, giving a modernist interpretation of Islam and praising the state's real accomplishments in educational progress for women.[22] A women's popular press, with papers in the different Ottoman languages, discussed many issues, and several writers and activists, male and female, also stressed women's status and spoke and wrote for reforms and for new professions and higher education for women, with some voicing more radical and populist positions after the 1908 Young Turk revolution.[23] Ottoman reformers increasingly adopted many Western ideas, whether as Ottomanists speaking for all people in the empire, or as Turkish nationalists, though there was also a more conservative Islamist trend. Nationalists found modern virtues, including greater gender equality, in the Turkish past, as did many Iranian nationalists in the pre-Islamic Iranian past. Some forms of secular Arab nationalism were similar, but Arab nationalisms mainly saw Islam as a progressive Arab achievement. Women participated in these discourses, and educated women expressed themselves in the arts, including poetry, and helped create an influential women's press, initially centering in Cairo and Istanbul.

Some women and male reformists strongly criticized predominant practices regarding marriage and sexuality. In Iran the nineteenth-century feminist Bibi Khanom Astarabadi wrote a treatise, *The Vices of Men*, which criticized loveless, male-dominant marriages, and included complaints of women whose husbands turned to sex with other men and boys instead of to their wives.[24] Condemnation of homosexuality in modern times was not always a sign of Victorianism or religious conservatism, but often had this feminist aspect of promoting greater respect, better treatment, and even love for wives.

The dramatic political and economic changes that led to Western dominance and to dependent economic relations also brought about changes in women's lives, which varied by class and region, but which initiated new health, education, and public roles while at the same time creating hardships for many women. Although the upper classes fared better than the popular classes, there were contradictory impacts even within a single class.

As indicated by the beginnings of women's press and women's activities and organizations focusing on education, health, and legal and other rights, some women were taking action before 1914 to better women's position. Some authors refer to nearly all such acts and women as "feminist," a word that different authors use differently, but it seems useful for this and later periods to consider the distinction noted by Julie Peteet, citing Temma Kaplan, between "female consciousness" and feminism: "Female consciousness is women's awareness of their rights within the prevailing system of labor and dominant ideology."[25] What is perceived as due in the prevailing system changes with time and place, but I would see new approaches as feminist only when they aim at novel rights and status that move significantly in a gender-egalitarian direction.

1914–45: Nationalism and Women's Movements

An Overview of Changes

The period 1914–45 saw further major political and socioeconomic changes with impact on women. Among these were World War I, in which some women were mobilized in new work and public roles, and the post-war dissolution of the Ottoman Empire, which lost its large remaining Arab territories. Successor states were Turkey—whose borders changed after a nationalist struggle against European occupiers led by Mustafa Kemal, later called Atatürk—and several Arab states. Although Arab nationalists expected independence, Great Britain and France had secret agreements that divided Arab Asia between them. Also, Britain in 1917 issued the Balfour Declaration saying they favored the establishment in Palestine of a Jewish homeland. This was incorporated into the League of Nations Covenant. This deliberately ambiguous declaration meant that Britain, supported by Western powers, promoted Jewish immigration in Palestine, and many saw it as meaning support for a Jewish state. At this time many Jews in the world were opposed or indifferent to Zionism. Western Jews became much more Zionist after the rise of Hitler, as did some Middle Eastern Jews.

Post–World War I treaties, decided by the victorious Allies, found a way to finesse Arab expectations and Woodrow Wilson's stand against territorial annexations with British and French imperial ambitions, by creating a system of "mandates"—areas put under the "trusteeship" of one of the Allied powers. Syria-Lebanon, Iraq, Transjordan and Palestine became Class A mandates, to be readied for independence soon, under Britain (Iraq, Transjordan, Palestine) and France (Syria and Lebanon). The Arabian Peninsula, aside from the British treaty–controlled coastal principalities, was divided into the prior independent states of Yemen and Najd, and the newly independent Hijaz, under the sharif of Mecca, leader of the Arab wartime revolt. Two of his sons were put on thrones in mandatory Iraq and Transjordan. The Saudi family from Najd conquered the Hijaz in 1924 and established Saudi Arabia. Control of oil reserves was a major point in Western policies, with Iran and Iraq the main known sources of oil at first, while Saudi oil, under an American company, came in the 1930s.

In the 1914–45 period the independent countries—Turkey, Iran, and Afghanistan—underwent important changes in government that brought in rulers who worked to lessen the control of foreign forces and their local feudal and religious allies. They worked to modernize and strengthen their countries with measures that included encouraging public roles for women via education, unveiling, and new job opportunities; these measures went deepest in already reformed Turkey, and were most resisted in barely reformed Afghanistan.

Both Turkey and the major Arab states had nationalist movements during and after World War I in which women participated significantly. Early Arab nationalism had been directed against Ottoman rule, except in Egypt and North Africa, where the real rulers were the British, the French, and, in Libya after 1911, the Italians. These Western countries became the focus of nationalism after the war. Arab nationalism was directed especially at achieving independence, which some nationalists tied to modernization and self-strengthening, including greater gender equality, although gender reforms were usually to be deferred until after independence.

The British declared Egypt a protectorate in World War I. A major nationalist struggle, often called the revolution of 1919, included significant participation by organized women's groups. Egypt gained formal independence in 1922, though the British retained much power. The greatest post–World War I changes came in noncolonized Turkey and Iran. The Allied powers at Versailles created a Turkey limited to central Anatolia with the sultan-caliph as their puppet. A nationalist movement, led by the World War I hero Mustafa Kemal and including many women, undertook a military struggle that ousted the Greeks and set up a new government in Ankara. The Allies were forced to recognize the new borders of Turkey in the Treaty of Lausanne, 1924—the only victory for nationalists against the Versailles Treaty. Mustafa Kemal abolished first the caliphate and then the sultanate and set up a modernizing republic with widespread support.

Iran suffered greatly from the war and emerged weakened. The Bolshevik Revolution, whose leaders renounced Russian treaty rights, removed Russia from the scene. The British tried a de facto protectorate, but nationalist and U.S., French, and Russian opposition prevented this. In 1921 a military officer with local British backing, Reza Khan, led a coup, and in 1925 ended the Qajar dynasty and set up the Pahlavi dynasty (1925–79). Although Iran was less modernized than Turkey, the two countries were alike in being independent and hence able to undertake nationalist modernization programs and end many foreign privileges. Their governments were highly centralizing and came to discourage independent organizations, including women's organizations, which were brought under government control. Some Arab countries kept both nationalist and independent women's organizations. By historical accident the main independent countries were non-Arab, and their nationalisms were expressed in terms of their pre-Islamic Turkish or Iranian ancestors, while various Arab nationalisms in this period often had an Islamic component. In both independent and foreign-ruled states, women's demands were subordinated to nationalist demands; in independent states activist women tried to influence the state to act for women, while in foreign-ruled states they often had to bow to nationalist demands not to insist on programs that might alienate conservatives.

Many Westerners saw the negative aspects of women's conditions as stemming directly from Islam. Such attitudes were expressed and felt most forcefully in colonized countries, which were, coincidentally, Arabic-speaking. This negative view of Arabs was reinforced by the widespread Aryan-Semitic division promulgated by many Westerners, as the Arabs were the main Middle Eastern speakers of a Semitic language. There were also differences in modern trends, on gender as other matters, in countries on different sides of the colonized-noncolonized divide. The timing of colonialism in different Arab countries also had an impact on women's movements. Egypt, with much internal independence from colonial rule after 1922, was able to pioneer in women's organization. Syria, Lebanon, Iraq, and Jordan achieved independence later, and their politics concentrated more on nationalist goals, while separate feminist organizations were discouraged.[1]

Two primarily Arabic-speaking countries were heavily settled by Western immigrants—Algeria and, increasingly, Palestine. Though the two cases are quite different, with Palestine having had some Jewish population since ancient times and the settlers, whether or not they invoked religious justification, seeing their settlement as a return, they had some common features. They experienced extensive settler appropriation of land and domination of the economy, which affected women in specific ways. They also had prolonged armed struggles, in which women played an important role, which continue in Palestine. Colonizers said Algeria was part of France, and some settlers originally said that Palestinians did not exist. In both areas activist women identified with nationalist struggles and did not prioritize women's rights.[2]

Family and lineage ties and power have remained important from 1914 until now even in many areas that were no longer formally tribal and those where conjugal families predominate. This is stressed for Lebanon by Suad Joseph and for the Maghreb by Mounira Charrad, both of whom note the importance for women's rights of overcoming the power of tribes and lineages.[3]

The interwar period saw the growth of women's organizations, especially in Egypt, where some were explicitly feminist, but most emphasized national liberation, though they also made demands for reforming family law, gaining the vote, and greater gender equality. Women's participation in nationalist struggles gave them experience, visibility, and respect. Those women who participated got a new sense of their roles as public persons and ventured further than before in activities outside family, kin, and household.

Most women's organizations had primarily educational and charitable goals. They pioneered in creating institutions for society as a whole—institutions that had not existed before or had, in different form, been limited to religious groups in which some women participated but did not direct. Before 1914 there were few state girls' schools, and girls' schooling was largely pioneered by foreign and missionary groups. From the late nineteenth century Christian, Muslim, or mixed women's groups and individuals formed girls' schools, which provided a model and impetus for states to launch such schools. Christian missionaries faced legal prohibitions on conversion and concentrated their religious work among non-Muslims, while also creating schools, clinics, and hospitals that served both Muslims and non-Muslims. Although missionaries often served imperialist goals, they also pioneered in founding educational and medical institutions. Such institutions were also founded by minority communities, by nonmissionary foreign groups, and by voluntary Muslim groups and individuals, male and female. In many countries it was such groups, not governments, that pioneered in girls' education, usually in separate girls' schools, and also in modern health care for women, including prenatal, birth, and postnatal care. Although these services reached a minority of women, they often provided models for later government services, and trained local women to participate in expanding these fields.

Turkey, already ahead in state-sponsored girls' schooling, extended it greatly under Atatürk, and most other states expanded girls' schools in the interwar period. The new universities set up in Turkey, Iran, Egypt, and elsewhere were overwhelmingly coeducational. Nationalists promoted female education to create good mothers and citizens. Some religious and traditional forces opposed girls' education, especially after puberty, saying that such education might threaten girls' chastity and devotion to their family. Women's groups promoting education and the schools they founded were often involved in difficult struggles.

Women's organizations attracted upper-middle-class women, and their charitable and social work usually embodied traditional views of charity and noblesse oblige. They were, however, innovative in setting up adult education in domestic skills, hygiene, and crafts, which improved health and developed salable skills. Some women combined such work with efforts for greater gender equality, among them the pioneering Egyptian feminist Huda Sha'rawi, who was the chief founder in 1923 of the Egyptian Feminist Union, and Iran's Sediqeh Daulatabadi, who created several feminist organizations and publications. Women's groups contributed to the women's press, sponsored lectures and cultural events for women, and gave women a greater and more organized public presence. Their efforts in health, education, and job promotion had a direct impact and encouraged governments to do more in these fields.

New roles for women, stressed in the writings and teachings of women's groups, were useful in adapting to modern needs and in creating more autonomous nuclear families, whatever limiting effects on women such families also had.[4] Conjugal rather than natal families had a growing role, with more power for husbands and less for birth relatives. This could be constraining or liberating for women, or both, depending on the circumstances. In much traditional Islamic thought and writing women were considered highly sexual and lustful, which was one justification for their veiling and seclusion. Those both within and outside governments who worked for public roles for women thus found it useful to self censor their language, stress their belief in chastity and fidelity, and refrain from talking or writing publicly about women's sexual interests. These constraints continued in many areas well beyond World War II, and positive discussions of female sexuality are primarily a recent and limited phenomenon.

Women were active in numerous nationalist movements that focused on unifying and modernizing independent states like Turkey and Iran, and on gaining independence in most Arab states. Nationalists wished to play down or overcome internal divisions, and many encouraged women's activism, though most postponed serious work for gender reform. Only in independent Turkey and Iran could governments enforce new gender policies.

The early twentieth century saw a reshaping of perceived group identities, which had formerly been primarily local or religious, and now increasingly became national, usually based on a common language. As in the West, nationalism accompanied socioeconomic change and had implications for women, who were increasingly seen as guardians of national identity. Arguments for women's education and public roles emphasized women's role in bringing up children and, later, their contribution to national economic strength. National identities were presented as eternal but in fact were modern and could be fluid, changing in one individual's lifetime from Ottoman to Turkish or Syrian or Arab, for example. In the twentieth century "Arab" changed in meaning from "Bedouin" to cover an ever-expanding group of nations, most of which had Arabic as their majority language. "Turk" similarly changed from denoting rural Anatolians to meaning, in practice if not theory, all Turkish-speaking Muslim Anatolians, and sometimes the many others who spoke Turkic languages (or even, in the official Turkish view, Kurdish-speakers). Nationalisms also began among minorities without countries, notably the Kurds in Turkey, Iran, Iraq, and Syria, and the Berbers of North Africa, many of whom, like religious minorities, are more secular than their Arab or Iranian rulers. Various tribal, religious, and other minorities also command strong loyalty.

Nationalisms varied somewhat in their view of women, with Turkey's Kemalism advocating near gender equality, while others often moved only slowly to modify shari'a family law and concentrated on women's public roles. Secular nationalists in power in the interwar years (Turkey and Iran) and after (Egypt, Syria, Iraq) significantly increased public roles and rights for women, and all nationalist governments accelerated the takeover of formerly ulama-dominated educational, charitable, and legal functions. These policies were among the many reasons for Islamic reactions to nationalist reforms, which began before 1945 and became widespread beginning in the 1970s.

Although Christians and some Jews pioneered in Arab nationalism, over time it took on a more Islamic cast, stressing Islam as an Arab contribution. Christian and Jewish males and females, who were a large population in Iran and several Arab countries, were the first to get Western-style educations and adopt some new roles for women, and many Muslims came increasingly to see them, and some other religious minorities like the Baha'is, as agents of Western imperialism. Some Muslims, especially in colonized Arab countries, saw the greater gender equality pioneered by such religious minorities as a Western imperial phenomenon. The rapid socioeconomic changes of the past century, including huge internal and external migration and accelerating urbanization, have also created a conservative reaction of trying to preserve in the family traditional male power under cultural and political attack and of identifying Islam with a conservative view of its gender component.

From the late nineteenth century on, the first emphasis of reformers was to say that women had to be educated and patriotic (or properly Islamic) in order to bring up sons with these qualities. Later, women's role in strengthening the nation through entering the public sphere and employment was stressed. Only more recently have significant numbers of women and men spoken and worked for gender equality. There was important and often active opposition to women's education and their entry into the public sphere, coming mostly from some ulama and their allies.

As the women's movements and changes in status varied by national units, the discussion below will deal with such units, but can include only a few countries, with some interwar background on the remaining countries given in the next chapter. Nearly everywhere there have been important changes in the status of women since 1914, including major expansion in female education and health services for women and children, and some new women's presence in public life.

TURKEY

Women's involvement in politics began before World War I, in the successful Young Turk movement, and in the earliest women's organizations and women's press. One scholar lists a dozen women's associations formed 1908–16, primarily philanthropic, but also some that worked for women's rights. The latter included one founded in 1908 by Halide Edib, with links to the British suffragettes, and also the militant Society for the Defense of Women's Rights, which highlighted women's access to the professions.[5] The Young Turk government (1908–18) undertook many reforms, a large number of which were centralizing and secularizing. These reforms encompassed the educational system and the legal system, and thus affected the status of women.

The year 1911 saw the establishment of the first lycée for women, Istanbul University opened to women in 1914, and business classes for women opened in the Advanced School for Commerce. Some women abandoned the face veil in Turkey's western cities, and the long period of armed conflict in the Balkan Wars, World War I, and Turkey's war of Independence (roughly 1912–23) deprived many Muslim households of men to support them. This led to a rise in prostitution, and, to some degree, an entrance of women into the paid workforce in urban areas.

Leading Ottoman writers who wrote in Turkish were divided into Islamist, Westernist, and Turkist positions. The first opposed reforms in women's status, while the latter two favored them. The Young Turks in power made some gender reforms. A law of 1916 recognized women's right to divorce for adultery or in the case of a husband's taking an additional wife without first receiving permission from an existing wife. The Family Law Code of 1917 incorporated these reforms and brought all questions of family law and civil status under the jurisdiction of civil authorities. The extent to which the Young Turks could carry out those reforms at a practical level, however, was limited owing to Ottoman participation in the war (on the German side) and to the regime's ensuing uneasy compromise with religious institutions. Wartime needs did bring measures to encourage women's work, while the government also tried to make marriage mandatory and gave financial aid at each birth. Official ambivalence concerning women's public presence appeared in contradictory measures—an imperial decree in 1915 allowed women to unveil at work, while in 1917 overzealous police posted an announcement, soon retracted by the government, against innovations in women's dress.[6]

The war and its aftermath increased nationalist struggles, and women participated in many of these, forming the Anatolian Women's Organization for Patriotic Defense in 1919. In postwar Turkey Mustafa Kemal Atatürk (r. 1923–38) promoted the extension of women's rights with a government that is often called secular, although its own term, the French *laïc*, is more suggestive of its militancy against religious institutions. Atatürk saw increased gender-egalitarianism and large public and work roles for women as central to modernization, nationalism, and destruction of conservative religious institutions.

The successful war to regain all of Anatolia, under the leadership of Mustafa Kemal Atatürk, created a republic with its capital in Ankara. Atatürk built on, but radically revised, Ottoman reforms, inaugurating the most secular state in the Islamic world, and promoting more radical reforms in women's status than have been realized elsewhere in the Middle East. Atatürk's military victories helped give him more internal support than any other Middle Eastern ruler. Turkey was not burdened by a colonial past, which elsewhere made modernizing changes in women's status suspect as imitations of the colonizer.[7]

Atatürk abolished the sultanate in 1922, proclaimed a republic in 1923, and abolished the caliphate in 1924. He made education a state monopoly, eliminated religious courts, and ended Islam's being the state religion in 1928. Such measures undermined the power of religious institutions and replaced them with institutions similar to those in Western countries. This was done on the basis of a governmental nationalist ideology. The Arabic call to prayer and alphabet were outlawed, a Latin script was developed for Turkish, and there was a partial purge of Arabic and Persian words. These changes had religious and gender implications, including limiting access to Arabic and Ottoman gender-inegalitarian texts. For decades there was no higher religious education and lower-level religious education was severely curtailed.

Turkish nationalists like Zia Gökalp said the pre-Islamic Turks had many modern values, including equality for women and monogamy, and that these had been undermined by Islamic, Iranian, and Byzantine institutions. Gökalp spoke of reviving "Turkish feminism," based on women's sacred power and abilities in all fields, including warfare. This view was adopted by many republicans. As the leading nationalist woman Halide Edib wrote: "In the recent changes in Turkey, a great many intellectuals believe that there is a . . . return to our origins. What is more important is that this belief is consciously propagated by a considerable number of intellectuals, partly for the sake of making these changes acceptable to the masses."[8]

The Young Turk government had enacted a slightly reformed Family Code in 1917, which remained in force in Turkey until 1926 and in the formerly Ottoman Arab countries for many decades. In the early 1920s, powerful groups favored different approaches to family law, and Atatürk had reasons for adopting a radical approach. According to Deniz Kandiyoti "the woman question became one of the pawns in the Kemalist struggle to liquidate the theocratic remnants of the Ottoman state, a struggle in which male protagonists engaged each other while women remained surprisingly passive onlookers."[9]

Alone among Muslim countries Turkey abolished use of the shari'a, which by then covered essentially only family, inheritance, and personal status matters. A slightly altered Swiss Civil Code was introduced in 1926. Women got equal rights in divorce and child custody, and polygamy was outlawed, though the Swiss code had inegalitarian features, including recognizing the husband as the head of the household. Atatürk launched campaigns favoring unveiling and wearing Western clothing. "Islamic dress," especially covering the hair and neck, was eventually outlawed for public employees and in governmental sites, including schools and universities. Women got to vote in municipal elections in 1930 and in national elections in 1934, well before they did in France, Italy, or Switzerland. Such provisions were elements of government laicism, as religious groups backed patriarchal interpretations of religion and saw women's rights as weakening their power. Many changes in gender laws were, however, not universally followed. In the rural interior, especially the eastern region, inhabited by Kurds and Turks, old ways often continued. The persistence of old marriage practices is shown by periodic Turkish governmental legitimation of children whose parents, including some polygamists, had not had the required civil marriage. Underage marriages also continued.[10] In western and urban areas the new rules were more widely followed, and general observance increased with time. In other parts of the Middle East the observance of reform laws was similarly variable but also increased over time.

In education and in public and professional activities women went further faster in Turkey than in any other Middle Eastern country. In several key professions, including university teaching, there existed in 1970 a higher percentage of women in Turkey than in most Western countries. Most educated women favored and benefited from Atatürk's policies, which were continued by his party after his 1938 death and began to be challenged only with the onset of the multiparty system after World War II. However, Atatürk did not allow women's independent mobilization. The government approved the Turkish Women's Association in 1924 but disbanded it in 1934, right after it hosted a congress of the International Federation of Women that highlighted woman suffrage and other Turkish achievements. Other independent groups like workers' organizations and cultural clubs were also abolished.

IRAN

Iran underwent many political changes, with the years 1905–14 dominated by a constitutional revolution and then Russo-British control. Though neutral in World War I, Iran became a battlefield for foreign forces and emerged from the war devastated. The Bolsheviks renounced concessions and unequal rights in Iran and elsewhere, leaving the British as the influential foreign power. Iran's leading ministers agreed to an abortive Anglo-Iranian 1919 treaty that would have made Iran a protectorate. Nationalist and leftist opposition to foreign control culminated in a military coup, led by Colonel Reza Khan in early 1921. He had help from British military commanders who preferred a strong government to disorder and leftist power. Most nationalists and feminists supported Reza's regime until near the end, when many opposed his brutality. After a short campaign for a republic on the Turkish model, Reza Khan had a constituent assembly depose the Qajar dynasty in 1925 and crowned himself shah of the new Pahlavi dynasty.

Iran had seen far less modernization than the Ottoman Empire or Egypt. It had stronger groups opposed to modernization and centralization, including nomadic tribal federations, and an independent ulama. Regarding women as on other matters, Iran was behind the Ottoman Empire in reform. The first girls' school was established in Istanbul in 1858, but in Tehran in 1907. A Teachers' Training College for women opened in 1870 in Istanbul, but only in 1918 in Tehran. The first women's periodical in Turkish came in 1869, but in Persian in 1911. Women got access to university education in 1911 in Istanbul, but in 1936 in Tehran.[11]

From 1906 through the early Reza Shah period there were independent women's organizations and publications, and opposition to women's activities came more from religious conservatives than from the government. There were several political parties, some of which had women's programs. The Communist Party created a women's section, and the Socialist Party called for equal rights, including the vote, for men and women.[12] The left nationalist Jangali movement in Gilan in 1920, with Communist Party participation, announced a short-lived socialist republic whose program included equal rights for women.

Women's autonomous political activities began during the 1906–11 revolution. The first women's newspaper was published in 1911. Independent women's groups emphasized girls' schools. Maryam Amid Mozayen al-Saltaneh founded the *Shokufeh* newspaper in 1913 and founded the Iranian Women's Society soon after, with a reported membership of five thousand. In 1918 the government extended public education to women, and public girls' schools were opened, followed by a women's teacher training college. From 1917 to 1927 several new women's newspapers and organizations were created. The leading woman in this activity was Sediqeh Daulatabadi, who was born in Isfahan and joined women's activities from 1911. A school she helped to found in Isfahan was attacked by mobs and had to close, but she set up a women's organization and newspaper there. When these were banned and she was expelled from Isfahan, she went to Tehran, where she resumed publication of her newspaper, which was banned anew in 1921. She went to France to study psychology in the 1920s. Another women's newspaper, *Women's Letter*, was founded in 1920 and banned after a year when it argued for abolishing the veil. Two more women's newspapers began in 1921, one of which, in Mashhad, was banned after implicitly criticizing the clergy, after which it was briefly re-created in Tehran. The longest-running women's periodical, *Women's World*, was founded in 1920 by the Association of Graduates of the American Girls' School in Tehran. It renounced politics, carried many articles relating to scientific domesticity, and campaigned for women's rights. It lasted thirteen years.[13]

Reza Khan's 1921 coup did not immediately have a great impact on women, but eventually his rule proved important for them. He was a rough soldier, often brutal to opponents, but his centralizing measures were in part a response to Iranian realities. Once he had built a strong conscript army, he was able to put down autonomy and tribal movements. He set about building a modern nation-state, ending Western privileges, and encouraging industry, communications, and transport; he promoted modern education, and also Iranian nationalist ideology with its stress on pre-Islamic virtues. He made the nomadic tribes settle, lessened the ulama's independence, and made parliament a rubber stamp. His expansion of a public school system, of a national judiciary under a Ministry of Justice, and of government-sponsored social welfare all weakened the power of the ulama, who had controlled these spheres.

Unlike Atatürk, Reza Shah did not take power as the leader of a nationalist movement, and he relied largely on straight autocratic and military power. His break with religious leaders was less sharp than Atatürk's. He introduced no major legal reforms regarding women's rights, though he extended these rights in other ways. Reza Shah greatly extended public education, including university education, for boys and girls, and created boy and girl scout movements. He asked women to contribute to building Iran, both via informed motherhood and in appropriate jobs, like teaching.

Women's autonomous activities continued until the mid-1930s. In 1927 Sediqeh Daulatabadi returned to Iran with a degree in psychology from Paris. She appeared in Tehran in European clothes, unveiled, and continued her feminist activities. The newspaper *Women's World* continued to publish until it was closed down by the government in 1934, a closure that, in public, its leaders accepted, saying that Reza Shah was bringing its programs to fruition. A young woman poet, Zandokht Shirazi, founded the Society for Women's Revolution in 1927 in Shiraz, later changing its name to the Society of Women's Movement. Its aims included struggle against veiling and promoting equal rights for women. The society was banned after nine months, and Zandokht moved to Tehran and started an illustrated newspaper, *The Daughters of Iran*. In the 1920s there were important socialist and communist women's organizations, tied to their respective parties. The largest one was the socialist Patriotic Women's League, founded in 1922 by Mohtaram Eskandari, a Qajar princess married to Sulaiman Eskandari, a prominent socialist. It carried out daring campaigns for women's rights, braving attacks from religious conservatives. It set up women's literacy classes, published books, and put on plays. The league continued until 1932, and it published a journal, *Patriotic Women*, to which Daulatabadi contributed after hers was banned. Some Communist women joined the Patriotic Women's League, but others founded the more militant Women's Awakening in 1923. As was true in some other Middle Eastern countries, Communist Party demands for women workers included no night shifts for women and children and paid maternity leave.[14]

The progressive nationalist Revival Party had links with feminists, mainly through their influential exile newspapers, begun before Reza Shah's coup, *Kaveh* and *Iranshahr*. The former was published by Sayyid Hasan Taqizadeh, a leader of the leftist nationalists in the 1906–11 revolution, who spent many years in Germany. He was then an advocate of total Westernization, including in women's rights. *Iranshahr*, published from Switzerland by the progressive reformist Husain Kazemzadeh Iranshahr took a similar approach toward women's rights.

As elsewhere, the women's movement was based on the educated middle and upper classes—even its socialist and communist streams. Reza Shah took increasing action against socialists and communists, which affected the women's movement. In 1931 he had the parliament pass a law declaring socialist and antimonarchical activities illegal and banned opposition parties. The Socialist, Communist, and Revival parties were banned, and the press was censored and controlled. Soon women's organizations were either suppressed or brought under state control, with leftists getting the harshest treatment. The last semi-independent activity was the Congress of Oriental Women organized in Tehran, 1932, which included some outspoken socialist and feminist speeches. By 1935 the independent women's movement was suppressed, and Reza Shah set up an official women's organization.

Reza Shah visited Turkey in 1934, and was impressed by the role of women in Atatürk's centralizing and modernizing reforms. On his return he called together some women and encouraged the formation of a Ladies Center under the honorary presidency of his daughter, Shams Pahlavi. His main objective was to prepare the ground for unveiling, which the center promoted. The 1930s, which brought the end of independent women's activities, continued to see some women's input into reforms, and such women often preferred the new official framework, with its protection against fanatical attacks. The government took over some of the programs of women's organizations and periodicals, including opening the university to women, speeding the implementation of primary and secondary education for girls, encouraging women's employment in the state sector, opening new public arenas to women, and outlawing the veil. While women who opposed the state's suppression of their organizations were silenced, other women leaders and their journals welcomed Reza Shah's activities to promote women's goals.[15]

In January 1936 Reza Shah decreed unveiling for all women. In some cities this was enforced by gendarmes' pulling off women's chadors. In a famous incident, when the queen and some companions tried to enter an important shrine unveiled, mullas prevented them. In response the shah stormed into the shrine without taking off his boots, and beat and arrested several mullas. There was some serious ulama-led unrest, especially in Mashhad. The sudden unveiling seemed to many like going out naked, and some women scarcely left their homes.

In the same period, education and teacher training were expanded; the University of Tehran opened in 1935, and some women attended from 1936. The Civil Service was opened to women, and the new Ministry of Health set up a midwifery school. The Civil Code, completed in 1931, made few changes in shari'a laws relating to women, but did establish minimum marriage ages of fifteen for women and eighteen for men. Minorities, as in most Muslim countries, could follow their own personal status laws. By a 1937 law, all marriages, divorces, births, and deaths had to be registered with the state.

Reza Shah's policies were at first popular among reformist men and women. Most reformist males retained a belief in fundamental male-female differences. Even female advocates of women's rights often gave priority to women's role in the family. Some Iranians turned against Reza

Shah in his last years, but this was based more on his increased arbitrary autocracy than on his treatment of women.

Reza Shah came under the influence of Nazi Germany. Although Iranian nationalists had earlier turned to Germany as an alternative to Russo-British control of Iran, Reza Shah and conservative nationalists were attracted by Nazi ideology, and stressed the common "Aryan" roots of Iran and Germany. Although Reza Shah's request that foreign countries use the local term "Iran" instead of the Western term "Persia" was reasonable, it was suggested by a German representative's noting that "Iran" and "Aryan" were linguistic cognates.

When Hitler invaded Russia in June 1941, Britain and Russia became allies and insisted on removing German influence in Iran, forcing Reza's abdication in favor of his son, Muhammad Reza. From 1941 to 1953 parliament and ministers regained power, and political parties were formed ranging from the pro-communist Tudeh to liberal and conservative parties and revived Islamic movements. Several liberal and leftist groups had women's programs or divisions, but these remained subordinate to the parties and their programs. Some Islamic groups called for a reversal of unveiling and reforms. When enforcement of unveiling ended after Reza Shah's 1941 abdication, it became clear that unveiling was part of a class cultural division, with modernized middle and upper classes wearing Western-style clothes, and the popular and bazaar classes returning to the all-covering chador, though without face veils.

The Reza Shah period saw gains for women in education, health, physical activity, public presence, and employment. Some women saw unveiling as a gain, but others as an imposition. Poor women, especially in the heavily taxed popular classes and settled tribes, gained little or nothing. Some women entered the public workforce as teachers, in government jobs, and in factories. Women and children worked in the growing carpet industry, which produced Iran's second largest export, after oil. Conditions in carpet and textile workshops were often terrible and pay was low, but carpet making added to family income, and in tribal carpet making the work was more flexible.

In Iran, as in several other countries, there developed what has been called "two cultures," especially in urban areas. Those classes who had Western-style education and government or Western-tied employment followed Western ways, while the popular and bazaar classes remained tied to many older ways, and also to the ulama who provided them legal and other services. As in many countries, the position of women was often the crucial element in this division, with one group favoring the chador, reluctant to educate girls, and so forth, while the others favored greater gender equality.

AFGHANISTAN

This mountainous country has long been dominated by tribal politics, in which rulers, themselves of tribal origin, have had a hard time imposing centralization and its accompanying reform on the tribal population. Afghanistan came into existence as a country only in the eighteenth century, but it has rarely had a strong state, owing to the predominance of tribal groups of multiple ethnicities, of which the Pushtuns are the largest and Persian-speakers the second largest. Two late nineteenth-century amirs and an early twentieth-century king tried to modernize and centralize the country and to lessen the restrictive tribal codes on women, but were ultimately unsuccessful. The most dramatic changes were attempted by Amanullah Khan, with the help of the reformist intellectual Mahmud Tarzi (1866–1935); the latter edited the paper *Siraj al-Akhbar*, which advocated modern reforms, including for women. Amanullah tried greatly to expand girls' and women's education, and to change the most patriarchal laws. He even advocated unveiling and Western dress for women, which he practiced at court and with his wife. His 1921 family law abolished forced marriage, child marriage, and the payment of tribal bride price, and it placed restrictions on polygamy and on huge wedding expenses, although such provisions were in most cases impossible to enforce. A conservative tribal and clerical reaction forced him to abdicate in 1929. This was a case where the reforms enacted by the ruler were far in advance of what the society of the time, and especially its tribal and ulama leaders, were willing to follow.

The reform policies on women's issues of Atatürk, the Pahlavi shahs, Amanullah, and some later postindependence Arab rulers—notably Habib Bourguiba of Tunisia—do not mean that women's rights were their central concern. They were primarily concerned with unifying and modernizing their countries and increasing the power of government. For these purposes, curbing the power of foreigners, tribes, elite households, and religious institutions was important. These rulers promoted greater freedom for women in the public sphere, replacing the near-absolute control of patriarchal families over women with partial state control, and mobilized some women in the project of modernization and national strength.[16]

EGYPT

Egypt, the most populous Arab country, has had the longest and best-documented women's movement in the Middle East. In Egypt and elsewhere, Christian and Jewish women, who had the most contact with

Western institutions, were the first to attend foreign and missionary schools and to adopt many Western ways and ideas, including unveiling. Previously class and urban-rural and nomadic divisions had been more important than religion in women's social practice, but in the twentieth century religious and ethnic ties became increasingly important elements in influencing women's behavior. Several Christians, both Coptic and Syrian, and Jews were important in Egyptian nationalism and in women's activities and publications. All were considered Egyptian, and the idea that Egypt was an Arab state became prominent only after World War II.[17] There were differences in the pace of modernization among communities. Most Muslim women covered their faces until the late 1930s. Many middle-class Copts, Jews, and Syrian Christian immigrants and some Muslims unveiled earlier.

Egypt had the strongest and most varied women's movement in the Middle East, and women's rights groups helped bring about significant change in health, education, family practices, and women's employment. Yet in reforming the laws affecting women, Egyptian governments have done less than those in Tunisia, Turkey, Morocco, or prerevolutionary Iran. Egyptian women's movements organized major demonstrations for nationalist and feminist goals, worked both within and outside political groups and parties, and pioneered in education and welfare. They had important impacts on education, job training, changing the image of women, expanding women's public roles and employment, and achieving woman suffrage and eligibility for election in 1956.

Egypt's uniquely varied women's movement was due both to its early exposure to Western and capitalist forces and to its having the longest period of any Middle Eastern country when independent feminist organization was possible, from about 1900 until 1956. In most Middle Eastern countries independent organization was constrained by colonial or indigenous governments. Egypt had a feminist organization of international importance and affiliations, the Egyptian Feminist Union (EFU), headed by the feminist pioneer Huda Sha'rawi, a woman of elite origin and multifaceted activities. Sha'rawi and the EFU campaigned on many issues and undertook extensive social service and educational activities. Some Egyptian feminists were more radical, like Doria Shafik and the leftist Inji Aflatun. Islamism (Islamic politics) also began in the interwar period, with its most important organization coming with Hasan al-Banna's creation of the Muslim Brotherhood in 1928. It had significant women's affiliates, and continued thereafter in Egypt and elsewhere. In the 1930s, Doria Shafik, who achieved a *Doctorat d'Etat* from the Sorbonne, founded another important Egyptian feminist organization, the Bint al-Nil Union. She was controversial, sometimes seen as too French, too Western, and too upper bourgeois, despite her strong nationalist record and influential leadership.[18]

In the interwar years leading women from all religious communities established philanthropic societies, breaking the control over philanthropy exercised by religious institutions, among Muslims ulama and waqf institutions. Some women found a way out of seclusion in social welfare work. Among prominent activist women was Mayy Ziyadeh, a Christian who created a mixed-gender salon in 1914. An outstanding intellectual and professional woman, Nabawiya Musa became inspector of girls' schools in 1924. She had to face conservatives who monitored girls' behavior and opposed her teaching Arabic. She published many books and articles, founded women's schools, and advocated anti-British nationalism.

Beth Baron has analyzed what was called at the time the women's awakening.[19] She shows that while males have been considered the important advocates of women's rights, many female writers expressed themselves on these rights and other issues in the new women's press, which began and flowered in the late nineteenth and early twentieth centuries. The women's press articulated a variety of positions. One theme was a campaign for what many call scientific domesticity, which soon became central throughout the Middle East. Today, a stress on domesticity might seem not at all liberating. However, the domesticity movement encouraged women to be educated, mainly in order to bring up educated sons, to adopt more healthful practices in homemaking and child rearing, and to take on new responsibilities. While some today stress the positives in premodern times, when women from different classes intermixed more, this intermixture was based on systems involving large households, harems, and slaves and servants, while the new domesticity was congruent with the decline of these conditions and the rise of autonomous nuclear families. Women who had little contact with manual work and few ideas of hygiene became educated, and educated others, on how to manage a new type of household, and women were encouraged not to rely on wet nurses and nannies but to use their own bodies and brains in new ways.[20] A seminal article by Afaf Marsot is often cited as showing the managerial capabilities and activities of premodern women, but what she vividly demonstrates is a situation already influenced by new ideas and practices among upper-class women with modern educations.[21] Gains often involve losses, and scientific domesticity in both East and West was also a straitjacket, binding women to unnecessarily long hours of cleaning, cooking, and child rearing, and placing new limits on their behavior and language. Those who see scientific domesticity and other new ideas as blind copying of the West, however, ignore the strong indigenous forces involved in modernization and the socioeconomic changes that made such ideas appropriate to capitalism, even partial or dependent capitalism, everywhere. Baron's recognition of the contradictory nature of scientific domesticity has been developed further by Afsaneh Najmabadi and others.[22]

Several influential women intellectuals in Egypt and elsewhere diffused a variety of new ideas regarding the roles and capabilities of women. Their role is often ignored in discussions of Middle Eastern intellectual history. Their writings on scientific domesticity included much practical advice on homemaking and child rearing, including health, hygiene, and child care at time when infant and child mortality was high. Many in Egypt and elsewhere used new ideas of domesticity to argue the need for women to be educated and knowledgeable about the world. Some advocated a public role, with women to repudiate seclusion, unveil, and work in various professions.

Women's specifically political—nationalist and feminist—activities are discussed in several books and are featured by Margot Badran.[23] Women organized militant nationalist demonstrations in 1919, in which several women were killed. In 1920 the nationalist Wafd Party set up a Women's Central Committee (WWCC), which often acted independently. In February 1922, the British, under nationalist pressure, issued a declaration of Egyptian independence, though they reserved several important powers. Huda Sha'rawi called the WWCC to her home in 1923, and they formed the EFU with Sha'rawi as president. They were more radically nationalist than the Wafd. Sha'rawi resigned from the WWCC, and she and many others thenceforth pursued their nationalist and feminist program from the EFU.

The EFU began an organized feminist struggle, pioneering in this and in setting up new organizational structures and international affiliations. The first public declaration of the EFU program came at the International Woman Suffrage Alliance congress in Rome, May 1923. Huda there said that Egyptian women were calling for restoration of their lost rights and reclaiming their national heritage, not imitating the West. She evoked two golden ages, the Pharaonic and the early Islamic. She said ancient Egyptian women had had equal rights, lost with foreign domination; original Islam granted women equal rights, which eroded with time. Nabawiya Musa said only a few thousand urban women lost their rights: "The Egyptian peasant woman still enjoys all her social rights." Egyptian and Arab feminist and nationalist discourse frequently idealized peasant women, used as a symbol of both women and the nation.

Returning from this congress, Sha'rawi and Saisa Nabarawi uncovered their faces at the Cairo railroad station as a political act, and some of the crowd did the same. The veil was seen as representing the old social system. Both women gave unveiled photographs to Egyptian papers. In 1925 the EFU founded a French-language monthly, *L'Egyptienne*, which discussed unveiling in the Middle East, including a notable book, *Unveiling and Veiling*, published in Beirut and discussed below. A feminist demonstration against the veil occurred during a state visit in 1928 of the Afghan king and queen, when the first Muslim queen to unveil was required by Egyptian court protocol to veil. Face covering waned in Egypt, and by the late 1930s it was largely gone.

Unveiling was not among the joint EFU-WWCC demands announced in 1924. These included the full independence of Egypt, educational opportunities, laws banning prostitution, and reforms in health and the economy. They said, "The Muslim religion ordains the equality of the two sexes in all domains, especially in education." They called for educational equality and for more women's schools and teachers. They suggested woman suffrage, to be instituted gradually, and reform of the personal status code. In time such demands became stronger. The feminist movement was essentially urban middle- and upper-class, though it provided services for other classes. It included women from different religions, and its discourse combined feminism, Islamic modernism, and nationalism.[24]

The EFU ran a dispensary for poor mothers and children, a center for domestic instructions, and a handicraft workshop. Their new headquarters in 1932 was called the House of the Women. By bringing women of varied backgrounds under one roof, they hoped to lessen the distance between them. That the EFU newspaper was in French, however, reflected the inability of elite women educated in French Catholic schools to read and write in Arabic, although they spoke it, but the existence of three major Arabic women's journals shows that many educated women read and wrote Arabic. Mass meetings and speeches were conducted in Arabic. In 1937 the EFU created an Arabic periodical, with an unveiled peasant woman on the cover, symbolizing both wider class appeal and unveiling. Both papers ended in 1940, with the onset of World War II.

Little of the feminist program for legal change was realized. A decree in 1923 set the marriage age at sixteen for girls, eighteen for men, but was laxly enforced. Divorce remained a male prerogative in the 1929 family law. Husbands could still get judges to order the forcible return of wives who left home without permission, a stricture that ended only in 1967. There was a partial victory in 1929 when child custody for divorced mothers was extended to age eleven for girls and nine for boys. Fifty years passed before significant changes were made in the personal status code.

More changes occurred in education, where the British had created no girls' secondary schools. The EFU campaigned for such schools with the same curriculum as boys' schools, and the first state secondary school for girls was begun in 1925. Women activists also had some success regarding physical education. Women gradually entered the university, where they often excelled. Few women got advanced education in music and the arts, however.

Paid work for middle-class women challenged patriarchal culture as it threatened men's control of the family and monopoly of the workplace. There was, however, a need for women to deal with girls and women in health and education. In Egypt and elsewhere nursing, which might bring contact with strange men, was devalued, and teaching was long the only respectable job. The EFU encouraged job training, especially in handicrafts, which they sold. Some women worked in textile and tobacco factories and sugar refineries. New jobs for women gradually opened.

Feminists favored protective labor laws. According to the provisions of a 1933 labor law, women were not allowed in work that was heavy or polluting, work that involved heavy machinery, or most night work, which often relegated women to lower positions. Women were not to work more than nine hours, or five without a break, and got maternity leave. The EFU welcomed these rules as a step to recognizing rights of women workers, though enforcement was a problem. After complaints, an inspector of women's work was appointed. Similar labor laws were passed over time in several Middle Eastern countries.

There was great growth in teacher training. The government prohibited some from teaching after marriage, however. Women began to study medicine abroad and began medical careers in the early 1930s. As laws were secularized, demand for trained lawyers grew, and women began to enter the field in the 1930s, though they were not allowed to become judges. Women now began to be professional journalists. Women also got state jobs, and the Ministry of Social Affairs became known as the women's ministry. Entertainment careers were traditional, but mostly not prestigious. This changed with the rise of the Egyptian film industry and the wide public following of a few singers, notably the world-famous Umm Kulthum, whose singing career and character made her for decades perhaps the best-known figure in the Arab world.

The EFU battled state-regulated prostitution, raising many contentious issues. Egypt had regulated prostitutes since the 1860s. Prostitutes were primarily poor women, ex-slaves, and women from southern and eastern Europe. State regulation in the name of disease control was abolished in England by 1886, but was imposed by the British in the empire, including Egypt. The state registered houses, and the police issued photo permits to prostitutes; weekly medical examinations were mandated. If infected, women had to stop working and pay for their treatment. Much of this was hard to enforce. As elsewhere, women, not men, had to pay the price. The 1923 international women's congress demanded an end to state-regulated prostitution and to traffic in women, and the EFU campaigned for these goals. Not until 1949 were state-licensed houses of prostitution ordered closed, and after the 1952 revolution state-regulated prostitution was outlawed.

While the 1923 Constitution said that all Egyptians had civil and political rights, the electoral law restricted voting and political office to men. Women were even barred from the opening ceremonies of the new parliament. The EFU suggested that the vote might initially be limited to educated women. Turkey's grant of votes to women in national elections in 1934 revived the issue. The congress of the International Federation of Women was held in Istanbul in 1934, and the EFU sent a large delegation. At the end of the conference the delegates went to Ankara and met Atatürk. Huda Sha'rawi recalls in her memoirs speaking "to the president of Turkey in his own language expressing the admiration and gratitude of Egypt's women toward the liberation movement he had led in his country. I said that it was highly exemplary for Muslim countries that their big sister had encouraged all the countries of the East to strive for liberation and advocate the rights of women."[25]

In some matters Egypt was close to Turkey in women's rights: a court case was pleaded by a woman lawyer for the first time in Turkey in 1929, and in Egypt in 1934. The first Turkish woman medical doctor graduated from the University of Istanbul in 1929, while in Egypt the first group of women entered the Medical Faculty at the university in 1932. Turkey, however, was radically different in having ended the political and social power of religious groups opposed to women's rights, and in having eliminated the conservative force of monarchy and of most aspects of foreign power.

Syria and Lebanon

Gender and society in post–World War I Syria and Lebanon, where France was the mandatory power, are analyzed by Elizabeth Thompson. The war began the politicization of women's charities; some worked for independence, and some for education, including schools in Arabic to counter the French schools that provided the only respectable female education. In 1924 the Women's Union in Syria and Lebanon was formed. It was multisectarian and Arab nationalist. By the 1930s many women's groups campaigned for public roles and legal changes. Though male liberal nationalists supported some women's goals, there also developed a populist Islamic trend that argued that girls' schools were a French weapon against Islam. Conservatives, colonial and noncolonial, undermined campaigns for woman suffrage and equal rights, and even nationalists often compromised on these questions.

The issue of veiling was especially contentious in Syria. In 1928 a twenty-year-old Druze, Nazira Zain al-Din, published a book, *Unveiling and Veiling*, which became a bombshell. The author condemned the top-to-toe garment with face cover and asserted she could speak on Islamic law, having been tutored by her father, a judge. She put forth arguments for separating religion from government and law, which should reflect changes in time, and said Islamic law should be restricted to matters in the Quran, and that new interpretation of its meaning was permissible. She argued that hijab violated Islam, which favored equal rights for women.[26]

Zain al-Din claimed that Muslim jurists had no jurisdiction on veiling. She requested French intervention, citing the congruence of Western liberal ideals with Islam's spirit. She sent ten copies of her book to the French high commissioner with an open letter, reprinted in newspapers, asking him "to extend his strong hand to save the weakened Muslim woman and lift her from the dark abyss of slavery where she was arbitrarily plunged, contrary to the Book of God."[27] In contrast to frequent French condemnation of the veil in North Africa, in Syria the French did not criticize veiling. In Syria and Lebanon debate raged for two years. Zain al-Din was initially supported by a few prominent Muslims; the Egyptian women's movement magazine hailed the book, and parts were translated into several languages. But hostile reviews soon overwhelmed praise. Zain al-Din was called the dupe of a foreign conspiracy of missionaries and Orientalists who themselves wrote the book to make Muslims doubt their religion, history, and nations.[28] Zain al-Din's appeal to the French backfired. While some secular nationalists continued to support her and unveiling, many rallied to the opposition. Islamic populists in Damascus, after a conservative became prime minister in 1928, mounted violent attacks on unveiled women and threw acid on women not "properly" covered. This caused reformers to withdraw from discussing this question for a time, but elite nationalists gradually came to favor unveiling. Islamic populists were countering a Francophile Westernized elite. Before these events several nationalist progressives openly admired the West; afterward nationalist discourse changed, and some implied that women's rights were a Western Christian conspiracy. Such charges were also made in French-ruled North Africa. French support for a Catholic missionary network encouraged the association of colonialism, Western ideas, and hostility to Islam.[29]

Women's campaigns for suffrage and legal reforms failed, and both nationalists and the French sacrificed women's rights to cooperation with powerful politicians and religious patriarchs. In Lebanon control of personal status was given to the courts of the multiple religious denominations, where it remains. Under a leftist Popular Front government the French tried to change personal status law, but there was a backlash that hurt reform as much as did the Zain al-Din case. A 1938 decree gave citizens the right to invoke civil law, effectively ending Islamic law as the overriding jurisprudence of Syria and Lebanon. It elicited huge demonstrations. Muslim opponents said the law downgraded Islam. They rejected state wedding registrations as meaning civil marriage, which would permit Muslim women to marry non-Muslims. Faced with violent protests, the French concluded such reforms were doomed and retracted the decree. A National Bloc leaflet said, "The French want to take from you your wives, your daughters, and your children!"

Most women's groups allied with nationalists and accepted the formula of "patriotic motherhood" in the 1930s. They united with their relatives in the nationalist elite and subordinated women's goals to national independence. The 1930s ended with neither legal gains nor a mass base for women's organizations, and little expansion beyond the 1920s. However, the state had to expand health, education, and labor protections for women, which laid a basis for later advances.

Syria and Lebanon had labor unions and significant Communist parties. The CP program condemned veiling and forced marriage, and created a women's wing in the mid-1930s. Labor and CP gains brought improved conditions for some urban working women, but labor laws were often violated, and, as elsewhere, labor law protections virtually blocked women's entry into high-paying industrial jobs just when employment in home industries was falling. Communists joined in opposing the 1938 personal status law reform. Leaders of women's movements worked for labor organization, but their focus was on helping poor women get home work. Communists, unions, and nationalists often abandoned women's demands when faced by opposition to them.

As more women went out in public in Syrian cities, populist Islamists and new proto-fascist groups attacked them. A debate ensued on where women should walk. Harassment of women and other conflicts brought, in the late 1930s, a masculinization of the streets and of mass politics. This occurred despite women's leading role in nationalist demonstrations, including a 1934 protest in Damascus, and in mass 1936 protests in Syria and Lebanon. In 1938–39 Damascene women organized four nationalist protests on their own. But political movements were male-dominated, and with growing violence the message was that the streets were too dangerous for women—a message reinforced by the emergence of proto-fascist paramilitary groups who increased the violence of street politics.

The leading Nazi-influenced group was the Syrian National Party. In Beirut the right-wing Christian Lebanese Phalange became important. Hitler and Mussolini were sometimes viewed as strong state builders, and anti-Zionism made antisemitism appealing to some. Nazi-influenced groups adopted violent methods, including street battles, and favored strongly male-dominant views. The interwar period saw largely successful campaigns to keep women from going to cinemas. The press also became remasculinized in the 1930s. Newspapers rarely mentioned women after the demise of the significant women's press of the 1920s. By 1933, nearly all women's magazines were defunct, disappearing just when the women's movement was holding high-profile conferences. In the 1930s the press printed complaints about educated wives and images of women in stories of sex, violence, and scandal. Such stories implied great risks to women if they ventured out.

World War II saw preparations for the French to leave and struggles among oppositional groups for roles in independent Syria and Lebanon. The women's unions of both reorganized in early 1944, into the Syrian-Arab Women's Union, and the Lebanese-Arab Women's Union. Under Huda Sha'rawi's leadership the first Arab Women's Conference was held in Cairo, December 1944. Just before this Damascus ordered the segregation of women tram riders during religious holidays, fulfilling an Islamist demand. In this problematic climate, a Syrian women's leader said that Syrian women were more concerned with national goals than with women's goals. She and the main Lebanese leader, while expressing higher hopes, dared only to demand partial suffrage for educated women. The Cairo women's conference, however, produced several resolutions aimed at all Arab governments, headed by the demand for women's political equality, especially the right to vote and hold office. They demanded restrictions on men's abuse of divorce and polygamy, a minimum marriage age of sixteen, universal education, and medical care for the poor. They also made demands regarding Arab unity and Palestine.

The conference aroused Syrian Islamists. An Islamist manifesto attacked the decisions of the women's conference in Cairo as potentially disastrous for the Arab Muslim nation. The Friday sermon at the Umayyad mosque, Damascus, condemned the government for authorizing Syrian women's attendance, and governmental responses were hostile to the conference. In Lebanon the situation was better, and the prime minister promised to study the Cairo resolutions.

Women were involved in struggles to hasten the French departure, and women factory workers in Lebanon were prominent in a wave of postwar strikes. Both Syria and Lebanon became independent in 1946, and their parliaments, under popular pressure, had to adopt labor codes in 1946. These extended protections for women and children, and paid maternity leave. But enforcement was weak, and the codes assigned workers to particular unions and limited strikes.

In the interwar mandate period there occurred rapid urbanization, economic crises, increasing numbers of women in the workforce, and challenges to old forms of male control. However, women's movements had no reliable allies. The Communists supported women workers but stopped calling for reforms in women's legal status, probably for fear of sectarian divisions and rivalry with Islamists for lower-class allegiance. Elite nationalists also appeased religious interests.

Arguably, colonial rule negatively affected women's rights. While in Turkey and Iran rulers curbed the power of religious leaders and increased women's rights and public roles, colonial powers rarely interfered overtly in religious or women's rights matters, and when they did, it could bring a backlash. Foreign rule strengthened conservative Muslims and increased ideological hostility to things Western or Christian. The appeal of women's movements was undercut by suspicion of foreigners and their ideas. Nevertheless, progress occurred in women's education, health, and entry into various occupations and laid the foundation for subsequent advances.

The women's movement in Syria and Lebanon was never strong enough seriously to challenge dominant colonial and local patriarchal structures and forces. As elsewhere, many women participated courageously in nationalist struggles for independence, but when independence came, the nationalist elite did very little for women, though later in the twentieth century new governments did more.

In colonized areas like Syria, Lebanon, and North Africa, where the main struggle was against foreign rule, nationalists wished to distinguish themselves from Europeans and were less open to a "Western" approach to women than were noncolonial Iran and Turkey. But particular situations are contradictory and complex: after independence colonized Tunisia behaved like some noncolonized countries, while in recent decades Iran saw an anti-Westernizing backlash; Syria and Iraq moved toward secular government with greater women's rights, though Islamists have grown in strength there in recent decades.

PALESTINE

When Palestine came under British mandate, there were from the earliest days struggles over British acts to fulfill the Balfour Declaration's pledge to create there a homeland for the Jewish people. This involved many contentious issues, including immigration levels and Zionist purchase of land from absentee owners and clearing out Arabs to bring in Jewish settlers. Socially, the British tended to preserve old ways and do little for modern education or social services, especially for women. This absence was one factor in women's forming educational and charitable associations and building schools and new institutions, which began even before the mandate but grew in the mandate period.

Palestine had a large Christian population, and Christians in west Asia had pioneered in Arab nationalism, stressing the Arab identity of Arabic-speaking Christians and Muslims (and, for a time, Jews). Conservative Muslims were less prominent in Palestine than in Syria and Iran, and there was less violence against such innovations as the opening of girls' schools.[30] As elsewhere, veiling and unveiling were central subjects of debate, and domesticity was a major topic. Again as elsewhere, while many men and women supported women's education and roles in nationalism, few spoke up for changing the status and role of women in the traditional family. Women were seen as guardians of national culture, religion, and the family. Starting in the 1920s the Palestinian press was full of heated, contentious articles on gender issues.[31]

Women's activity began with primarily charitable, reformist organizations. Most worked within one religious group. Missionary and Christian groups often pioneered in women's activities that extended to Muslims. Although the charitable groups were in many ways conservative, they also tied in to the growing nationalist movement. The more political Arab Women's Association was founded, and it organized the first Arab Women's Conference in 1929. Nationalist riots and large-scale arrests in that year and the death sentences imposed on three men brought a variety of women's protests and activities. These continued with the struggles of the 1930s, culminating in a 1936–39 general strike and Arab revolt. Women, like men, were radicalized and, especially in peasant communities, participated in the revolt in many ways. Some writers note a conservative reaction regarding women's dress and activities in the late 1930s; Ellen Fleischmann, however, believes this to be overstated, and that its main feature was to get Muslim and Christian women to dress conservatively, to show they were Arabs (and not Jews).[32]

As in many women's movements, a dominant approach was that the national struggle took precedence, and that reforms favoring women could be achieved only after national independence. While in Turkey, Iran, Egypt, Tunisia, Iraq, and Syria secular nationalist rulers did make reforms in women's status after achieving national independence, in Palestine independence was not achieved, and hence prioritizing nationalism limited women there more than it did elsewhere. Activist women continued to be overwhelmingly elite women, and they bore the burden of maintaining national and religious traditions while at the same time being active and militant in new ways. The women's movement increasingly identified and cooperated with movements in other Arab countries and expressed Pan-Arab as well as local nationalist views. Although some women's organizations came to speak out for legal and other gender reforms, nationalist preoccupations had a conservative influence. In 1944 the main leader of the movement, Zilkha al-Shihabi, said that "women in Palestine and Trans-Jordan will not demand more rights than what is allowed under Islamic law and the holy Qur'an. Demanding political rights for women is before its time."[33] The primacy of nationalist concerns continued with the UN partition of Palestine into Jewish and Arab sectors, the subsequent wars, and Israeli occupation of the Arab sectors.

Other Arab countries, including Iraq and the countries of North Africa, have not yet had as much scholarly study of the 1914–45 period as have the countries covered in this chapter, but some aspects of their interwar history are discussed in the next chapter. Some general trends were similar in most countries. This period saw a great growth in women's participation in political and social organizations and movements—feminist, nationalist, socialist, communist, and Islamist. Women's public roles and employment expanded, as did public debate by women and men regarding women's issues. Women gained self-confidence, new skills, and greater male respect through their participation in social and political organizations and movements and through their public roles. These trends were found in North Africa and Iraq as well as in the countries covered in this chapter, while they were less important in the countries of Arabia and the Gulf. The most important ideological trend was nationalism, which in noncolonized countries involved strengthening and centralizing the nation, while in colonized countries it was directed at national liberation. Nationalist men and women often stressed the contributions that newly educated women could make both to their children and to national development, though they were mostly not gender-egalitarian and discouraged women's independent demands. Nationalists tended to favor greater secularization and tried to restrict the power of the ulama and of traditional conservative interpretations of Islam that greatly limited women's rights. On the other hand some, especially popular-class, women and men had new problems resulting largely from rural-urban migration and exploitative employment, and both socialist movements and right-wing religious ones were often able to appeal to them as well as to disaffected men and women from other classes.

1945–Today: New States and Trends, Women's Activism, and the Rise of Islamism

GENERAL FEATURES

The period since 1945 has seen a great variety of developments affecting women, many of which have been studied especially by anthropologists and sociologists, but there have been few narrative treatments of the history of women in this period in any of the many countries of the Middle East. Within the limits of this book I can only suggest a few major points and note some lacunae regarding what is known about women in recent decades. I will primarily go country by country, an approach that allows distinctions among laws and governmental structures and practices of different countries, though it cannot give equal space to internal variations or the general features discussed immediately below. I will not stress statistical comparisons among countries, an approach available in several recent human and women's rights reports that are cited.

The period was characterized by an extension of modern economic trends, a growth in the importance of oil and of Western influence in the region because of oil and strategic interests, rapid population growth only partially countered by family planning, and a dramatic growth in migration, both from countryside to city and between countries. Much of this migration was, either temporarily or permanently, by males, leaving many women to do rural and other labor not formerly open to them. In some but not all cases this increased the power and economic control of women, though male-dominant ideology remained resistant. Large-scale migration of families from countryside to cities resulted in the rapid growth and large size of urban areas, and the spread of shantytowns that often reproduced many village customs and patterns. Since 1970 Islamist groups have frequently been more successful in reaching and often helping poor migrants and other urban dwellers than have secular groups and parties.

The early decades of this period saw the growth of both nationalist and leftist movements in the most populous countries—movements in which women participated and succeeded in putting forth some important women's demands, although these were subordinated and sometimes sacrificed to nationalist and leftist demands by male leaders. In several Middle Eastern states the early postwar years, which saw some coups, revolts, and other changes in who held state power, gave way to authoritarian states with strongman rule in which women's organizations were limited to those sponsored by the state. Several of these authoritarian states, notably Pahlavi Iran, Egypt, Tunisia, Iraq, and Syria, passed legal and other reforms favorable to women. On state power as on several matters Turkey was an important exception, with a trend, among many vicissitudes, toward decreased strongman authoritarianism and increased autonomy and influence of women's groups after Atatürk's death. From about 1920 to 1990 it was mostly rulers who had replaced traditional monarchies with modernizing nationalist governments who extended women's rights while instituting control of autonomous women's organizations. More recently and perhaps by chance, hereditary rulers—as in Morocco, Jordan, Oman, and Kuwait—have taken more steps to advance women's rights than have nonhereditary rulers.

Overall women's education increased, often dramatically, at all levels, as did women's labor force participation, less dramatically, and below what was found, for example, in East Asia. Women entered into a greater variety of industrial, agricultural, white-collar, and professional jobs, though there were still barriers to both entry and respect, with Turkey having the most nearly egalitarian record and Saudi Arabia being the most limited of the major states. Slow rates of economic development and the imbalances and discouragement of industry that resulted largely from the primacy of oil income brought high rates of unemployment and underemployment and hindered the rapid opening of new spheres of employment to women. Resistance to women's employment in some countries and spheres, though often expressed in traditional ways, was also partly based on this economic reality.

Few men gave significant help in housework or child care. Personal choice in marriage grew, though at different rates in different regions and classes, and the ideals of virginity and fidelity for women remained strong, though not always followed. Nearly all areas had important cultural divisions between the classes whose members had modern jobs, educations, and some new ideas on gender relations and those, both male and female, who identified with more traditional ways. These divisions were intersected in various ways, including by some women and men who offered more gender-egalitarian versions of Islam. These versions, put forth largely by newly educated Islamist women, stressed both new interpretations of existing texts, especially the Quran, and insistence on defending the rights granted to women by Islam. However, Saudi Arabian oil income allowed that country to subsidize mosques and schools throughout the Muslim world that taught their restricted gender-segregated and male-dominant minority version of Islam.

International influences were contradictory. Islamists and conservative nationalists used Western support for gender reforms and more freedoms for women as a ground to attack them and the women who favored them as parts of an imperialist/Christian/Zionist plot to undermine Muslim countries and their culture. These attacks were often effective in times of general impoverishment, discontent, and reaction to foreign occupation. Private foundations and international organizations that included countries in the Global South were often more able to influence gender questions than were Western governments. The First World Conference on Women was held in Mexico City in 1975, and a UN Convention on the Elimination of All Forms of Discrimination Against Women (CEDAW) was opened for signatures at the 1980 World Conference on Women. Several Middle Eastern governments have since signed the declaration, though mostly with reservations based on their interpretation of Islamic laws. In many cases reservations virtually nullify the convention, though in some others governments have tried to meet several of the convention's prescriptions on women's rights, and the convention and its promoters probably influenced reforms in family law.[1] The United States has not ratified CEDAW, which may make it easier for Muslim countries to include reservations. Most Middle Eastern countries have long been, and still are, more reformist in laws regarding women's labor and education than in those regarding family, sexuality, and other matters stressed in Islamic law.

Subsequent UN-based conferences on women were also influential, particularly in creating networks of activists that continued in contact. One of the most productive was the UN Conference on Population and Development in Cairo, 1994.[2] At the Beijing world conference in 1995, a Catholic-Muslim alliance on several questions regarding women and sexuality developed, but the conference nonetheless had a major influence in furthering women's activism and international contacts.[3] Recent years have seen a proliferation of women-oriented nongovernmental organizations (NGOs) in most countries, with various forms of international and (despite their name) governmental support and influence. They have done important work and helped develop female leadership, but competition for money, power, and recognition and the frequent lack of grassroots autonomy have also been aspects of the NGO movement. Some NGOs as well as governmental birth control and health programs have been hurt by the recent U.S. government refusal to fund programs that mention or include abortion and do not stress abstinence only.

Except in Turkey, Tunisia, and Morocco reform in personal status law has been slow. In most countries Muslim women cannot marry non-Muslim men, which often means a pro forma conversion. Foreign Muslim men generally cannot gain citizenship through marrying a local woman and residing in her country, nor can citizenship rights be automatically passed to children of the couple.[4] Matters that have been introduced in only some Western laws very recently are, not surprisingly, rarely found in Middle Eastern laws: abortion is illegal in several countries, though enforcement is variable, and some countries recognize earlier Islamic permission of abortion in the first few months. Most law codes do not punish sexual harassment or marital rape. In many countries marital violence must be extreme to be punished. On the other hand, most women live in countries with paid maternity leave and protective employment provisions for women, often including equal pay for equal work.

In most countries, especially in rural or recently urbanized areas, family and local custom is in many cases still more important than law and the courts. Such custom, especially in countries with tribal populations or powerful family elites, is often less favorable to women than is the written law, despite the existence of some tribal groups that are more gender-egalitarian than nontribal ones. There are movements to enforce written laws, however, and urbanization and expanded education favor such enforcement, at least in the urban areas where most Middle Easterners now live.

Since 1945 the non-Arab and noncolonized states of Iran, Turkey, and Afghanistan have evolved in different directions. Iran began with constitutional monarchical rule, then after the U.S.-backed coup in 1953 developed monarchical autocracy, and since the 1979 revolution has developed a clerical-bourgeois rule that has allowed some opposition but repressed many activities. Turkey, after many vicissitudes, may be evolving into a real democracy, while Afghanistan has been devastated by decades of civil war and invasion and lacks central rule and development. The Arab states, again after vicissitudes, have mostly become partial autocracies, and in a few cases full autocracies, although a few monarchies and emirates, notably Morocco, Jordan, and some Arabian and Gulf states, have initiated significant electoral and parliamentary forms. Nonmonarchical rulers have had long reigns, and some of them have passed, or are planning to pass, rule on to their sons. Human and civil rights are violated in various ways. Opposition to rulers now often, except in Iran, takes the form of Islamist movements that usually seek to limit women's rights. Women's oppositional responses, while sometimes secular, increasingly take the form of new interpretations of Islam. Overall there have been advances in women's education and employment, while changes in law and in patriarchal culture have been mixed.

Autocratic rule has been encouraged by the importance of oil income, which has brought large nontax revenue to governments unfettered by public opinion. Oil income may enrich a state either directly or indirectly, partly through remittances sent home to nonoil countries by millions of foreign workers laboring in oil-rich Gulf states. Oil exports have several aspects inimical to democracy and balanced development. They allow governments to have large incomes independent of taxation, to have large security forces, and to subsidize basic foodstuffs in order to deflect opposition. Oil income discourages balanced development of spheres not tied to oil, creating several states where government employees outnumber and outweigh independent middle classes, and spurs an inflation that hinders launching independent capitalism in the form of small low-paid factories, as in East Asia. Large income in a few hands encourages corruption, monopolistic practices, and overblown bureaucracy. In several oil-based states, especially in Arabia and the Gulf, there is little demand for local labor or women's employment, and conservative forces are strengthened by oil income. Western powers, especially the United States, but also others, have overwhelmingly provided support to authoritarian governments, including direct financial assistance. The current U.S. talk of democracy is generally greeted skeptically in view of this history, and most people doubt that the United States would welcome democratically elected governments that oppose the superpower. The United States and other Western governments supported Algeria's suppression of elections in 1992 when they would have favored the Islamist party, and this suppression was one cause of the ensuing civil war. Autocratic governments have taken some steps favorable to women but have not permitted autonomous women's movements.

In the first post-1945 decades secular nationalists often came to power, and communists and socialists had considerable strength in several countries. The programs and some actions of these groups favored the expansion of women's rights. Since 1970 Islamist groups have grown, and have incorporated many former nationalists and leftists. Among the reasons for this are the failures of secular nationalist governments significantly to improve economic and political conditions, heavy migration to cities from traditionalist rural areas, growing hostility to the West and to Israel, which discouraged purely Western ideologies, overall stagnation and high unemployment, and Islam's no longer being associated with existing rulers, as it was under the Ottoman Empire, which meant that Islam could be seen as oppositional. The role of women has been a changing one and differs from country to country.

Unfortunately there are no published women's history narratives for this period for any country but Iran. Hence it is difficult to construct such a narrative for most Middle Eastern countries, and what follows is necessarily partial. Existing sources too often differ even on elementary facts and dates. Even for such a basic question as the reform of Islamic law, only partial sources exist that cover the whole Middle East.[5] Research has, however, brought to light details of previously little-understood phenomena. For example, the widespread influence of Western penal law has been used in several countries to reinforce customary practices. Honor killings, not sanctioned in Islamic law, have, beginning with the Ottoman penal code of 1858 and going on to twentieth-century Arab codes, often been codified as Western "crimes of passion," subject to reduced penalties. And Western-inspired reduced sentences for minors have meant that families have chosen minors to do the killings—this has been shown in Palestine; in Jordan, where there is an active countercampaign; and in Turkey, which has now abolished the reduced sentences for minors and "crimes of passion."[6]

Several issues relating to women have come to be written about and acted upon for the first time in the past few decades. Birth control has gone from being widely considered un-Islamic, despite medieval Islamic authorizations of it, to being the policy of many governmental and other entities. Early abortion is legal in Turkey and allowed under certain conditions in Iran and some other countries. There is increasing discussion and activity regarding such issues as violence against women and children, FGC, and trafficking in (mostly foreign) women. With growing urbanization, rising marriage ages, and female participation in public life there is an apparent rise in premarital and extramarital sex, though it is not widely sanctioned, and also an increase in operations to restore hymens. Prostitution, rape, child abuse, and incest have begun to be discussed in print in some areas, as has female and male homosexuality. As in many countries there is a gap between dominant law and discourse and sexual realities. Some memoirs and anthropological works stress the ignorance of many boys and girls regarding sex and even menstruation, which results in much distress,[7] but this is gradually changing. One study has noted that books by traditional clerics are more open about sex, though from the viewpoint of male dominance, than are books by reformers, who probably wish to stress the social capabilities of women rather than their purely sexual aspect.[8]

As is the case of law and narrative history, there is a need for a more comprehensive scholarly literature on these subjects. Such a literature could base itself on the increasing discussion of sexual relations for over a century in fiction, memoirs, and poetry and more recently in the press, in interviews, and in scholarly works. There is resistance to public discussion of such issues, in part similar to such resistance in Western history, and in part from hostility to imitating the "licentious" West on sexual matters, and to "washing one's dirty linen in public," thus encouraging Western and local criticism of local mores and of Islam. Increased discussion of such phenomena does not mean that they are now more prevalent than they were formerly, any more than recent discussion of child and spousal abuse in the West means that they have increased. Rather, discussion indicates efforts to deal with such issues, which have resulted in some new laws and action.

On questions ranging from sexuality to religious attitudes and everyday behavior, there continue to be great differences not only between countries and regions but, within countries and regions, between different classes and among groups with different views toward religion and secularism. It is thus both unfortunate and inaccurate to make large generalizations about Middle Easterners or about any of the ethnic groups they comprise, generalizations that often confuse very different countries or groups within one country.[9] Writing a history inevitably involves generalization, as not every individual, group, action, or idea can be covered, but can avoid sweeping timeless generalizations about such things as "Arab women" or "Islam."

NON-ARAB STATES

Iran

The story of Iran's women includes dramatic examples of many contemporary forces involving Middle Eastern women in recent decades, and is worthy of extended treatment that may shed light on these forces and ideas elsewhere. Strong political movements of Communists, nationalists, and Islamists emerged in this period, which saw three major political phases—parliamentary monarchy 1941–53; autocratic monarchy 1953–79; and Islamic Republic after 1979. The latter two had distinctive state programs regarding women.

During World War II there were Russian troops in the north, and British and U.S. forces in the south. Autonomy movements in Kurdistan and Azerbaijan, protected by Soviet troops, also expressed local desires. The leftist Democratic Party of Azerbaijan took control and instituted autonomy. It had an active women's section, and Azerbaijan's Provisional Government had women vote in elections for the first time in Iran. It established equal pay for equal work and paid maternity leave. This ended when Azerbaijan's autonomous government was conquered by central government troops in 1947.[10] Elsewhere in Iran, the pro-Communist Tudeh Party, formed during the war, promised women political rights and equal pay; it created a Women's Association with a gender-egalitarian program, activities, and a magazine, *Our Awakening*. It joined the International Democratic Federation of Women in 1947, but was outlawed along with the Tudeh in 1949. In 1951 a similar Democratic Association of Women was created, promoting social and political rights, protections, and equal pay for women workers.

The formerly semiofficial Ladies' Center became independent as a training center. Sediqeh Daulatabadi worked for it and on the journal *Women's Language*. Several other women's magazines were published, often with radical names and programs. One, *Banu*, advocated woman suffrage. In 1942 the editor of *Today's Woman*, Badr al-Moluk Bamdad, founded the Iranian Women's League, and Safiyeh Firuz founded the Iranian Women's Party, with a periodical, *Women of Iran*. The party promoted woman suffrage and other rights. In 1946 it became the National Council of Women, including women of different views, with an egalitarian social, political, and economic program.[11] It had mainly leftist leaders and a large active membership, and it participated in international conferences. Another women's organization worked for suffrage, prison reform, and legal training. Also created were the Women's Medical Association, the Association of Iranian Nurses, the Women's Art Committee, and other associations. Ethnic-religious groups included the Armenian Women's Charity Organization, founded in 1927, and the Iranian Jewish Ladies' Organization in 1947.

Women were involved in nationalist politics. The control of Iran's oil by a British company that paid low royalties and trained few Iranians became the focus of nationalism. In 1949 a coalition of diverse parties formed the National Front, led by a prominent democratic nationalist, Mohammad Mosaddeq. The National Front demanded (compensated) nationalization of the Anglo-Iranian Oil Company. The *majles* (parliament) voted for nationalization in March 1951 and chose Mosaddeq as premier, bringing a British boycott of Iranian oil, which other countries upheld. The United States secretly instigated a coup against Mosaddeq in August 1953.[12] His overthrow led to the increasingly autocratic rule of Mohammad Reza Shah with strong U.S. influence.

Women were active in nationalist struggles, but Islamic groups inside and outside the National Front discouraged reforms like woman suffrage, as some parties advocated. After the 1953 coup the Tudeh and most National Front parties were outlawed, as was the Islamist extremist Feda'iyan-e Islam. In 1956 the Ministry of Labor founded the Welfare Council for Women and Children, run by women, which worked to improve conditions. Social work was led by Sattareh Farman Farmaian, Iran's first trained social worker, active in Iran from 1954 to 1979.[13] Women volunteers carried out various social programs, many with government and foreign support.

Women's periodicals and professional associations grew, within government-approved or sponsored limits. Independent groups campaigned for women's votes and rights: these included the New Path Society, founded by Mehrangiz Daulatabadi in 1955; the League of Women Supporters of the Declaration of Human Rights, which began campaigning for suffrage in 1956; and the Association of Women Lawyers. These three established the Federation of Iranian Women's Organizations with fourteen groups. They worked to negotiate concessions from the government. They presented the shah with a comprehensive list of demands for equal rights, legal status, and opportunities for women.[14] In 1961 the shah replaced the Federation of Iranian Women's Organizations with the semi-official High Council of Women's Organizations, installing his twin sister Ashraf as president.

Votes for women were achieved during a period of reforms that were seen by John Kennedy and some leading Iranians as needed to strengthen the state and forestall opposition threats in a crisis period from 1960 through 1963. After wide electoral protests the shah appointed Ali Amini, a pro-American reformer, prime minister in 1960. His minster of agriculture, Hasan Arsanjani, launched a major land-reform program, but Amini and Arsanjani were soon dismissed and the land reform was revised in a conservative direction. In 1962 Prime Minister Alam announced that local elections, under a new electoral law, would not exclude women. Clerics, including Ayatollah Ruhollah Khomeini, opposed the law, and the Second National Front opposed the whole process. After clerically led demonstrations Alam cancelled the law. The High Council of Women's Organizations protested. In January 1963 the shah announced his reform program and presented it to a referendum in which women voted. This "White Revolution" comprised several reforms, including votes for women. A March 1963 decree made women's votes official, and women were elected to the majles and appointed to the Senate. In June 1963 a clerically led uprising was mounted against the autocracy, capitulation to foreign powers, and the reform program; the revolt was repressed, with many deaths. New demonstrations followed the arrest of the leading oppositional cleric, Ayatollah Khomeini, who was exiled to Iraq in 1964.

From 1963 to 1979 the shah launched rapid modernization, fueled by rising oil income. He also, like many modernizing rulers, recognized the important role women could play as workers and professionals, and encouraged state-sponsored educational and health programs for women. In 1966 the High Council of Women's Organizations was abolished in favor of the Women's Organization of Iran (WOI), under the shah's twin sister Ashraf, with the queen's mother as vice president. The WOI had several programs in education, training, child care, and other fields, and lobbied the government for women's rights. In 1975 its secretary, Mahnaz Afkhami, became the first minister for women's affairs. Women's concerns were also brought into the planning of several ministries and of the Plan Organization. The WOI and governmental bodies contributed to a growth in women's education, access to health care, and labor-force and public participation, though some women objected to aspects of their work and role.[15]

In 1967 a bill codrafted by the WOI was passed as the Family Protection Law (FPL). It secularized marriage and divorce registration, and made divorce subject to adjudication by new family protection courts. The courts decided child custody and maintenance if parents disagreed. New grounds for divorce included taking a second wife without the consent of the first. Husbands also needed court permission for a second wife. These were major changes to shari'a-based law. After women's groups advocated improvements, the majles passed an amended law in 1975 that, among other points, raised the marriage age to eighteen for women and twenty for men, and tightened restrictions on polygamy. The state began a family-planning program in 1967. In 1977 abortion was legalized with some restrictions, although this was not publicized for fear of clerical reaction. These reforms, like those in most Middle Eastern countries, fell short of gender equality, as men remained household heads, who could still force their wives to have intercourse, and polygamy was not ended. Wives still needed husbands' permission to travel or reside separately; for first marriages brides still needed a male guardian's permission; and honor killings were not punished. The WOI and many women advocated further reforms.

There were significant increases in girls' and women's education, and in women's public role, with a few cabinet appointments; the range of women's jobs grew, including the legal, medical, and business professions. In 1968 the judiciary was opened to women, and most female high school graduates had to enter the Women's Literacy and Health Corps and, like males, serve in rural or backward areas for two years.

As elsewhere, legal reforms and changes in employment opportunities mainly affected modern-educated middle- and upper-class women. Women in rural or urban popular-class sectors might have fewer productive activities than before, and even if they worked for money, they rarely controlled their own income. Rapid rural-urban migration was often disruptive and could increase women's isolation. Growing cultural and income distribution gaps, dislocations brought by top-down modernization, and the unpopularity of autocratic repressive measures led many popular-class men and women to heed the growing oppositional discourse.[16] New opposition movements grew in the 1960s and 1970s. Forced underground and influenced by foreign guerrilla movements, some groups advocated violent action to precipitate mass uprisings. Such groups included the Marxist Feda'iyan and the variable "Islamic Marxist" Mojahedin-e Khalq. Both had women activists and members, but both postponed women's equal rights until victory.[17]

Some reformers, like Jalal Al-e Ahmad, author of the polemic *Westoxication*, and Ali Shari'ati, moved toward a reformist interpretation of Islam, without gender equality. The ulama opposition concentrated on the regime's autocracy, frequent brutality, and subservience to the United States. Khomeini's statements from exile circulated in Iran. He said the FPL was null and void, and marriages, divorces, and births under it were illegitimate.[18]

Ayatollah Mortaza Motahhari presented another position in articles republished as *The System of Women's Rights in Islam*. He argued that women, while primarily wives and mothers, could undertake public occupations and activities as long as they avoided close interaction with men. He defended temporary marriage for the otherwise unmarried, and sought to limit polygamy.

Ali Shari'ati, who presented a modern, activist Islamic position and became popular throughout the Muslim world, considered women's oppression a result of cultural imperialism, depriving Third World nations of their values in order to exploit them. Women were becoming "Western dolls," distracting men from opposition, and encouraging a Western consumption society. This view remains widespread in Iran's popular and bazaar classes and in several other Muslim countries. Shari'ati constructed the Prophet's daughter, Fatima, as the model for a modern Muslim woman. She was chaste, virtuous, and modest in dress. He wrote: "Although Islam is strongly against 'prejudice' against women, it does not support 'equality' for them. . . . Nature has created man and woman as complementary beings. . . . This is why, unlike Western civilization, Islam offers men and women their 'natural rights' and not 'similar rights.' "[19] Modern Shi'i discourse increased as corruption and repression worsened, the shah created a single political party, socioeconomic disruptions and income gaps grew, and the shah was seen as a tool of U.S. policy.

By the 1970s, some women working for gender equality were allied with a disliked government, while the opposition increasingly accepted the leadership of Khomeini, who opposed gender reform. Most liberals and leftists thought they would lead Iran after the revolution and that clerics could never rule. Clerics were supported by the urban popular classes and bazaaris, who had close ties to the clergy and followed what they considered Islamic norms, including chadors and traditional family practices. Partly because the autocracy had a Westernizing culture, Islamic culture became a rallying cry for the opposition. With political groups suppressed, while the clergy were harder to attack, politically activist clerics allied with Khomeini gained in strength. Some secular women in the 1970s wore the chador or a more modern hijab (headscarf, loose smock, pants) to show opposition to the shah.

After the February 1979 victory of the revolution, leftist and liberal revolutionaries were suppressed and eliminated from government from 1979 through 1983. For modernized women clerical power was negative. Women were defined in the 1979 constitution by their family status and duties; the Family Protection Law was annulled, and Islamic law reinstated, including polygamy, child marriage, child custody to the father or his family, free divorce for men but not for women, and, for a time, a minimum age of nine for brides. A governmental announcement of enforced hijab was temporarily derailed after a huge and unprecedented mass demonstration on International Women's Day, March 8, 1979, but was gradually reimposed. In the early years of the Islamic Republic women were discouraged from working outside the home, and women's labor-force participation declined in most spheres, with a gradual comeback since the 1990s.[20]

Several factors led to a gradual partial reinstatement of women's rights. Prerevolutionary reforms were deeper than many realized. Women felt it when they were annulled, and also felt the campaign that reduced their employment and job access. In response, women went to work in the private sphere, and many became independent entrepreneurs and professionals. Khomeini encouraged women's pro–Islamic Republic activism, but soon even Islamist women in parliament and elsewhere demanded legal change. In the Iran-Iraq War 1980–88 the government called on women to be active on the home front, which they were. The war showed up major problems. War widows according to shari'a had to transfer custody of their children to their husbands' families. Many women protested, and some changes were made in laws and practices.

Women's active participation in revolutionary and postrevolutionary politics aroused the consciousness of many women about their political and socioeconomic potential. The new rulers, despite their traditionalism on many gender questions, encouraged girls' education, participation in public health programs, and certain women's public activities. Girls' education was promoted even in distant tribes and villages, so that almost universal literacy has now been achieved for girls.[21] While the regime closed some spheres to women, many circumvented these limitations, entered the private sphere in novel ways, and went into areas such as teaching, medicine, and the arts.[22]

A novel trend for Iran, of women interpreting Islam in more gender-egalitarian ways, became important. Many women felt the shock of being deprived of rights, and opposed severe controls and punishments regarding behavior. Some mastered technical forms of Islamic argument after the government opened religious education to women. More women were politically active, and more girls were educated. There developed a new group of Islamic women, some related to major political figures, who promoted women's case. The women's press was both a profession and a rallying point.

The most vocal opposition to restrictions on women came from the women's press. The magazine *Zan-e Ruz* (Today's Woman), which began in the 1960s and changed tone after the revolution, often opposed new laws and practices with novel interpretations of Islam. Women's magazines featured stories of women's suffering under despotic husbands. Such publicity and activism brought some legal remedies, such as limits on a husband's right to prevent his wife from taking a job. A new marriage contract was introduced that spelled out wives' rights and grounds for women to divorce, similar to those in the Family Protection Law.[23] However, these provisions were valid only if both the bride and groom signed them. The government tried to mitigate some gross injustices by instructions to the courts. A limited divorce reform bill passed parliament in 1989, saying that (as under the FPL) divorces had to have court permission.[24]

The women's press flourished in the liberalization of the 1990s. The weekly *Zan-e Ruz* reflected the views of women activists, including advocacy of women's demands. In 1992 its editor Shahla Sherkat quit and launched the monthly *Zanan* (Women), which became notable for its gender-egalitarian stance. It raised forbidden subjects and published articles by men and women, Islamic and secular, including Iranian women abroad. The prominent secular lawyer Mehrangiz Kar was a frequent contributor, as was the reformist cleric Hojjat ol-Islam Mohsen Saidzadeh.

Many articles cited the spirit of Quranic verses that address men and women equally, and explained inegalitarian verses as due to temporary circumstances. After *Zanan*'s articles on women judges, the journal of the Islamic Center in Qom published notes by the late Ayatollah Motahhari, who said the hadiths cited to exclude women from judgeships were either inauthentic or did not justify the exclusion. Women were allowed in 1995 to be consulting judges, and today there are a few regular women judges. In 1997 there was discussion over whether a woman could be elected president of Iran. Several women presented themselves as candidates, but the Guardian Council disallowed their candidacies, along with those of many men; this recurred in the 2005 presidential elections.

The struggle for women's causes involved cooperation between secular and Islamic female activists, some secular men, and a few reformist clerics. Reformist interpretations of Islam are not new, but in the Middle East they had not previously been adopted by so many men and women. There has been unprecedented gender solidarity among Islamic and secular activists, including the secular lawyer and writer Mehrangiz Kar, the reformist Muslim attorney Shirin Ebadi (winner of the 2003 Nobel Peace Prize), and many others. Women's magazines must have a theoretical Islamic orientation, but many include secular contributors. In the absence of po-litical parties the press was key to organizing pressure for reform and change; until the crackdown in 2000 the press was increasingly free, and it continued to have some freedom after the crackdown.[25]

With the recrudescence of the hard-liners since 2000, many women have continued to feel the legal, behavior, and dress restrictions of the regime. There was an apparent unwritten agreement that the regime would usually allow much pushing of the envelope regarding dress, con-tact with the opposite sex, and other behavioral matters, though not in politics or truly free written expression, but some random harassment and physical punishment by various official agencies or semiofficial vigilantes continued. Azadeh Moaveni describes the discontent and frustration of middle-class women, and says that most male reformers continue to un-derrate women's issues.[26] She also describes an atmosphere among some classes of hypersexuality, promiscuity, and aping Western excesses, espe-cially in private. This has evoked anger among the popular and bazaar classes, as has the growing economic, cultural, and consumption gap be-tween rich and poor and the prevalence of financial corruption. The 2005 presidential victory of conservative Mahmud Ahmadinejad was based in part on the economic and cultural reactions of these classes.

Given problems with interpreting statistics, authors arrive at different conclusions regarding women and work. Census figures show that the percentage of women in the labor force fell in the years after the revolu-tion, when the government discouraged many forms of women's work, and that this percentage has not recovered to prerevolution levels. Like most censuses in the Middle East and the Global South, however, Iran's seriously undercounts women's work, even though improvements have been made in counting, as in most countries. The low figures for women's work in the countryside, including among nomadic tribes, are almost meaningless. Rural and tribal women often do more work than the men—caring for animals and plants, working in the harvest, gathering food, and doing all the weaving, including carpets that are sold and con-tribute significantly to family income. They usually are not counted in the labor force.

Maryam Poya has used observation and interviews in addition to offi-cial figures. She writes that such figures exclude many women workers, including many in towns whose employers do not declare them, in order to evade taxes and insurance, a phenomenon found in many countries. In the countryside, officials do not ask about or list most women's work. She says that many women are small commodity producers and traders, and others are employed in shops and workshops without being regis-tered.[27] Erika Friedl has noted the contradictions brought by the Islamic Republic's effective programs to improve roads, electricity, water, birth control, and education, which have overall made women's lives easier and longer, but, along with sexual segregation policies, have meant greater isolation and a lesser feeling of accomplishment for some women.[28]

Aside from the many working-class women in a now predominantly urban Iran, women have made their mark in a variety of professions. Women shut out after the revolution were more resourceful than similar men in creating new working lives. They set up small businesses in manufacture and sales, entered educational institutions in such numbers that they now comprise more than 63 percent of university entrants, and went into professions like medicine and law and also into writing and the arts, including filmmaking. A women-endorsed measure to allow part-time work without loss of benefits has encouraged this trend.

After a decade of denouncing birth control as an imperialist plot, during which the population doubled, the government reversed itself and launched one of the world's most effective birth control programs, with free contraceptives and widespread education, including sessions for all newlyweds. This program, along with the rise in education, urbanization, and effective public health programs, has brought birthrates down to replacement levels. Women in all urban and rural regions and classes have been helped by the decline in pregnancies and in infant mortality and the rise in educational and employment opportunities, even though they suffer from the cultural restrictions and economic failures of the Islamic Republic.[29] Smaller families ease burdens on women and bring more into the labor force, though the current large number of children and youths and economic decline since the revolution create many problems for women. Abortion is legal under certain limited conditions; sources on the scene say that it is becoming more widely practiced by doctors in government hospitals without punishment and is the subject of liberalizing debate, though most abortions are apparently done outside the law.[30]

Despite the huge electoral victories of reformist President Khatami in 1997 and 2001 and a reformist parliament in 2000, victories that were especially supported and promoted by women and young people, clerical conservatives and reactionaries retained most control under Khomeini's successor, Khamenei, and the appointed Guardian Council, which rejected or weakened progressive laws passed by parliament. A majles law to raise the minimum marriage age for girls to fifteen was changed to thirteen, though the vast majority of marriages occur at higher ages, and the average marriage age for women, as in most Middle Eastern countries, is now in the twenties and rising. Conservative power grew after the Guardian Council disqualified thousands of candidates in the 2004 parliamentary elections. There are disagreements among reformers inside and outside Iran; President Khatami lost popularity when he could not implement reform and many people thought he could have done more.[31] An increasing number think that no regime that styles itself Islamic will become truly gender-egalitarian, as shari'a law is inegalitarian. Others think Iran can become something akin to Christian democracy, a largely secular and democratic form of rule. This is suggested by the popular intellectual Abdol Karim Soroush, who says that true Islam is unknowable, and so we must work with varying interpretations of it.

The disqualification of reform candidates for the majles in February 2004 showed that the traditionalists would not easily give up their governmental and legal powers. Discontent with the government is active and widespread, but recently has taken more individual forms of personal behavior and Internet communication, rather than group protests that bring jail and suppression. The Internet has allowed women and men who use it to communicate and express themselves publicly in writing as never before.[32]

In the June 2005 presidential elections, Mahmud Ahmadinejad, an almost unknown conservative noncleric, beat ex-president Rafsanjani and the reformists, who had no strong candidate. Reformers were shocked. Though there were credible charges of electoral manipulation, these did not account for Ahmadinejad's majority. The most likely explanation lies in divisions among reformers and in Ahmadinejad's stress on attacking poverty and corruption, with ordinary people highly conscious of the increasing income distribution gap and the malfeasance of the rich and of ruling clerics, with Rafsanjani in both categories. During the campaign there was a significant women's demonstration on June 12 that for the first time questioned the constitution of the Islamic Republic and called for systemic changes in the legal system toward equal rights.[33] But the election results underlined a split between liberal urban reformers and many in the popular classes. It is too early to predict the results for women of Ahmadinejad's conservative past and cabinet. It seems unlikely, however, that there will be either significant new gender reforms soon or a major return to earlier restrictions. Also, all groups want some form of nuclear energy independence, and threats against Iran by the United States strengthen the hard-liners.

Afghanistan

Afghanistan has remained a country dominated by tribes where, at least in rural areas, gender segregation and male control of girls and women have remained prevalent. After the forced abdication of the reformist king Amanullah (1919–29) in 1929, not until the 1950s were reforms attempted again, with a moderately reformed marriage law. King Zahir Shah (1933–73) did little for women. His cousin Daoud Khan (1973–78), who overthrew him and established a republic, attempted a new marriage reform law in 1977, but it was little enforced. A communist-oriented People's Democratic Party of Afghanistan (PDPA) was formed in 1965 and included women's equality in its program. A parallel Democratic Organization of Afghan Women was also formed. In 1970 two mullas shot and threw acid at women in Western dress. One of the perpetrators was Gulbeddin Hekmatyar, the later and continuing Mojahedin leader; this was followed by an unprecedented protest of five thousand school-girls in Kabul.

In a 1978 coup the PDPA took over and instituted a series of rapid land and gender reforms, outlawing forced marriage, establishing free marital choice, setting minimum marriage ages of sixteen for women, eighteen for men, and limiting the male dower. They also took measures to protect mothers' and children's health, legislated compulsory girls' education, and instituted a compulsory literacy campaign. Many tribal elements opposed the reforms, and many went to refugee camps in Pakistan, where girls and women had very few educational opportunities and were extremely isolated.

In September 1979 President Nur Mohammad Taraki (1978–79) was killed on the orders of his deputy, Hafizullah Amin (1979–79), whose policies alienated many people. The Pakistani regime of Zia ul-Haq supported an armed uprising of Mojahedin against the government. In December 1979 the Soviet army intervened, killed Amin, and installed Babrak Karmal (1979–86), who instituted a far more gradual reform program. The United States, largely via aid to Pakistan, supported the most reactionary Islamist groups in this war, as did Saudi Arabia, and many Saudis and other Arab Islamists acquired arms and training from Pakistanis and Americans. Despite the state's slowing of educational and marriage reforms, opposition spread. Many urban women, however, benefited from educational and employment opportunities, and popular-class women benefited from the training and services offered by the Afghan Women's Council, which claimed a membership of 150,000.

The Mojahedin took Kabul in April 1992, declared all women had to veil, and fired women who appeared on television. Civil war continued, accompanied by kidnappings and rapes of women, and many welcomed the Taliban, who took over in 1996 as a force of order. The Taliban were Pushtuns, largely educated in "Wahhabi" schools in Pakistan. They declared women could not work, could not go out unless accompanied by a male relative, and had to wear an all-covering *burqa* when out. Afghan organizations, notably the Revolutionary Association of Women of Afghanistan, and also the international feminist movement, including Women Living under Muslim Law and the U.S.-based Feminist Majority, campaigned effectively against the Taliban, which helped prevent most countries from recognizing the government.

After September 11, 2001, the United States, aided by Mojahedin, attacked Afghanistan and overthrew the Taliban. Though they succeeded in installing a liberal president, Hamid Karzai, and getting an Afghan assembly, including women delegates, to approve a liberal constitution (ambiguous about the role of Islamic law), the power of the central government did not extend much beyond Kabul. In other areas warlords have ruled, and the United States has engaged them as allies in the hunt for Osama Bin Laden. Girls and women are encouraged to go to school and to work; in practice, however, as a result of continued tribal, warlord, and clerical power, and also insecurity, few girls go to school, few women work, and nearly all are insecure and uncertain about the future. Several killings of women in 2005 underlined the dangers women face in many regions, especially if they move outside of strict traditional ways. The major cultural changes needed to ensure greater women's rights have barely begun, and as of 2005 the United States had done little to help extend the power of the center or of reform beyond Kabul and faced rising internal violence.[34]

Turkey

Turkey since 1945 has seen a growth of competing political forces and also of women's organizations, some of which identify with one of these forces. The secular nationalist Kemalists have remained a significant group who tend to think that Kemalism has solved most women's problems and needs only to be extended. The Turkish army, which has taken over the government temporarily several times, most recently indirectly in 1997, is Kemalism's most powerful defender. Another force is the secular Left, which is divided among militant activists who were strong in the 1970s, Communists, and moderate left republicans. A growing force has been Islamists or Islamic-tending movements who, as elsewhere, taking advantage of secular parties' failure to solve major social and economic problems, present Islam as the solution to those problems. They have their roots in the immediate postwar period but have become especially strong since the 1990s, having taken over the prime ministership 1995–97, when they were forced out by the threat of a military coup. The more moderate Justice and Development Party, the AK Party, with partially Islamist roots, has ruled Turkey since its electoral victory in November 2002.

A largely secular women's movement began in the 1980s, and it has become a significant political force. It succeeded in having the Constitutional Court rule unconstitutional an article of the civil code requiring husbands' permission for wives to work. It also broke the silence regarding violence against women and brought about the establishment of several shelters, both official and autonomous. It founded Women for Women's Human Rights and other organizations, and was instrumental in the government's founding of the Women's Library and Resource Center. A few mainly radical feminists stress bodily and sexual issues, but most feminists have been more concerned with the moderate or leftist gender-egalitarian secularism they advocate. Feminists are mostly urban professional women; they have been criticized as insensitive to rural, minority, and poor women, and some have tried to meet these criticisms. Feminists have benefited from the Kemalist reforms, including secularism, and defend these reforms and work to further gender equality. They also represent the emergence of a voice for women that does not depend on the state, and they have made women's rights more than a state-defined issue. Most of them have opposed the rising tide of Islamism, but Islamist women, who have drawn heavily from the huge number of poor migrants to cities, found Islamist parties more helpful to them with food, health, and social services than were secular parties and governments. In the 1980s and 1990s the Islamist Welfare Party was particularly active among these migrant women. A few women have combined feminism and Islam.[35]

Although women have long had full political rights, fewer than 5 percent of the members of parliament are women, and women gravitate less to politics and more to professions like medicine, law, and university teaching where their percentages are high by international comparison. In 1993–95 Turkey had a woman prime minister, Tansu Çiller (who was not related to a dead male leader, as were women prime ministers in Pakistan and Bangladesh), but her record was problematic. In 1995 she formed a coalition government with the (Islamist) Welfare Party under Prime Minister Necmettin Erbakan, which had to resign in the wake of an army-led campaign against it, based largely on fears it was violating secularism. The current government of the AK Party has roots in the Welfare Party, but drew many votes from those angry at the corruption, cronyism, and lack of achievement of previous governments, and the party rejects being called Islamist. Mainly owing to Turkey's eagerness to enter the European Union (EU), the government has expressed willingness to settle the Cyprus issue and has played down its Islamist past. A combination of EU pressure and campaigns and suggestions by women's groups led to a series of legal changes that virtually ended the remnants of gender discrimination in Turkish laws, making Turkey's legislation more favorable to women than is that of several U.S. states.[36] The AK Party's 2004 local election victories increased pressure on it to end the ban on headscarves in public buildings, an issue that many secularists see as embodying the conflict between a secular Turkey and the threat of reviving Islam, while Islamists speak of freedom. AK Party members introduced legislation to criminalize adultery, but the government withdrew it under pressure from the EU and from women's groups.

Some hope that the relatively successful experience of AK Party government and its mixture of pragmatism and nationalism with a relatively light promotion of some elements of Islam may open the way for true democracy in Turkey. To achieve this, government, with the population's support, will have to address the lingering problems of repression of the Kurds, arrests for political reasons, and the continuation of patriarchal practices, especially in the popular classes. There are still differences in women's de facto rights between urban areas and the west of Turkey, on the one hand, and rural and tribal groups in the east, where most Kurds live, but these are less dramatic than they were decades ago. Overcoming the gulf between legal equality and some local practices requires both enforcement of law and efforts to change popular attitudes. In 2005 the government began such efforts with a media campaign, using Turkish celebrities, against honor killings.

ARAB STATES

Overview

The Arab states under British and French mandates gained independence in the 1930s and 1940s. There were some similarities in economic and political developments in most Arab states after 1945, aside from some very conservative ones in the Arabian Peninsula. In the others, independence often led to a variety of political movements, with ideologies of nationalism, socialism, and communism becoming important, and including programmatic reforms for women, some of which were carried out by those who took power, although all subordinated women's demands to other considerations. Nationalist governments wanted to use the talents and work of women, and to weaken vested feudal, tribal, and religious forces, for which mobilizing women helped, but only Tunisia, and in 2004 Morocco, made major changes in Islamic family law. There was little progress toward democracy, and strongman rule, for increasingly long periods, was the norm. Two major revolutions, in Egypt in 1952 and in Iraq in 1958, overthrew monarchies, which weakened conservative groups. The Jordanian, Moroccan, and some Gulf monarchies have, however, recently been progressive regarding women. Since the 1970s Islamists have increasingly dominated the opposition to existing governments; they are harder to suppress than political parties, express a variety of discontents, and sometimes influence parliaments and legislation. They generally favor legal and other restrictions on women in the name of Islam and the shari'a, but have some women's support.

Palestine was the scene of intense nationalist struggles by Arabs and Jews, in which women participated, in the interwar period. Palestine experienced UN-sponsored partition in 1947; further Israeli expansion after Israeli victories in 1948, with the rest of Palestine taken over by Jordan (the West Bank) and Egypt (the Gaza Strip); and Israeli occupation of the West Bank and Gaza since the 1967 war. Egypt achieved total independence with the officers' coup in 1952 and the abolition of the monarchy. Tunisia and Morocco got independence from France in the 1950s, while Algeria, with a heavy settler population, had a long struggle for independence in which women played a key role but did not achieve gender reforms. Iraq had an antimonarchist revolution in 1958. Syria, after an initial period of coups, has seen autocratic government for decades under President Hafez al-Assad and his son, while Lebanon, after a long civil war, returned to arrangements that included representation for its numerous religious communities. In recent decades most Middle Eastern governments have seen long-lived regimes and uncontested successions, but most are highly centralized and largely or completely authoritarian, whether they have a leftist or nationalist origin, like the governments of Syria, Egypt, and Tunisia, or are monarchies, though some have increased electoral and parliamentary roles. The primacy of oil in the economy of the region gives many governments the income they need to be arbitrary, discourages balanced economic development, and encourages interference, often in the form of propping up undemocratic governments, by Western countries, especially the United States. Certain rights for women have been legislated by left-nationalists like Nasser, by the Ba'th Party regimes of Syria and Iraq, and more recently by monarchies in Morocco and Jordan. Most Middle Eastern countries have seen the growth of women's rights movements that have helped bring about reforms, and also of various Islamic women's groups that often promote the recognition of such women's rights as are covered in recent interpretations of the Quran and Traditions, though some act primarily in a conservative direction.

Egypt

The policies of Gamal Abdel Nasser, who (de facto) ruled from 1952 until his death in 1970, began with state-centered nationalism and, in the 1960s—partly because of Western acts against him—moved toward socialism. Nasser, like several other modernizing nationalists, encouraged women's work and education while discouraging women's independent organization and leaving family law and patriarchal culture largely untouched. Less than a year after Doria Shafik established the Bint al Nil Party in 1953, it and all other independent organizations were closed, and no women were in the Constitutional Assembly in 1954. In protest Shafiq and several associates began a hunger strike for votes and representation for women, which the government granted. The EFU was permitted only as a social welfare society, the Huda Sha'rawi Association. Nasser granted woman suffrage, but initially women who wanted to register had to petition the state, and few did at first, though their numbers grew and restrictions ended.

The 1956 constitution included woman suffrage and gender equality before the law and in employment and wages. There was compulsory free education for six years, and female education rose rapidly at all levels. Many women got jobs, especially teaching and clerical jobs, for the first time. The state guaranteed university and high school graduates jobs in the state bureaucracy and free health care.

After the United States and Britain withdrew aid for the Aswan Dam because of Nasser's growing ties with the Soviet bloc, and after England, France, and Israel attacked Egypt in the 1956 Suez War, Nasser appropriated assets of British, French, and Belgian nationals, and from 1960 on, nationalized many Egyptian enterprises. He also passed progressive labor laws, giving legal rights and special protection to working women, including paid maternity leave, breaks for mothers of infants, and day care, to facilitate the entrance of mothers into the labor force. (Other Arab countries have also passed progressive labor laws covering women, though in all enforcement is a problem.) Nasser's 1962 socialist Charter for National Action endorsed gender equality and all citizens' right to medical care, education, and work. Children for the first time were called the responsibility of the working generation, not specifically of women. The charter also approved birth control, which was pioneered by Aziza Hussein. In 1967 the Egyptian Family Planning Association was put under the Ministry of Social Affairs.

The regime did not question family structure, patriarchal power and culture, or religious family law. Men continued to dominate the family, the workplace, and the government. Feminist organizations, like other autonomous groups, were prohibited from 1954. In 1957 Nasser shut down Doria Shafik's *Bint al-Nil* magazine and in 1960 put her under several years' house arrest. In near seclusion, she jumped to her death in 1975. Inji Aflatun was imprisoned in 1959 with hundreds of other communists, as was the Islamist woman leader Zeinab al-Ghazzali in 1965. Nasser helped to create new political and economic space for women, but did not allow independent action or try to reform patriarchal culture or family law. Women remained absent from most top positions. However, they entered education and the economy in greater numbers and with greater protections, and this gave them more of a public presence and more options than before.[37]

Ex–Vice president Anwar Sadat consolidated presidential power after Nasser's death, and suppressed Nasserists and leftists. He ended ties with the Soviets, took measures to open a market economy, and launched closer ties with the West. Like several other ruling entities, including the shah of Iran, the Israeli government, and various U.S. administrations, he early encouraged the Islamist movement against his leftist secular enemies. Dependence on the West, unemployment, and economic inequality grew. Religious conservatives worked to reverse women's advances, though near the end of his life Sadat promoted women's rights with new laws. Sadat's "Open Door" market policies helped bring Egypt near to bankruptcy, and Sadat had to call in the International Monetary Fund. Their "structural adjustment," as usual, reduced subsidies on essentials, resulting in 1977 in the largest riots in decades. Structural adjustment hit women as the state trimmed programs in health and education, women had fewer job opportunities, and the social welfare network was reduced.

Sadat at first worked with Islamists, who shared his aim of ending Nasserist power in universities and in professional and trade associations. This alliance hurt women's rights. In 1971 the constitution was redefined to say gender equality applied only when it did not contradict shari'a, opening the way for attacks on women's rights. In practice, however, the number of educated and working women kept rising. Sadat amended the constitution in 1976 to make Islam the main source of law, and Islamists chipped away at women's gains. But feminist pressure and the UN Decade of Women 1975–85 were reflected in Sadat's establishing the Egyptian Women's Organization and the National Commission for Women to deal with family planning, illiteracy, and child welfare.

Sadat's wife, Jihan, set up women's welfare organizations, but was unpopular with many for her ties to the West and for her reputed ego. As in Iran, the ties of some feminists to the regime were used by Islamists to discredit them. After Islamists killed a minister in 1977, the government broke with them. In the later 1970s Sadat supported women's rights, decreeing gender quotas to increase women's numbers in parliament and in regional councils. Sadat also decreed the first reform in family law in half a century. His decree-law said husbands must register divorces and immediately inform wives. It gave first wives the right to refuse polygamy and stopped the practice of husbands' using the authorities to force wives' return to the marital home. Wives who refused to return could now divorce. The law provided substantial alimony and said wives had rights to the home if they had child custody. Custody to wives was raised to age ten for boys, twelve for girls, and could be extended. Fathers had to pay child support until children could take adult roles. Women's right to work was confirmed, as were equal salaries. Islamists opposed the law, popularly called "Jihan's law," and many disliked its autocratic imposition when there was no parliament to vote on it.

A nongovernmental Committee for the Defense of the Rights of Women and Family at first united diverse groups, but Aziza Hussein, the family-planning pioneer, soon withdrew. A 1980 law gave the government new excuses to arrest opponents, and in September 1981 hundreds of religious extremists, leftists, and others, including the prominent feminist author and activist Dr. Nawal al-Saadawi, were arrested and jailed for months.[38] Sadat was assassinated in 1981 by a member of a militant Islamist group. He was succeeded by Vice President Husni Mubarak, who still rules, increasingly autocratically under a periodically renewed state of emergency.

The Constitutional Court nullified Sadat's family law in May 1985. Parliament replaced it in July 1985 with a weaker reform law that said a first wife could seek divorce from a polygamous husband only if she proved, within a year, that the new marriage harmed her. It reduced the divorced wife's right to housing and alimony, while leaving custody essentially as under Sadat's law.

Mubarak suppressed militant Islamists but acceded to some Islamist demands, including reversals that affected women. Previous women's electoral quotas were reversed in 1986, resulting in a great drop in the number of women in parliament. The Arab Women's Solidarity Association, permitted to form in 1984 and sparked by Dr. Nawal al-Saadawi, was active and called for gender equality and democracy. It participated in the 1985 Nairobi International Conference on Women and other conferences, and published a journal. In 1991 the government shut it down, especially for having opposed the first Gulf War.

From the late 1960s on, many middle-class citizens and intellectuals increasingly leaned toward moderate Islamism. This trend is often dated from Nasser's 1967 defeat by Israel, after which some said Israelis won because they had faith in their religion while Muslims had lost their faith and virtue. Many Egyptians who had migrated temporarily to Arabia became more conservative there. A new type of urban veiling began, first among students, which, with modifications, soon spread in many Muslim countries. The pro-veil discourse in Egypt and elsewhere often implied that unveiled women were responsible for male harassment of them. Urban veiling has various causes: it protects against harassment, hides economic need, and protects women from criticism for working alongside men, as well as affirming Islamic identity. It enables women who could not work or undertake public activities unveiled to do so, but limits women who previously went unveiled. Women's education continued to rise impressively, and more women were employed. Employed women remained a small minority, and many more who wanted employment could not get it. Female unemployment rose much more than male. Studies have shown that despite their disadvantages, poor Egyptian women cooperate effectively to defend and help themselves. But there has been no significant attack on the male-supremacist elements of culture.

Most Egyptian girls, like their counterparts in some Arabian and Gulf countries, still experience female genital cutting (FGC), which some consider Islamic, even though it is not and the great majority of Muslims worldwide do not practice it. The important UN International Conference on Population and Development held in Cairo in 1994 was subject to attacks regarding three agenda points—contraception, abortion, and FGC—but nonetheless made headway on these points. A ministerial decree in 1996 forbade FGC in state-run medical facilities and was affirmed by a higher constitutional court in 1997. On most matters, however, Mubarak's government has tried not to offend the powerful nonviolent Islamists.

Nasser's successors stopped guaranteeing jobs to all graduates, which hurt women, who were concentrated in government jobs. Some women, especially in rural areas, have, however, gained new independence and experience by managing all farm and other work while their husbands work in Gulf countries. This is true in several other Middle Eastern countries as well, and applies also to families where the husband has gone to Europe, although women's ideological and cultural independence often lags behind economic autonomy.

The popularity of Islamist groups in Egypt and elsewhere has been boosted by their founding clinics, schools, and other needed welfare organizations that give services not supplied by the state. The government funds some clinics for family planning and other needs, but, although family size has decreased as it has in most of the world, the success of family planning does not nearly match Iran's recent results. Egypt's continued crises of weak development, population growth, Islamist trends limiting women, and suppression of opposition are of concern to Egyptian advocates of women's and human rights and of democracy, many of whom continue to struggle against autocracy.

The government still responded to some pressures for reform, however. A major reform came with Egypt's divorce law of 2000, which instructs courts to accept a wife's petition for divorce in return for monetary compensation to the husband, even if he does not agree (as he must in traditional khul' divorces). Also significant were reforms in 2004, including revisions to the nationality law to extend nationality rights to the children of Egyptian mothers and non-Egyptian fathers, and the creation of family courts.[39]

Recently there has been, in Egypt and elsewhere, a burgeoning of nongovernmental organizations (NGOs) of variable merit, involved in women's projects and often competing for foreign funding. An NGO law that came in force in 2003 restricts activity through licensing and security rules, and gives the Ministry of Social Affairs the right to dissolve NGOs and put its representatives on NGO boards.[40] Egypt, like several Arab countries, has also seen growing concern about "authenticity," both Islamic and national, in part against feminisms that are tainted as being Western. In 2000 President Mubarak decreed the formation of the National Council for Women (NCW), a governmental body to advance women's status. Women's NGOs must register and must accept the hegemony of the NCW and the Ministry of Social Affairs, though some have refused and the judiciary has declared the 2003 NGO law to be in conflict with the constitution.

Egyptian women have expanded their economic roles and legal rights in recent years, though they have suffered along with men from weak economic development, population increase, and the decline of tourism. Family-planning programs, women's legal status, and literacy levels are improving but have not equaled those in Turkey or several Arab countries.

Iraq

In Iraq a military-led revolution in 1958 toppled the monarchy and was followed by a period in which leftist forces like those of the Iraqi Communist Party were prominent. The left-oriented government of Abdul Kasem Qasim instituted a major and more gender-egalitarian reform of family law in 1959 in face of religious and conservative opposition. Under the 1959 law personal status courts replaced shari'a courts, making rulings based on codified state law, although non-Muslims followed their own laws. The reform restricted polygamy and empowered wives to initiate divorce and make financial claims. It also gave equal inheritance shares, including shares of land, to male and female heirs. Qasim was overthrown in a 1963 Ba'th Party coup, in which Abdul Salem Aref emerged victorious. Under religious pressure, the new junta restored the old inheritance rules and a few other features of the prereform law, but many key features of the 1959 reform law have continued operative until the present, and further reforms were added in the 1970s and 1980s.

After another Ba'th coup in 1968, this secular nationalist party worked to consolidate power and to achieve economic growth. Women's participation was needed, and the government passed laws to improve women's status. Prior to 1968 there were several independent organizations, including women's organizations. The Ba'th dismantled most independent groups and in 1972 established the General Federation of Iraqi Women (GFIW). The GFIW helped implement state policy, running rural and urban community centers that offered job-training, educational, and other social programs for women, and serving as a channel for communicating state policies. The GFIW also played a role in implementing legal reforms and in lobbying for further reforms in the personal status code. Some activists opposed its official nature, however.[41]

The Iraqi Provisional Constitution of 1970 declared all citizens equal before the law regardless of sex, lineage, language, social origin, or religion. Iraq adopted an education law making primary education compulsory for both sexes. A 1979 law required all illiterate persons from fifteen to forty-five to attend literacy classes. Labor and employment laws gave women equal opportunities in the civil service, maternity benefits, and freedom from harassment in the workplace. Partly because of these laws, women's employment grew and opposition to it lessened.

Saddam Hussein took power in 1979. Like several Middle Eastern authoritarian nationalist rulers, Hussein wanted to subordinate the traditional power of patriarchy, tribes, and religion to his centralized state, and hence was generally progressive on social issues and women's rights. Until the late 1980s more opportunities were opened to women in public life, education, and the professions. During the Iran-Iraq War (1980–88), women at first assumed greater roles in the workforce, reflecting the shortage of working-age men, but in 1988, to make room for demobilized soldiers, women were encouraged to return home. Until the 1990s, the number of women working continued to grow. On the other hand, Iraq's aggressive policy in launching the long Iran-Iraq War and its 1991 invasion of Kuwait resulted in wars and long-term UN sanctions that impoverished men and women, reduced female school attendance, and harmed most women and girls even more than men and boys. The once-advanced health care system declined from the mid-1980s, and by the 1990s the system was in crisis.

While most advances in women's status occurred in the political and economic spheres, the government also reformed the personal status laws in the 1970s and 1980s. Divorced mothers were granted custody of their children until the age of ten (previously seven for boys and nine for girls), at which time, at the discretion of a state judge, custody could be extended into the teens, after which the child could choose with which parent to live. Reforms were also made in inheritance, in the conditions in which a woman could seek divorce, and in requiring the first wife's permission for her husband to take a second wife, and all divorces had to be court-sanctioned. These reforms reflected the Ba'th's attempt to modernize Iraqi society and supplant loyalty to extended families and tribal society with loyalty to the government and ruling party.

Women attained the right to vote and run for office in 1980. In 1986, Iraq became one of the first countries to ratify the CEDAW but, like several other Muslim countries, made important reservations with regard to family law. As with other countries in the region, most advancement in the status of Iraqi women occurred in the public sphere.

The regime's attitude changed after the 1991 Gulf War and subsequent UN sanctions. Saddam turned to religion and tribes to legitimize and reinforce his power base and as instruments of social control. The increasing control of these patriarchal authorities hurt women. In 1990 the penalty for "honor killing" was reduced from eight years to a maximum of six months. In 1993 Saddam reversed his prior decree with a new decree allowing men to marry plural wives without the first wife's consent. Tribal jurisdiction, which had prevailed under the monarchy, reappeared, and civil and personal matters were often left to tribal chiefs and tribunals.

After the 1991 Gulf War, the government issued laws and decrees that somewhat weakened women's status in the labor code, criminal justice, and personal status. UN sanctions had a disproportionate impact on women and children (especially girls), causing hundreds of thousands of deaths from shortages in food, medicine, and pure water. The gender gap in school enrollment increased dramatically owing to families' financial inability to send all children to school. One source says that female literacy rates were the highest in the region in the early 1990s and among the lowest, at under 25 percent, in 2003.[42] Though such a rapid fall in one decade is improbable, a dramatic fall in schooling and literacy did occur. As the economy shrank, the government pushed women out of the labor force and government jobs in order to promote employment for men. Women's freedom to travel abroad was legally restricted, and formerly coeducational high schools were required to provide single-sex education only, reflecting the reversion to religious and tribal traditions. As a result of these forces, by the last years of Saddam Hussein's government most women and girls had returned to traditional roles within the home.

In late 2003, after the invasion by the U.S.-dominated coalition, the Coalition Provisional Authority set up the Iraq Governing Council. The council, by a small majority, voted to reestablish shari'a family law and religious courts, but this was quickly reversed in 2004. Many of the council members were chosen to represent religious communities in the absence of political and civil bodies. Religious and ethnic groups also dominated the 2005 elections, with a Shi'i party, many of whose leaders advocate a return to shari'a, winning the most votes.

The temporary constitution adopted in March 2004 and the constitution ratified by popular vote in October 2005 have shari'a only as *a* main source of law, but shari'a and Islamic judges could be emphasized once the Iraqis begin to legislate. The constitution guarantees women equal rights and 25 percent representation in the National Assembly. Some Shi'i and Sunni leaders are calling for compulsory veiling and other limits on women's rights, however, and though many women and secularists are fighting this, it is not clear they will ultimately win. Women and girls suffer from lack of security, kidnappings, and rapes. There is real fear that women's position will be worse than under Saddam Hussein despite resistance by women and secular groups and the constitution's assurances. In Shi'i controlled cities like Basra in the south, women de facto must veil and not mix with men. The increasing incidence of killings, kidnappings, and rapes in 2005 has meant that many girls and women have had to stay at home and live a life of far greater restriction and fear than under the previous government.[43]

New women's organizations like the Iraqi Women's League, the Iraqi Higher Council for Women, and the Organization of Women's Freedom are working hard to guarantee women's rights. Kurdish women in the north, effectively a Kurdish autonomous region since 1991, live under a secular government that recognizes many women's rights. They have many well-financed NGOs and have successfully lobbied for a law against "honor crimes." With violent and nonviolent opposition in Iraq focusing on ending the U.S. occupation, the recrudescence of Shi'i and Sunni Islamist forces, and the salience of ethnoreligious politics countering the liberal effects of feminist groups and secular parties, it is impossible to predict the outcome of the current situation. In the debate and struggle over a new constitution in 2005, women's rights were a major point of contention, and it is possible that women's legal status will vary significantly by region and religious community, as they already do between the Shi'i south and the secular Kurdish north. While the United States has supported women's rights, the hostility evoked by the U.S. presence has encouraged Islamist identities that have been inimical to even the full preservation of women's previous rights and status.

Palestine

Palestinians have experienced a traumatic history since the UN voted to partition Palestine in late 1947. International Arab resistance to partition in the 1948 war brought Israeli annexation of more Palestinian territory, Egyptian occupation of the Gaza Strip, and Jordanian annexation of the West Bank and the old city of Jerusalem. Most Israeli Arabs fled, chiefly to camps in nearby Arab states. Over a million Palestinian women, men, and children have ever since lived a marginal existence in camps, probably 800,000 of them in Palestine, and only a minority of refugees have found a decent living elsewhere. According to the Palestinian Central Bureau of Statistics (PCBS) 66.5 percent of Palestinian households lived below the poverty line in 2002, and the situation is now worse.[44]

The Palestine Liberation Organization (PLO) was founded in 1964. After threats from Egypt's Nasser, Israel launched war in June 1967 and quickly took the Sinai Peninsula from Egypt, the West Bank and East Jerusalem from Jordan, and the Golan Heights from Syria. The war made the PLO a resistance organization. Besides its mainstream component, Yasir Arafat's Fatah, the PLO included leftist groups. These guerrilla groups also operated in Jordan and Lebanon, until Jordan fought and expelled them in 1970–71 and the PLO transferred its base to Lebanon. In 1973 Egypt's president Anwar Sadat launched a partly successful war along with Syria against Israel. At a Camp David meeting hosted by President Jimmy Carter in 1978, Israeli prime minister Menachem Begin and President Sadat signed the Camp David Accords, which brought Israeli withdrawal from Sinai and withdrew the strongest Arab state from the Palestinian struggle via a separate peace. In 1987–91 a major Palestinian uprising, or *intifada*, primarily called on Israel to stop building settlements, confiscating land, and putting restrictions on Palestinians, and to recognize an independent Palestinian state. In 1988 the Islamist organization Hamas was formed and refused to accept a two-state solution. The intifada was a factor in the Oslo Accords between Israel and the PLO's Yasir Arafat in 1993, which provided a flawed path toward a two-state solution. Continued Palestinian impoverishment and disillusionment helped strengthen Hamas. Labor Party prime minister Yitzhak Rabin's assassination by an Israeli religious extremist in 1994, and subsequent Hamas suicide bombings, contributed to a narrow victory of the conservative Likud Party, but Labor won in 1999 under Ehud Barak. President Clinton's Camp David II summit in 2000 failed to bring agreement.

General Ariel Sharon's provocative visit to Jerusalem's sacred Muslim shrines sparked the second intifada, followed by Sharon's defeat of Barak in 2001. This intifada was far bloodier than the first, with suicide bomber attacks followed by much more deadly military attacks from Israel that killed many civilians. Yasir Arafat's death in 2004 brought a new leader and elections, but expanding Israeli settlements, confiscations, the "wall" under construction, and Sharon's declarations showed that he had no intent of returning to anything like the 1967 lines. The Sharon-led Israeli withdrawal from Gaza in August 2005 was significant, but the question remains of whether it will be followed by further meaningful steps toward the creation of a viable and peaceful Palestinian state centering on the West Bank. Sharon's major stroke and the unexpected victory of Hamas in the February 2006 Palestinian parliamentary elections created additional problems.

Many authors stress Palestinian women's continued participation in nationalist struggles against Israeli occupation, with women found participating in or supporting all the major political groups. In the period 1948–67 women's groups and activities were mostly elite and charitable. In 1965, after the creation of the PLO, a women's branch of it, the General Union of Palestinian Women, was set up in the West Bank. From the time of Israeli occupation of the West Bank women joined in nationalist struggles, but a new generation of more activist and feminist women wanted more independent women's action, and in 1978 the first of a series of activist women's committees was created. This was the Women's Work Committee, whose leaders were close to the leftist Democratic Front for the Liberation of Palestine. Three other committees soon followed, two of them close to the Communist Party and the leftist Popular Front for the Liberation of Palestine, and a somewhat less militant one close to Fatah. Although the committees differed and sometimes struggled against one another, the existence of four groups spurred recruitment for membership, and in 1984 the four committees set up a framework for cooperation. All four were secular and nationalist, and voiced some demands for women. The women's movement in Gaza also allied with these committees and grew from the mid-1980s despite repression.[45] Israeli authorities have restricted women's activities and their leaders in various ways, including travel restrictions, and the committees responded by building up international, including Israeli, networks of support. International ties were strengthened at several conferences, especially at the UN-sponsored International Women's Conferences in Nairobi, 1985, and Beijing, 1995, which were also important for strengthening the international ties of women from other Middle Eastern countries. The new women's committees succeeded in recruiting women from all classes. They were generally decentralized and able to deal with local women's needs. In addition to their nationalist activity some of them worked on economic, social, family, educational, and health problems, and set up child care centers, literacy courses, clinics, and income-generating projects. They also helped to organize some women in trade unions. Although the main stated aim of the committees has been freeing Palestine from Israeli rule, they have also dealt with women's issues and given women public leadership roles.

Women were active in both intifadas, which increased their political prominence. In recent years a number of independent women's centers and organizations have been formed, with a wide variety of programs, including university and other women's studies programs, and these have helped call national attention to women's needs and demands. However, women suffer from the economic, political, and military oppression by the Israelis and some Palestinians. They also face the autocratic and patriarchal tendencies of the Palestinian Authority, which has done little to promote able women or women's rights. Although one woman, Hanan Ashrawi, has been a national leader for decades and very prominent in struggles for a state and then for democracy and human rights, very few other women have risen in the Palestinian Authority or its components. Many nationalists stress a home and family orientation for women and encourage large families in order to reach an Arab majority in Israel/Palestine. Rising women's urbanization and education have, as elsewhere, brought some fall in birthrates, but they are now near the highest in the region, with a women's fertility rate of 5.7, while in most comparable Arab countries rates are now far lower.[46]

Annelies Moors has written an important book on Palestinian women, with conclusions applicable to other areas.[47] She demonstrates that legal and judicial protections for women, many of them emphasized in recent historical works based on Ottoman records, predominantly benefit certain classes of women, and that court judgments are often not enforced. She shows how recent developments have affected different classes, with middle and upper classes especially benefiting from educational opportunities to get professional jobs that provide some economic independence. Rural women, however, have seen their role in agriculture decline, often rendering them more dependent on men and less in control of property than before. A trend, also found elsewhere in the Middle East, toward greater importance for the conjugal family has led to more pooling of conjugal property and more choice of marriage partners.[48]

Illuminating the subtleties of the reality that urban more than rural women inherit according to Islamic law, Moors notes, as do some other sources, that rural women rarely inherit and often renounce inheritance so as not to impoverish their brothers (a phenomenon also predominant in Jordan and widespread elsewhere). Moors discusses relations with the Israeli occupiers, with many women used as cheap labor in textile factories, and others impacted by the jailing of male relatives and/or refusing to work for Israelis. Many of the women she studied were involved in struggles against the occupation, and advocates of women's rights are concerned about the increasingly Islamist orientation of that struggle.

Women are discriminated against in penal codes, derived from unreformed Egyptian codes in Gaza and, in the West Bank, from prereform Jordanian codes, which do not reflect Jordan's 2001 ending of impunity for honor crimes. A new draft criminal code that treats men and women equally had not been put in force as of early 2005. Statistics show a pattern, probably similar to that in other countries of the region, of low women's property ownership and inheritance. In a 1999 survey they showed only 7.7 percent of women own real estate, only 5 percent own land, and 20 percent of women entitled to inheritance claimed their share.[49]

Many Palestinian women have been affected in dress, behavior, and restriction of reform possibilities by the rise in Islamist trends, particularly the rise of Hamas, which in the late 1980s launched a largely successful campaign demanding that women wear hijab in Gaza and some West Bank towns. Islamists have grown in importance in recent years and have interfered with some women's programs, although they also have some women's support.[50] Hamas has, like Islamist groups elsewhere, created a network of schools and clinics that help many women.

With the fall of the Soviet Union and the declining importance of the Left in Palestine and elsewhere, the role of the Left in women's activism has fallen since its heyday of the 1980s. The probable nature of personal status law under the Palestinian Authority and any future Palestinian state is unclear. From the 1990s on, much of women's activity was, as in many countries, taken over by NGOs, a reality that increased their international and official financing and sometimes their scope, but also put limits on their autonomy and initiative.[51] Nearly all Palestinians, male and female, have been affected by the great difficulties of movement and of work in Israel since the Israelis instituted pervasive checkpoints and roadblocks during the second intifada and favored non-Muslim foreign workers. Growing difficulties, including Israeli incursions on Arab land and water and the increase in poverty, have moved some men and women to take hope from what are conceived to be traditional and Islamic ways, many of which do not help women's status. As elsewhere, there is a continuing struggle between those who want egalitarian reforms and those who advocate a return to laws and practices seen as Islamic. As in other countries under occupation, national liberation takes priority and it is difficult to stress reforms in the status of women.

Jordan

Jordan has, since its post–World War I creation as the British mandate of Transjordan, been a monarchy with monarchs often favoring reform from above but confronting strong conservative tribal power and more recently Islamist power. After the 1948 war, Jordan annexed the West Bank of the Jordan River, and Palestinians to this day make up a majority of Jordan's population, though Jordanian Arabs of tribal origin are also strong. In the 1967 war Jordan lost the West Bank and East Jerusalem to Israel. There has long been a parliament, but only in some recent years has it had any real power. The first significant women's organization, the Arab Women's Federation (AWF), was formed in 1954, and had a program of raising women's status and literacy and for legal reforms. A coup attempt in 1957 led to the dissolution of many groups, including the AWF. After 1967 much Jordanian attention, including that of activist women, turned to the Palestine question. A crackdown on Palestinian activists in 1970–71 was followed by a revival of "tradition," encouraged by the regime and negative for many women.

Partly moved by the declaration of a forthcoming UN International Decade of Women 1975–85, and also from a desire to appear progressive, in 1974 King Hussein ended Jordan's position as the last non-Gulf Arab state where women could not vote by issuing a decree giving women the vote. Women activists met before the first UN Decade of Women conference in Nairobi, 1975, and got a license for the Women's Federation in Jordan (WFJ). This had a range of progressive goals for women, and its leadership included both Palestinian and Transjordanian women of several political persuasions. It operated numerous women's services and had a varied membership in several regions. The first woman minister was appointed in 1980. In 1981 a state-sponsored General Federation of Jordanian Women (GFJW) was formed; the government effectively took most powers away from the independent WFJ and thenceforth dominated most activities regarding women.

The period 1989–94 was one of political and economic liberalization, and candidates with many views, including twelve women, ran for parliament in 1989. All the women lost, however, and Islamists emerged as the strongest bloc in parliament. The GFJW opened individual memberships, and both leftists and Islamists joined. After major struggles over voting procedures for GFJW leadership, non-Islamists boycotted the election and Islamist women won. A new minister of social affairs granted new GFJW elections in 1991, which Islamists boycotted and non-Islamists won. Challenges continued, and in 1992 the higher court ruled members had to belong to registered social organizations. This led to a leadership with little serious commitment, countered by the reemergence of the more independent WFJ, now called the Jordanian Women's Union (JWU), with many leftists and Pan-Arabs. It campaigned for major legal changes and to raise awareness of family problems.

In 1992 Princess Basma, King Hussein's sister, became head of a Jordanian National Committee for Women, and it developed a National Strategy for Women in 1993. Princess Basma has remained the leading figure representing the royal family's interest in the gradual improvement of women's condition. The National Strategy resulted in ninety-nine women's appointments to municipal and village councils. Several women won positions in the 1995 municipal elections. In 1995 a quasi-governmental organization under Princess Basma, the Jordanian National Women's Forum, was formed, undercutting the independent groups. The princess and Queen Noor were able to attract most external donor funds, and the undermining of independent activity with growing control by the royal family was one aspect of the demise of the liberal period.[52]

An outspoken progressive activist journalist, Toujan Faisal, was the first woman elected to Jordan's parliament, for 1993–97, but she and all other women candidates were defeated in 1997. She had aroused conservative Islamists, beginning in 1984 when a seminar she ran with the Business and Professional Women's Club showed a high incidence of child abuse. In a 1988 TV program she maintained that violence against women was being protected by the state. She also published an article criticizing, without naming her clerical target, "those who hold women to be intellectually deficient and in need of being treated like minors." An Islamist army officer and an army private sued her in shari'a court for apostasy. The case aroused an effective countercampaign, and, probably moved by public reaction and royal pressure, the court ruled it had no jurisdiction, and the plaintiffs' appeal was unsuccessful.[53] The case was one of several instances of a royal balancing act in face of the conservative power of Islamists and army and tribal elements. In 2002 Faisal accused the government of corruption and was arrested and tried under laws limiting free speech passed after the events of September 11, 2001. She and three male journalists were sentenced to eighteen months in jail. After a hunger strike and international campaign King Abdullah released her in June 2003.

Many shari'a inheritance and family laws remain in effect, but there have been important legal reforms. A provisional law passed in 2002 added to the circumstances under which a woman may file for divorce. Women's and human rights groups have campaigned against legal leniency for "honor killings," and in 2001 the government cancelled the article acquitting perpetrators of this crime; still, unpunished or lightly punished killings, often as elsewhere entrusted to minors to lighten punishments, continue, as does the campaign against them. Reforms in family law raised the minimum marriage age to eighteen. As in many countries marriage and divorce matters for Christians are adjudicated by special courts for each denomination. In 2003 there were nineteen female judges in Jordan.

Civil law grants women equal pay for equal work, but this is sometimes ignored. Women are in a wide variety of professions. According to 2002 government statistics, women constituted 14.7 percent of the workforce and 49.8 percent of university students. Female literacy is 84 percent, and 67 percent of women have a secondary education. Jordan's universities, like a few elsewhere in the Middle East, offer courses in women's studies. The Business and Professional Women's Club holds seminars on women's rights and assists women in establishing small businesses. It and other organizations offered programs for potential female voters and candidates leading up to the parliamentary elections. Members of the royal family have worked to improve women's status, but they and semiofficial NGOs also limit the independence of groups working for women's rights.[54] Such groups, which are often progressive and activist, must thus deal both with the aroused conservatism of tribal and Islamist forces and the "moderate" approach of the royal family—problems that are paralleled elsewhere in the Middle East.

Syria

The French proclaimed Syrian and Lebanese independence in 1941, but all foreign troops were not withdrawn until 1946. Participation in the defeat by Israel in 1948–49 and frustration with the urban landowning elites' stranglehold on parliamentary government helped cause three coups in 1949, culminating in the strongman rule of Col. Adib al-Shishakli until 1954, when there were elections and the Communists gained strength. The rival Ba'th Party, originally socialist, nationalist, and secular, allied with a peasant movement, was first centered in the army but gradually became the strongest party. Partly to counterbalance growing Soviet influence, Syria joined with Egypt in the United Arab Republic from 1958 to 1961, when they broke apart. A 1963 coup brought in a joint Ba'th-military government, which nationalized much of the economy and distributed land to peasants. After its 1967 victory Israel took over Syria's Golan Heights, and negotiations for its return have failed, partly because Syria, unlike Egypt, has insisted on tying their resolution to a general settlement on Palestine. Further conflicts in the Ba'th brought Gen. Hafez al-Assad to power in 1970, and he brought in a new constitution in 1973 but ruled semiautocratically for decades. The Muslim Brotherhood challenged his rule, and attempted an uprising in the city of Hama in 1982, which was brutally put down with thousands killed. Syrian troops were in Lebanon from 1976 until their 2005 withdrawal; they helped forestall civil war and fought Israel's 1982 invasion, but were increasingly opposed by many Lebanese.

The Ba'th and Assad started out with some major reforms that lessened the power of landlords and ulama and stressed equal rights for women and for all religious and national groups, but later Assad tried to appease more conservative and Islamic tendencies. Assad died in 2000 and was succeeded by his less able son Bashar al-Assad, who has attempted some reforms but overall did not greatly change his father's policies.

After independence the strongest movements were nationalist elites, the Communist Party, and the Muslim Brotherhood, and women continued to be active in the nationalist Women's Union and in Communist women's groups. There were public demonstrations for women's rights and against veiling, and most urban women unveiled after 1946. The rising Ba'th Party was committed to integrating women fully into public and national life. Once they took power, their 1973 constitution spoke of rights for all citizens; it includes an article promoting the advancement of women in all public spheres, though no laws or mechanisms protect women from discrimination.[55] The Ba'th did promote reforms, especially in education, that raised women's status. The government sought to overcome traditional discriminatory attitudes toward women and encouraged women's education by ensuring equal access to educational institutions, including universities. However, its reforms of discriminatory shari'a and secular laws have been limited. Independent women's organizations were changed into government-sponsored ones, and the Ba'th came to control all aspects of public life.

Women went to school and university in increasing numbers, and growing percentages entered formerly masculine professions, including medicine and engineering. By 1995, the women's illiteracy rate was down to 31.6 percent.[56] The existing Women's Union was incorporated into the party structure in 1968 as the General Women's Union (GWU). The GWU works for women's welfare and participation in public life. It is very difficult for women's groups to operate independent of the GWU. By 1995 the government included a female minister, and there were several female members of parliament. However, economic stagnation and the continued strength of Islamist forces and beliefs made the government move slowly regarding women's status, and it did not introduce major reforms in personal status law. Some women adopted various forms of hijab, sometimes, as in prerevolutionary Iran, as a sign of opposition to the regime, but others because of a rise in Islamic identification.[57]

A Code of Personal Status was passed in 1953 and applies in toto to Syrian Muslims, but has many exemptions for Druze, Christians, and Jews, who follow their own personal status law on important matters. Some reforms were passed in a 1975 revision of the previous predominantly Ottoman code that sets the minimum marriage age at eighteen for males, seventeen for females, with some exceptions. Judges may refuse to permit polygamous marriages unless the husband can establish lawful cause and financial capacity. The wife's financial rights are, however, forfeited if she works without her husband's permission or leaves the home without justification or refuses to cohabit with her husband. Male unilateral divorce is permitted, with some limits, while a wife's divorce is allowed only for specified reasons, though either spouse may apply for divorce on the grounds of irreconcilable differences. Divorced wives may get compensation of up to three years' maintenance if the judge finds the male divorce arbitrary. The mother gets custody of girls to age eleven and boys to age nine, extendable by courts. Husbands may prevent wives' travel abroad. As in some other Middle Eastern legal systems, honor killings get little or no punishment, rape can be exonerated if the parties marry, and punishment for adultery is more severe for women than for men.[58]

Women participate actively in public life and are represented in most professions, including the military.[59] Women in the professions are mostly from the elite, and they are encouraged to quit their jobs when they have children. In a country without open politics, women's strong role in writing and other arts has political and social significance, and the woman minister of culture for many years, Najah al-Attar, has had considerable power, as has another minister and writer, Bouthaina Shaaban. The secular orientation of the state has been helpful for women's public participation. Any significant further concessions to Islamists could increase the power of the Sunnis, who are a majority of Syria's Muslims, and decrease that of the Alawi Shi'i sect, to which the Assads belong, and of the other Shi'is. As is true of several Arab countries, the most likely alternative to an undemocratic state that has promoted some reforms in women's status is a populist Islamist rule that might reverse a number of reforms.

Lebanon

Lebanon, which gained independence from France in 1943, is a parliamentary republic that has incorporated sectarian differences in its government structure. By custom the president is a Maronite Christian, the prime minister a Sunni Muslim, and the speaker of the Chamber of Deputies a Shi'i Muslim. No government has held a census, which would be bound to show the Shi'is, who hold the least powerful top post, as the largest single community. As in several Muslim countries each religious community follows its own family and inheritance law, and in Lebanon this means many separate codes, most of them Christian. As elsewhere, many Christian codes are in some ways more limiting than Muslim ones, as in not allowing or strictly limiting divorce.

From the time of independence, the Lebanese women's movement focused on gaining full political rights, and achieved the right to vote in 1951–52. Lebanon has long been ruled by powerful elite families; this, along with its sectarian structure, has made it difficult to reduce the power of sects and lineages. However, Lebanon was early exposed to modern and Western influences, including educational institutions that came to include both a French Catholic university and an American, originally Protestant, one, and these have helped to make it more modern in many respects, including women's education, than many Arab countries. Prior to the civil war Beirut was an intellectual center in the Arab world, and a center of free Arab publication, which it remains to some degree. Women have long been prominent in intellectual and social life. Among feminist authors was Leila Baalbaki, whose book *I Live* was banned by the authorities, making it a cause célèbre. Although Lebanese society was one of the most liberal, educated, and diverse, it also suffered the most from religious and sectarian divisions and from proximity to the problems of neighboring Israel, Palestine, and Syria. A large population of Palestinian refugees has not been granted citizenship but has been politically important.

From 1975 to 1990 Lebanon experienced sixteen years of originally sectarian civil war, which came to involve Palestinians, Israel, Syria, and the United States. The war brought more women into public life, but was traumatic and harmful for many women and had mixed effects on their status. Maronite Christians lost some of their previously predominant power, and Shi'i Muslims, who had become the largest single religious group, increased in power, often with socially conservative views and practices that affected women. The Lebanese president invited Syria to send in troops to help stabilize the situation in 1976, and Syria remained a power behind the scenes until their troop withdrawal in 2004–5. Israel invaded Lebanon in 1978 and 1982, partially withdrawing in 1985, and the resistance movement led by the Iranian-influenced Shi'i Hizbullah forced Israel to leave in 2000. The Hizbullah party, called terrorist by the United States, is a recognized political party with substantial representation in parliament.

Lebanon pioneered in the Middle East with an Institute for Women's Studies in the Arab World, located at the Lebanese American University since 1973 and offering courses on women's issues. It has a sophisticated feminist English-Arabic journal, *al-Raida*. Premarital cohabitation and even single motherhood have begun to be openly practiced by a few in major cities, where Lebanon's relative modernism is evident.[60] Despite women's presence in most arts and professions, there are still forms of discrimination that are fought by women's organizations. There are numerous governmental and nongovernmental women's organizations; they are active on many political, social, and cultural fronts, and several now stress economic programs for poor rural women.

While the personal status and inheritance codes vary by religious community, all have some elements of gender inequality. As in Syria, penal codes coming in part from unreformed French law allow a man who kills a female relative to receive a reduced sentence if he shows he was responding to the victim's having engaged in a sexual relationship. Several instances of honor crimes are reported in the media every year, and no one has been convicted in a case legally considered an honor crime. However, a number of laws that discriminated against women in various spheres of public life have been repealed beginning in 1983, and in 1997 the Convention on the Elimination of All Forms of Discrimination against Women was ratified, with reservations, after a long struggle.[61]

North Africa

The contrasting twentieth-century gender history of Algeria, Morocco, and Tunisia is analyzed by Mounira Charrad.[62] In all three, tribal groups were historically powerful and governments were limited in their control of tribes. Charrad sees Islamic family law as reflecting the interests of the extended male family line and making them far more important than those of the conjugal family. She interprets wives' property being separate from husbands' and women's carrying their fathers' second names less as rights for women than as signs of the superior role of the agnatic family. This is also reflected in the ease of divorce and divorcees' and widows' return to the agnatic family. Much of this is applicable in other parts of the Middle East, as is the discussion of tribal law and custom, which, though varied, was and is predominantly even more favorable to the agnatic patriarchal family than is Islamic law. Charrad shows that Tunisia, which put down the power of the tribes and effectively centralized rule, could eliminate most of the patriarchal features of law. In 2003–4, the Moroccan king, supported by women's and progressive movements, proposed and had ratified by parliament a reform in family law that goes further than that in any Arab country except Tunisia.

TUNISIA

In Tunisia during the struggle for independence from the French, nationalist leaders, including Habib Bourguiba, defended traditional and Islamic practices, while a pioneering male writer for women's rights, Tahir Haddad, had to leave his professorship and died in disgrace. There was a turnabout when nationalists under Bourguiba achieved independence in 1956 and within a few months promulgated what is to this day the most reformed Personal Status Code (PSC) in the Arab world. This code abolished polygamy, eliminated husbands' repudiation, allowed women to file for divorce, set marriage age minimums of seventeen and twenty, and increased women's child custody rights. Such radical reform was enacted partly to break the power of tribes, lineages, and ulama, and was not preceded by a significant feminist movement. There were serious and continuing efforts to enforce the new law, which, as in Iranian and Moroccan later major reforms, was officially based on new interpretations of Islam.

In the 1980s and 1990s gender relations were affected by new developments. A new Islamist movement arose, and although some in this movement said they would preserve the PSC, others spoke of repealing it or subjecting it to a referendum.[63] Partly in response, new women's and feminist groups arose and were a factor in 1992–93 laws that expanded women's rights under the government of Zine el-Abedine Ben Ali, who deposed Bourguiba for health reasons in 1987 and has ruled increasingly autocratically ever since. Feminist and women's groups organized to defend and expand women's rights, and the state encouraged them, fearing the growth of Islamist power, especially as Islamists became very strong in neighboring Algeria in the early 1990s. The state, influenced by women's groups and its own women's commissions, in July 1993 dropped the PSC's statement that wives must obey husbands, expanded women's custody rights after divorce, and created a fund to guarantee alimony and child support to women whose ex-husbands did not supply them, after which it would try to recover the money from delinquent fathers (an innovation in advance of most Western countries). Parents were given joint authority over children, and divorced mothers can sue for guardianship of children in some cases. Domestic violence was criminalized, and men were no longer allowed reduced sentences for honor crimes.[64] Many women's rights advocates are thus among the important supporters of the government.

Tunisia, however, has also seen increasing autocracy and jailing and harassment both of Islamists and of human rights advocates, who as elsewhere often advocate human rights for Islamists. About 30 percent of the workforce is female, and the law, as in several Arab countries, requires equal pay for equal work. A slight majority of university students are women, and women's literacy and education continue to grow impressively. Women serve in high levels of the government as ministers and secretaries of state, making up more than 13 percent of the total. Women constitute 37 percent of the civil service and 24 percent of Tunisia's jurists. However, women still face discrimination in certain categories of private sector employment.[65]

Tunisia adopted CEDAW in 1985, with fewer reservations than most Arab states, and has worked to meet international standards. Unofficial women's and other organizations are, however, limited. Civil law is largely based on the Napoleonic Code, although judges may use shari'a as a basis for customary law in cases involving inheritance. As elsewhere Muslim women are not permitted to marry outside their religion. Tunisian law punishes rape, spousal abuse, and sexual harassment. There is a Ministry for Women's Affairs, Family, and Childhood, with money allotted to ensuring the legal rights of women and improving their socioeconomic status. The government supports its Women's Research Center and funds women's professional associations. Several NGOs deal with women's advocacy and research on women's issues. There is still an Islamist movement whose party has been outlawed, but it is less militant and less influential than in several other Muslim countries, though it attracts many who are hostile to what is seen as an autocratic government.

Algeria

In colonial Algeria, European settlers took over much of the land and economy from Algerians, denigrated Algerian culture, and presented French ways, including those regarding women, as essential to civilization. In this situation many Algerians reacted by trying to reinforce Islam and the traditional family. Many saw women's seclusion as a defense against French cultural attacks.

1. Pre-Islamic Syria

Fully veiled women, bas-relief, Palmyra, ca. 200 C.E. (Kodachrome).
Photo © Nikki R. Keddie

2. QASHQAI PEOPLE OF SOUTHERN IRAN 1976–78

a. Grandmother and grandson. Photo © Nikki R. Keddie

b. Spinning wool in tent (Kodachrome). Photo © Nikki R. Keddie

c. Carpet school south of Shiraz. Photo © Nikki R. Keddie

d. Tribal school in tent (Kodachrome). Photo © Nikki R. Keddie

e. Shepherd. Photo © Nikki R. Keddie

f. Women migrating. Photo © Nikki R. Keddie

3. IRAN 1973–79

a. Silk-reeling factory, Gilan, northern Iran. Photo © Nikki R. Keddie

b. Reeling yarn. Photo © Nikki R. Keddie

c. Weaving. Photo © Nikki R. Keddie

d. Woman in Tehran postrevolution. Photo © Nikki R. Keddie

4. Morocco 1975–83

a. Two girls playing, northern Morocco town. Photo © Nikki R. Keddie

b. Girl on steps, northern Morocco town. Photo © Nikki R. Keddie

c. Girl in carpet workshop, Tangier. Photo © Nikki R. Keddie

d. Girl on country road to Fez (Kodachrome). Photo © Nikki R. Keddie

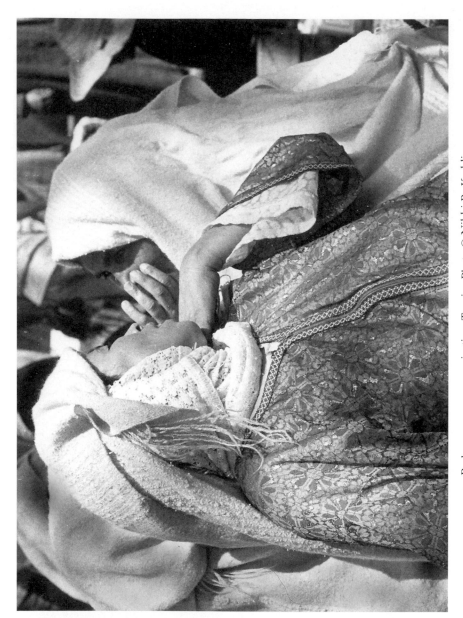

e. Berber women communicating, Tangier. Photo © Nikki R. Keddie

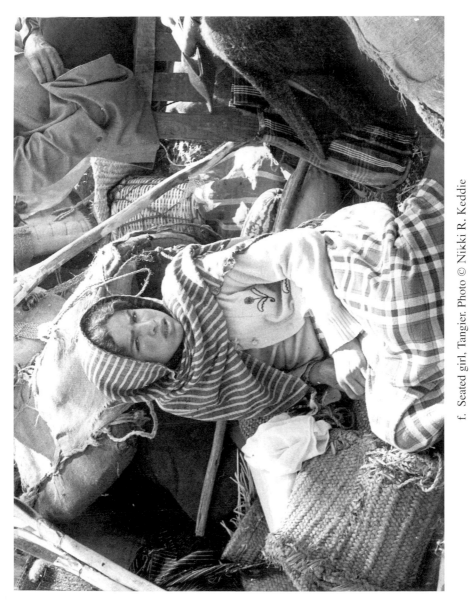

f. Seated girl, Tangier. Photo © Nikki R. Keddie

g. Women on the road to Marrakesh (Kodachrome). Photo © Nikki R. Keddie

5. Syria, Tunisia 1976–83

a. Jewish girl with bread, Damascus (Kodachrome). Photo © Nikki R. Keddie

b. Girls' volleyball class, Tunis. Photo © Nikki R. Keddie

c. Five women, Tunis. Photo © Nikki R. Keddie

d. Islamist activist, Tunis. Photo © Nikki R. Keddie

6. NIKKI KEDDIE, PHOTOGRAPHER

a. Persepolis (Kodachrome)

b. Lahore, Pakistan (Kodachrome)

In the armed liberation struggle against the French, 1954–62, Algerian women fought in various brave ways, mainly behind the lines, but also by carrying bombs and arms. They thought their contribution would lead to an improved position for women; indeed the 1962 constitution did prohibit sex discrimination and included woman suffrage, and ten women were elected to the new National Assembly. But the leaders of the ruling National Liberation Front (FLN) soon turned out to be culturally conservative, in some measure as a reaction to prior French efforts at cultural assimilation to French ways. Birth control and women's work were discouraged, so that women's labor-force participation became and remained one of the lowest in the region, partly with the excuse of high unemployment.

After the death of longtime FLN leader Col. Houari Boumedienne (1965–78) there was a trend away from state socialism and toward a market economy. In response to growing Islamist trends, a proposed Islamist-influenced Family Code in 1981 brought the first major feminist counterdemonstration in December. The national assembly passed an even more conservative code in 1984. It was and remains based on a conservative interpretation of Muslim law, saying women cannot marry without permission of their male guardian, must obey their husbands, and do not have the right to divorce or to guardianship of their children. Feminists have continued to fight for major changes in the code, which they note contravenes equality provisions of the constitution, the labor code, and international conventions including CEDAW that Algeria has signed.[66]

Women's organizations and actions grew from 1981 on, but in the same period the Islamist movement also grew. In April 1989 a demonstration of 100,000 women favoring Islamism and gender segregation startled progressive women. After the government permitted opposition parties and elections, the Islamist party FIS grew rapidly, largely as an expression of opposition to a government that had done little to meet Algeria's major economic and other problems, and had instituted austerity programs that hurt many. In the virtual civil war launched by one faction of this Islamist party after national elections were cancelled in 1991, women were attacked, raped, killed, taken without consent into "temporary marriages" (not licit in Sunni Islam), and forced to dress and behave in ways decreed by Islamists. Even though Islamists lost this civil war, and although local and international women's and human rights groups work to protect women against spousal abuse, kidnapping, violence, and rape by terrorists, such problems remain. This reflects a major deviation from what women who fought heroically in the liberation war expected. Islamist gender conservatism is partly due to a reaction against the denigration of Arab-Islamic culture by the French colonialists, partly to the strength of conservative tribal and household groups, and partly to the domination of public school education by an Arab-Islamic curriculum, taught largely by teachers of small-town traditional origin. Not only many male and female activists but also the sizable and largely secular Berber population resist this conservative interpretation of Islam and tradition, but Islamists opposed to extending women's rights remain strong.[67]

Women's organizations have fought with increasing effect and sophistication, and a cabinet-level position for women and children was created in 2002. Today divorce remains difficult for wives, and husbands generally get the family home after divorce. Although child custody normally is awarded to the mother, she may not enroll children in school or take them out of the country without the father's authorization. Polygamy is legal, though a wife may sue for divorce if her husband does not inform her of his intent to marry another woman before the marriage.

Despite some laws and regulations providing equality between men and women, women face discrimination in employment. Leaders of women's organizations report that discriminatory violations are common, and Labor Ministry inspectors do little to enforce the law. Women make up over half of university students but constitute only a small percentage of the official workforce. However, women may own businesses, enter into contracts, and pursue most careers. About 25 percent of judges are women, a percentage that has been growing. Women's fertility rate has fallen to 2.8 percent, and female literacy is 60 percent and rising as 92 percent of girls aged six to fourteen attended school in 2003, and women made up 53 percent of university enrollees.[68]

There are several women's rights groups, mostly small, in addition to women's professional, charitable, and other organizations. The women's rights groups work for women's economic welfare and to amend aspects of the Family Code. In March 2003 women's rights groups launched a new campaign to reform the Family Code and the government hosted two closed-door conferences to discuss the code, but no changes were made. The major reform of Morocco's family code in 2004 has given additional impetus to the strong movement to reform Algeria's code. Women's education, workforce participation, organization, and consciousness have been growing, and women's activity and consciousness have been promoted by NGOs, often with foreign help, and by the long series of international conferences on the rights of women since 1975.[69]

Morocco

Morocco is a parliamentary monarchy, in which the recent kings, who are also religious leaders as "Commanders of the Faithful," have managed to balance and control a variety of political parties, tribes, and ulama. It achieved independence from France in 1956 under Muhammad V. Hassan

II ruled 1961–99, and Muhammad VI has ruled since 1999. In the early 1950s, before independence, Allal al-Fasi, the leader of Morocco's main nationalist party, proposed a reform program in the name of Islam but incorporating women's rights. He opposed polygamy. Other nationalists supported his program, and his cousin, Malika, was involved in the independence movement and became a model and patron for later generations of female activists. However, his proposals were not adopted by the postindependence commission, on which he served, set up to unify Morocco's personal status codes. Instead, in Morocco as in Algeria, the family code (*Mudawwana*) adopted in 1957 retained inegalitarian practices, including need of a guardian's consent for a woman to marry; consent of a father or husband for her to work, carry out business, or travel; unilateral male rights to polygamy and repudiation; and a widow's child custody's being conditional on her remaining unmarried and in the same city. There were minor reforms, including a minimum marriage age of fifteen for women, the end of forced marriage, and a woman's right to alimony in case of abusive repudiation. Although in the early postindependence period women's employment grew, it later shrank as economic conditions deteriorated and priority was given to males.[70]

Women's groups in political parties undertook women's rights activities, and women intellectuals, notably the prolific writer and sociologist Fatima Mernissi, were important in putting forth a women's perspective. While nationalist parties and leaders spoke for women's rights, they did little in power for such rights. One problem, also found in Algeria, was that the French had divided law into Islamic law for the Arabs and tribal law for the Berbers, and nationalists chose to unify the country culturally by making all follow Islamic law, which disfavored women in certain ways. Also as in Algeria, there was a program of Arabization, especially in the schools, to reduce the importance both of French and of Berber languages. As in Algeria, Arabization was accompanied by an emphasis on Islam in the schools and elsewhere, which ultimately helped Islamists and delayed women's rights.

A long struggle against the Mudawwana and in favor of egalitarian laws led in 1992 to the One Million Signatures petition campaign, demanding gender-egalitarian extensions of women's legal rights and spearheaded by the Democratic Association of Moroccan Women, which was formed in 1985. It was the first women's organization independent of a political party, although its leaders were affiliated with the leftist Party of Progress and Socialism. More than a million signatures were collected in a few months, but at the same time Islamist activists in schools and universities collected three million signatures against the campaign. Islamist newspapers launched a major attack on the campaign, implicitly questioning the king's religious primacy. King Hassan asked women to end their campaign and address their demands to him, and he would decide. The women's groups were pessimistic about the outcome. However, in 1993 Hassan issued some reforms, limiting the power of the marriage guardian, affirming widows' guardianship of their children, and requiring the presence of both parties to register a divorce and compensation for some repudiated women. Polygamy now required a judge's permission and informing the first wife. These were far from meeting egalitarian demands, and women activists were disappointed. However, the reform question had been reopened, and King Hassan in 1998 brought opposition parties, including Socialists, into his government who drafted a comprehensive plan to integrate women into development. The plan argued the need for extensive reform of the Mudawwana on the lines of the Million Signatures campaign. Ulama and Islamists, strong among the urban masses and on university campuses, opposed the plan, and the leader of a predominantly Islamist party declared the matter to be "a war between the believers and the apostates."[71] King Muhammad, who acceded in 1999, instituted extensive political and economic liberalization, and pursued the extension of women's rights.

The government in 1999 issued a National Plan for Integrating Women into Development that included major egalitarian changes in the Mudawwana. This plan revealed the polarization within society, as on March 12, 2000, hundreds of thousands demonstrated in Casablanca against the plan, and fifty thousand in the capital, Rabat, in its favor. Officially in face of the strong opposition the plan was then dismissed, but behind the scenes King Muhammad moved to implement it. He closed the royal harem and publicly married a modern woman. A deadly terrorist bombing in Casablanca was followed by harsh measures, some of them doubtful from a human rights perspective, against Islamists. The king determined to revive family law reform, and late in 2003 he issued, and the parliament in 2004 approved, a major change in family law, which brought it close to Tunisia's almost egalitarian 1956 code, except that polygamy was not completely outlawed. As in Tunisia, the king's speech grounded the changes in Islam. These changes outlaw polygamy except in rare circumstances and with the judge's and first wife's permission. They raise girls' marriage age from fifteen to eighteen and give wives joint responsibility with husbands in family matters. Although the 2004 reforms in Morocco are very important, they do not go quite as far as those in Tunisia or Turkey, both because polygamy is still possible in Morocco, and also because the reforms on divorce are less thorough in Morocco in that they leave more room for interpretation by individual judges.[72] The crux of the matter will be in the implementation of the new laws. Liberal forces, including Berber cultural associations, were heartened by the king's decision and the reforms, while those who opposed reform, as elsewhere in the Middle East, continued to attack the reformers as agents of Zionists and Western imperialists. Again as elsewhere, some female Islamists favored family law reforms, however, and all sides now use Islamic language. According to Bruce Maddy-Weitzman:

> Like Allal al-Fasi, the new generation of reformers seeks to reconcile Islam with the modern world, and to show that the very notion of progress in fact derives from the principles of Islam. However . . . the plan's formulators and supporters were more interested in seeking religious legitimization for their essentially modern, secular project than in genuinely engaging Islamic sources in a real dialogue. Sociologist Fatima Mernissi is an exception in this regard. However, her radical reformulation of Islamic texts to promote democracy and women's rights has not resonated widely.[73]

While many well-educated Moroccan women pursue careers, few rise to top positions. Women constitute approximately 35 percent of the workforce, with most in the industrial, service, and teaching sectors. In 1998 the government reported that the illiteracy rate for women was 67 percent compared with 41 percent for men, though percentages are much lower for school-age children. There has been a dramatic drop in birthrates, from 3 percent in the 1960s and 1970s to 1.3 percent today. The average marrying age for urban women is now twenty-five to twenty-six, reflecting a trend also found in other Middle Eastern countries.[74] Poverty is a major problem, and poor women and women in rural areas are most affected by inequality and least likely yet to have reaped the full benefit of new laws.

Many NGOs work for women's rights and issues. Among them are the Democratic Association of Moroccan Women, the Union for Women's Action, and the Moroccan Association for Women's Rights, which advocate enhanced political and civil rights, as well as numerous NGOs that provide shelters for battered women, teach women basic hygiene, family planning, and child care, and promote literacy. In 1998 the government created a ministry responsible for the status of women. The state has also adopted programs in the past six years to increase young women's access to education, improve women's health, decrease maternal mortality, and combat violence against women. Women's and other organizations are relatively free to organize and demonstrate. For the parliamentary elections of 2002 the government, prompted by women's groups, reserved thirty seats for women, which increased women's representation.[75]

Today the two ex–French protectorates in North Africa, Tunisia and Morocco, have the most reformed laws and practices in the Arab world regarding women, with Tunisia having the longest record of major reform. This openness to reform may relate to these countries' preprotectorate history and culture, and possibly to a lesser colonialist attack on local culture and economy than in Algeria and in other colonies. Other possible causes are a lesser impact than in eastern Arab countries of oil income, and a lesser involvement in the Palestine issue. Only further comparative study can answer such questions.

Libya

There has been little scholarly access to, or scholarly study of, Libya, whose population is about 5,500,000. According to a summary by the UN Development Program, women in Libya have significant opportunities in education and employment, but face substantial social discrimination. Right after the 1969 coup that overthrew the monarchy and brought President Qadhafi to power, the new leader supported traditional Islamic laws and values. But in the mid-1970s, Qadhafi turned away from this and began to implement his own personal revolutionary vision. This vision, embodied in his Green Book, advocated social equality for men and women. Women were mobilized in the military and in the political system of revolutionary councils in the late 1970s and early 1980s. During the late 1980s, Qadhafi challenged tenets considered Islamic, such as the obligation of women to travel with a male guardian and female veiling. But by the mid-1990s, the Qadhafi government had begun to reverse its stance, supporting a larger role for Islam in the law. This seemed designed to preempt the regime's Islamic opposition. Hence it is difficult to ascertain a clear government stance on the status of women in public life. The Libyan government ratified CEDAW in 1989 with reservations, like those in many Muslim countries, for conflicts with Islamic law in four areas of the personal status code: property rights, marriage, divorce, and parental rights.

President Qadhafi's autocratic government claims to have improved the status of women, and has introduced antidiscriminatory legislation, taken measures to increase women's education and employment, and encouraged women's participation in social and economic life. The government has established the Department of Women's Affairs as part of the secretariat of the General People's Congress, the national legislative body. The department collects data and oversees the integration of women into public life. The government has also established the General Union of Women's Associations as a network of nongovernmental organizations that address women's employment and other matters. However, no autonomous or independent organizations, female or male, are permitted to function.

The government provides free health care and education to all citizens, though quality is not always high, especially for those women who are not permitted to see male doctors. The World Bank estimated that nearly 100 percent of boys and girls were enrolled in primary education by 1998.

In 2002, adult female illiteracy had fallen to 29 percent, though it continues to exceed illiteracy among men. Women constitute 22 percent of the labor force, but discrimination still exists in the workplace. Men and women are guaranteed equality under the law, but lack of enforcement has led to continued social inequality.

As elsewhere, clear differences exist across generational lines. Women who were born before the 1969 revolution tend to stay in the home and have low education levels. Younger women are much more likely to receive a public education and show much higher rates of participation in the public sphere.[76]

Recent years have seen growing urbanization and increasing mixing of the sexes, choice of marriage partners, and importance for the conjugal rather than the natal family—all trends found elsewhere in the Middle East. Change has been fueled by both oil income and revolution, with the country being transformed from an overwhelmingly traditional tribal monarchy into a modernizing state and society, with the contradictory elements this involves. Conservative tribal and Islamist groups remain strong, and de facto changes in male-dominant patterns have been far slower than a listing of reforms might suggest. Several personal status laws have been reformed, but some remain unequal, such as the permission of polygamy with the agreement of the first wife or a judge.[77] With current improving Western relations with Libya, it may become open to more scholarly study.

Saudi Arabia

Saudi Arabia since its founding has promoted an atypical restrictive version of Islam, of eighteenth-century Arabian origin, often called Wahhabi. The Saudi state is a monarchy with a strong tribal-kinship basis, in which members of the royal family are the most powerful members of a wealthy elite. Saudi wealth, like that of several Middle Eastern countries, is based on oil, which was discovered between the world wars and was owned by a U.S. company until nationalization. Saudi relations with the United States have always been close. Oil income allowed the Saudis, after World War II, to promote their version of Islam through the creation of schools, mosques, and other institutions throughout the world in both Muslim-majority and Muslim-minority countries. The Saudi version of Islam is particularly restrictive regarding women, especially since 1979, which saw both the Iranian revolution and an Islamist attempt to take over a main Saudi mosque and subsequent attempts by the Saudi state to defend itself against Islamist challenges.

Saudi rulers were more open to change in the 1960s and 1970s than they were in the 1980s and 1990s, and the state allowed or promoted for women more education, including abroad, more job opportunities, and fewer constraints than before. After an Islamist takeover of the main Saudi mosque in 1979, the Saudi government reverted to a strict enforcement of its interpretation of Islamic law, education, and practice, though in the past few years there has been discussion of more rights for women and a few steps in this direction. Women have economic rights but few political or social ones. Women may not legally drive and must enter city buses by separate rear entrances and sit in designated sections. Women may not undertake domestic or foreign travel alone. In public, women have to wear an *abaya* (a black garment that covers the entire body) and must cover their head and hair. The religious police often expect Muslim women to cover their faces, although this varies by region. Since 1979 potentially oppositional Islamism has grown among both men and women, and some women have used this trend to meet together and to reinterpret the Quran.[78]

Women have access to free, segregated education through the university level, and women's education has increased rapidly since publicly funded girls' education began in 1960. Women constitute more than 58 percent of all university students, but are excluded from studying such subjects as engineering, journalism, and architecture. Women make up approximately 15 percent of the formal citizen workforce and about 16 percent of the officially unemployed, although many more women might work if they could. Citizen women reportedly own about 20 percent of businesses, but they must deputize a male relative to represent them in financial transactions. Although women are not supposed to interact with men in the workplace, many do and have found ways to do so discretely.[79] Most women's jobs are in education and health care. Some women have studied abroad and returned to work in professions such as architecture, law, and journalism. Many foreign women work as domestic servants and nurses, and, as in several Gulf countries, they are often mistreated without possibility of redress.

Workplaces are segregated by gender. The degree of segregation varies by region. Women cannot get business licenses for work where they might supervise foreign workers, interact with male clients, or deal regularly with officials. However, in hospital settings and in energy and several other spheres, women and men work together, and some women supervise male employees. Elite women with ties to ruling families are favored when the rules are bent.

In late 1990 during the buildup to the Gulf War, when U.S. soldiers, including women, were present in large numbers in Saudi Arabia, some women with international drivers' licenses and their husbands' permission, decided to test the ban on women drivers by driving in the capital, Riyadh. They were all arrested, dismissed from their (mainly teaching) jobs, and put under house arrest. Later the government quietly ended the punishment. Some Saudi women thought the movement was badly timed, given the war situation, but it may ultimately have helped liberalization.[80]

Some changes have occurred since 2002, when religious police prevented girls who were not in full hijab from leaving a school that was on fire and fourteen girls died. King Fahd dismissed the director of the General Presidency for Girls' Education and put girls' education under the Ministry of Education. The school curriculum still emphasizes the Saudi interpretation of religion and teaches girls to conform to male-dominant views of Islam. In May 2003 the king called for expanding the role of women in society, and in June, an official conference endorsed this and a reexamination of customary restrictions; in December this conference included ten women for the first time. Also for the first time, the Jiddah Economic Forum devoted a day to the role of women in business.

There has been increased attention in the press to women's issues, including discrimination, health, rising divorce rates, employment, driving, and legal problems women face in business. The government held municipal elections in 2005 with no women's participation, but it talks of possible future woman suffrage, which elicits conservative resistance. After the Jiddah conference, in which women participated, separated from men, the chief Saudi cleric issued an edict that said: "Allowing women to mix with men is the root of every evil and catastrophe. It is highly punishable. Mixing of men and women is a reason for greater decadence and adultery."[81] However, the number of vocal male and female reformers is growing, despite threats and jailings. The first independent poll in Saudi Arabia showed that 90 percent wanted to grant women more rights, and 63 percent thought women should be allowed to drive. These changes have a social component—Saudi women have proven themselves in the academic and professional spheres in the past decades—and also reflect economic realities. Economic problems have necessitated decreased reliance on foreign workers and made barring Saudi women from parts of the workforce increasingly untenable.[82]

Yemen

Yemen for decades was divided between South Yemen, which emerged from the 1959 British-sponsored Federation of South Arabia, and included the port city of Aden and British tribal protectorates, and North Yemen, independent since the collapse of its former suzerain, the Ottoman Empire, under an inherited imam of the Zaidi branch of Shi'ism. Before 1962 North Yemen was very conservative, with almost no contact with the outside world, and a very strong role of patriarchal tribes, which continues. A republican revolution in 1962 was followed by an eight-year civil war, with Nasser supporting the republic and Saudi Arabia the imam, ending in victory for the Yemen Arab Republic (YAR). Only with the coming to power of President Ali Abdallah Salih in 1978 was there enough stability for the state to address social questions. Women were already experiencing results from the huge outmigration of Yemeni men to oil-rich countries in Arabia, which left women in charge of agricultural and other traditionally male activities (similar results were found in Turkey and other countries with male outmigration). Between 1975 and 1986 female labor-force participation increased from 8 percent to 22 percent, and between 1969 and 1988 girls in primary schools rose from 8 percent to 23 percent. Women's enrollment in secondary schools and the new University of Sana'a also rose, and in the Faculty of Medicine women outnumbered men by 1985.[83]

Women participated in the single-party General People's Congress formed in 1982, when women were also given the right to vote, though religious pressure kept most women from being electoral candidates. The first Family Law of 1979 included polygamy; unilateral male divorce, while wives had to sue for divorce for limited reasons; and a minimum marriage age of fifteen for girls (badly enforced). Protective labor and civil service laws were scarcely enforced, and the state took control of the main women's organization, the Women's Union. Society remained sexually segregated, with most urban women wearing some form of head-to-toe veiling, aside from one commercially active and colorfully dressed group in the south of the YAR. Only a few elite women were active socially or politically, but they made some important advances in education and work.

South Yemen was very different. After five years of guerrilla fighting against the British and between parties in Aden Colony, South Yemen declared independence in 1967; after a Communist victory in 1969, the People's Democratic Republic of Yemen (PDRY) was born in 1970. It pursued leftist policies and passed a secular constitution in 1970, modified in 1978, which declared all citizens to have equal rights and said the state would work to enable women to fulfill both family and work roles, including the establishment of state-supported child care. Wanting the work and active participation of women, the state passed a revolutionary family law in 1974. It declared that marriage needed explicit consent of both parties, who had equal rights and duties, with minimum ages of sixteen for girls and eighteen for boys; abolished polygamy except in exceptional circumstances and with the agreement of the first wife; greatly reduced the male dower; gave women and men equal rights in court regarding divorce; and increased women's right to child custody. This was accompanied by measures to reduce the power of lineages and ulama. Outside of Aden, however, the law was difficult to enforce. Women got the vote under universal suffrage laws in 1970. A General Union of Yemeni Women was formed and was active in many women's issues, including a literacy campaign. Women could vote and·run in elections, and some were elected to office. Women worked in many fields, including professional ones, and by 1983 an equal number of males and females graduated from the University of Aden. Still, outside of Aden prejudices against girls' education and women's working remained strong and limiting, despite the state's efforts, and poverty persisted.[84]

In May 1990 the two Yemens were unified after an agreement between their presidents, following the loss of aid from the USSR to the PDRY. The new state's coalition government allowed multiple parties, and a new Islamist party, the Reform Party, challenged the previously official parties of North and South. The Islamists (and Northern tribes) opposed the new constitution's statement that Islamic law is the main source of law, and favored the former YAR constitution's statement that Islamic law is the only source of law. Islamists also wanted state funds for religious schools and a more Islamic public school curriculum. Further, they said women's main role was in the home, and women should not mix with men in school or at work. The old ruling parties resisted demands for such constitutional changes, but times were difficult for advancing women's rights.

The new constitution and the 1992 Family Law were mainly based on laws of the North and rescinded rights held by women in the PDRY. The 1992 law follows unreformed shari'a in most ways, saying wives must obey husbands and may not leave home (implying work) without their consent. Male relatives may marry off a woman. There is free divorce for husbands, and very limited divorce for wives. Divorced women return to their paternal family, and the home and older children are often awarded to husbands. The minimum marriage age for girls is fifteen. There were unsuccessful protests by women in Aden.[85]

Recent years have seen the formation of numerous NGOs, often with international funding, devoted to women's issues. As in several Middle Eastern countries, they have done good work, but their record has been mixed as they compete for funds and position, and governments often give them jobs that governments themselves should do. After unification the Women's Unions of North and South merged into one Women's Union, aided by the government and Western donors, which initially concentrated on fighting Islamist efforts to change the education curriculum. However, some northern branches of the Union sympathized with the Islamists.

Partly to present a progressive face to Western funders, the Yemeni government, in preparation for the 1995 Beijing Women's Conference, established the National Committee for Women, which produced a position paper and, in 1996, a National Strategy. The committee has produced impressive research and guidelines, but has had little influence on policy. In January 1997 an Islamist-oriented Committee to Enact Laws Based on the Shari'a drafted a revised personal status law that further hurt women, proposing to end the minimum marriage age of fifteen and accepting in court the testimony of only male witnesses. A bloc of professionals, feminists, and human rights activists succeeded in preventing these changes but only by having the president refuse to sign the law after its passage by parliament.

Women gained the right to candidacy in the multiparty 1993 parliamentary elections. Two women of the many who ran won seats, and two came in second with large votes. Women candidates faced slanders and also attacks by the Reform Party. A 1994 war between armies of the North and South brought flight from Yemen by many Yemen Socialist Party leaders. This destroyed that party and increased the power of the Reform Party, which got several ministries and changed the constitutional article prohibiting gender discrimination to an ambiguous statement that Islamic law guarantees women's equality. Women's groups were very active in the 1997 parliamentary elections, and women's rights became a central issue after a hard-line Reform Party leader criticized the promotion of a woman to be deputy minister of information and in an interview said, "God made women emotional and did not give them strong character, and emotion does not suit leadership."[86] This hurt the Reform Party, which lost seats;it encouraged women activists, who won a victory in 2003 in a successful national campaign to cancel a proposal that would have authorized judges to force married women to return to their conjugal homes.[87]

Although individual women are often powerful, the government does not yet give central attention to women's issues. Socially, as in many countries, the frequent migration of men abroad for work for long periods has created much de facto independence and managerial experience for the women who remain, even though many men returned as the Saudi Arabian oil economy declined and oil was found in Yemen. The Saudi experience gave an impetus to the spread of a restrictive view of Islam and the emergence of violent jihadist groups. Educated Yemeni women have countered with gender-egalitarian versions of Islam. Girls' education is progressing, though the gap between girls and boys is unusually large. In 2001 primary school attendance was 76 percent for boys and 40 percent for girls; total female literacy was 28.5 percent and male 69.5 percent.[88] The laws protecting women, setting female minimum marriage age at fifteen and outlawing rape and violence against women, are not well enforced. Nonetheless, Yemeni women have begun to take advantage of the parliamentary and multiparty structure to put forth their issues and candidates. The long cultural isolation and poverty of Yemen, along with the power of patriarchal tribes, and now of Islamists, have created major obstacles to women's equality, but Yemeni women are notably assertive and may be able to add to their social and educational gains if they continue to organize more effectively.[89]

Oman

Oman, in southeast Arabia, has long been the center of the Ibadi sect of Islam, descended from early Khariji Islam. With coastal areas ruled by a sultan and the interior by Ibadi imams, the country, like most of the western and southern Arabian coast, was under considerable British control until Britain pulled out of the Gulf beginning in the late 1960s. Oil was discovered in 1964, and there was a major leftist revolt in the southern Dhofar region 1965–75. In 1970 a coup brought in Sultan Qaboos Bin Said, who undertook a liberalization and modernization program in a country that had seen little of either.

Oman has made considerable progress in women's rights. In 2000–2001 girls and boys had equal numbers in primary education, and women constituted 54 percent of entering students at Sultan Qaboos University in 2002. Educated women have attained positions of authority in government, business, and the media. In 2002, approximately 33 percent of all civil servants were women. In both the public and private sectors, women were entitled to maternity leave and equal pay for equal work. The government, the country's largest employer of women, observes such regulations, as do many private sector employers. However, many women still face job discrimination. Approximately 24 percent of students who study abroad under the sponsorship of the Ministry of Higher Education are women.[90]

The Ministry of Social Development handles women's affairs. The ministry funds the Oman Women's Association (OWA) and local community development centers. OWA activities include health or sociological lectures, kindergarten services, and handicraft-training programs. The OWA also provides counseling and support for women with divorce-related difficulties, girls forced to marry, and women experiencing domestic abuse. The government allows and sometimes aids other women's organizations, but not any that work for women's or human rights.

The basic law of 1996 included a consultative council elected by limited suffrage. The sultan decreed in 1997 that women could vote and stand for elections, and made voting universal in 2003. Eight women serve in the appointed fifty-seven-seat State Council. In March 2004 a woman was appointed to a ministerial rank for the first time, and in October two women were elected to the Consultative Council. Women hold other senior government positions, including, as of 2004, four undersecretaries and one ambassador. Three women serve on the twelve-member Main Election Committee of the Consultative Council.

As elsewhere, social practice often lags behind law, and family law is still shari'a-based and hence unequal for women in several spheres. Oman was a highly traditional country with little contact with the outside world before the discovery of oil and Sultan Qaboos's 1970 coup, and so it is not surprising that social reality has changed slowly. Also, women's activism and organizations have been limited to those tied to the government and, like the government, have not yet challenged many unequal legal and traditional practices, particularly those involving family relations. Until now, however, reformist trends in education, health, family planning, citizenship rights, and employment have continued, even though there is Islamist and other opposition to some of the reforms.[91]

The Small Gulf States

The smaller states in the northern Gulf area are all ruled by hereditary rulers, mostly emirs, and are all areas formerly controlled by the British. All have large oil incomes and rely heavily on foreign labor. Foreign workers, especially women, are often deprived of most rights and protections, while their occupation of many jobs limits possibilities for local women's employment. On the other hand, large oil income finances expansion in education and health services from which local women benefit. Several states have instituted partial representative government, and all now have instituted woman suffrage. Conservative forces like most ulama and tribal leaders remain strong, while central governments often favor modernizing projects, some of which help women, and there are some women's movements and reformist NGOs. The difficulty or impossibility for foreigners, even Arabs, to obtain citizenship creates two-class societies (also found to a degree in Saudi Arabia), which put special disabilities on foreign women workers and limit the roles of local women.

KUWAIT

Kuwait—with a population of about two million persons, of whom about 700,000 are Kuwaiti nationals—was in the twentieth century ruled by a combination of British agents and local emirs until independence in 1961. The 1962 constitution, like several in the Middle East, gives equal rights to men and women, but, again as in many cases, several laws are unequal. With the large and growing income from oil there was much modernization, but real power remained in the hands of the hereditary emirs and the wealthy and well connected, despite a constitution and an elected National Assembly, which can reject the emir's proposals. Citizenship and electoral rights were limited to a minority even of men, with several categories of residents denied such rights. The country is about 70 percent Sunni and 30 percent Shi'i, and each community follows its own shari'a-based courts in personal status matters. Shari'a is little reformed, and Sunni women have no right to marry without the consent of their wali (guardian).

The 1960s saw an expansion of women's roles in work, education, and freedom of dress, and the formation of two women's organizations, one of which, the Arab Women's Development Society (AWDS), worked for legal reform and suffrage, while the other was more limited to elite concerns. Women's organizations and activism grew in the 1960s and 1970s, and some campaigned for equal rights and on other issues important to women. They were, however, hurt by divisions between upper-class and middle-class women, and were increasingly challenged by conservatives and by a growing Islamist trend among men and women since the 1970s. The government dissolved the AWDS in 1980 and accused its energetic and intelligent leader, Nouria al-Sadani, of a crime and exiled her. Since then there has been little autonomous women's organization permitted.

As elsewhere, the greatest advances have come in education at all levels, with women making up almost two-thirds of university students (with more male than female students abroad). In an affirmative action for men, in the mid-1990s the university introduced higher GPA requirements for women than men in fields like engineering and medicine.[92] Islamic law has remained dominant in family law, and a major issue has been the struggle for women's electoral rights. Activist women particularly put forth their case after the first Gulf War, in which women's activities in resisting Saddam Hussein's invasion of Kuwait were of central importance, and women participated bravely in the resistance in a variety of ways. Conservative Islamists, with tribalists, for years successfully blocked parliamentary expansion of women's rights. In 1996 Islamists succeeded in passing a bill requiring colleges and the university to ensure gender segregation.

In May 1999, the emir issued several decrees, one of which granted women full electoral rights. This was approved by the Council of Ministers and was seen as a deliberate abandonment of the emir's prior alliance with Islamists. The government, however, failed to lobby the new parliament to support the decree, and a bitter struggle between women's organizations and Islamists ensued. In November, the decree was rejected by the new parliament. In April 2005 parliament voted to enfranchise women in municipal elections, an act that was negated by a temporary parliamentary maneuver. In May, however, parliament voted to give women full electoral rights, which they will exercise in parliamentary elections in 2007. Today women vote in every Middle Eastern country except Saudi Arabia (and the United Arab Emirates, where nobody votes). In June 2005 a women's rights activist and professor of political science, Massouma Mubarak, became the first woman to be appointed as a minister in Kuwait's cabinet.

A variety of reasons have been given for the emir's interest in woman suffrage—to lessen the power of the opposition; to influence foreign democracies; to open more government posts to the emir's family; or to strengthen the dynasty's popular base. Many Kuwaiti women, including Islamist women, campaigned to vote, and some have worked to restore and expand women's presence in public life. The strong appeal of Islamism to women led many Islamists to support woman suffrage.

Women's NGOs are required to receive offered government funds and cannot accept funds from outside donors. Women's NGOs have been transformed into a government-support network.[93] The combination of Islamists and tribal conservatives has limited basic social and legal reforms, but the modernization largely due to oil income has given many women new roles in education, public health, and employment, despite the setbacks since the more liberal 1960s and 1970s.[94]

UNITED ARAB EMIRATES (UAE)

The United Arab Emirates, previously called the Trucial States, became independent in 1971 when Britain withdrew from the Gulf. It is a federation of seven monarchies, whose rulers choose the UAE president every five years. The population is officially about four million, but fewer than 20 percent are citizens. Per capita GDP is a high $22,000, owing to oil, the exploding free trade zone in Dubai, and manufacturing, banking, and tourism. The UAE's states, much like Kuwait, mostly profit from recent oil income, have high average incomes, have many migrant and émigré male and female workers, and are led by hereditary tribal leaders. Most of their governing elites support some extension of women's rights, but strong traditional and Islamist sentiment against this exists, as do a variety of inegalitarian practices.

Women's equality is not established in the constitution, and women's rights differ in part according to their citizenship and employment. There are no known independent organizations working on gender equality. There is a semigovernmental General Women's Union founded in 1975 by the then president's wife. It is an umbrella organization monitoring other women's groups, which are mostly charitable and business organizations. Family law is mostly unreformed shari'a, though a man must have the permission of his first wife to marry a second wife. UAE law, however, does criminalize rape, abuse, and harassment, and in Dubai divorces granted women for domestic violence have increased, which suggests more reporting rather than more violence. Those who report rape, as in some other countries, risk being punished for illicit sexual relations.

Female literacy in 2003 was 81 percent, higher than the male 76 percent. Women make up 75 percent of the students at the National University, though, as elsewhere, many men study abroad. The UAE has held no elections, and nobody has the right to vote. Women get paid maternity leave but face employment discrimination and low employment levels. As is true of several countries in the Arabian Peninsula, women are trafficked into the country, despite laws against it, for exploitation in work and sex. Citizens, but not the 80 percent of the population who are foreign, have access to good free health services, including prenatal and maternal care. In the past twenty-five years the number of children per woman has dropped from 5.23 to 3, even though only about 28 percent of women use contraception—a low figure for the Middle East.[95]

QATAR

Qatar is a hereditary emirate that gained independence from Britain in 1971. Like other small Gulf states, Qatar has a high average income, from oil and natural gas. Only about 150,000 of its estimated population of 600,000 are citizens with rights to free education and health care.

Emir Sheikh Hamid al-Thani deposed his father in a bloodless coup in 1995 and has introduced reforms, some of them beneficial to women. A 1998 decree established a national advisory council for municipal affairs and gave men and women the right to vote and stand for elections. Six women candidates ran, but none won. Qatar's constitution, approved in a 2003 referendum, grants women equality and the right to vote and stand for election. One woman won a seat in the April 2003 council elections, the first time a woman was elected by universal suffrage in the group of Arab Gulf state countries called the Gulf Cooperation Council (GCC). In 2003 the emir of Qatar appointed women to cabinet and high university positions, indicating a commitment to women's advancement on the part of the Qatari leadership and the first lady.[96]

BAHRAIN

The small island country of Bahrain, with a population of about 700,000 and a two-thirds Shi'i majority, gained independence from Britain in 1971. In 1975 its emir dissolved the National Assembly and suspended the 1973 constitution for twenty-five years. The new constitution issued in 2002 by the ruler, now called king, creates a parliamentary monarchy but leaves most power with hereditary kings. The current king has implemented various reforms since his accession in 1999.

Bahrain is a rich, tax-free country with a high per capita income and wide access for males and females to education and free health care. It gives few rights to the many migrant or expatriate workers, including female domestics, some of whom are trafficked and/or indentured. The government and various NGOs have recently taken some steps to address women's problems and to codify shari'a law, but results are not yet clear. The government ratified CEDAW in 2002, with major reservations, and has since taken some steps to improve women's political rights and representation. The number of NGOs devoted to women's issues has grown, but the government severely regulates NGOs. Women in the past participated in nationalist struggles and recently have demonstrated, in some cases for women's rights and in others for Islamist aims. Women are active in political NGOs.

Health care, including maternity care and birth control, are free and available, and the high level of education and of living standards makes women aware of their health needs. Women are the great majority of university students but do not have access to sufficient employment opportunities. Having been aided by one women's NGO, women in the garment industry can now join an established trade union that protects their rights. Some women have been increasingly influenced by Islamist movements, while others work for greater organizational independence and political power for both women and men.[97]

ISLAMIST AND NON-ISLAMIST TRENDS IN THE MIDDLE EAST

Islamist movements have become increasingly important throughout the Middle East since 1970; they incorporate many young men and women, rural migrants, and people from all classes, even former nationalists and communists. Islamism is the name given to Islamic political movements, but these vary greatly from those, who are a majority, who do not countenance violence (except, often, against territorial occupation) and the minority that do countenance violence. There is also a difference in targets; for years most movements were directed primarily against their own governments, but now a minority accept attacks on civilians in other countries. Although among the countries considered here, Islamists rule only in Iran, they have long ruled in Sudan and are also powerful in Afghanistan, Iraq, and Pakistan, and strong in Egypt and some other countries. The Islamist Hamas also won a majority in Palestine's 2006 parliamentary elections. Saudi Arabia has combined an older form of monarchical-Islamic rule with major financial encouragement throughout the Muslim world of the strictest and most potentially militant and male-supremacist Islamist tendencies, via schools, mosques, and propaganda. Saudi-style education has been a factor in the turn to militant Islamism among a minority of young people. Only recently have economic constraints and fear of terrorism by stricter Islamists begun very slowly to change this Saudi policy.

Contemporary Islamic political movements have largely called for shari'a as state law. Shari'a comprises the obligations of all Muslims, whether legally enforceable or not, and was never before modern times a state law code but rested on flexible judgments by Muslim judges.[98] Often, as seen in this book, strict shari'a rules were not enforced, especially for sexual offenses, and some rulers, including major Ottoman sultans, issued laws that significantly reduced shari'a-based punishments. Islamic law was codified for the first time in the Ottoman Empire in the late nineteenth century, and much of this codification passed to the Ottoman successor states of western Asia. However, most criminal and civil law was put under Western-style codes, which themselves had a number of gender-inegalitarian elements. What remained under shari'a covered most of the matters of concern to women and the family—marriage, divorce, child custody, and inheritance. Some important scholars and thinkers maintain that a proper interpretation of Islam would bring gender-egalitarian interpretations of the shari'a, but in practice steps advocated, sometimes successfully, by Islamists in the name of "restoring" the shari'a have until now been antiegalitarian and restrictive for women.

Legal changes in women's status in recent decades have varied by country and have gone in contradictory directions. On opposite ends are Iran's reinstatement of shari'a and Morocco's 2004 passage of major reforms. In most of Arabia there have been few reforms, and in nearly all Middle Eastern countries reform in personal status law lags behind reforms in labor, health, and education, where shari'a is not involved and legal changes that favor women have been notable. In most countries, women's and reformist groups have actively campaigned for reform, while clerics and Islamists have campaigned for what they present as the shari'a, though their shari'a is to be codified and inflexible, unlike that of the past. In several countries influenced by Islamism shari'a courts in practice deal more often and more harshly with sexual crimes than such courts traditionally did. Islamists are often joined by tribal and other conservatives, who tend to emphasize issues regarding women, and the issues have been, and continue to be, fiercely contested. It remains true that rulers, like Egypt's Mubarak, the kings of Morocco and Jordan, and Oman's sultan, have often been essential to introducing reform, but women's movements, parliaments, and political activities on both sides of the question have been more important than is usually realized, and reformist women and their male allies have sometimes mounted decisive pressures.

In recent decades women's roles and status in education and work have expanded in many ways but have been affected by the rise of Islamic politics. The popularity of Islamism has numerous causes, including the failures of secular or non-Islamic governments to meet people's needs, poverty, economic and cultural crises, and struggles against Western powers and Israel, which is generally seen in the Middle East as a colonial implantation. A point of appeal for young men, who make up a large part particularly of extremist Islamism, is the contrast between the sexual freedoms they see in their media and elsewhere and their own sexual frustration, which leads some to idealize a more unified and regulated Islamic past, and a few to long for a sexualized paradise. Some women, too, find new sexual and cultural ways upsetting, while others gain new mobility and knowledge from belonging to moderate Islamist groups. To all this is added the economic and political frustrations of both men and women. Though Islamic politics involve many tendencies, they are similar in wanting states to implement Islamic beliefs and practices, including the shari'a, which often involves the literal application of its punishments.[99] Many shari'a punishments, especially those for sexual crimes, were rarely applied in those periods for which we have documentation, and so the "revival" of such punishments is often really an innovation.

Islamists mostly read Islam as endorsing polygamy, male control in marriage and elsewhere, veiling, and strong punishments for sexual relations outside of marriage. Literally, the Quran does not require veiling, and its requirement of four eyewitnesses to adultery should make convictions almost impossible, as it did in the past, but on these questions most Islamists follow their more restrictive interpretations of shari'a. Female Islamist groups have often stressed the protective aspects of Islam, including the protection of property rights that have often been denied in practice. Female Islamists also often have a very different and more woman-friendly interpretation of Islam than do male Islamists, even when they belong to the same party. Islamist and Islamic groups sometimes empower women from traditional families, providing them with a way to meet and act together in the public sphere, to attend schools and universities, and to work if their bodies are covered.[100]

Most Islamists do not advocate the older urban elite practices of facial veiling and seclusion, but give interpretations that take into account many features of the modern world.[101] Increasing numbers of people interpret hijab to mean new forms of "Islamic" dress and wear it, whether from conformism or as a badge of morality and cultural authenticity. Girls' and women's participation in education and in the workforce, including the major professions, is continually growing. For some believers it is hijab that makes such participation acceptable.

With the spread of Islamist ideologies, many defenders of women's rights have reinterpreted the Quran and original Islam as being gender-egalitarian, and some secularists find it prudent to use Islamic arguments. These arguments often advance the practices of Islamic modernists favoring the early or Meccan moral texts—texts that treat and address male and female believers equally—over the late, legalistic, Medinan texts that are seen as time-related. Islamists frequently try to show that the Quran treats men and women as equal although having distinct natures. They note that the Quran says both men and women should behave modestly and wear modest dress, which for men usually means covering the arms, legs, and torso.

On the feminist and liberal side, there have been some new approaches by those who wish to preserve adherence to Islam. One of them, pioneered by the Sudanese reformer Mahmud Mohamed Taha in the 1960s, and developed by his follower Abdullahi Ahmed An-Na'im and others, says that only the Meccan ethical Quranic verses have eternal binding significance, and the Medinan laws are time-bound, so that modern laws enforcing equal human and women's rights are compatible with true Islam.[102] Several Iranian and other thinkers have put forth new liberal interpretations of Islam that do not depend on the above distinction but involve new interpretations of other points.[103]

Many women have suggested more nearly egalitarian approaches to Islam. They have included feminist theologians, like Riffat Hassan, a Pakistani now teaching in an American university, who stresses in more detail the egalitarian verses of the Quran. Also in this group is the Moroccan feminist sociologist Fatima Mernissi, whose early work was more critical of Islam, but who has subsequently done textual studies of Islamic Traditions and early history. She stresses the active public role of Muhammad's wives and of other women in the initial period of Islam. She says Muhammad's vision of Islam was egalitarian, and he lived this ideal. However, Muslim males were not ready to accept such dramatic changes. Finally, the Prophet had to sacrifice his egalitarian vision for the sake of communal cohesiveness and the survival of Islam. To Mernissi, the seclusion of Muhammad's wives was a symbol of Islam's retreat from the principle of gender equality.[104]

Among the issues discussed today are whether Islam can become egalitarian for women; and whether states that call themselves Islamic can fully implement women's rights. Islamic countries average lower on international indexes of women's welfare than economically equivalent non-Muslim countries, and this is probably connected with widespread beliefs and practices that those who profess them consider Islamic, even though many such beliefs and practices are doubtfully Islamic. All revealed religions have male-supremacist content, but appeals to inegalitarian texts are today more common in Islamic areas than in non-Muslim ones. States that call themselves Islamic have, on average, a more subordinate legal status for women than states that do not stress Islam. Those who want to reinterpret Islam have a difficult weight of custom and vested interests to confront, but they have major successes to signal in Tunisia,

Morocco, Turkey, and some countries outside the Middle East and lesser successes elsewhere.

Islamism came, from the 1970s onward, to be seen as the most politically potent counterideology to existing regimes, rejecting failed secular Westernizing rule, unsuccessful communism, and imperialism. Many liberals and leftists allied with Islamists. Some women adopted the hijab as a form of protest, and some saw positive aspects to it, such as reducing class differences in female display, reducing sexual harassment, and ending sexual distractions at work. Just as the position of women had been a central question for early oppositional nationalists, so, with a new and powerful framing, Islamists saw it as central to resistance to imperialism and the restoration of morality. Women's hijab came to be a major symbol showing that Islamist movements and states were truly Islamic.

Islamism and the persistence of traditional culture are far from the only problems for women in the Middle East. There have been a number of international and local efforts, some quite successful, to promote the active participation of women in development, and many organizations have come to realize and address the central importance of women in all aspects of change that could benefit the entire population. However, the weakness of economic development in the area contrasts not only with the West, but increasingly with East Asia. This has several local and global socioeconomic and political causes, including the distorting economic and political effects of oil, which, along with outside support for existing governments, helps to maintain authoritarian regimes and their vested economic interests. Many experts agree that despite recent progress, including some improvements in women's status and activity, ongoing disparities for women—among them legal inequalities, low female labor-force participation, and the persistence of male-dominant beliefs and practices—are important contributing causes of regional political and socioeconomic underdevelopment.[105]

Some who fight for women's rights have begun to stress the need for women to control their bodies and sexuality, the theme of many literary works, and of a regional conference of NGO representatives in Malta organized by the Turkish-centered group Women for Women's Human Rights in spring 2004. The conference issued a report stressing a variety of violations of women's sexual and bodily rights that still occur despite progress in several countries, and the need for further legal, educational, and cultural change. Public actions and written works by Middle Eastern women about various aspects of sexuality and the sexual repression of women are increasing, although there are also frequent attacks on discussing or acting upon these subjects, and most people today reject Western models of sexuality.[106]

Despite the persistence of problems, women have also scored many gains in the past few decades. Women's educational levels, access to health centers and birth control, and labor-force participation have all risen. The number and variety of women's organizations have grown, and they have done important and often successful work in many fields. The international connections of Middle Eastern women's movements and NGOs have given them significant support, including that generated by UN-sponsored conferences and programs, and by work underwritten by various foundations and governments, and there has been a broader and more equal interchange of ideas than in the colonial period.[107] Given the rapid advances in women's education and awareness in nearly all Middle Eastern countries—an awareness that includes international influences and ties and new interpretations of religious and national heritages—there is every reason to hope that the overall trend toward greater rights will continue, though it may face temporary setbacks.

Conclusion

THE HISTORY OF WOMEN in the Middle East is so varied and complex as to defy simple generalization. Apart from the influence of different views on how the limited evidence should be interpreted, there have been major variations in women's roles by class, region, ethnicity, religion, and period. Many of the features of women's status often attributed to Islam turn out to have been borrowed from prior civilizations in the Near East and from other religions, notably Judaism. The Quran is no more male-supremacist than several other major religious texts, including the Old Testament. As in many cultures, women were legally subordinate to men in several spheres, and the agnatic family, with its age and gender hierarchies, was a central institution. As compared to the West until late modern times, Muslim women had more property and inheritance rights, though in several other spheres they had fewer rights and were treated like minors, needing male permission to marry, work, or travel. Most Westerners have little idea how recent in the West are most of the women's rights they now take for granted, and hence exaggerate the historical differences between Middle Eastern and Western women. The ideal of sexual segregation, based on a patriarchal compulsion to control women's sexuality, was wrongly taken by outsiders to mean an absence of almost any positive features in women's lives.

Although documentation for early periods is scarce, once documents become available, they show us women enjoying a social, cultural, and religious life together that had many satisfactions. Evidence from literature and legal cases shows that in the medieval and early modern periods adherence to Islamic law, texts, and punishments was often far from strict or universal. Certain peoples, notably the Turks and Egyptians, and also many Sufis and unorthodox groups, were noted for the greater freedom of their women. This said, it is also clear that many women suffered, and a large number still suffer, from bad arranged marriages, domestic violence, limited rights or communication in the family, widespread cultural acceptance of male superiority and prerogatives, and denigration of women's character and potential.

The development of Islamic law and of local practices regarding women was influenced by socioeconomic and political circumstances, notably the importance of patriarchal tribes and extended families in which older men, and to a degree older women, exercised strong control over the lives and marriages of younger relatives, and boys and men had significant controls over girls and women. Control over sexual missteps was especially important and occasionally violent, though we also hear of many freer sexual practices that were not sanctioned by religious texts. Women in many cases had greater freedoms than were envisaged in either Islamic or tribal laws. On the other hand, contemporary research shows that poor women, rarely studied in older documents, often had fewer rights and protections than elite women, and that idealization of the status of peasant and tribal women based on their having been less segregated than elite women is unwarranted. Women's status varied greatly among different tribal groups. Violence against women and limits on women's rights in the public sphere were among the problems that many women and some men combated in modern times, as was the authority of family elders over the marriages and behavior of young men and women.

For various historical reasons more Muslims than adherents of other scriptural traditions have remained tied to premodern gender practices attributed to their religious texts. One major reason for this has been the role of imperialism, and especially its cultural aspects. Westerners to this day have attacked Islam especially for its treatment of women, which has encouraged many Middle Easterners to defend this treatment as part of its reaction against imperialism. Even today more of the Middle East than of any other region is under foreign occupation—today including the occupied Palestinian territories, Iraq, and, in the minds of some, Afghanistan. The area with the longest history of occupation—Algeria—has seen more backlash reaction regarding women than have most areas of shorter and lesser occupation. That all colonized areas were predominantly Arab has contributed to greater Arab conservatism regarding women's status. It is surely no accident that the country that could free itself soonest from Western control—Turkey—could also undertake the strongest reforms regarding women. This said, there are clearly also other cultural forces at work, as conservative Saudi Arabia was never colonized.

Also important in gender practices has been the strength, from pre-Islamic times and in many cases down to the present, of patriarchal tribal and extended familial forms of social organization. The honor-shame complex, with its sanctions and stress on control of female sexual behavior, is even today tied to such social structures. This form of social organization arose in part because of the ecology of the Middle East, including large arid and mountainous areas where nomadic tribes must migrate in order to feed their flocks. In part it also reflects the inability of premodern central governments to control large territories, so that much local control devolved onto powerful tribal or familial leaders. Tribal and familial patterns of control varied, but in general, although women had some freedoms, they were also often subject to strong sanctions for unauthorized behavior, especially sexual behavior. Patriarchal familial, tribal, local, and even national structures have limited the emergence of egalitarian societies with greater possibilities of economic, social, and political development.[1]

Central governments' frequent direct or indirect access to large oil income has increased the power of autocrats, discouraged economic development, and sometimes hindered fundamental participation and changes in society and politics that could benefit women. High and rising oil prices, today augmented by U.S. failure to implement conservation, bolster the power of conservative governments with large oil incomes, notably those of Saudi Arabia and Iran. Widespread Western denigration of Islam has brought about a cultural backlash, in which people feel they must defend their beliefs against cultural attack. Such a defense for some Muslims involves a stricter interpretation of Islamic rules and laws than was common in the past, while for others it has contributed to a liberal restatement of Islam with an emphasis on women's rights and greater democracy. Until now Islamic politics have more often limited than expanded women's legal rights.

This work has barely had space to touch upon the complexities of life of either past or contemporary Middle Eastern women. There is today huge variation by class within countries and by country, ranging from Turkey and Tunisia on the modernizing side to Saudi Arabia on the side of resistance to social, political, and gender-related changes. All countries' laws and practices regarding women have, however, changed in important ways in the past two centuries. As a gross generalization, women's education, workforce participation, and access to health services—including birth control and pediatric care, with improvements in health and declining birthrates—have been increasing in nearly all countries, often with major input both from governments and from women's and other civic organizations. Legal gains have continued in some countries, but in most countries there remain important legal gender inequalities, and there have been a few reinstatements of Islamic law under Islamist pressure. In most countries husbands and male kin retain significant legal power over girls and women and greater rights than women in marriage, divorce, custody, inheritance, and freedom of movement.

International bodies, including UN agencies and international conferences, have encouraged attention to women's issues and organization. There are now local, regional, and international organizations working on a wide variety of issues, including, in some countries, formerly taboo issues. In several countries there has been a growth, encouraged by international agencies, of NGOs focusing on women's issues; this has brought gains but has also meant that some governments have turned over some of their proper functions to NGOs, and that NGOs are often in competition for money and influence, and officially sponsored ones may replace truly autonomous organizations. Changes in male supremacist cultural ideas and practices have often lagged, partly because of the lack of major political and economic development, so that many widespread ideas and actions based on male supremacy and control over girls and women continue strong, especially among the popular classes. These classes have often not seen benefits from modernization or from governments, and often can get needed social and health benefits only from Islamist institutions, a situation that helps account for their attraction to groups that speak in the name of Islamic traditions familiar to these classes.

The persistence of major problems like economic stagnation, foreign occupation or undue influence, widespread autocracy, and denial of human rights has meant that popular and even elite discontent and protests have for many decades been more often directed to such problems than to the rights of women. Some measures to improve women's freedoms have been associated with unpopular autocracies or an equally unpopular West, and even with licentiousness. All this makes the job of women working in this field more difficult and has dissuaded, or been an excuse for, some liberal men who do not stress women's rights. In these circumstances and with the rise of Islamic identification, many reformers, whether or not they are sincere believers, turn to new interpretations of Islam, which often center on rethinking the position of women. Books and arguments that focus on the earliest Islamic centuries are common both inside and outside the Muslim world, but their real concern in most cases is to provide Islamic sanction for their own views, especially about women. There are still some vocal secularist proponents of women's rights, and their number is rising in Iran, where clerical rule has been tried and has largely failed. Despite all obstacles and disagreements, improvements in women's status and rights have continued, and newer forms of organization around women's issues can boast important achievements.

As a generalization, one may say that in premodern times women were widely considered inferior, as they were in other societies, but that women's power and agency were always greater than most outsiders imagined. Today many women's socioeconomic role in a variety of jobs and professions and, in increasing numbers, in the home is more independent and powerful than a simple reading of laws or a report on the prevalence of veiling might make one think. However, modern trends have not been uniformly beneficial, and many rural, tribal, and popular-class women have harder lives and fewer economic roles and possibilities than before. Working women of all classes often have the double burden of all the housework and care of their husbands and family in addition to their jobs, even if they have access to more and better jobs.[2] Such issues are important in much of the world beyond the Middle East. A major problem is the continued strength of ideas and customs that privilege men, whether based in religious concepts or other aspects of culture, which mean second-class status and mistreatment for many women. While women's situation is not nearly as bad overall as it is often depicted, and many women have advanced toward greater equality and independence, there still remains a great deal to be done if more gender equality is to be achieved—and many women and men recognize this and are acting upon it. Islamist movements have been contradictory in their impact, giving some formerly secluded girls and women a chance to be educated, to meet together, and to develop their own interpretations of Islam, while at the same time most Islamists legitimate superior male power and privilege. Whether feminist interpretations of Islam will increase in importance and influence, and whether formerly important secularist ideas and movements will see widespread revivals—perhaps in new forms, as in today's Iran—is for the future to tell. The dramatic rise in female education, the increased awareness of women's rights, and the growth of women in the workforce and in public positions give reason for hope.

Notes to Book One

Issues in Studying Middle Eastern
Women's History

1. The one narrative I know of is Parvin Paidar, *Women and the Political Process in Twentieth-Century Iran* (Cambridge: Cambridge University Press, 1995). Even the admirable and comprehensive multivolume *Encyclopedia of Women and Islamic Cultures*, ed. Suad Joseph and Afsaneh Najmabadi (Leiden: Brill, 2003–), does not plan to have historical narratives covering any country, region, or period, though the first volume has a useful section on historical methodologies and several historical questions are discussed in later volumes.

2. Some of the issues raised in this introduction are discussed at greater length in the essays in Book Two of this volume.

I
Regional Background and the Beginnings of Islam

1. Deniz Kandiyoti, "Islam and Patriarchy: A Comparative Perspective," in *Women in Middle Eastern History: Shifting Boundaries in Sex and Gender*, ed. Nikki R. Keddie and Beth Baron (New Haven: Yale University Press, 1991).

2. Nikki R. Keddie, "Material Culture and Geography: Toward a Holistic History of the Middle East," in *Comparing Muslim Societies: Knowledge and the State in a World Civilization*, ed. Juan R. I. Cole (Ann Arbor: University of Michigan Press, 1992); Jared M. Diamond, *Guns, Germs, and Steel: The Fates of Human Societies* (New York: W. W. Norton, 1997).

3. Jane Schneider, "Of Vigilance and Virgins: Honor, Shame, and Access to Resources in Mediterranean Societies," *Ethnology* 10, no. 1 (January 1971): 1–24. Several articles by anthropologists discussing Schneider's theses followed. For a complex view of honor and the centrality to male domination of an (often fictitious) deflowering of a bride by a groom, see Nancy Lindisfarne, "Variant Masculinities, Variant Virginities: Rethinking 'Honour and Shame,' " in *Dislocating Masculinity: Comparative Ethnographies*, ed. Andrea Cornwall and Nancy Lindisfarne (Routledge: London, 1994).

4. See, for example, John Esposito with Natana J. DeLong-Bas, *Women in Muslim Family Law*, 2nd ed. (Syracuse: Syracuse University Press, 2001), chap. 2. Various writers present the view that Muhammad's revelations were dramatically and overwhelmingly beneficial for women. Many of them have not closely studied what is known about pre-Islamic Arabia.

5. Cf. Denise A. Spellberg, "Political Action and Public Example: 'Ai'sha and the Battle of the Camel," chap. 3 of Keddie and Baron, *Women in Middle Eastern History*; Spellberg summarizes the different views on the Quran's role regarding women. See also her *Politics, Gender, and the Islamic Past: The Legacy of 'A'isha bint Abi Bakr* (New York: Columbia University Press, 1994). For a brief statement of the more positive view of the pre-Islamic period, see Ghada Karmi, "Women, Islam and Patriarchalism," in *Feminism and Islam: Legal and Literary Perspectives*, ed. Mai Yamani (New York: New York University Press, 1996), 69–86.

6. Leila Ahmed, *Women and Gender in Islam: Historical Roots of a Modern Debate* (New Haven: Yale University Press, 1992), 49, citing Ibn Sa'd; Gertrude Stern, *Marriage in Early Islam* (London: The Royal Asiatic Society, 1939), 34.

7. The most thorough documentary study and analysis of questions regarding marriage in pre-Islamic and early Islamic times is Stern, *Marriage in Early Islam*. Similar views are summarized in Wiebke Walther, *Women in Islam*, trans. C.S.V. Salt (Princeton: Markus Wiener, 1981), 57.

8. This and the immediately subsequent Quran quotations are taken from Barbara Freyer Stowasser, *Women in the Qur'an, Traditions, and Interpretation* (Oxford: Oxford University Press, 1993), here 90.

9. Ibid., 91.

10. Ahmed, *Women and Gender in Islam*, 55–56.

11. Stowasser, *Women in the Qur'an*, 99.

12. Ibid., 92–93.

13. Ahmed, *Women and Gender in Islam*, 42.

14. Ibid., 45.

II
From the Pious Caliphs through the Dynastic Caliphates

1. Leila Ahmed, *Women and Gender in Islam: Historical Roots of a Modern Debate* (New Haven: Yale University Press, 1992), 61.

2. The origins and nature of Islamic law on adultery and other sexual matters, and the lack of stoning in the court records she studied, are discussed in Vivian Elyse Semerdjian, " 'Off the Straight Path': Gender, Public Morality and Legal Administration in Ottoman Aleppo, Syria" (Ph.D. diss., Georgetown University, Washington, DC, 2002), chaps. 1, 2. The author's wording makes it seem that she accepts the attribution of hadiths to the Prophet, although she herself shows how many of them incorporated Jewish and other non-Islamic legal traditions. Writings by several scholars indicate that past Islamic courts very rarely imposed death or physical punishment for adultery, partly because of the near impossibility of meeting Islamic requirements for proof.

3. E. A. Salem, *Political Theory and Institutions of the Khawarij* (Baltimore: Johns Hopkins University Press, 1956), 86–87, 100. .

4. For women in biographical dictionaries, see Ruth Roded, *Women in Islamic Biographical Collections: From Ibn Sa'd to Who's Who* (Boulder, CO: Lynne Reinner, 1994).

5. See Paula Sanders, "Gendering the Ungendered Body: Hermaphrodites in Medieval Islamic Law," in *Women in Middle Eastern History: Shifting Boundaries in Sex and Gender*, ed. Nikki R. Keddie and Beth Baron (New Haven: Yale University Press, 1991), chap. 5.

6. See Everett K. Rowson, "Gender Irregularity as Entertainment: Institutionalized Transvestism at the Caliphal Court in Medieval Baghdad," in *Gender and Difference in the Middle Ages*, ed. Sharon Farmer and Carol Braun Pasternack (Minneapolis: University of Minnesota Press, 2003). Abdelwahab Bouhdiba, *Sexuality in Islam*, trans. Alan Sheridan (London: Routledge and Kegan Paul, 1985), 142–45 lists among the few surviving medieval erotic texts, out of numerous originals, one titled *Concubines and Youths in Competition*, and another in which "[p]ederasty and its advantages are described at some length. . . . Lesbianism and nymphomania are the subjects of a well-documented and salacious chapter."

7. Patricia Crone, *Roman, Provincial and Islamic Law: The Origins of the Islamic Patronate* (Cambridge: Cambridge University Press, 1987); Joseph Schacht, *The Origins of Muhammadan Jurisprudence* (Oxford: Oxford University Press, 1979).

8. John Esposito with Natana J. DeLong-Bas, *Women in Muslim Family Law*, 2nd ed. (Syracuse: Syracuse University Press, 2001), 7.

9. Noel J. Coulson, *Conflicts and Tensions in Islamic Jurisprudence* (Chicago: University of Chicago Press, 1969), chap. 2. For a fine analytic narrative, see Sami Zubaida, *Law and Power in the Islamic World* (London: I. B. Tauris, 2003), which unfortunately does not take account of the extensive recent revisionist work on Ottoman law.

10. Esposito, *Women in Muslim Family Law*, chap. 1.

11. Barbara Freyer Stowasser, *Women in the Qur'an, Traditions, and Interpretation* (Oxford: Oxford University Press, 1993), chap. 2.

12. See Denise A. Spellberg, *Politics, Gender, and the Islamic Past: The Legacy of 'A'isha bint Abi Bakr* (New York: Columbia University Press, 1994).

13. Summaries of traditional Islamic marriage practices are in Wiebke Walther, *Women in Islam*, trans. C.S.V. Salt (Princeton: Markus Wiener, 1981), 54–61, and in Guity Nashat, "Marriage in the Qajar Period," in *Women in Iran from 1800 to the Islamic Republic*, ed. Lois Beck and Guity Nashat (Urbana: University of Illinois Press, 2003), chap. 1, which is broader in scope than its title suggests.

14. Fatemeh Etemad Moghadam, "Women and Labor in the Islamic Republic of Iran," in Beck and Nashat, *Women in Iran from 1800 to the Islamic Republic*, 165.

15. Shahla Haeri, *Law of Desire: Temporary Marriage in Shi'i Iran* (Syracuse: Syracuse University Press, 1989).

16. Semerdjian, " 'Off the Straight Path,' " 40–51: "Stoning in the Judeo-Christian Tradition."

17. Mounira M. Charrad, *States and Women's Rights: The Making of Postcolonial Tunisia, Algeria, and Morocco* (Berkeley and Los Angeles: University of California Press, 2001).

18. Bouhdiba, *Sexuality in Islam*, chap. 9.

19. Ahmed, *Women and Gender in Islam*, 92, and Basim Musallam, *Sex and Society in Islam: Birth Control before the Nineteenth Century* (Cambridge: Cambridge University Press, 1983).

20. C. Cahen, "Réflexions sur le Waqf ancien," *Studia Islamica* 14 (1961): 54–54 (my translation). Joseph Schacht, "Law and Justice," in *Cambridge History of Islam*, ed. P. M. Holt, Ann K. S. Lambton, and Bernard Lewis (Cambridge: Cambridge University Press, 1970), 2:561, says that, in great measure, the rapid development and spread of waqf "arose from the desire of the Muslim middle classes to exclude daughters and, even more so, the descendants of daughters from the benefits of the Qur'anic law of succession; in other words, to strengthen the old Arab patriarchal family system." Both citations and a discussion are in Nahid Yeganeh [Parvin Paidar] and Nikki R. Keddie, "Sexuality and Shi'i Social Protest in Iran," in *Shi'ism and Social Protest*, ed. Juan R. I. Cole and Nikki R. Keddie (New Haven: Yale University Press, 1986), reprinted in Book Two of this volume. According to Bouhdiba, *Sexuality in Islam*, 113, even waqfs that did not exclude daughters passed in the following generations exclusively to male descendants.

21. Ülkü U. Bates, "Women as Patrons of Architecture in Turkey," in *Women in the Muslim World*, ed. Lois Beck and Nikki Keddie (Cambridge, MA: Harvard University Press, 1978), chap. 12, and *Women, Patronage, and Self-Representation in Islamic Societies*, ed. D. Fairchild Ruggles (Albany: SUNY Press, 2000).

22. E. W. Fernea has pioneered in presenting women's religious lives. See her *Guests of the Sheik: An Ethnography of an Iraqi Village*, reissue ed. (New York: Anchor, 1995).

23. For an analysis of Shahrzad and other medieval and modern literary figures, see Fedwa Malti-Douglas, *Woman's Body, Woman's Word: Gender and Discourse in Arabo-Islamic Writing* (Princeton: Princeton University Press, 1991).

24. S. D. Goitein, *A Mediterranean Society: An Abridgement in One Volume*, rev. and ed. Jacob Lassner (Berkeley and Los Angeles: University of California Press, 1999), 446.

25. Ibid., 447.

26. Ibid., chap. 15, "The World of Women."

27. Ibid., 404.

28. Ibid., 418.

III
From the Turkish and Mongol Invasions to 1798

1. Thomas Barfield, "Tribe and State Relations: The Inner Asian Perspective," in *Tribes and State Formation in the Middle East*, ed. Philip S. Khoury and Joseph Kostiner (Berkeley and Los Angeles: University of California Press, 1990), and idem, "Turk, Persian and Arab: Changing Relationships between Tribes and State in Iran and along Its Frontiers," in *Iran and the Surrounding World 1501–2001: Interactions in Culture and Cultural Politics*, ed. Nikki R. Keddie and Rudi Matthee (Seattle: University of Washington Press, 2001), chap. 3.

2. On elite Turkish and Mongol women in the Seljuk and subsequent periods, see the chapters on the Seljuks, Timurids, and Safavids by Carole Hillenbrand,

Beatrice Forbes Manz, and Maria Szuppe in *Women in Iran from the Rise of Islam to 1800*, ed. Guity Nashat and Lois Beck (Urbana: University of Illinois Press, 2003); chapters on the Timurids, Ottomans, and Safavids by Priscilla P. Soucek, Yvonne J. Seng, Leslie Peirce, Fariba Zarinebaf-Shahr, Maria Szuppe, and Kathryn Babayan in *Women in the Medieval Islamic World: Power, Patronage, and Piety*, ed. Gavin R. G. Hambly (New York: St. Martin's Press, 1998), chaps. 10, 12–16; and Ann K. S. Lambton, *Continuity and Change in Medieval Persia: Aspects of Administrative, Economic and Social History 11th–14th Century* (Albany: State University of New York Press, 1988), chap. 8, "The Constitution of Society (2): Women of the Ruling House."

3. Geoffrey Lewis, "Heroines and Others in the Heroic Age of the Turks," in Hambly, *Women in the Medieval Islamic World*, chap. 7.

4. Maria Szuppe, "Status, Knowledge, and Politics: Women in Sixteenth-Century Safavid Iran," in Nashat and Beck, *Women in Iran from the Rise of Islam to 1800*, chap. 7.

5. Guity Nashat and Judith E. Tucker, *Women in the Middle East and North Africa* (Bloomington: Indiana University Press, 1998), 58.

6. Ibn Batuta, *Travels in Asia and Africa 1325–1354*, trans. and selected by H.A.R. Gibb (1929; reprint, London: Darf Publishers, 1983), 146–47.

7. David J. Duncan, "Scholarly Views of Shajarat al-Durr: A Need for Consensus" (1999), available at http://www.ucc.ie/chronicon/duncfra.htm.

8. Wiebke Walther, *Women in Islam*, trans. C.S.V. Salt (Princeton: Markus Wiener, 1981), 120–21.

9. Personal communication from Leslie Peirce (June 2004).

10. Carl F. Petry, "Class Solidarity versus Gender Gain: Women as Custodians of Property in Later Medieval Egypt," in *Women in Middle Eastern History: Shifting Boundaries in Sex and Gender*, ed. Nikki R. Keddie and Beth Baron (New Haven: Yale University Press, 1991), chap. 7.

11. Jonathan P. Berkey, "Women and Islamic Education in the Mamluk Period," in Keddie and Baron, *Women in Middle Eastern History*, chap. 8.

12. See Huda Lutfi, "Manners and Customs of Fourteenth-Century Cairene Women: Female Anarchy versus Male Shar'i Order in Muslim Prescriptive Treatises," in Keddie and Baron, *Women in Middle Eastern History*, chap. 6.

13. Leslie Peirce, *The Imperial Harem: Women and Sovereignty in the Ottoman Empire* (New York: Oxford University Press, 1993).

14. Maria Szuppe, "The 'Jewels of Wonder': Learned Ladies and Princess Politicians in the Provinces of Early Safavid Iran," Priscilla P. Soucek, "Timurid Women: A Cultural Perspective," and Kathryn Babayan, "The 'Aqa'id al-Nisa': A Glimpse at Safavid Women in Local Isfahani Culture," all in Hambly, *Women in the Medieval Islamic World*; and Rudi Matthee, "Prostitutes, Courtesans, and Dancing Girls: Women Entertainers in Safavid Iran," in *Iran and Beyond: Essays in Middle Eastern History in Honor of Nikki R. Keddie*, ed. Rudi Matthee and Beth Baron (Costa Mesa, CA: Mazda, 2000).

15. The pioneering works by men include R. C. Jennings, "Women in Early-Seventeenth-Century Ottoman Judicial Records: The Shari'a Court of Anatolian Kaiseri," *Journal of the Economic and Social History of the Orient* (Leiden) 18 (1975): 53–114; Haim Gerber, "Social and Economic Position of Women in an

Ottoman City, Bursa, 1600–1700," *International Journal of Middle East Studies* 12 (1980): 231–44; and articles by Abraham Marcus, reflected in his *The Middle East on the Eve of Modernity: Aleppo in the Eighteenth Century* (New York: Columbia University Press, 1989).

16. Among the important books using legal and endowment documents for the Ottoman period are Margaret L. Meriwether, *The Kin Who Count: Family and Society in Ottoman Aleppo, 1770–1840* (Austin: University of Texas Press, 1999); Leslie Peirce, *Morality Tales: Law and Gender in the Ottoman Court of Aintab* (Berkeley and Los Angeles: University of California Press, 2003); Judith E. Tucker, *In the House of the Law: Gender and Islamic Law in Ottoman Syria and Palestine* (Berkeley and Los Angeles: University of California Press, 1998); and *Women in the Ottoman Empire: Middle Eastern Women in the Early Modern Era*, ed. Madeline C. Zilfi (Leiden: Brill, 1997). See also in *Women, the Family, and Divorce Laws in Islamic History*, ed. Amira El-Azhary Sonbol (Syracuse: Syracuse University Press, 1996), the chapters by F. Zarinebaf-Shahr, A-R.A-R. Abdal-Rehim, Iris Agmon, Nelly Hanna, Mary Ann Fay, Dina Rizk Khouri, Najwa al-Qattan, Amira El Azhary Sonbol, D. Largueche, and M. C. Zilfi.

17. Meriwether, *Kin Who Count*, 211.

18. Afaf Marsot, *Women and Men in Late Eighteenth Century Egypt* (Austin: University of Texas Press, 1995).

19. Annelies Moors, "Debating Islamic Family Law: Legal Texts and Social Practices," *Social History of Women and Gender in the Modern Middle East*, ed. Margaret L. Meriwether and Judith E. Tucker (New York: Westview, 1999). The major problems of Ottoman court records as sources were earlier noted in Dror Ze'evi "The Use of Ottoman Shari'a Court Records as a Source for Middle Eastern Social History: A Reappraisal," *Islamic Law and Society* 5,: no. 1 (1998): 35–57.

20. Tucker, *In the House of the Law*, chap. 5; Dror Ze'evi, "Women in 17th-Century Jerusalem: Western and Indigenous Perspectives," *International Journal of Middle East Studies* 27 (1995): 157–73.

21. Fariba Zarinebaf-Shahr, "Women and the Public Eye in Eighteenth-Century Istanbul," in Hambly, *Women in the Medieval Islamic World*, chap. 14.

22. Peirce, *Morality Tales*.

23. Dror Ze'evi, *Producing Desire: Changing Sexual Discourse in the Ottoman Middle East, 1500–1900* (Berkeley and Los Angeles: University of California Press, 2006); Rudi Matthee, *The Pursuit of Pleasure: Drugs and Stimulants in Iranian History* (Princeton: Princeton University Press, 2005), 169–74; Janet Afary and Kevin B. Anderson, *Foucault and the Iranian Revolution: Gender and the Seductions of Islamism* (Chicago: University of Chicago Press, 2005), 155–62; and Everett K. Rowson, "Gender Irregularity as Entertainment: Institutionalized Transvestism at the Caliphal Court in Medieval Baghdad," in *Gender and Difference in the Middle Ages*, ed. Sharon Farmer and Carol Braun Pasternack (Minneapolis: University of Minnesota Press, 2003).

24. Afsaneh Najmabadi, *Women with Mustaches and Men without Beards: Gender and Sexual Anxieties of Iranian Modernity* (Berkeley and Los Angeles: University of Californian Press, 2005), stresses the limits of modern, as compared to earlier, discourse. Afary and Anderson, *Foucault and the Iranian Revolution*, chap. 5, however, stress the modern critique of even married men's homosexual

interests as a part of women's liberation. The point about the relative freedom with which many popular-class women discuss sex comes mainly from my observation and discussions regarding several countries. Women's mocking of men and discussing sex in their private gatherings and in theater games is documented for Iran and Yemen; e.g., Kaveh Safa-Isfahani, "Female-Centered World Views in Iranian Culture: Symbolic Representations of Sexuality in Dramatic Games," *Signs* 6, no. 1 (Autumn 1980): 33–53; Claudie Feyein, *A French Doctor in the Yemen*, trans. Douglas McKee (London: R. Hale, 1957); and Marjane Satrapi, *Embroideries* (New York: Pantheon, 2005). It appears that the limits on sexual speech mainly affected the mixed-gender public sphere and helped women to enter this sphere.

25. Judith E. Tucker in *Women in the Middle East and North Africa*, 80–81.

26. Ze'evi, "Women in 17th-Century Jerusalem."

27. See Billie Melman, *Women's Orients: English Women and the Middle East, 1718–1918: Sexuality, Religion and Work*, 2nd ed. (Ann Arbor: University of Michigan Press, 1995), chap. 3.

28. Quoted in Nashat and Tucker, *Women in the Middle East and North Africa*, 72.

29. See the discussion of Mary Lucy Garnet's views in Melman, *Women's Orients*, 106–7.

30. Among the leftist Arab critics of Said's classic *Orientalism* is Sadiq Jalal al-'Azm, "Orientalism and Orientalism in Reverse," in *Forbidden Agendas: Intolerance and Defiance in the Middle East: Khamsin, an Anthology*, ed. Jon Rothschild (London: Al-Saqi Books, 1984). See also *Orientalism: A Reader*, ed. A. L. Macfie (New York: New York University Press, 2000), and the intelligent discussion in Zachary Lockman, *Contending Visions of the Middle East: The History and Politics of Orientalism* (Cambridge: Cambridge University Press, 2004), chap. 6.

31. The literature on modern Western racism is huge. One may start with Stephen J. Gould, *The Mismeasure of Man*, rev. ed. (New York: Norton, 1996); Leon Poliakov, *The Aryan Myth: A History of Racist and Nationalist Ideas in Europe*, trans. Edmund Howard (New York: Basic Books, 1974); and Tzvetan Todorov, *On Human Diversity: Nationalism, Racism, and Exoticism in French Thought*, trans. Catherine Porter (Cambridge, MA: Harvard University Press, 1994). For an accessible discussion, incorporating the results of scholarly works, of antiblack and anti-Jewish racial views among scholars until well into the twentieth century, see Claudia Roth Pierpont on Franz Boas and his opponents and disciples, "The Measure of America: The Anthropologist Who Fought Racism," *New Yorker*, March 8, 2004.

IV

Change in the Long Nineteenth Century 1798–1914

1. The key revisionist work is Jane Hathaway, *The Politics of Households in Ottoman Egypt: The Rise of the Qazdağlis* (Cambridge: Cambridge University Press, 1997), which includes an important chapter titled "Marriage Alliances and the Role of Women in the Household."

2. Afaf Marsot, *Women and Men in Eighteenth Century Egypt* (Austin: University of Texas Press, 1995); Judith E. Tucker, *Women in Nineteenth Century Egypt* (Cambridge: Cambridge University Press, 1985); and Guity Nashat and Judith E. Tucker, *Women in the Middle East and North Africa* (Bloomington: Indiana University Press, 1998), 76–77.

3. Donald Quataert, personal correspondence, and "Ottoman Women, Households, and Textile Manufacturing, 1800–1914," in *Women in Middle Eastern History: Shifting Boundaries in Sex and Gender,* ed. Nikki R. Keddie and Beth Baron (New Haven: Yale University Press, 1991), chap. 9.

4. See Marsot, *Women and Men,* and Dror Ze'evi, "Women in 17th-Century Jerusalem: Western and Indigenous Perspectives," *International Journal of Middle East Studies* 27 (1995): 157–73.

5. An illustrative warning against idealizing traditions is found in Michael Gilsenan, *Lords of the Lebanese Marches: Violence and Narrative in an Arab Society* (London: I. B. Tauris, 1996), 189–92, summarizing the ways of a partly "traditional" area in the 1970s, rejected by the more modernized:

> Sharaf, the honour of person and family which is particularly identified with the control of women's sexuality, was crucial to the public, social identity of men. It was intimately linked with hierarchy. Beys and aghas who wished to assert the more "traditional" sense of a strict order of prestige and rank regarded speaking of the sharaf of any of the fellahin groups as a source of mockery. . . . They alone guarded and preserved the sanctity of their women, while showing deliberate disregard for that of men beneath them. So the lower orders might be said by such speakers not to have sharaf, and that principle was illustrated and "proven" by reference to the violation of anonymous fellahin victims so necessary to the discourses of power. . . . Work, money, favour was at stake, and the bosses could take advantage. These women laboured in the fields, not within the privacy of the house. . . . They were treated as available.
>
> The sharaf of the mighty was thus linked with . . . the denial that . . . others either had or might presume to possess such a quality.

The mighty also freely broke taboos against a variety of homosexual and heterosexual practices.

6. See the penetrating discussion in Leila Ahmed, *Women and Gender in Islam: Historical Roots of a Modern Debate* (New Haven: Yale University Press, 1992), chap. 8.

7. Dalenda Largueche, "Confined, Battered, and Repudiated Women in Tunis since the Eighteenth Century," in *Women, the Family, and Divorce Laws in Islamic History,* ed. Amira El-Azhary Sonbol (Syracuse: Syracuse University Press, 1996).

8. Nashat and Tucker, *Women in the Middle East and North Africa,* 98.

9. Alan Duben and Cem Behar, *Istanbul Households: Marriage, Family and Fertility, 1880–1940* (Cambridge: Cambridge University Press, 1991).

10. Beth Baron, *Egypt as a Woman: Nationalism, Gender, and Politics* (Berkeley and Los Angeles: University of California Press, 2005).

11. On this school and its later history, see especially Khaled Fahmy, "Women, Medicine, and Power in Nineteenth-Century Egypt," in *Remaking Women: Femi-*

nism and Modernity in the Middle East, ed. Lila Abu-Lughod (Princeton: Princeton University Press, 1998), chap. 1; also Amira El-Azhary Sonbol, *The Creation of a Medical Profession in Egypt, 1800–1922* (Syracuse: Syracuse University Press, 1991).

12. Margot Badran, *Feminists, Islam, and Nation: Gender and the Making of Modern Egypt* (Princeton: Princeton University Press, 1995), 52–54.

13. Deniz Kandiyoti, "End of Empire: Islam, Nationalism and Women in Turkey," in *Women, Islam and the State*, ed. Deniz Kandiyoti (London: Macmillan, 1991), 27–30.

14. Janet Afary, *The Iranian Constitutional Revolution, 1906–1911: Grassroots Democracy, Social Democracy, and the Origins of Feminism* (New York: Columbia University Press, 1996); Mangol Bayat-Philipp, "Women and Revolution in Iran, 1905–1911," in *Women in the Muslim World*, ed. Lois Beck and Nikki Keddie (Cambridge, MA: Harvard University Press, 1978), chap. 15.

15. Beth Baron, *The Women's Awakening in Egypt: Culture, Society, and the Press* (New Haven: Yale University Press, 1994); Jasamin Rostam-Kolayi, "The Women's Press, Modern Education, and the State in Early Twentieth-Century Iran, 1900–1930s" (Ph.D. diss., UCLA, 2000).

16. An argument that male authors' emphasis on the status of women relates to the distortions of boys' upbringing resulting from this status is one of several important points in Deniz Kandiyoti, "The Paradoxes of Masculinity: Some Thoughts on Segregated Societies," in *Dislocating Masculinity: Comparative Ethnographies*, ed. Andrea Cornwall and Nancy Lindisfarne (Routledge: London, 1994), chap. 9.

17. Barbara Freyer Stowasser, *Women in the Qur'an, Traditions, and Interpretation* (Oxford: Oxford University Press, 1993), 132; Malcolm H. Kerr, *Islamic Reform; the Political and Legal Theories of Muḥammad 'Abduh and Rashīd Riḍā* (Berkeley and Los Angeles: University of California Press, 1966), 189 ff.

18. See Baron, *Women's Awakening*, chaps. 6, 7, and passim.

19. Stowasser, *Women in the Qur'an*, 127.

20. Ahmed, *Women and Gender in Islam*, 163–64. For a general discussion of the tendency of intellectuals in colonies first to accept, but then to react against, Western ideas, see Nikki R. Keddie, "Western Views versus Western Values: Suggestions for a Comparative Study of Asian Intellectual History," *Diogenes* 26 (1957): 71–96.

21. On these men, see Şerif Mardin, *The Genesis of Young Ottoman Thought: A Study in the Modernization of Turkish Political Ideas* (Princeton: Princeton University Press, 1962).

22. Carter Findley has written several important articles and papers on Fatma Aliye and other aspects of late Ottoman women, especially "La soumise, la subversive: Fatma Aliye, romancière et feministe," *Turcica* 27 (1995): 153–76, and "Fatma Aliye: First Ottoman Woman Novelist, Pioneer Feminist" (unpublished paper, 1993). According to Nüket Sirman, "In view of the dominant position of an Islamic discourse whereby any attempt to criticize veiling, segregation or polygamy was immediately branded as a sacrilege . . . a moderate Islamic approach to the position of women gained prominence. The main proponent of this moderate view was Fatma Aliye Hanim, who even wrote a polemical essay against

the view . . . that polygamy was sanctioned by Koranic law. By contrast, Fatma Aliye argued that polygamy was an Arab custom that had been adopted in the course of the centuries. To prove her point, she gave extensive references to the life of the prophet and to the exalted position of the women of his time. It is interesting that these same arguments are now being put forward by contemporary Islamist young women." Nüket Sirman, "Turkish Feminism: A Short History," Women Living under Muslim Laws, *Dossier 5–6* (December 1988–May 1989), available at http://www.wluml.org/english/pubsfulltxt.shtml?cmd[87]=i-87-2616.

23. Elizabeth Brown Frierson, "Unimagined Communities: State, Press, and Gender in the Hamidian Era" (Ph.D. diss., Princeton University, 1996); Ayfer Karakaya-Stump, "Debating Progress in a 'Serious Newspaper for Muslim Women': The Periodical *Kadin* of the Post-revolutionary Salonica, 1908–1909," *British Journal of Middle Eastern Studies* 30, no. 2 (November 2003): 155–81. A. Holly Shissler is working on the centrality of the woman question among Turkish writers of this period and has written about one such writer in *Between Two Empires: Ahmet Ağaoğlu and the New Turkey* (London: I. B. Tauris, 2003), chap. 6.

24. The book is frequently cited, but this part is stressed by Janet Afary and Kevin B. Anderson in *Foucault and the Iranian Revolution: Gender and the Seductions of Islamism* (Chicago: University of Chicago Press, 2005), 160.

25. Julie Peteet, *Gender in Crisis: Women and the Palestinian Resistance Movement* (New York: Columbia University Press, 1991), 71.

V
1914–45: Nationalist and Women's Movements

1. Margot Badran, *Feminists, Islam, and Nation: Gender and the Making of Modern Egypt* (Princeton: Princeton University Press, 1995), chap. 12.

2. Elizabeth Thompson, *Colonial Citizens: Republican Rights, Paternal Privilege, and Gender in French Syria and Lebanon* (New York: Columbia University Press, 2000); Julia Clancy-Smith, *Rebel and Saint: Muslim Notables, Populist Protest, Colonial Encounters—Algeria and Tunisia, 1800–1904* (Berkeley and Los Angeles: University of California Press, 1997); and Ellen L. Fleischmann, *The Nation and Its "New" Women: The Palestinian Women's Movement 1920–1948* (Berkeley and Los Angeles: University of California Press, 2003). See also *Domesticating the Empire: Race, Gender, and Family Life in French and Dutch Colonialism*, ed. Julia Clancy-Smith and Frances Gouda (Charlottesville: University Press of Virginia, 1998).

3. See the chapters and bibliographical items by Suad Joseph and Mounira Charrad in *Gender and Citizenship in the Middle East*, ed. Suad Joseph (Syracuse: Syracuse University Press, 2000), and Mounira M. Charrad, *States and Women's Rights: The Making of Postcolonial Tunisia, Algeria, and Morocco* (Berkeley and Los Angeles: University of California Press, 2001).

4. *Remaking Women: Feminism and Modernity in the Middle East*, ed. Lila Abu-Lughod (Princeton: Princeton University Press, 1998); Beth Baron, *The*

Women's Awakening in Egypt: Culture, Society, and the Press (New Haven: Yale University Press, 1994).

5. Deniz Kandiyoti, "End of Empire: Islam, Nationalism and Women in Turkey," in *Women, Islam and the State*, ed. Deniz Kandiyoti (London: Macmillan, 1991), 29, citing research in Turkish by T. Z. Tunaya. Further information provided by Holly Shissler.

6. Cited in Kandiyoti, "End of Empire," 31.

7. On these points, see Nikki R. Keddie, "Secularism and the State: Towards Clarity and Global Comparison," *New Left Review* 226 (November–December 1997): 21–40.

8. Quoted in Kandiyoti, "End of Empire," 35–36.

9. Ibid., 38.

10. See, for example, Paul Stirling, *Turkish Village* (London: Weidenfeld and Nicolson, 1965).

11. Afsaneh Najmabadi, "Hazards of Modernity and Morality: Women, State and Ideology in Contemporary Iran," in *Women, Islam and the State*, 55.

12. Parvin Paidar, *Women and the Political Process in Twentieth-Century Iran* (Cambridge: Cambridge University Press, 1995), chap. 3; Eliz Sanasarian, *The Women's Rights Movement in Iran: Mutiny, Appeasement, and Repression from 1900 to Khomeini* (New York: Praeger, 1982).

13. Camron Michael Amin, *The Making of the Modern Iranian Woman: Gender, State Policy, and Popular Culture, 1865–1946* (Gainesville: University Press of Florida, 2002); Paidar, *Women and the Political Process*, 93–95; Jasamin Rostam-Kolayi, "The Women's Press, Modern Education, and the State in Early Twentieth-Century Iran, 1900–1930s" (Ph.D. diss., UCLA, 2000); *Iran and the Surrounding World 1501–2001: Interactions in Culture and Cultural Politics*, ed. Nikki R. Keddie and Rudi Matthee (Seattle: University of Washington Press, 2001), chap. 8; and Jasamin Rostam-Kolayi, "Expanding Agendas for the 'New' Iranian Woman: Family Law, Work, and Unveiling," in *The Making of Modern Iran: State and Society under Riza Shah, 1921–1941*, ed. Stephanie Cronin (London: RoutledgeCurzon, 2003), chap. 9.

14. Paidar, *Women and the Political Process*, 95–98.

15. Rostam-Kolayi, "The Women's Press"; Sanasarian, *The Women's Rights Movement*, 71; Najmabadi, "Hazards of Modernity."

16. Much of this is clearly argued by Charrad, *States and Women's Rights*.

17. See especially Leila Ahmed, *A Border Passage: From Cairo to America— A Woman's Journey* (New York: Farrar, Straus and Giroux, 1999), chap. 11, "On Becoming an Arab."

18. Cynthia Nelson, *Doria Shafik, Egyptian Feminist: A Woman Apart* (Gainesville: University Press of Florida, 1996).

19. Baron, *Women's Awakening*.

20. See Afsaneh Najmabadi, "Crafting an Educated Housewife in Iran," in Abu-Lughod, *Remaking Women*.

21. Afaf Lutfi al-Sayyid Marsot, "The Revolutionary Gentlewoman in Egypt," in *Women in the Muslim World*, ed. Lois Beck and Nikki Keddie (Cambridge, MA: Harvard University Press, 1978), chap. 13. Marsot makes the important point that women's managerial ability in households was later translated into

various public activities. Beth Baron (personal communication, July 2004) notes that the women Marsot discusses were educated at French Catholic schools and had many servants, while the domesticity movement was mainly aimed at middle- and lower-class women.

22. See especially the articles by Najmabadi and others in Abu-Lughod, *Remaking Women.*

23. Badran, *Feminists, Islam, and Nation.*

24. Ibid., 91–95.

25. Ibid., 213.

26. For discussions, with some translated passages, of this book, see Bouthaina Shaaban, "The Muted Voices of Women Interpreters," in *Faith and Freedom: Women's Human Rights in the Muslim World,* ed. Mahnaz Afkhami (Syracuse: Syracuse University Press, 1995), and the several references in Nazik Saba Yared, *Secularism and the Arab World (1850–1939)* (London: Saqi Books, 2002), indexed under *D* as "al-Din." Two previously translated sections of the book are reprinted in *Liberal Islam: A Sourcebook,* ed. Charles Kurzman (New York: Oxford University Press, 1998), chap. 11.

27. Thompson, *Colonial Citizens,* 131.

28. Ibid., 134. In 1998 the prominent Syrian intellectual and later government minister Bouthaina Shaaban edited and reissued Zain al-Din's book and her second book responding to hostile reviews, and since then her work has been noted by sympathetic authors, usually without mention of her Druze origins or her appeal to the French. See Miriam Cooke, *Women Claim Islam: Creating Islamic Feminism through Literature* (London: Routledge, 2001), xiv–xv.

29. See Elizabeth Thompson, "Neither Conspiracy nor Hypocrisy: The Jesuits and the French Mandate in Syria and Lebanon," in *Altruism and Imperialism: Western Cultural and Religious Missions in the Middle East,* ed. Eleanor H. Tejirian and Reeva Spector Simon, Columbia University, Occasional Papers 4 (New York: Middle East Institute, 2002) 66–87.

30. Fleischmann, *The Nation and Its "New" Women,* 72. This is the most comprehensive work on its subject.

31. Ibid., 67.

32. Ibid., 133–36.

33. Quoted in ibid., 189.

VI
1945–Today: New States and Trends, Women's Activism,
and the Rise of Islamism

1. Jane Connors, "The Women's Convention in the Muslim World," in *Feminism and Islam: Legal and Literary Perspectives,* ed. Mai Yamani (New York: New York University Press, 1996), 351–71. For a more critical view, see Ann Elizabeth Mayer, "Rhetorical Strategies and Official Policies on Women's Rights: The Merits and Demerits of the New World Hypocrisy," in *Faith and Freedom: Women's Human Rights in the Muslim World,* ed. Mahnaz Afkhami (Syracuse: Syracuse University Press, 1995), chap. 7. I disagree with Mayer that "[w]henever

governments decide that changes are in order shari'a rules give way to government-sponsored initiatives, even if the latter conflict with Islamic principles" (115). Reforms are often delayed, amended, or negated under pressure from Islamists and others, especially where governments are not completely autocratic, as in cases in Egypt under Sadat, Jordan, and Kuwait discussed below.

2. Irene Tinker and Aziza Hussein, "Crossroads for Women at the UN," in *Developing Power: How Women Transformed International Development*, ed. Arvonne S. Fraser and Irene Tinker (New York: The Feminist Press at the City University of New York, 2004), 3–13.

3. See *Globalization, Gender, and Religion: The Politics of Women's Rights in Catholic and Muslim Contexts*, ed. Jane Bayes and Nayereh Tohidi (New York: Palgrave, 2001).

4. See *Gender and Citizenship in the Middle East*, ed. Suad Joseph (Syracuse: Syracuse University Press, 2000), esp. 8.

5. For some basic facts and bibliography, see Sherifa Zuhur, *Gender, Sexuality and the Criminal Laws in the Middle East and North Africa: A Comparative Study* (Istanbul: Women for Women's Human Rights [WWHR]—New Ways, 2005), available at www.wwhr.org/images/GenderSexualityandCriminalLaws .pdf. The same group has issued other relevant works, both on-line and in hard copy, including the multiauthored *Turkish Civil and Penal Code Reforms from a Gender Perspective: The Success of Two Nationwide Campaigns*, available at http://www.iwhc.org/resources/wwhrcodereforms.cfm (2005). It reqires 68 pages to cover concisely twenty-first-century gender-egalitarian reforms. There is need for a cooperative effort to present comprehensible comparative summaries of the legal situation for women throughout the Muslim world, which could be updated on-line; such a project was begun, but needs new financial support, expansion, and updating.

6. *Turkish Civil and Penal Code Reforms* and Lama Abu-Odeh, "Crimes of Honour and the Construction of Gender in Arab Societies," in Yamani, *Feminism and Islam*.

7. See Paul Vieille, "Iranian Women in Family Alliance and Sexual Politics," in *Women in the Muslim World*, ed. Lois Beck and Nikki Keddie (Cambridge, MA: Harvard University Press, 1978), chap. 22, and Sana al-Khayyat, *Honour and Shame: Women in Modern Iraq* (London: Saqi Books, 1990).

8. Ziba Mir-Hosseini, "Sexuality, Rights, and Islam: Competing Gender Discourses in Postrevolutionary Iran," in *Women in Iran from 1800 to the Islamic Republic*, ed. Lois Beck and Guity Nashat (Urbana: University of Illinois Press), chap. 8.

9. In addition to general Western prejudices, it is common for Westerners to think, for example, that Iranian or Arab women cannot drive (only true in Saudi Arabia) or have any dealings with men; *The West Wing*, a TV program that prided itself on accuracy, in 2004 claimed that Turkey was about to execute a woman for sleeping with her fiancé, at a time when Turkey had adopted a series of resolutely gender-egalitarian laws and withdrawn a brief proposal to make adultery a (noncapital) crime, which it still is in many U.S. states.

10. For a longer treatment on this and other points on modern Iran, see Nikki R. Keddie, *Modern Iran: Roots and Results of Revolution*, new ed. (New Haven:

Yale University Press, 2006), and Ervand Abrahamian, *Iran between Two Revolutions* (Princeton: Princeton University Press, 1982).

11. Parvin Paidar, *Women and the Political Process in Twentieth-Century Iran* (Cambridge: Cambridge University Press, 1995), 126–27, citing Ruth Woodsmall, *Women and the New East* (Washington, DC: The Middle East Institute, 1960).

12. The extensive literature on these events includes *Musaddiq, Iranian Nationalism and Oil*, ed. James A. Bill and Wm. Roger Louis (London: I. B. Tauris, 1988); Mark J. Gasiorowski, *U.S. Foreign Policy and the Shah: Building a Client State in Iran* (Ithaca, NY: Cornell University Press, 1991); *Mohammad Mosaddeq and the 1953 Coup in Iran*, ed. Mark J. Gasiorowski and Malcolm Byrne (Syracuse: Syracuse University Press, 2004); and Stephen Kinzer, *All the Shah's Men: An American Coup and the Roots of Middle East Terror* (New York: John Wiley & Sons, 2003).

13. Sattareh Farman Farmaian with Dona Munker, *Daughter of Persia: A Woman's Journey from Her Father's Harem through the Islamic Revolution* (New York: Crown Publishers, 1992).

14. Leonard Binder, *Iran: Political Development in a Changing Society* (Berkeley and Los Angeles: University of California Press, 1962), 198.

15. The role of the shah's regime and of the WOI regarding women was at the time controversial, given the unpopularity of the shah with various groups. Today many former opponents of the shah would grant that in order to modernize he, like several Middle Eastern autocrats, objectively opened new doors that women used to improve their position. For a summary by the former head of WOI and minister for women's affairs, see Mahnaz Afkhami, "The Women's Organization of Iran: Evolutionary Politics and Revolutionary Change," in Beck and Nashat, *Women in Iran from 1800 to the Islamic Republic*, chap. 4.

16. See Nayereh Tohidi, "Modernity, Islamization, and Women in Iran," in *Gender and National Identity: Women and Politics in Muslim Societies*, ed. Val Moghadam (London: Zed Books, 1994), 110–41.

17. Paidar, *Women and the Political Process*, 169–72, and Haideh Moghissi, *Populism and Feminism in Iran: Women's Struggle in a Male-Defined Revolutionary Movement* (New York: St. Martin's Press, 1994).

18. Ruhollah Khomeini, *Resaleh-ye Tauzih al-masa'el*, quoted in Paidar, *Women and the Political Process*, 174.

19. Quoted in Paidar, *Women and the Political Process*, 181. See also Adele Ferdows, "Shari'ati and Khomeini on Women," in *The Iranian Revolution and the Islamic Republic*, ed. Nikki R. Keddie and Eric Hooglund (Syracuse: Syracuse University Press, 1986), pt. 4.

20. See Fatemeh Etemad Moghadam, "Women and Labor in the Islamic Republic of Iran," in Beck and Nashat, *Women in Iran from 1800 to the Islamic Republic*, 163–81.

21. On education and family planning, see Keddie, *Modern Iran*, 285–89, and its sources. On girls and education, see Golnar Mehran, "The Paradox of Tradition and Modernity in Female Education in the Islamic Republic of Iran," *Comparative Education Review* 47, no. 3 (2003): 269–86; idem, "Khatami, Political Reform and Education in Iran," *Comparative Education* 39, no. 3 (2003): 311–29; and idem, "The Presentation of the 'Self' and the 'Other' in Postrevolutionary

Iranian School Textbooks," in *Iran and the Surrounding World 1501–2001: Interactions in Culture and Cultural Politics*, ed. Nikki R. Keddie and Rudi Matthee (Seattle: University of Washington Press, 2001), 232–53.

22. Haleh Esfandiari, *Reconstructed Lives: Women and Islam's Islamic Revolution* (Washington, DC: Woodrow Wilson Center Press, 1997).

23. Paidar, *Women and the Political Process*, 282–84.

24. Ziba Mir Hosseini, *Marriage on Trial: A Study of Islamic Family Law*, rev. ed. (London: I. B. Tauris, 2000).

25. Azam Torab, "The Politicization of Women's Religious Circles in Postrevolutionary Iran" (chap. 9), and Hossein Shahidi, "Women and Journalism in Iran" (chap. 5), both in *Women, Religion and Culture in Iran*, ed. Sarah Ansari and Vanessa Martin (Curzon Press: Richmond, UK, 2002).

26. Azadeh Moaveni, *Lipstick Jihad: A Memoir of Growing Up Iranian in America and American in Iran* (New York: Public Affairs, 2005), chaps. 2–3.

27. Maryam Poya, *Women, Work and Islamism: Ideology and Resistance in Iran* (London: Zed Books, 1999), 20. Women's changing socioeconomic roles in Iran and the Middle East are discussed in several articles by Valentine Moghadam and in her *Modernizing Women: Gender and Social Change in the Middle East*, 2nd ed. (Boulder, CO: Lynne Reinner, 2003). Fatemeh Etemad Moghadam has convincingly theorized the labor roles of women, with Islamic law stressing women's sexual and reproductive roles, while modernizing rulers favor public labor; see her "Commoditization of Sexuality and Female Labor Participation in Islam: Implications for Iran, 1960–90," in *In the Eye of the Storm: Women in Postrevolutionary Iran*, ed. Mahnaz Afkhami and Erika Friedl (Syracuse: Syracuse University Press, 1994), chap. 5.

29. Erika Friedl, "Rural Women's History: A Case Study from Boir Ahmad," in Beck and Nashat, *Women in Iran from 1800 to the Islamic Republic*, chap. 9.

29. For the effects of birth control, education, and other government policies on rural and tribal women, see the works of two anthropologists who have worked in rural and tribal areas since the revolution, i.e., Friedl, "Rural Women's History," and Lois Beck, "Qashqa'i Women in Postrevolutionary Iran," both in Beck and Nashat, *Women in Iran from 1800 to the Islamic Republic*, chaps. 9, 10.

30. Clinic and hospital abortions have become more widely available as health reasons have been interpreted more broadly. This may be related to the government's desire to limit births, but also demonstrates its pragmatism in many spheres. Homa Hoodfar (personal communications, September 2005 and January–February 2006) gave me details on the expansion of medical abortion in Iran, but says this is mainly for educated women who can work the system, while most abortions are still not done by medical personnel.

31. See Haideh Moghissi, *Feminism and Islamic Fundamentalism: The Limits of Postmodern Analysis* (London: Zed Books, 1999), and Haleh Afshar, *Islam and Feminisms: An Iranian Case Study* (New York: St. Martin's Press, 1998).

32. See Fereshteh Nouraie-Simone, "Wings of Freedom: Iranian Women, Identity and Cyberspace," in *On Shifting Ground: Muslim Women in the Global Era*, ed. Fereshteh Nouraie-Simone (New York: The Feminist Press at the City University of New York, 2005).

33. See Nayereh Tohidi, "Women at the Forefront of the Democracy Movement in Iran" *International Journal of Not-for-Profit Law* 7, no. 3 (June 2005), available at http://www.icnl.org/JOURNAL/vol7iss3/ar_tohidi.htm.

34. Moghadam, *Modernizing Women*; Nelofer Pazira, "Curtailed Rights, Lost Dignities: A Century of Afghan Women's Struggle for Equality," in "Women's Movements and Gender Debates in the Middle East and North Africa," ed. Homa Hoodfar (forthcoming); Seymour M. Hersh, "The Other War: Why Afghanistan Is Going Badly," *New Yorker*, April 12, 2004, 40–47; Ahmed Rashid, *Taliban: Militant Islam, Oil, and Fundamentalism in Central Asia* (New Haven: Yale University Press, 2001).

35. Nilüfer Göle, *The Forbidden Modern: Civilization and Veiling* (Ann Arbor: University of Michigan Press, 1997); *Women in Modern Turkish Society: A Reader*, ed. Şirin Tekeli (London: Zed Books, 1995); Jenny B. White, *Money Makes Us Relatives: Women's Labor in Urban Turkey* (Austin: University of Texas Press, 1994).

36. Soli Ozel, "Turkey at the Polls: After the Tsunami," in *Islam and Democracy in the Middle East*, ed. Larry Diamond, Marc F. Plattner, and Daniel Brumberg (Baltimore: Johns Hopkins University Press, 2003); *Turkish Civil and Penal Code Reforms*.

37. On Egyptian women since 1952, see Nadje Al-Ali, *Secularism, Gender and the State in the Middle East: The Egyptian Women's Movement* (Cambridge: Cambridge University Press, 2000); Mervat F. Hatem, "Economic and Political Liberation in Egypt and the Demise of State Feminism," *International Journal of Middle East Studies* 24 (1992): 231–51; Leila Ahmed, *Women and Gender in Islam: Historical Roots of a Modern Debate* (New Haven: Yale University Press, 1992), chaps. 10–11; Selma Botman, *Engendering Citizenship in Egypt* (New York: Columbia University Press, 1999); and Sherifa Zuhur, *Revealing Reveiling: Islamist Gender Ideology in Contemporary Egypt* (Albany: State University of New York Press, 1992). There are numerous relevant monographic social science studies, including Homa Hoodfar, *Between Marriage and the Market: Intimate Politics and Survival in Cairo* (Berkeley and Los Angeles: University of California Press, 1988); *Development, Change, and Gender in Cairo: A View from the Household*, ed. Diane Singerman and Homa Hoodfar (Bloomington: Indiana University Press, 1996); Arlene Elowe MacLeod, *Accommodating Protest: Working Women, the New Veiling, and Change in Cairo* (New York: Columbia University Press, 1991). Marilyn Booth, *May Her Likes Be Multiplied: Biography and Gender Politics in Egypt* (Berkeley and Los Angeles: University of California Press, 2001), covers biographies of Egyptian and other women both before and after 1945.

38. Nawal El Saadawi has written both fictionally and nonfictionally about her jail experience. Her best-known work is *The Hidden Face of Eve: Women in the Arab World* (London: Zed, 1980).

39. Amira El-Azhary Sonbol, "Egypt," in *Women's Rights in the Middle East and North Africa: Citizenship and Justice*, ed. Sameena Nazir and Leigh Tomppert, A Freedom House publication (Lanham, MD: Rowman & Littlefield, 2005); available at http://www.freedomhouse.org/research/menasurvey/, 70–71.

40. Sonbol, "Egypt," 79.

41. On Iraq, see Amal Rassam, "Iraq," in Nazir and Tomppert, *Women's Rights in the Middle East*, 87–104; Human Rights Watch Briefing Paper, "Background on Women's Status in Iraq prior to the Fall of the Saddam Hussein Government" (November 2003), available at http://www.hrw.org/backgrounder/wrd/iraq-women.htm, citing numerous primary and secondary sources.

42. Rassam, "Iraq," 89, 96. I was unable to access the UN report cited by Rassam for the 2003 figure.

43. Information on Iraq from Human Rights Watch Briefing Paper, "Background on Women's Status," and Sami Zubaida, "The Next Iraqi State: Secular or Religious," available at www.opendemocracy.net/debates/article-2-95–1737.jsp. On Iraqi women's lives at different times, see the still-relevant pioneering classic, Elizabeth W. Fernea, *Guests of the Sheik: An Ethnography of an Iraqi Village*, reissue ed. (New York: Anchor, 1995), and Khayyat, *Honour and Shame*.

44. Suheir Azzouni, "Palestine," in Nazir and Tomppert, *Women's Rights in the Middle East*, 219–20.

45. Joost R. Hiltermann, *Behind the Intifada: Labor and Women's Movements in the Occupied Territories* (Princeton: Princeton University Press, 1991), chap. 5, has a detailed description of the women's committees and of women's trade union activities; Anan Ameri, "Conflicts in Peace: Challenges Confronting the Palestinian Women's Movement," in *Hermeneutics and Honor: Negotiating Female "Public" Space in Islamicate Societies*, ed. Asma Afaruddin (Cambridge, MA: Harvard University Press, 1999), 29–54; *Palestinian Women: Identity and Experience*, ed. Ebba Augustin (London: Zed Books, 1993).

46. Azzouni, "Palestine," 232, citing "2003 World Population Data Sheet" (Washington, DC: Population Reference Bureau, 2003).

47. Annelies Moors, *Women, Property and Islam: Palestinian Experiences 1920–1990* (Cambridge: Cambridge University Press, 1995).

48. This trend toward increased central importance of the frequently nuclear conjugal family is discussed in other works, including Singerman and Hoodfar, *Development, Change, and Gender in Cairo*; *Remaking Women: Feminism and Modernity in the Middle East*, ed. Lila Abu-Lughod (Princeton: Princeton University Press, 1998); and Beth Baron, "The Making and Breaking of Marital Bonds in Modern Egypt," in *Women in Middle Eastern History: Shifting Boundaries in Sex and Gender*, ed. Nikki R. Keddie and Beth Baron (New Haven: Yale University Press, 1991), chap. 15.

49. Azzouni, "Palestine," 227.

50. Mona Morshy, "Palestinian Women's Organizational Activism: Contradictions and Trade-offs," in Hoodfar, "Women's Movements"; Julie M. Peteet, *Gender in Crisis: Women and the Palestinian Resistance Movement* (New York: Columbia University Press, 1992).

51. See Ameri, "Conflicts in Peace," 42–53.

52. Laurie A. Brand, "Jordan: Women and the Struggle for Political Opening," in *Women and Globalization in the Arab Middle East: Gender, Economy, and Society*, ed. Eleanor Abdella Doumato and Marsha Pripstein Posusney (Boulder, CO: Lynne Reinner, 2003); Laurie A. Brand, *Women, the State, and Political Liberalization: The Moroccan, Jordanian, and Tunisian Cases* (New York: Columbia

University Press, 1998); and Amira El-Azhary Sonbol, *Women of Jordan: Islam, Labor, and the Law* (Syracuse: Syracuse University Press, 2003).

53. Nancy Gallagher, "Human Rights on Trial in Jordan: The Triumph of Toujan al-Faisal," in Afkhami, *Faith and Freedom*, chap. 12; Brand, *Women, the State, and Political Liberalization*, 145–49; Ibtesam al-Atiyat, *The Women's Movement in Jordan: Activism, Discourses and Strategics* (Berlin: Friedrich Ebert Stiftung, 2003).

54. U.S. Department of State, *Jordan: Country Reports on Human Rights Practices—2003* (Washington, DC, 2004).

55. Catherine Bellafronto, "Syria," in Nazir and Tomppert, *Women's Rights in the Middle East*, 276–77.

56. *Women and Men in the Arab Region: A Statistical Portrait 2000* (New York: United Nations, 1999). Elisabeth Longuenesse, "Ingénieurs et développement au Proche-Orient: Liban, Syrie, Jordanie," *Sociétés Contemporaines* 6 (June 1991), and "Femmes médecins en pays arabe: L'exemple de la Syrie," *Sociologie Santé* 9 (1993).

57. Elizabeth Thompson, "Women, Gender, and Revolutionary Movements: Syria," in *Encyclopedia of Women and Islamic Cultures* (Leiden: Brill, 2006), 2:662–64.

58. Bellafronto, "Syria," 277–78; *Islamic Family Law in a Changing World: A Global Resource Book*, ed. Abdullahi A. An-Na'im (London: Zed Books, 2002), and www.law.emory.edu/IFL/legal.

59. U.S. Department of State, *Syria: Country Reports on Human Rights Practices—2003* (Washington, DC, 2004), available at http://www.state.gov/g/drl/rls/hrrpt/2003/27938.htm. "Memorandum to the United Nations Human Rights Committee: Syria's Compliance with the International Covenant on Civil and Political Rights. 3. Discrimination against Women," available at http://www.hrw.org/press/2001/04/syriam-0405.htm.

60. Zeina Zaatari, "Lebanon," in Nazir and Tomppert, *Women's Rights in the Middle East*, 141–63.

61. On Lebanon, in addition to Zaatari, "Lebanon," see *Women and War in Lebanon*, ed. Lamia Rustum Shehadeh (Gainesville: University Press of Florida, 1999); *Arab Women: Between Defiance and Restraint*, ed. Suha Sabbagh (Brooklyn, NY: Olive Branch Press, 1996); and U.S. Department of State, *Lebanon: Country Reports on Human Rights Practices—2003* (Washington, DC, 2004).

62. Mounira M. Charrad, *States and Women's Rights: The Making of Postcolonial Tunisia, Algeria, and Morocco* (Berkeley and Los Angeles: University of California Press, 2001).

63. Mounira M. Charrad, "From State Action to Women's Agency: Gender Debates in Tunisia," in Hoodfar, "Women's Movements"; for interviews with two male and one female Islamist leaders, see Nikki R. Keddie, "The Islamist Movement in Tunisia," *Maghreb Review* 11, no. 1 (January–February 1986): 26–39. See also Brand, *Women, the State, and Political Liberalization*, pt. 3.

64. V. M. Moghadam, "Tunisia," in Nazir and Tomppert, *Women's Rights in the Middle East*, 300.

65. U.S. Department of State, *Tunisia: Country Reports on Human Rights Practices—2003* (Washington, DC, 2004).

66. Valentine M. Moghadam, "Organizing Women: The New Women's Movement in Algeria," *Cultural Dynamics* 13, no. 2 (2001): 131–54.

67. On Algeria, see Sakina Brac de la Perrière, "Algeria," in Nazir and Tomppert, *Women's Rights in the Middle East*, 33–50; idem, "The Algerian Women's Movement: Coming of Age in the Maghrib," in Hoodfar, "Women's Movements"; Marnia Lazreg, *The Eloquence of Silence: Algerian Women in Question* (New York: Routledge, 1994); Peter Knauss, *The Persistence of Patriarchy: Class, Gender and Ideology in Twentieth Century Algeria* (New York: Praeger, 1987); Juliette Minces, "Women in Algeria," in Beck and Keddie, *Women in the Muslim World*, chap. 7; and U.S. Department of State, *Algeria: Country Reports on Human Rights Practices—2003* (Washington, DC, 2004).

68. Brac de la Perrière, "Algeria," 33, 41. Though this text, like many others, lists more problems for women than are found in most Middle Eastern countries, the book's numerical figure assessing women's rights in Algeria is, strangely, higher than for most Middle Eastern countries.

69. See sources listed in previous notes.

70. On Morocco, see Charrad, *States and Women's Rights*; Zakia Salime, "Reframing Religion and Politics: The Women's Movement and Family Law in Morocco," in Hoodfar, "Women's Movements"; Brand, *Women, the State, and Political Liberalization*; and Bruce Maddy-Weitzman, "Women, Islam, and the Moroccan State: The Struggle over the Personal Status Law," *Middle East Journal* 59, no. 3 (Summer 2005): 395–410.

71. Maddy-Weitzman, "Women, Islam, and the Moroccan State," 403.

72. Mounira Charrad (personal communication, June 2004).

73. Maddy-Weitzman, "Women, Islam, and the Moroccan State," 408–9.

74. U.S. Department of State, *Morocco: Country Reports on Human Rights Practices—2003* (Washington, DC, 2004), and Maddy-Weitzman, "Women, Islam, and the Moroccan State."

75. Rabéa Naciri, "Morocco," in Nazir and Tomppert, *Women's Rights in the Middle East*, 183–202.

76. United Nations Development Programme: "Programme on Governance in the Arab Region; Gender: Libya," available at http://www.pogar.org/countries/gender.asp?cid=10. I have partly summarized and partly quoted this document; it would be awkward to distinguish quotations and summaries. I have also used Alison Pargeter, "Libya," in Nazir and Tomppert, *Women's Rights in the Middle East*, 165–81, which stresses more than the UNDP the continued conservatism of Libya's tribally based society. The Libyan state does not regularly produce statistics about women or allow many independent studies, so good information is limited.

77. Pargeter, "Libya," 170.

78. Mai Yamani, "Some Observations on Women in Saudi Arabia," in Yamani, *Feminism and Islam*.

79. Eleanor Abdella Doumato, "Education in Saudi Arabia: Gender, Jobs, and the Price of Religion," in Doumato and Posusney, *Women and Globalization*; U.S. Department of State, *Saudi Arabia: Country Reports on Human Rights Practices—2003* (Washington, DC, 2004); Soraya Altorki, *Women in Saudi*

Arabia: Ideology and Behavior among the Elite (New York: Columbia University Press, 1989).

80. Lisa Wynn, "The Women's Movement and the Driving Protest in Saudi Arabia: Social Identity and the Politics of Traditions," in Hoodfar, "Women's Movements."

81. "Saudi Arabia's Top Cleric Condemns Calls for Women's Rights," *New York Times*, January 22, 2004.

82. See Eleanor Abdella Doumato, "Saudi Arabia," in Nazir and Tomppert, *Women's Rights in the Middle East*, 257–74.

83. Janine A. Clark, "Yemen Women in Public Politics: The Struggles and Strategies for Women's Rights," in Hoodfar, "Women's Movements." There are also several useful anthropological studies of Yemeni women, including Carla Makhlouf, *Changing Veils: Women and Modernization in North Yemen* (Austin: University of Texas Press, 1979), and Susan Dorsky, *Women of 'Amran: A Middle Eastern Ethnographic Study* (Salt Lake City: University of Utah Press, 1986).

84. Moghadam, *Modernizing Women*, 95–97. Maxine Molyneux, "Legal Reform and Socialist Revolution in Democratic Yemen: Women and the Family," *International Journal of Sociology of Law* 13 (1985): 147–72, Clark, "Yemeni Women."

85. Maxine Molyneux, "Women's Rights and Political Contingency: The Case of Yemen, 1990–1994," *Middle East Journal* 49, no. 3 (Summer 1995).

86. Clark, "Yemeni Women," quoting *Al-Shura*, April 23, 1997.

87. Amal Basha, "Yemen," in Nazir and Tomppert, *Women's Rights in the Middle East*, 342.

88. Ibid., 337. Some sources give lower percentages for female literacy.

89. Clark, "Yemeni Women"; U.S. Department of State, *Yemen: Country Reports on Human Rights Practices—2003* (Washington, DC, 2004). During my 1983 stay in Yemen I noted the independence and assertiveness of even veiled and secluded Yemeni women.

90. Mary-Jane Deeb, "Oman," in Nazir and Tomppert, *Women's Rights in the Middle East*, 203–18.

91. On Oman, see Deeb, "Oman"; Carol J. Riphenburg, "Changing Gender Relations and the Development Process in Oman," in *Islam, Gender and Social Change*, ed. Yvonne Yazbeck Haddad and John L. Esposito (New York: Oxford University Press, 1998); U.S. Department of State, *Oman: Country Reports on Human Rights Practices—2003* (Washington, DC, 2004). Unni Wikan, *Behind the Veil in Arabia: Women in Oman* (Baltimore: Johns Hopkins University Press, 1982), among other points, gives important information about "transsexual" men who identify as women. See also Christine Eickelman, *Women and Community in Oman* (New York: New York University Press, 1984).

92. Haya Al-Mughni, "Kuwait," in Nazir and Tomppert, *Women's Rights in the Middle East*, 132.

93. Ibid., 138.

94. On Kuwait, see Haya al-Mughni, *Women in Kuwait: The Politics of Gender* (London: Saqi Books, 2001); Margot Badran, "Gender, Islam, and the State: Kuwaiti Women in Struggle, Pre-invasion to Postliberation," in *Islam, Gender*

and Social Change; U.S. Department of State, *Kuwait: Reports on Human Rights Practices—2003* (Washington, DC, 2004), available at http://www.state.gov/g/drl/rls/hrrpt/2003/27931.htm; and Ebtisam Al Kitbi, "Women's Political Status in the GCC States," *Arab Reform Bulletin* 2, no. 7 (July 2004), available at http://www.ceip.org/files/Publications/ARB-7-19-04.asp.

95. Shatha K. Al-Muttawa, "U.A.E.," in Nazir and Tomppert, *Women's Rights in the Middle East*, 313–33.

96. Al Kitbi, "Women's Political Status in the GCC States"; Jill Crystal, "Qatar," in Nazir and Tomppert, *Women's Rights in the Middle East*, 241.

97. See Sabika al-Najjar, "Bahrain," in Nazir and Tomppert, *Women's Rights in the Middle East*, 51–67; May Seikaly, "Women and Religion in Bahrain: An Emerging Identity," in *Islam, Gender and Social Change*.

98. R. Stephen Humphreys, *Between Memory and Desire: The Middle East in a Troubled Age* (Berkeley and Los Angeles: University of California Press, 1999).

99. On women and the new religious politics, see the relevant chapters on the Muslim world by Valentine M. Moghadam and others, *Journal of Women's History*, special issue, "Women and Twentieth-Century Religious Politics: Beyond Fundamentalism," ed. Nikki R. Keddie and Jasamin Rostam-Kolayi, 10, no. 4 (Winter 1999), including the article in it by Nikki R. Keddie, "The New Religious Politics and Women Worldwide: A Comparative Study." See also Tohidi, "Modernity, Islamization, and Women in Iran"; Bayes and Tohidi, *Globalization, Gender, and Religion*; and Ziba Mir-Hosseini, *Islam and Gender: The Religious Debate in Contemporary Iran* (Princeton: Princeton University Press, 1999).

100. See Jenny B. White, *Islamist Mobilization in Turkey: A Study in Vernacular Politics* (Seattle: University of Washington Press, 2003).

101. Barbara Freyer Stowasser, *Women in the Qur'an, Traditions, and Interpretation* (Oxford: Oxford University Press, 1993), 128–29.

102. Mahmūd Mohamed Tāhā, *The Second Message of Islam*, English trans., introd. Abdullahi Ahmed An-Na'im (Syracuse: Syracuse University Press, 1987), and Abdullahi Ahmed An-Nai'im, *Toward an Islamic Reformation: Civil Liberties, Human Rights, and International Law* (Syracuse: Syracuse University Press, 1990).

103. On the Iranian thinkers, see Keddie, *Modern Iran*, chap. 12 and the sources it mentions. Among important contemporary Arab thinkers is Khaled Abou El Fadl, a scholar of Islamic law, who has written several important books with fresh interpretations of Islam, including *Speaking in God's Name: Islamic Law, Authority and Women* (Oxford: Oneworld, 2001).

104. Fatima Mernissi, *Women and Islam: An Historical and Theological Enquiry*, trans. Mary Jo Lakeland (Oxford: Blackwell Publishers, 1991); idem, *The Veil and the Male Elite: A Feminist Interpretation of Women's Rights in Islam*, trans. Mary Jo Lakeland (Reading: Addison-Wesley, 1991).

105. See the views of Arab experts in the *Arab Human Development Report 2002: Creating Opportunities for Future Generations* and the *Arab Human Development Report 2003: Building a Knowledge Society* (New York: United Nations Development Programme: Regional Bureau for Arab Studies, 2003).

106. The Women for Women's Human Rights conference report is at www.wwhr.org. See also *Al-Raida* (Beirut) 20, no. 2 (Fall 2002/2003), issue titled "Sexuality and Arab Women."

107. See Nayereh Tohidi, "International Connections of the Iranian Women's Movement," in Keddie and Matthee, *Iran and the Surrounding World*, chap. 9.

Conclusion

1. See Hisham Sharabi, *Neopatriarchy: A Theory of Distorted Change in Arab Society* (1988; reprint, New York: Oxford University Press, 1992).

2. For vivid presentations of women's problems in the family, based on extensive interviews, see Sana al-Khayyat, *Honour and Shame: Women in Modern Iraq* (London: Saqi Books, 1990), and Bouthaina Shaaban, *Both Right and Left Handed: Arab Women Talk about Their Lives* (Bloomington: Indiana University Press, 1991), which presents women's activism as an effective means to improve some husbands' behavior.

Bibliography of Books

Abu-Lughod, Lila, ed. *Remaking Women: Feminism and Modernity in the Middle East*. Princeton: Princeton University Press, 1998.

Afaruddin, Asma, ed. *Hermeneutics and Honor: Negotiating Female "Public" Space in Islamic/ate Societies*. Cambridge, MA: Harvard University Press, 1999.

Afary, Janet. *The Iranian Constitutional Revolution, 1906–1911: Grassroots Democracy, Social Democracy, and the Origins of Feminism*. New York: Columbia University Press, 1996.

Afary, Janet, and Kevin B. Anderson, *Foucault and the Iranian Revolution: Gender and the Seductions of Islamism*. Chicago: University of Chicago Press, 2005.

Afkhami, Mahnaz, ed. *Faith and Freedom: Women's Human Rights in the Muslim World*. Syracuse: Syracuse University Press, 1995.

Afkhami, Mahnaz, and Erika Friedl, eds. *In the Eye of the Storm: Women in Postrevolutionary Iran*. Syracuse: Syracuse University Press, 1994.

Afshar, Haleh. *Islam and Feminisms: An Iranian Case Study*. New York: St. Martin's Press, 1998.

Ahmed, Leila. *A Border Passage: From Cairo to America—A Woman's Journey*. New York: Farrar, Straus and Giroux, 1999.

———. *Women and Gender in Islam: Historical Roots of a Modern Debate*. New Haven: Yale University Press, 1992.

Al-Ali, Nadje. *Secularism, Gender and the State in the Middle East: The Egyptian Women's Movement*. Cambridge: Cambridge University Press, 2000.

Al-Atiyat, Ibtesam. *The Women's Movement in Jordan: Activism, Discourses and Strategics*. Berlin: Friedrich Ebert Stiftung, 2003.

Al-Khayyat, Sana. *Honour and Shame: Women in Modern Iraq*. London: Saqi Books, 1990.

Al-Mughni, Haya. *Women in Kuwait: The Politics of Gender*. London: Saqi Books, 2001.

Altorki, Soraya. *Women in Saudi Arabia: Ideology and Behavior among the Elite*. New York: Columbia University Press, 1989.

Amin, Camron Michael. *The Making of the Modern Iranian Woman: Gender, State Policy, and Popular Culture, 1865–1946*. Gainesville: University Press of Florida, 2002.

An-Nai'im, Abdullahi A. *Toward an Islamic Reformation: Civil Liberties, Human Rights, and International Law*. Syracuse: Syracuse University Press, 1990.

———, ed. *Islamic Family Law in a Changing World: A Global Resource Book*. London: Zed Books, 2002.

Ansari, Sarah, and Vanessa Martin, eds., *Women, Religion and Culture in Iran*. Richmond, UK: Curzon Press, 2002.

Augustin, Ebba, ed. *Palestinian Women: Identity and Experience*. London: Zed Books, 1993.

Badran, Margot. *Feminists, Islam, and Nation: Gender and the Making of Modern Egypt.* Princeton: Princeton University Press, 1995.

Baron, Beth. *Egypt as a Woman: Nationalism, Gender, and Politics.* Berkeley and Los Angeles: University of California Press, 2005.

———. *The Women's Awakening in Egypt: Culture, Society, and the Press.* New Haven: Yale University Press, 1994.

Batuta, Ibn. *Travels in Asia and Africa 1325–1354.* Translated and selected by H.A.R. Gibb. 1929. London: Darf Publishers, 1983.

Bayes, Jane, and Nayereh Tohidi, eds. *Globalization, Gender, and Religion: The Politics of Women's Rights in Catholic and Muslim Contexts.* New York: Palgrave, 2001.

Beck, Lois, and Nikki Keddie, eds. *Women in the Muslim World.* Cambridge, MA: Harvard University Press, 1978.

Beck, Lois, and Guity Nashat, eds. *Women in Iran from 1800 to the Islamic Republic.* Urbana: University of Illinois Press, 2004.

Bill, James A., and Wm. Roger Louis, eds. *Musaddiq, Iranian Nationalism and Oil.* London: I. B. Tauris, 1988.

Binder, Leonard. *Iran: Political Development in a Changing Society.* Berkeley and Los Angeles: University of California Press, 1962.

Booth, Marilyn. *May Her Likes Be Multiplied: Biography and Gender Politics in Egypt.* Berkeley and Los Angeles: University of California Press, 2001.

Botman, Selma. *Engendering Citizenship in Egypt.* New York: Columbia University Press, 1999.

Bouhdiba, Abdelwahab. *Sexuality in Islam.* Translated by Alan Sheridan. London: Routledge and Kegan Paul, 1985.

Brand, Laurie A. *Women, the State, and Political Liberalization: The Moroccan, Jordanian, and Tunisian Cases.* New York: Columbia University Press, 1998.

Charrad, Mounira M. *States and Women's Rights: The Making of Postcolonial Tunisia, Algeria, and Morocco.* Berkeley and Los Angeles: University of California Press, 2001.

Clancy-Smith, Julia. *Rebel and Saint: Muslim Notables, Populist Protest, Colonial Encounters—Algeria and Tunisia, 1800–1904.* Berkeley and Los Angeles: University of California Press, 1997.

Clancy-Smith, Julia, and Frances Gouda, eds. *Domesticating the Empire: Race, Gender, and Family Life in French and Dutch Colonialism.* Charlottesville: University Press of Virginia, 1998.

Cole, Juan R. *Comparing Muslim Societies: Knowledge and the State in a World Civilization.* Ann Arbor: University of Michigan Press, 1992.

Cooke, Miriam. *Women Claim Islam: Creating Islamic Feminism through Literature.* London: Routledge, 2001.

Cornwall, Andrea, and Nancy Lindisfarne, eds. *Dislocating Masculinity: Comparative Ethnographies.* London: Routledge, 1994.

Coulson, Noel J. *Conflicts and Tensions in Islamic Jurisprudence.* Chicago: University of Chicago Press, 1969.

Crone, Patricia. *Roman, Provincial and Islamic Law: The Origins of the Islamic Patronate.* Cambridge: Cambridge University Press, 1987.

Cronin, Stephanie, ed. *The Making of Modern Iran: State and Society under Riza Shah*. London: RoutledgeCurzon, 2003.

Diamond, Jared M. *Guns, Germs, and Steel: The Fates of Human Societies*. New York: W. W. Norton, 1997.

Diamond, Larry, Marc F. Plattner, and Daniel Brumberg, eds. *Islam and Democracy in the Middle East*. Baltimore: Johns Hopkins University Press, 2003.

Dorsky, Susan. *Women of 'Amran: A Middle Eastern Ethnographic Study*. Salt Lake City: University of Utah Press, 1986.

Doumani, Beshara, ed. *Family History in the Middle East: Household, Gender, Property*. Albany: State University of New York Press, 2003.

Doumato, Eleanor Abdella, and Marsha Pripstein Posusney, eds. *Women and Globalization in the Arab Middle East: Gender, Economy, and Society*. Boulder, CO: Lynne Reinner, 2003.

Duben, Alan, and Cem Behar. *Istanbul Households: Marriage, Family and Fertility, 1880–1940*. Cambridge: Cambridge University Press, 1991.

Eickelman, Christine. *Women and Community in Oman*. New York: New York University Press, 1984.

El Saadawi, Nawal. *The Hidden Face of Eve: Women in the Arab World*. London, Zed, 1980.

Esfandiari, Haleh. *Reconstructed Lives: Women and Islam's Islamic Revolution*. Washington, DC: Woodrow Wilson Center Press, 1997.

Esposito, John, and Natana J. DeLong-Bas. *Women in Muslim Family Law*. 2nd ed. Syracuse: Syracuse University Press, 2001.

Farmaian, Sattareh Farman, and Dona Munker. *Daughter of Persia: A Woman's Journey from Her Father's Harem through the Islamic Revolution*. New York: Crown Publishers, 1992.

Farmer, Sharon, and Carol Braun Pasternack, eds. *Gender and Difference in the Middle Ages*. Minneapolis: University of Minnesota Press, 2003.

Fernea, E. W. *Guests of the Sheik: An Ethnography of an Iraqi Village*. Reissue ed. New York: Anchor, 1995.

Feyein, Claudie. *A French Doctor in the Yemen*. Translated by Douglas McKee. London: R. Hale, 1957.

Fleischmann, Ellen L. *The Nation and Its "New" Women: The Palestinian Women's Movement 1920–1948*. Berkeley and Los Angeles: University of California Press, 2003.

Fraser, Arvonne S., and Irene Tinker, eds. *Developing Power: How Women Transformed International Development*. New York: The Feminist Press at the City University of New York, 2004.

Frierson, Elizabeth Brown. "Unimagined Communities: State, Press, and Gender in the Hamidian Era." Ph.D. diss., Princeton University, 1996.

Gasiorowski, Mark J. *U.S. Foreign Policy and the Shah: Building a Client State in Iran*. Ithaca, NY: Cornell University Press, 1991.

Gasiorowski, Mark J., and Malcolm Byrne, eds. *Mohammad Mosaddeq and the 1953 Coup in Iran*. Syracuse: Syracuse University Press, 2004.

Gilsenan, Michael. *Lords of the Lebanese Marches: Violence and Narrative in an Arab Society*. London: I. B. Tauris, 1996.

Goitein, S. D. *A Mediterranean Society: An Abridgement in One Volume.* Revised and edited by Jacob Lassner. Berkeley and Los Angeles: University of California Press, 1999.

Göle, Nilüfer. *The Forbidden Modern: Civilization and Veiling.* Ann Arbor: University of Michigan Press, 1997.

Gould, Stephen J. *The Mismeasure of Man.* Rev. ed. New York: Norton, 1996.

Haddad, Yvonne Yazbeck, and John L. Esposito, eds. *Islam, Gender and Social Change.* New York: Oxford University Press, 1998.

Haeri, Shahla. *Law of Desire: Temporary Marriage in Shi'i Iran.* Syracuse: Syracuse University Press, 1989.

Hambly, Gavin R. G. *Women in the Medieval Islamic World: Power, Patronage, and Piety.* New York: St. Martin's Press, 1998.

Hathaway, Jane. *The Politics of Households in Ottoman Egypt: The Rise of the Qazdağlis.* Cambridge: Cambridge University Press, 1997.

Hiltermann, Joost R. *Behind the Intifada: Labor and Women's Movements in the Occupied Territories.* Princeton: Princeton University Press, 1991.

Hoodfar, Homa. *Between Marriage and the Market: Intimate Politics and Survival in Cairo.* Berkeley and Los Angeles: University of California Press, 1988.

———, ed. "Women's Movements and Gender Debates in the Middle East and North Africa." Forthcoming.

Howard, Jane. *Inside Iran: Women's Lives.* Washington, DC: Mage Publishers, 2002.

Humphreys, R. Stephen. *Between Memory and Desire: The Middle East in a Troubled Age.* Berkeley and Los Angeles: University of California Press, 1999.

Jansen, Willy. *Women without Men: Gender and Marginality in an Algerian Town.* Leiden: Brill, 1997.

Joseph, Suad, ed. *Gender and Citizenship in the Middle East.* Syracuse: Syracuse University Press, 2000.

Joseph, Suad, and Afsaneh Najmabadi, eds. *Encyclopedia of Women and Islamic Cultures.* Leiden: Brill, 2003.

Kandiyoti, Deniz, ed. *Women, Islam and the State.* London: Macmillan, 1991.

Keddie, Nikki R. *Modern Iran: Roots and Results of Revolution.* New ed. New Haven: Yale University Press, 2006.

Keddie, Nikki R., and Beth Baron. *Women in Middle Eastern History: Shifting Boundaries in Sex and Gender.* New Haven: Yale University Press, 1991.

Keddie, Nikki R., and Rudi Matthee, eds. *Iran and the Surrounding World 1501–2001: Interactions in Culture and Cultural Politics.* Seattle: University of Washington Press, 2001.

Kerr, Malcolm H. *Islamic Reform; the Political and Legal Theories of Muḥammad 'Abduh and Rashīd Riḍā.* Berkeley and Los Angeles: University of California Press, 1966.

Khoury, Philip S., and Joseph Kostiner, eds. *Tribes and State Formation in the Middle East.* Berkeley and Los Angeles: University of California Press, 1990.

Kinzer, Stephen. *All the Shah's Men: An American Coup and the Roots of Middle East Terror.* New York: John Wiley & Sons, 2003.

Knauss, Peter. *The Persistence of Patriarchy: Class, Gender and Ideology in Twentieth Century Algeria.* New York: Praeger, 1987.

Lambton, Ann K. S. *Continuity and Change in Medieval Persia: Aspects of Administrative, Economic and Social History 11th–14th Century.* Albany: State University of New York Press, 1988.

Lazreg, Marnia. *The Eloquence of Silence: Algerian Women in Question.* New York: Routledge, 1994.

Lockman, Zachary. *Contending Visions of the Middle East: The History and Politics of Orientalism.* Cambridge: Cambridge University Press, 2004.

Macfie, A. L., ed. *Orientalism: A Reader.* New York: New York University Press, 2000.

MacLeod, Arlene Elowe. *Accommodating Protest: Working Women, the New Veiling, and Change in Cairo.* New York: Columbia University Press, 1991.

Makhlouf, Carla. *Changing Veils: Women and Modernization in North Yemen.* Austin: University of Texas Press, 1979.

Malti-Douglas, Fedwa. *Woman's Body, Woman's Word: Gender and Discourse in Arabo-Islamic Writing.* Princeton: Princeton University Press, 1991.

Marcus, Abraham. *The Middle East on the Eve of Modernity: Aleppo in the Eighteenth Century.* New York: Columbia University Press, 1989.

Mardin, Şerif. *The Genesis of Young Ottoman Thought: A Study in the Modernization of Turkish Political Ideas.* Princeton: Princeton University Press, 1962.

Marmon, Shaun E., ed. *Slavery in the Middle East.* Princeton: Princeton University Press, 1999.

Marsot, Afaf. *Women and Men in Late Eighteenth Century Egypt.* Austin: University of Texas Press, 1995.

Matthee, Rudi, and Beth Baron, eds. *Iran and Beyond: Essays in Middle Eastern History in Honor of Nikki R. Keddie.* Costa Mesa, CA: Mazda, 2000.

Melman, Billie. *Women's Orients: English Women and the Middle East, 1718–1918: Sexuality, Religion and Work.* 2nd ed. Ann Arbor: University of Michigan Press, 1995.

Meriwether, Margaret L. *The Kin Who Count: Family and Society in Ottoman Aleppo, 1770–1840.* Austin: University of Texas Press, 1999.

Meriwether, Margaret L., and Judith E. Tucker, eds. *Social History of Women and Gender in the Modern Middle East.* New York: Westview, 1999.

Mernissi, Fatima. *The Veil and the Male Elite: A Feminist Interpretation of Women's Rights in Islam.* Translated by Mary Jo Lakeland. Reading: Addison-Wesley, 1991.

———. *Women and Islam: An Historical and Theological Enquiry.* Translated by Mary Jo Lakeland. Oxford: Blackwell Publishers, 1991.

Mir Hosseini, Ziba. *Islam and Gender: The Religious Debate in Contemporary Iran.* Princeton: Princeton University Press, 1999.

———. *Marriage on Trial: A Study of Islamic Family Law.* Rev. ed. London: I. B. Tauris, 2000.

Moaveni, Azadeh. *Lipstick Jihad: A Memoir of Growing Up Iranian in America and American in Iran.* New York: Public Affairs, 2005.

Moghadam, Valentine. *Modernizing Women: Gender and Social Change in the Middle East.* 2nd ed. Boulder, CO: Lynne Reinner, 2003.

———, ed. *Gender and National Identity: Women and Politics in Muslim Societies.* London: Zed Books, 1994.

Moghissi, Haideh. *Feminism and Islamic Fundamentalism: The Limits of Post-modern Analysis*. London: Zed Books, 1999.

———. *Populism and Feminism in Iran: Women's Struggle in a Male-Defined Revolutionary Movement*. New York: St. Martin's Press, 1994.

Moors, Annelies. *Women, Property and Islam: Palestinian Experiences 1920–1990*. Cambridge: Cambridge University Press, 1995.

Mundy, Martha. *Domestic Government: Kinship, Community and Polity in North Yemen*. London: I. B. Tauris, 1995.

Musallam, Basim. *Sex and Society in Islam: Birth Control before the Nineteenth Century*. Cambridge: Cambridge University Press, 1983.

Najmabadi, Afsaneh. *Women with Mustaches and Men without Beards: Gender and Sexual Anxieties of Iranian Modernity*. Berkeley and Los Angeles: University of California Press, 2005.

Nashat, Guity, and Lois Beck, eds. *Women in Iran from the Rise of Islam to 1800*. Urbana: University of Illinois Press, 2003.

Nashat, Guity, and Judith E. Tucker. *Women in the Middle East and North Africa*. Bloomington: Indiana University Press, 1998.

Nelson, Cynthia. *Doria Shafik, Egyptian Feminist: A Woman Apart*. Gainesville: University Press of Florida, 1996.

Nouraie-Simone, Fereshteh, ed. *On Shifting Ground: Muslim Women in the Global Era*. New York: The Feminist Press at the City University of New York, 2005.

Paidar, Parvin. *Women and the Political Process in Twentieth-Century Iran*. Cambridge: Cambridge University Press, 1995.

Pamuk, Orhan. *Snow*. New York: Alfred A. Knopf, 2004.

Peirce, Leslie. *The Imperial Harem: Women and Sovereignty in the Ottoman Empire*. New York: Oxford University Press, 1993.

———. *Morality Tales: Law and Gender in the Ottoman Court of Aintab*. Berkeley and Los Angeles: University of California Press, 2003.

Peteet, Julie. *Gender in Crisis: Women and the Palestinian Resistance Movement*. New York: Columbia University Press, 1991.

Poliakov, Leon. *The Aryan Myth: A History of Racist and Nationalist Ideas in Europe*. Translated by Edmund Howard. New York: Basic Books, 1974.

Poya, Maryam. *Women, Work and Islamism: Ideology and Resistance in Iran*. London: Zed Books, 1999.

Rashid, Ahmed. *Taliban: Militant Islam, Oil and Fundamentalism in Central Asia*. New Haven: Yale University Press, 2001.

Roded, Ruth. *Women in Islamic Biographical Collections: From Ibn Sa'd to Who's Who*. Boulder, CO: Lynne Reinner, 1994.

Rostam-Kolayi, Jasamin. "The Women's Press, Modern Education, and the State in Early Twentieth-Century Iran, 1900–1930s. Ph.D. diss., UCLA, 2000.

Rothschild, Jon, ed. *Forbidden Agendas: Intolerance and Defiance in the Middle East: Khamsin, an Anthology*. London: Al-Saqi Books, 1984.

Ruggles, D. Fairchild. *Women, Patronage, and Self-Representation in Islamic Societies*. Albany: State University of New York Press, 2000.

Sabbagh, Suha, ed. *Arab Women: Between Defiance and Restraint*. Brooklyn, NY: Olive Branch Press, 1996.

Salem, E. A. *Political Theory and Institutions of the Khawarij.* Baltimore: Johns Hopkins University Press, 1956.

Sanasarian, Eliz. *The Women's Rights Movement in Iran: Mutiny, Appeasement, and Repression from 1900 to Khomeini.* New York: Praeger, 1982.

Schacht, Joseph. *The Origins of Muhammadan Jurisprudence.* Oxford: Oxford University Press, 1979.

Sharabi, Hisham. *Neopatriarchy: A Theory of Distorted Change in Arab Society.* Reprint, New York: Oxford University Press, 1992.

Shehadeh, Lamia Rustum, ed. *Women and War in Lebanon.* Gainesville: University Press of Florida, 1999.

Shissler, A. Holly. *Between Two Empires: Ahmet Ağaoğlu and the New Turkey.* London: I. B. Tauris, 2003.

Singerman, Diane, and Homa Hoodfar, eds. *Development, Change, and Gender in Cairo: A View from the Household.* Bloomington: Indiana University Press, 1996.

Sonbol, Amira El-Azhary. *The Creation of a Medical Profession in Egypt, 1800—1922.* Syracuse: Syracuse University Press, 1991.

———. *Women of Jordan: Islam, Labor, and the Law.* Syracuse: Syracuse University Press, 2003.

———, ed. *Women, the Family, and Divorce Laws in Islamic History.* Syracuse: Syracuse University Press, 1996.

Spellberg, Denise A. *Politics, Gender, and the Islamic Past: The Legacy of 'A'isha bint Abi Bakr.* New York: Columbia University Press, 1994.

Stern, Gertrude. *Marriage in Early Islam.* London: The Royal Asiatic Society, 1939.

Stirling, Paul. *Turkish Village.* London: Weidenfeld and Nicolson, 1965.

Stowasser, Barbara Freyer. *Women in the Qur'an, Traditions, and Interpretation.* Oxford: Oxford University Press, 1993.

Tāhā, Mahmūd Mohamed. *The Second Message of Islam.* English translation, introduction by Abdullahi Ahmed An-Naim. Syracuse: Syracuse University Press, 1987.

Tekeli, Şirin, ed. *Women in Modern Turkish Society: A Reader.* London: Zed Books, 1995.

Thompson, Elizabeth. *Colonial Citizens: Republican Rights, Paternal Privilege, and Gender in French Syria and Lebanon.* New York: Columbia University Press, 2000.

Todorov, Tzvetan. *On Human Diversity: Nationalism, Racism, and Exoticism in French Thought.* Translated by Catherine Porter. Cambridge, MA: Harvard University Press, 1994.

Toledano, Ehud R. *Slavery and Abolition in the Ottoman Middle East.* Seattle: University of Washington Press, 1998.

Tucker, Judith E. *In the House of the Law: Gender and Islamic Law in Ottoman Syria and Palestine.* Berkeley and Los Angeles: University of California Press, 1998.

———. *Women in Nineteenth Century Egypt.* Cambridge: Cambridge University Press, 1985.

Walther, Wiebke. *Women in Islam.* Translated by C.S.V. Salt. Princeton: Markus Wiener, 1981.

White, Jenny B. *Islamist Mobilization in Turkey: A Study in Vernacular Politics.* Seattle: University of Washington Press, 2003.

———. *Money Makes Us Relatives: Women's Labor in Urban Turkey.* Austin: University of Texas Press, 1994.

Wikan, Unni. *Behind the Veil in Arabia: Women in Oman.* Baltimore: Johns Hopkins University Press, 1982.

Woodsmall, Ruth. *Women and the New East.* Washington, DC: The Middle East Institute, 1960.

Yamani, Mai, ed. *Feminism and Islam: Legal and Literary Perspectives.* New York: New York University Press, 1996.

Yared, Nazik Saba. *Secularism and the Arab World (1850–1939).* London: Saqi Books, 2002.

Ze'evi, Dror. *Producing Desire: Sexuality in the Ottoman Empire.* Berkeley and Los Angeles: University of California Press, 2006.

Zilfi, Madeline C., ed. *Women in the Ottoman Empire: Middle Eastern Women in the Early Modern Era.* Leiden: Brill, 1997.

Zubaida, Sami. *Law and Power in the Islamic World.* London: I. B. Tauris, 2003.

Zuhur, Sherifa. *Gender, Sexuality and the Criminal Laws in the Middle East and North Africa: A Comparative Study.* Istanbul: Women for Women's Human Rights (WWHR)—New Ways, 2005. www.wwhr.org.

———. *Revealing Reveiling: Islamist Gender Ideology in Contemporary Egypt.* Albany: State University of New York Press, 1992.

BOOK TWO

Approaches to the Study of Middle Eastern Women

PART 1

Shifting Boundaries in Sex and Gender
1991

THE POSITION OF WOMEN in the Middle East has aroused much interest, but serious scholarly work on Middle Eastern women's history has been limited, in comparison both with the study of women's history elsewhere and with the study of contemporary problems. Existing volumes of articles about women in the Middle East contain little that is historical. This [i.e., *Women in Middle Eastern History: Shifting Boundaries in Sex and Gender*, ed. Nikki R. Keddie and Beth Baron (New Haven: Yale University Press, 1991)] is the first scholarly collection to stress Middle Eastern women's history, and it also includes the work of several social scientists whose theoretical perspectives are useful to the study of the past.

The relative neglect of women's history has occurred mainly because historians, unlike social scientists, cannot construct their own research projects based on people who can be directly observed, interviewed, or given questionnaires. Most historical work relies chiefly on written sources, which are heavily male oriented, and a great mass of documents needs to be unearthed or restudied with women's questions in mind.

Discussions of Middle Eastern women's history are also often ideologically charged. Such discussions may be wrenching ones for scholars who wish to overcome widespread prejudices against Islam, but not ignore the problems of Muslim women. One group denies that Muslim women, who comprise the great majority of women in the Middle East, are any more oppressed than non-Muslim women, or argues that in key respects they have been less oppressed. A second says that oppression is real but extrinsic to Islam; the Quran, they say, intended gender equality, but this was undermined by Arabian patriarchy and foreign importations. An opposing group blames Islam for being irrevocably gender-inegalitarian. There are also those who adopt intermediate positions, as well as those who tend to avoid these controversies by sticking to monographic or limited studies that do not confront such issues. Some scholars favor shifting emphases away from Islam to economic and social forces.

Given the paucity of studies and the abundance of controversy, surveying major questions in the field might seem premature. It is perpetually too early to survey any field, but such surveys are vital for nonspecialists who wish to understand a field, and they help situate the field's problems and useful directions for research.

This chapter stresses the Muslim majority in Middle Eastern history, as do the chapters following, although research on minorities also exists. Differences between Muslims and non-Muslims concerning gender status are usually attributed mainly to the Quran, to early Muslim tradition and holy law. There are also other, including pre-Islamic, roots of difference. Differences between the Middle East and other cultures regarding gender relations were in most ways smaller in the past than in modern times. Muslim resistance to Western-sanctioned change is tied to a centuries-old hostility between the Muslim Middle East and the West, which has increased in modern times. The home has become a last line of defense against a West that has won out in political and economic spheres. So-called fundamentalists, or Islamists, see Western practices toward and views on women as part of a Western Christian and Jewish cultural offensive, accompanying political and economic offensives, and turn to their own traditions as a cultural alternative.

The origin of gender inequalities in the ancient Near East is disputed, but it is known that hunter-gatherers and other pre-plow peoples are more egalitarian between genders than are people who have experienced the neolithic and agricultural revolutions. Technological developments that made possible a surplus, states, and ruling classes were accompanied by a greater division of labor, including class hierarchies and slavery, and encouraged the limiting of many urban women to domestic occupations. Class differences developed among women as well as among men, with some being slaves who filled menial or sexual roles, others who performed both nondomestic and domestic labor, and upper-class women who did not have to venture outside the home.[1] Veiling and seclusion developed in the pre-Islamic Near East and adjacent areas as markers for urban upper- and middle-class women, showing that they did not have to work and keeping them from strangers.

As women in ancient societies became more subordinate, often treated as property, many peoples developed myths about them as the source of evil and sexual temptation—dangerous and needing control. Once inheritance in the male line became important, female virginity and fidelity became central concerns. Males in most cultures were not required to be faithful, and male polygamy was often legal. Muslims note that female polygamy would raise doubts about fatherhood, which is unthinkable. Women had to be controlled largely to minimize their chances of contacts with outside men.

The guarding of women has been strong in Near Eastern and Mediterranean societies from ancient times. As many "Islamic" customs go back to the pre-Islamic Near East, something should be said about that before discussing Islam. In the first known reference to veiling, an Assyrian legal text of the thirteenth century B.C.E., it is restricted to respectable women and prohibited for prostitutes. From the first, veiling was a sign of status. Respectable Athenian women were often secluded, and veiling was known in the Greco-Roman world. Veiling and seclusion existed in pre-Islamic Iran and the Byzantine Empire, the two areas conquered by the first Muslims, though we do not know how widespread they were.[2]

A husband who had the means to keep his wife veiled and secluded showed that she was protected from advances and did not have to work or shop outside. Full veiling has been both a class phenomenon and an urban one. Early Muslims adopted veiling from conquered peoples, and both non-Muslims in Muslim societies and Mediterranean women in Christian societies were subject to many of the same forms of control and isolation from men. Mediterranean societies, Muslim and Christian, also had the same idea of the centrality of a man's honor, which lay chiefly in the purity of the women of his natal family.

Similarities in Mediterranean attitudes toward male-female relations are discussed by Germaine Tillion, who says that Mediterranean peoples favor endogamy, which increases the tendency to control women in tightly interrelated lineages. She notes that ancient Egyptians and Persians favored "incestuous" unions, whereas most Mediterranean peoples favor cousin marriage.[3] Building on Tillion, one could say that tribal groups, who are numerous among the Muslims of the Middle East, have special reasons to want to control women and to favor cousin marriage, and that the interaction of tribes with urban groups practicing seclusion added segregation to control.

The term *tribe* has been so misused that many, especially Africanists, avoid it. Whereas those who study Africa may justly react to a word misused to characterize groups with millions of people, there is a role for the word *tribe* in the Middle East. It translates terms in the main Middle Eastern languages that refer to contiguous groups claiming descent from one ancestor. A tribe is a political-economic unit, and its leaders, generally chosen from one lineage, command more loyalty than the central government, though they may now have little real power. In recent times tribes tend to be strong when central governments are weak, and central governments usually try to weaken tribes.

Tribes are not a primitive form of social organization. Pastoral nomadic tribes, the most common in the Middle East, can evolve only after animals are domesticated and there is a settled population with whom to trade animal products for agricultural and urban ones. Cohesion requires group decisions, which are facilitated in groups tied by kin. This favors cousin marriage, as does the Islamic provision for female inheritance, which encourages strategies to keep property in the lineage. Gertrude Stern documents that Muslim Arabs increased cousin marriage after the Quran required female inheritance.[4] When women inherit according to Muslim law, there are clear advantages in cousin marriage. Certain familial controls may be tied to the prevalence of tribal structures. In other areas, however, many tribes have strong and quite liberated women, and veiling and seclusion are more urban than tribal phenomena. The interaction between tribal and urban controls on women was an important influence on Middle Eastern gender relations.

The Quran was written in a context of different levels of sexual inequality among Arab tribes and in adjacent non-Arab empires. How it affected the position of women is controversial.[5] The classic Muslim view is that pre-Islamic Arabs lived in ignorance and barbarism and that the divinely revealed Quran provided a great step forward on all questions. Some scholars, however, have documented (especially in Arab poetry) conditions of matriliny, greater activity for women, even on the battlefield, and freer divorce.[6] Such sources do indicate some matrilineal and matrilocal customs, as well as freer divorce for women in certain tribes, and a greater outspokenness and activity for many women than became common after the rise of Islam, but we do not know how widespread these patterns were.

The Quran did bring in some reforms, however, including the outlawing of infanticide and the payment of the male dower to the bride, not to her guardian. The Quran also prescribed female inheritance—half that of a male heir—and women's control over their property (which was known earlier, however, as seen in Muhammad's first wife, the merchant Khadija). Unfavorable features were free divorce for men but not for women and polygamy for men (which already existed).

Although Islamic traditions say veiling and seclusion for all Muslim women are in the Quran, this is a tendentious reading. One verse tells women to veil their bosoms and hide their ornaments, later taken to mean all except the hands, feet, and perhaps the face. This interpretation makes no sense, because if everything was to be veiled, there would be no point in ordering bosoms to be veiled separately. Another verse tells women to draw their cloaks tightly around them so they may be recognized and not annoyed. These are the only words generally taken to refer to veiling.

Other verses suggest seclusion for Muhammad's wives, and these stricter rules for an elite later spread, encouraged by the example of the conquered Near East, to the urban middle and upper classes. Later veiling was not, however, simply in emulation of the Prophet's wives. Nabia Abbott notes that Muhammad's veiling of his wives reflected the growing prosperity of the Muslim ruling group, enabling them to have servants and to keep women from nondomestic work, and also the Muslims' growing contact with surrounding societies where women were veiled.[7] As

Muslim society became state centered and class divided like those of the surrounding and conquered peoples, many of their practices concerning women, appropriate to stratified social structures, and their reliance on family regulation to maintain social control were naturally also found appropriate by the Muslims.

The Quran gives men control of their wives, which extends to beating for disobedience, and adulterers of both sexes are to be punished by lashing when there is either confession or four eyewitnesses to the act. Islamic law and tradition changed this to the far more severe punishment of stoning to death, but in practice women were often killed by their brothers and many escaped punishment.

Islamic practices about women are often said to be resistant to change because of their Quranic sanction, believed to be the word of God. This has some truth, but there has been much breaking and bending of Quranic admonitions throughout Muslim history. The Quran has been interpreted, against the meaning of its text, as enjoining veiling, whereas Quranic rules on adultery are rarely followed. Quranic inheritance rules were hard to follow in rural and nomadic societies, as daughters married out of the family, with only a minority marrying paternal first cousins. Land or flocks inherited by an out-marrying woman reduced the property of the patrilineal line. Hence means were found, in most rural and a minority of urban areas, to evade women's inheritance rights. Also, the general inheritance rules of the Quran were interpreted in a more patriarchal way by Islamic law.

In all these cases, later practice was more patriarchal than the Quranic text warrants. In general, the Quran was followed when it was not too inconvenient to men or to the patriarchal family to do so, and not followed when it was. This gives some basis to modern feminists and reformers who want to return to, and reinterpret, the Quran, although their interpretation sometimes moves as far in a new direction as the old one did in the opposite one. Islamic law and Traditions tended to stress and rigidify gender distinctions, seen as crucial to an ordered world, and went to great lengths to avoid gender ambiguities.

Urban middle- and upper-class women, traditionally the most veiled and secluded, were also much more likely to inherit Quranically. This is a paradox only to a Westerner who reads back our concepts of women's rights into the past and thinks that "disadvantaged" veiled women should have fewer rights in other spheres. Urban residence in fact both made women's inheritance easier, by not involving flocks and fields, and encouraged veiling, because contact with unrelated strangers was more likely; also there were more middle- and upper-class women with more servants and slaves. Differences in class, place, and time meant that there was never one set of Muslim women operating under one set of rules.

A variety of historical and anthropological works contribute to the following overall picture of different female statuses: in general, rural and tribal women do not inherit as the Quran and Muslim law say they should, though "in return" they generally get permanent protection from their natal family, and in some cases their sons may get all or part of their share. Court records past and present suggest that urban women, however, usually do inherit and are willing and able to go to Islamic courts to protect their property rights, generally successfully. Sources also suggest that urban women have had more rights than agriculturalists, although the great freedoms and powers of tribal nomadic women are also noted. These differences are accentuated by a class-difference pattern, with ruling-class and upper-class women in both tribes and towns often notable for their powers and independence whereas poorer women were more dependent. Hence modern differences in styles of living among town, tribe, and countryside and between classes in town originate in earlier times and in continuing functional differences.[8]

This does not mean that the prescriptions of the Quran and Muslim law counted for little. The rules on polygamy, divorce, and child custody (to the father's family after a young age) were widely followed. If polygamy and divorce were less general than Westerners might imagine, they remained a threat to a wife. Divorce was generally common, but polygamy seems to have been a rare, mainly upper-class, custom.

The condition of most women seems to have been broadly comparable to that in the ancient Near East and the later Mediterranean and eastern and southern Asia. Most women were valued mainly as producers of sons and were brought up to marry, produce children, and safeguard the family honor by not transgressing rules of sexual conduct and segregation. Most were married young in arranged marriages in which the husband's family had to pay a dower. This often included a delayed payment in case of divorce or death, which provided some protection for the wife when it was observed. Brides frequently lived in the husband's father's household, often with a menial position until the first son might be born. Young brides were often dominated by mothers-in-law more than by husbands, and they gained status mainly through their maturing sons. By the time the sons became adults, their mother might be very powerful in the household, ready to dominate her sons' wives in turn.

This brief outline cannot suggest the variety and satisfactions that went along with the difficulties of women's lives. In the long preindustrial period when nuclear and extended families were the main productive units—whether in agriculture, herding, crafts, or trade—the organization of society around families and the superior power of dominant males and of male and female elders probably seemed natural to most people all over the world. It was only modern changes in economy, politics, and society that made these structures less functional and called them into question. Even before they were widely questioned, structures of male domination caused much suffering, however.

Dramatic differences between Muslims and non-Muslims came with nineteenth- and twentieth-century Muslim resistance to change, and with contemporary Islamic revivalism. Regarding gender relations, Islamism has no strict parallel in other civilizations, even though some practices in India and elsewhere indicate that the Muslim world is not the area of the worst atrocities toward women.

Whereas some scholars think the limitation of women's roles after the rise of Islam was due to borrowing from non-Muslims, others stress that this restriction began in Muhammad's time. The strongest women appeared at the beginning of Islam. Khadija, the merchant, who employed and married Muhammad, fifteen years her junior, was his first convert and helped him in every way. Muhammad's young wife A'isha, whom he married when she was a child and whose heedlessness of opinion sometimes caused trouble, exercised much power. After Muhammad's death she joined the coalition against Muhammad's son-in-law Ali and participated in the crucial battle against him.

If these figures were unparalleled in later generations, neither internal nor external forces were exclusively responsible. As Islamic society became more like the societies around it in stratification and patriarchy, it was natural to adopt their ways. Families wealthy enough to have slaves or servants could afford seclusion. Women often acquiesced in veiling and seclusion when to be less covered and to work outside were marks of low status.

Muslim women's lives have varied greatly by class, mode of production, time, and place. What generalizations one can make in a brief essay are partly based on Islamic laws and practices, even though their observation varied. Islamic law developed in the first few centuries of Islam, and recent scholarship has shown how much it reflected regional Middle Eastern customs—hence it is not surprising that much of it, though far from all, was in fact followed more in the Middle East than elsewhere. There were four orthodox law schools, plus Shi'i schools, which differed on some points important to women. Regarding marriage, schools differed as to whether a virgin's consent was needed, or only that of her father or guardian. In all schools marriage is a contract, not a sacrament, and the man must provide materially for the wife and perform sexually. The wife must have sex whenever the husband wishes, but she has no material obligations. A man may divorce a wife by a thrice-pronounced declaration, whereas women can divorce only for specified causes, agreed to by a judge in court. Polygyny up to four wives was permitted, although the

Quran says only if all are treated equally, which came to mean a norm of equal space and rotated sexual relations and overnight stays. Men were permitted concubines and female slaves, and their children's status was regulated. Another Shi'i practice goes back to pre-Islamic Arabia and seems to have been condoned by the Prophet, though it was outlawed for Sunnis by the caliph Umar. This is temporary marriage—a contract entered into for a definite period. As in all marriages there is a payment to the woman, and children are legitimate. It flourishes especially in pilgrimage centers where men may come alone. It is wrong to consider it prostitution, and it has uses besides satisfying men's sexual desires.[9] Women are supposed to obey their husbands, and the Quran authorizes beating if they do not. This is one of several verses that has been reinterpreted by modernists.

Women could hold and manage any amount of property, although seclusion often made effective management difficult. Regarding the two-thirds or more of inheritance that followed fixed rules, women were supposed to receive half the share of men. In Shi'i law daughters without brothers inherited everything, whereas in Sunni law they generally got no more than half. In spite of the presumption of female inheritance by all schools, it was common for women not to inherit, especially land. This kept land from passing outside the paternal family. Partial compensation in the form of gifts or sustenance in case of divorce or widowhood was sometimes given to a woman who renounced inheritance. In addition, the institution of *waqf*, inalienable endowment, was sometimes used to endow descendants in the male line, thus avoiding both property division and female inheritance. Some waqfs, however, benefited women particularly, both as recipients and as guardians.

Regarding the most effective form of birth control then known, coitus interruptus, most jurists and theologians allowed it, but some said it was licit only if the wife agreed, as she might want children or object to limiting her pleasure.[10] Some say the authorization of birth control came mainly because powerful men had slaves and concubines by whom they might not want children.

As in many societies, particularly Mediterranean ones, the code of honor and shame has been central. A family's honor was seen as resting mainly on the purity of its girls and women, and shame lay in any aspersions cast on this. Purity meant not only virginity for girls and fidelity for wives, but also the impossibility that anyone should think or say these were in doubt. Neither girl nor wife should talk to an outside man. The ideal of segregation from gossip-provoking situations encouraged veiling and seclusion. Some wealthy families kept women from going out of the house except fully covered to see close relatives. In less wealthy families women might have to have some business interaction with men, but they were supposed to keep talk to a minimum and their eyes down. It seems that outdoor dress for the upper classes usually included a facial veil and loose covering for the body. Working, rural, and tribal women usually had no facial veil. Most women passed the greater part of their lives in homes, where they could wear and show off their more important clothing and ornaments. Fashion was important, and current reporters who are surprised that Arabian and Iranian women may wear jeans or miniskirts below their veils are really reporting nothing new, as Muslim women at home have long followed fashions, often ones from far away.

Honor and shame encouraged early marriage, as leaving a girl unmarried after puberty was seen as creating a situation in which she might be violated or impregnated. Mothers often played a greater role than fathers in finding a groom, and matchmakers were sometimes used. Paternal cousin marriage, which kept property in the patrilineal line, was favored. Despite this, only a minority of marriages were to paternal first cousins; even when this is claimed, investigation often shows a more distant relationship. This may have limited bad genetic effects from such marriages, although today many educated Muslims oppose cousin marriage for genetic reasons.

As in much of traditional Mediterranean Europe, that a girl and a man alone can be doing only one thing is widely assumed, and the girl is often punished. Traditional ideology assumes that a woman who behaves immodestly arouses uncontrollable urges in men. She is a cause of *fitna*, serious trouble, a word that also means revolt or civil war. Fathers, husbands, and brothers are given formal control over women and the family, as in many traditional societies, but observers often note the real power of women in the home and family.

In spite of formal and legal male dominance, Middle Eastern women followed a number of strategies to increase their sphere of power and freedom. Although men might control the quantity of sex, women had much control over its quality and the amount of pleasure the man had. Women controlled cooking, which many men found important, and they could keep the home neat or messy, noisy or tranquil, attractive or unattractive for the husband's visitors. Throughout Islamic history many rulers were ruled by their wives or mothers, and the same thing happened in many private homes. More equal husband-wife relations were also known. Women taught one another how to overcome formal inequalities, and the theoretical rules of Islamic law and the honor code were often not enforced.

Too little research has been done to provide a true history of how women fared over time in the Middle East. Here we can essay a few generalizations. There seem to be four periods that saw the greatest freedom of action for a significant number of Middle Eastern women: the earliest period of Islam; its first two centuries; the periods of nomadic and steppe-based rule (those of the Seljuks, Mongols, Mamluks, early Safavids); and the period of modern reform. In the first of these, the activities of Khadija and A'isha have been mentioned, and there were also many lesser power-ful women, not to mention women who participated as aides in battle, or even fought (as they had in pre-Islamic times). The next period was more mixed, but women continued to be important and powerful as queens, as traditionists, and in mystical and sectarian religious move-ments. At the same time, however, slavery and class divisions were spread-ing. The invasions of Turkic and other military groups and nomads from the eleventh century on, and their rule over much of the Middle East, brought in, at least for the ruling classes and the nomads, more egalitarian treatment of women. Powerful women participated in rule in the Seljuk, Mongol, and Mamluk Empires, where restrictions on women appear to have been lessened.

Through the centuries nonorthodox religious spheres have provided a forum for female power. Shi'ism has women mullas, and Sufi (mystic) orders include powerful and creative women leaders, and all had many women followers.

Since the nineteenth century there have been modern, mainly legal and economic, reforms in the position of women, and the growth of reformist and feminist ideas. Although, as elsewhere, changes have been contradic-tory in their impact, the general trend thus far has been toward greater legal equality between the sexes and greater real equality among the urban Westernized middle and upper classes, although some in other classes have suffered.

Women's position, past and present, tended to become limited in times of economic contraction. At the very top, however, the role of women was determined most by court conditions. Where royal heirs were brought up within palace walls, they might be subject to the influence of women or eunuchs. One example is the Ottoman Empire, where from the late sixteenth century potential heirs to the throne were kept from threatening the ruler by being immured in the harem. This greatly in-creased women's and eunuchs' influence on them, even after they came to rule. The negative phrase "harem rule" will probably have its revisionist historians, though it is probably true that sultans with experience of the outside world ruled better than those without. The influence of Ottoman queens and queen mothers, as with their lesser-known counterparts in Mamluk, Mongol, and Seljuk times, not to mention Safavid and Qajar Iran, shows how possible it was for women to exercise great power, given the right circumstances.

The common Western view of the harem has little relation to reality. The Arabic word *harim* does not have sexy connotations, but means the part of the house forbidden to men who are not close relatives. For the nonelite it mostly was not polygamous and had no slaves or concubines. The harem was where the indoor work of the family was planned and carried on, usually under the supervision of the wife of the eldest male. In polygamous households and those with servants and slaves, the activities of the harem were more complex, but it was not the den of idleness and voluptuousness depicted from their imaginations by Western painters. (Westerners who saw photographs of harems were disappointed to find the clothing and furniture to be in keeping with Victorian propriety, bearing no resemblance to the paintings of Delacroix.) The main work of household production, including its textiles and other crafts, and of reproduction, was done in the harem.[11]

Partly owing to difficulties of documentation, little study has been done of premodern working women, rural or urban, or of slaves. Slavery in Islam was rarely characterized by heavy gang labor, but was overwhelmingly either household or male military slavery. Muslims could not be enslaved, and so slaves were either war captives or purchased from among non-Muslims. Slaves were often sexually subject to their masters. Unlike those in the medieval West, their children were free. Some slaves rose very high—slaves could be queens—and many were freed by their masters. Although slavery was less onerous than, say, in the New World, it still entailed a lack of freedom and a sexual subjugation that were more severe than those experienced by free women. Slaves were often trained to be singers and dancers—professions that were not quite respectable in the Islamic world or in many other traditional areas.

Although it was suggested above that many tribes are highly concerned about the purity of lineage, in most other respects treatment of women among tribal peoples tends to be more egalitarian than among urbanites. It may be something about the long-term confluence of nomadic and urban cultures that helps explain Middle Eastern patterns of gender relations and controls. The greater gender egalitarianism of tribal peoples shows up among pre-Islamic and early Islamic Arab women, and among the Seljuks and Mongols in Iran, with their powerful women in government. Early European accounts and indigenous painting suggest that tribal women did not veil. The Safavids in Iran (1501–1722), who made Shi'ism Iran's state religion, came in supported by the military backing of Turkic nomadic tribes, and early Safavid miniatures are full of unveiled women. Italian travelers to Iran in those years wrote that women were shockingly exposed! By late Safavid times, the influence of the religious classes had grown, and women were increasingly veiled and secluded.

In recent decades, as veiling and seclusion were rejected by many modernists and feminists, and as local nationalisms grew, those who opposed veiling ascribed it to a different nationality from their own. Many

Arabs say veiling was imposed on them by the Ottoman Turks. In fact, Turks began to veil only when they became assimilated in Islam, and if many Ottomans in Arab lands veiled, this was mainly because ruling classes veiled, not because Turks in particular did. There is abundant evidence that widespread Arab veiling preceded the Ottomans, although it appears that pre-Ottoman Mamluk Egypt was freer in this respect than Ottoman Egypt. Iranian modernists often blame veiling on Arabs, and Turks on Arabs or Persians. As noted, veiling and seclusion are ancient Near Eastern customs, long adopted by all major language groups in the Middle East.

Some writers, reacting to Western hostility to veiling, deny its significance. Although veiling and seclusion do not prevent women from living varied and significant lives, they are parts of a system where males are dominant and females are to be controlled. The system affects even nonsecluded women, who are expected to be modest and circumspect and are subject to sanctions if they transgress the rules. It is true that the overall system is more important than veiling as such.

The degree to which women follow the rules should not be exaggerated, however. Outside observers may see only heavily veiled shapes and assume that these women's lives are completely controlled by their menfolk. When seen from the inside, however, the same women may give quite a different impression. Thus two eighteenth-century Englishwomen wrote admiringly of the lives and freedom enjoyed by Ottoman ladies,[12] whereas their Western male colleagues reported no such views. Various peoples have reported transgressions of the rules by Egyptian women. Even in parts of the Middle East where Western influence is small, there have been recent reports of great independence on the part of women. These center on the Arabian Peninsula and Berber-influenced North Africa, both areas of tribal strength. In the latter, among several signs of a freer position for women is the institution of the free woman, who may take lovers after divorce or widowhood without loss of respect or of opportunities for remarriage. In Arabia, where women are veiled and secluded, Leila Ahmed and Unni Wikan report deviant and independent behavior and views by women in the United Arab Emirates and Oman. Ahmed thinks that the relative success in organizing women to assert their rights in Marxist South Yemen owes much to the Arabian women's independence in views and action.[13] From both Yemen and Iran come reports of women's theater games in which male arrogance and other male cultural qualities are mercilessly mocked, and such mockery must have existed in the past. Egyptian women have also been noted for their independence from pre-Islamic times to the present, indicating that local traditions and conditions can be as important as tribal background in variability. Differences not only by country but among city, tribe, and countryside and between classes in degrees of women's independence have already been noted, and further research will surely show more variation. Women's independent attitudes are also expressed in folktales, popular poetry, and women's religious ceremonies.[14] Female religious leaders and ceremonies express women's initiative. It would be wrong, however, to ignore the widespread oppression and enforced subordination of women.

Changes in economy and society in the past two centuries, along with the Western cultural impact, brought about forces within Middle Eastern societies favoring changes in the conditions of women. At first this did not involve legal changes, but rather such things as women's education. Changes in Islamic law pertaining to women have met considerable resistance. Only the Catholics, of major religions, vie with the Muslims for tenacity regarding women's position and control of her body. Islamic conservatism as it affects family law comes partly from the prominence of laws on women in the Quran. Also, however, change concerning women was felt by Muslim men to be a final invasion in the last sphere they could control against aggressive infidels, once sovereignty and much of the economy had been taken over by the West. The need to guard women from the stares of the traditional Christian enemy has been documented since the French came to Egypt with Napoleon, and veiling increased as a reaction to their presence.[15]

In the past two centuries those Muslims who became Westernized tended to be those in the middle and upper classes who had profitable contacts with Westerners. For larger if less visible groups, Westernization was generally unpopular. The petty bourgeoisie and bazaar traders tended to support traditional Islamic ways. Modernizing liberals generally belonged to the higher social classes, whereas those who defended traditional ways appealed to the traditional small bourgeoisie.[16] The upper classes were in alliance with Westerners, but the small bourgeois classes competed with larger Western trade and tended to reject Western ways partly from a desire to defend their own position. Women were and are used in a game that is really more about politico-ideological questions, including relations with the West, than about women per se. The petty bourgeoisie in most Middle Eastern countries have stuck to essentially traditional positions on women. Some traditional bourgeois and lower-class women also prefer the old ways to being forced to obtain unpleasant and low-paying jobs.

Until recently battles for women's rights in the Middle East resulted in broadening those rights. The first names associated with those struggles were male, but from the beginning women, too, were involved. Public and independent activity for women's rights became widespread in the twentieth century.[17] These movements are only one aspect of complex changes that include those in marriage, the family, the economic role of women, their social role, their ability to be public figures, and the like. Rural women have also undergone major transformations, often becoming more stratified and more secluded, but sometimes also more political. Modernization has had contradictory results in the Middle East and elsewhere, and whereas some women's positions have changed for the better, some poorer women have suffered from modernization's economic effects, becoming more, rather than less, restricted; having to work in unhealthful and poorly paid positions; and often removed from the community security of rural life. Veiling and seclusion spread in the countryside among the status conscious as they declined among Westernized city dwellers, and women's roles were sometimes limited by the economic effects of Western contacts. These contradictions have been reflected in conflicting women's attitudes on modernization versus tradition.

Although the success of reform was tied to economic and social changes, its immediate problems were often ideological; mainly, what attitude to take toward the holy law. A few, notably the reforming Turkish ruler Atatürk, took a secular position, legislating substantial legal equality for women on the basis of European law. Far more widespread have been modernist interpretations of the Quran and Islamic law. Attachment to these is strong not only because they are sacred texts, but also for identity vis-à-vis the West. There is an impetus to ground arguments in Islam, even for many who are privately secularists.

Varied modernist arguments have some widespread features. One is that the Quran has several meanings, with its literal one for its own time, and later interpretations to be made by modernists. Some stress the "spirit of the Quran," which is said to be egalitarian (largely true), and argue that several passages show that rights and egalitarianism were intended for women. There has been much reinterpretation of key verses. Modernists hold that the Quran opposes polygamy, because it says the conditions for it cannot be met. Various passages are seen to mean male-female equality, as the Quran sees them as equal believers and often explicitly addresses both men and women.

Reformists usually refer to the earliest sources—the Quran and selected Traditions about Muhammad—and reject most later interpretation. Subsequent Islamic law is rightly seen as more patriarchal than the Quran. If the Quran is reinterpreted, law can be reshaped. Such new interpretations could end polygamy and improve women's rights.

Reformist arguments arose partly because of a rapidly changing economy and society that were undergoing the influence of the capitalist and imperialist West. As in the West, the rise of capitalism and of paid jobs created new positions in the labor market for women, who had worked chiefly in the household economy. In the Middle East early demand was for nurses, midwives, doctors for women, and teachers. Demand soon spread to low-paid factory and white-collar work. As elsewhere, the development of capitalist relations had a contradictory impact on different women. Putting women in the paid labor force could change rules about sexual segregation, although not always. Some popular-class women became more restricted than before. Wealthier families, in contact with Westerners, saw advantages in women's education and participation in the wider world. Women's education was favored by reformists to improve child rearing and to prepare some women for jobs. The first arguments said that women's education would improve the rearing of sons, but women and men soon argued for women's rights. Although steps toward women's education, jobs, and freedom met resistance, until recently change was in the direction of greater equality.

Women's schools and women's or mixed universities were built in almost every Muslim country; new jobs were opened; and laws were reformed almost everywhere. The most radical reforms were those of Atatürk in Turkey. He took the unique path of adopting Western codes that outlawed polygamy and created substantial legal equality for women. Women got the vote in Turkey earlier than in France and Italy. Turkey was able to move radically owing to long contact with the West; to its experience of long, gradual reform; to the discrediting of Islamic leaders after World War I; and also to Atatürk's huge popularity, as a leader who, uniquely in the Middle East, had taken territory back from Western powers. The next most thorough reforms, outside Eastern Europe, were in Tunisia and Marxist South Yemen. In Tunisia, Habib Bourguiba's Personal Status Code of 1956 outlawed polygamy on Muslim reformist grounds and created substantial legal equality for women, while retaining a few Islamic features and male privileges. In South Yemen polygamy is allowed in a very few circumstances, but family law is otherwise egalitarian, and as important, women's organizations were encouraged to carry out education and propaganda.[18] Elsewhere legal reform is more limited, but significant. In spite of Islamist agitation there has until now been little retreat in reform except in Iran and, on a few matters, in Pakistan.

The main thrust of legal reform where it is not egalitarian is to place restrictions on divorce, polygamy, and age of marriage, often by means of Islamic precedents and often by making men justify divorce or polygamy to the courts. This is in line with a modern trend to put personal and family matters increasingly under state control and reduce the power of Islamic courts. Reforms are, however, called Islamic, and Islamic courts generally keep some power. Equally important, women's roles in education, politics, and most parts of the workforce have continued to grow.

Since World War II, a number of trends have undermined liberal reformism and encouraged Islamic revival. Among these are: (1) the growing cultural gap between the Westernized elite and the majority; (2) the growth in the power of the West and of Israel; (3) socioeconomic dislocations resulting from rapid urbanization, oil-backed modernization, and growing income distribution gaps; and (4) disillusionment with the failures of Westernized rulers and theories in the Middle East. The gap between the elite and the masses has created two cultures in the Middle East. Elite cultures tend to be Western-oriented, with young people getting a Western-style education and having little contact with the traditional bourgeoisie or the masses. Sometimes the two speak different languages, as in North Africa. The popular classes identify much more with Islam than the elite does. Among students and migrants from rural or small-town Islamically oriented backgrounds who migrate to overcrowded cities, alienation and Islamic revival are strong. It is also strong among some urban groups who stress identity and anti-imperialism.

Western consumer goods and experts are more evident than ever. Most important to Islamism, Western cultural influence is pervasive—in consumption, the media, and all cultural forms. Although many of these are items of choice, the backlash of rejection of Western cultural dominance is not surprising. Also, Israel is widely seen as a Western bastion of neocolonialism, bringing further reactions against pro-Western leaders and ways.

Socioeconomic dislocations, reinforced by fluctuations in oil income, include rapid urbanization, with the rich but rarely the poor getting richer; the problems of migrants; and the breakdown of accustomed family and rural ways. Islamism provides a social cement that appears familiar in the face of new problems.

Disillusionment with postcolonial governments that had nationalist and Westernizing, not Islamic, ideologies has focused on the Pahlavis in Iran, Anwar Sadat in Egypt, the National Liberation Front in Algeria, and Bourguiba in Tunisia. Nationalist and Western ideologies were discredited among many attracted instead by new visions of Islam, with major implications for women. Islam had the advantage of familiarity and of not having ruled recently, which could have discredited it.

Modern Islamic revivalism has roots in the Egyptian Muslim Brethren founded in 1928 and in the work of Abu al-A'la Maududi for Islamic government in Muslim India. Islamism grew after World War II, and especially after the 1967 Arab defeat by Israel and the 1973 oil price rise, with its resultant economic and social dislocations. In advocating state enforcement of Islamic law Islamism is innovating, as traditional Muslim states since the development of Islamic law have not applied it as states or in a centralized, codified way. What is demanded is novel, a modern centralized theocracy, using many modern economic and technical means, sometimes renamed.

Islamist movements are populist in appeal, stressing the rights of the oppressed and the socially egalitarian nature of the Quran. They are far from egalitarian about women, however, and take what they see as the Islamization of women's role as a touchstone of Islam. This is partly because matters affecting women make up much of the legislation in the Quran, and also because a return to Quranic injunctions on dress, polygamy, and so forth is a highly visible way to show one is a good Muslim. Dress is a symbol of Islamist beliefs, and the dress adopted by Islamist women is almost as important as a badge of ideology as it is a means to modesty or seclusion, In fact, Islamist women are not secluded from the world, but are found heavily among students, young working women, and the like, and are also engaged in political activity. The dress of most Islamist women also is not traditional, but newly fashioned.

There is separation of the sexes among Islamists. This is part of an ideology that can be stated, in terms familiar to the American past, as one of "separate but equal." Islamists often say that men and women are equal, but have different capacities according to their different roles. They stress the importance of homemaking and child rearing, and are divided on whether women can work provided it does not interfere with child rearing.[19] Practices in Islam that are unequal are justified as based on men's and women's different natures and needs. Polygamy is seen as better than the West's prostitution and mistresses, and early marriage as better than Western-style promiscuity. (Many Western ways shock strict Muslims just as many Muslim ways shock Westerners.) As in the former U.S. Supreme Court separate-but-equal doctrine for blacks, however, separation, in fact, means inferior rights—whether in education, work, or the family. The real strains of recent decades encourage nostalgia for an idealized past, including its sexual roles.

Though in most countries the leading Islamists tend to have partly Westernized educations, this was not true of Khomeini's clerical group in Iran, who took a hard line on reversing reforms concerning women. Other governments with Islamic claims, like those of Sudan, Saudi Arabia, Pakistan, and Libya, have been varied in their approach to women. And in Algeria, Pakistan, and Egypt threats of Islamist legislation have been a catalyst to mobilize women against this. Iran today is becoming less strict about women, but other countries are becoming more restrictive.

Islamist movements have had an appeal for some women, especially among students in some faculties and among the traditional classes. In Iran more women demonstrated for Khomeini than against him. Elsewhere Islamist women are also active and organized. Islamists encourage women's participation in many spheres. Many women have chosen to wear Islamic dress, and one of the reasons they give is that it keeps men from bothering them in street or social contacts. Islamic dress is again a badge—here saying that this is a serious respectable woman who should not be touched or annoyed.

Other aspects of Islamism that appeal to many women include their frequent women's circles and organizations, where women discuss important matters in all-woman surroundings that are not intimidating. They are also encouraged to undertake propaganda activities. Girls and women whose parents or husbands do not normally let them out allow them to go to mosque meetings, and some even reject proposed marriage partners on the grounds that they are not good Muslims.[20]

Many Islamist women experience protection and respect. The legal reforms in Muslim countries affected chiefly the elite, so that for many women Islamism may not seem a step backward and may even restore recently lost protections. Those who had experienced benefits, however, often suffer under Islamist rule or pressures. Hence there are radically different views about Islamism, often and understandably voiced and acted on with vehemence.

Feminists disagree about whether they should continue trying to interpret Islam in reformist ways or rather should stand foursquare for secularization, saying that Islam should be a matter for private belief and worship only. This is one of the key problems for Middle Eastern feminists today, extending from Pakistan's influential Women's Action Forum to the arguments among Middle Eastern women in many journals, including the *New Left Review*.[21] Those who stress the reinterpretation of Islam hope to meet some of the cultural needs of ordinary women, including Islamists, but their opponents say they are prolonging the repressive life and practices of political Islam.

A few modernists in a sense combine the two positions, presenting an Islam that does not require following Quranic practices regarding women. One Egyptian scholar claimed that the legal parts of the Quran were intended only for the lifetime of the Prophet. And a small group of Sudanese say that only the Meccan suras of the Quran (which have religious rather than legal content) and not the legalistic Medinan ones are valid after the Prophet.[22] Such views are rejected by most Muslims today, but they could fare better in the future.

Islamist trends will not necessarily continue strong far into the future. Khomeini was able to appeal to various kinds of discontented people, but once in power he aroused discontent. Even where Islamists do well in elections, many elements of a protest vote are involved. The Islamist phase of the 1970s and 1980s may continue, but it seems unlikely in radical form to outlive widespread experience with so-called Islamic governments. Only Iran in the Middle East to date has repealed major legislation favorable to women, although women's groups in Egypt and Pakistan have had to struggle to forestall major changes, which could still occur there or elsewhere.

Economic realities bring women in the Middle East more and more into the labor force and the public sphere, and this continues, despite Islamist trends. Yet women's legal struggles today are mostly defensive. Both the feminists who are convinced that Islamic theory must be reinterpreted in their cause and those who say that this approach will only play into the hands of antifeminists are trying to find the most promising way to bring back a situation in which women's rights may be actively furthered. It may be that both the Islamic reformist and the secularist path can contribute to this, especially if they concentrate more on the needs and desires of popular-class women. And although the study of history is not simply a pragmatic exercise, understanding the reasons for the positions of women in the near and distant past can also help us formulate how those positions might be changed.

NOTES

Some of the material in this essay was used in Nikki R. Keddie, "The Past and Present of Women in the Muslim World," *Journal of World History* 1, no. 1 (1990): 77–108. Where points differ, this text has priority. In addition to written sources, the essay is based on wide travel, residence, and interviews in many Muslim countries.

1. The wide literature on these subjects includes Guity Nashat, "Women in the Ancient Middle East," in *Restoring Women to History* (Bloomington, IN: Organization of American Historians, 1988); Gerda Lerner, *The Creation of Patriarchy* (New York: Oxford University Press, 1986); and Karen Sacks, "Engels Revisited: Women, the Organization of Production, and Private Property," in *Women, Culture, and Society*, ed. Michelle Zimbalist Rosaldo and Louise Lamphere (Stanford: Stanford University Press, 1974).

2. Nashat, "Women in the Ancient Middle East," discusses ancient Near Eastern practices and influences. See also Lois Beck and Nikki Keddie, eds., *Women in the Muslim World* (Cambridge, MA: Harvard University Press, 1978), 21, 32n12.

3. Germaine Tillion, *Le harem et les cousins* (Paris: Seuil, 1966).

4. Gertrude Stern, *Marriage in Early Islam* (London: Royal Asiatic Society, 1939).

5. On this issue, see especially Leila Ahmed, "Women and the Advent of Islam," *Signs* 11 (1986): 665–91.

6. Works that stress women's power but have been criticized by more recent scholarship are W. Robertson Smith, *Kinship and Marriage in Early Arabia* (Cambridge: Cambridge University Press, 1885), and W. Montgomery Watt, *Mohammad at Medina* (Oxford: Clarendon, 1956). More limited reports of women's

independence are largely based on pre-Islamic poetry found in the collection *al-Aghani*.

7. Nabia Abbott, *Aishah, the Beloved of Mohammed* (Chicago: University of Chicago Press, 1942).

8. See Shahla Haeri, *Law of Desire: Temporary Marriage in Shi'i Iran* (Syracuse: Syracuse University Press, 1989).

9. Among many sources, see Judith E. Tucker, *Women in Nineteenth-Century Egypt* (Cambridge: Cambridge University Press, 1985); the articles of Martha Mundy on Yemen; and *Embassy to Constantinople: The Travels of Lady Mary Wortley Montagu*, ed. and comp. Christopher Pick, with an introduction by Dervla Murphy (London: Century, 1988). Elizabeth N. Macbean Ross, *A Lady Doctor in Bakhtiari Land* (London: Leonard Parsons, 1921), shows leading tribal women managing lands, flocks, and accounts during their husbands' long absences. Recent literature shows how often urban women went to court and defended their legal and property rights, and stresses the independence of many tribal women, but indicates less independence for the rural and urban popular classes. These findings have not been coordinated, however, and some authors take a single group as typical of women as a whole.

10. B. F. Musallam, *Sex and Society in Islam* (Cambridge: Cambridge University Press, 1983).

11. See Afaf Lutfi al-Sayyid Marsot, "The Revolutionary Gentlewoman," in Beck and Keddie, *Women in the Muslim World*; and Sarah Graham-Brown, *Images of Women: The Portrayal of Women in the Photography of the Middle East, 1860–1950* (New York: Columbia University Press, 1988).

12. See the citation in R. C. Jennings, "Women in Early Seventeenth Century Ottoman Judicial Records: The Sharia Court of Anatolian Kayseri," *Journal of the Economic and Social History of the Orient* 28 (1975): 53–114 (56–57n5).

13. Unni Wikan, *Behind the Veil in Arabia* (Baltimore: Johns Hopkins University Press, 1982); Leila Ahmed, "Feminism and Feminist Movements in the Middle East, a Preliminary Exploration: Turkey, Egypt, Algeria, People's Democratic Republic of Yemen," *Women's Studies International Forum* 5, no. 2 (1982): 153–68. The women I met in North Yemen, externally a country of heavy veiling and seclusion, included the following, all of whom were typical according to the Yemeni specialist who accompanied me: a woman who said that the best thing that could occur in a pregnancy was miscarriage, and that it was best to have no children; three women who said that the longer their migrant husbands stayed away the better; and a woman who had left her husband and returned to her family and was then bargaining conditions for her return. In addition, many of Yemen's divorced and married women are known to have had affairs. Such conditions are not limited to tribally based societies, as indicated as early as Lady Mary Montagu's reports on upper-class women's freedoms in Turkey in the early eighteenth century; but specialists who compare southern Arabia and certain other tribal areas with other parts of the Middle East note "liberated" features that seem to owe nothing to Westernization.

14. Claudie Feyein, *A French Doctor in the Yemen*, trans. Douglas McKee (London: R. Hale, 1957), esp. 191; Lila Abu-Lughod, *Veiled Sentiments* (Berkeley

and Los Angeles: University of California Press, 1986); and the chapters by Vanessa Maher, Daisy Hilse Dwyer, and Erika Friedl in Beck and Keddie, *Women in the Muslim World.*

15. Nada Tomiche, "The Situation of Egyptian Women in the First Half of the Nineteenth Century," in *Beginnings of Modernization in the Middle East,* ed. W. R. Polk and R. L. Chambers (Chicago: University of Chicago Press, 1968).

16. Juan R. Cole, "Feminism, Class, and Islam in Turn-of-the-Century Egypt," *International Journal of Middle East Studies* 19 (1981): 387–407.

17. On twentieth-century feminist movements, see Ahmed, "Feminism"; Eliz Sanasarian, *The Women's Rights Movement in Iran* (New York: Praeger, 1982); Azar Tabari and Nahid Yeganeh, eds., *In the Shadow of Islam: The Women's Movement in Iran* (London: Zed, 1982); and Margot Badran, "Dual Liberation: Feminism and Nationalism in Egypt, 1870s—1925," *Feminist Issues* 8, no. 1 (1988): 15–34.

18. Maxine Molyneux, "Legal Reform and Socialist Revolution in Democratic Yemen: Women and the Family," *International Journal of the Sociology of Law* 13 (1985): 147–72.

19. Many statements by Islamist leaders against women's working are cited in Yvonne Y. Haddad, "Islam, Women, and Revolution in Twentieth Century Arab Thought," *Muslim World* 74 (1984): 137–60. My interviews with Tunisian, Egyptian, and other Islamist women, however, show that many of them work or expect to work, even if they sometimes justify it as less than ideal. Haddad's article also includes the results of interviews in several countries. There has been a considerable literature on Islamist women, including such authors as Fadwa al-Guindi, Afaf Marsot, Nesta Ramazani, John Alden Williams, and others. See also Sherifa Danielle Zuhur, "Self-Image of Egyptian Women in Oppositionist Islam" (Ph.D. diss., University of California, Los Angeles, 1990).

20. See Nikki R. Keddie, "The Islamist Movement in Tunisia," *Maghreb Review* 11, no. 1 (1986): 26–39.

21. Mai Ghoussoub, "Feminism—or the Eternal Masculine—in the Arab World," *New Left Review* 161 (1987): 3–18; Reza Hammami and Martina Rieker, "Feminist Orientalism and Orientalist Marxism," *New Left Review* 170 (1985): 93–106; Mai Ghoussoub, "A Reply to Hammami and Rieker," *New Left Review* 170 (1958): 108–9.

22. See especially Mahmoud Mohamed Taha, *The Second Message of Islam,* trans. with an introduction by Abdullahi Ahmed An-Na'im (Syracuse: Syracuse University Press, 1987), and Abdullahi Ahmed An-Na'im, *Toward an Islamic Reformation* (Syracuse: Syracuse University Press, 1990).

PART 2

Scholarship, Relativism, and Universalism
2000

BACKGROUND TO RECENT ACHIEVEMENTS AND PROBLEMS IN MIDDLE EASTERN WOMEN'S STUDIES

The continued flowering of studies of Middle Eastern women since about 1970 is part of a general movement, bolstered and originally largely inspired by the wave of feminist organization and thought that began in the 1960s. These studies have not only shed important new light on the roles and achievements of women, but also, in many cases, helped to recast whole academic fields. There remains much more to be done, and many male scholars continue to ignore the implications of women's studies and women's roles for their own fields.[1] The trend, however, is for both male and female scholars to take increasing note of works in women's studies, including women's history, and this is bound to continue.

While works in Middle Eastern women's studies, including women's history, have contributed enormously to our knowledge, they are often marked by a certain defensive and apologetic tone or tend to accentuate the positive while minimizing the negative. To understand this tendency, we should take into account the history of Western and Western-influenced attitudes toward the Muslim Middle East against which many recent authors have reacted. Islam has received worse press in the West than has any other religion, and the status of women has been a key issue in this bad press. Today, this press is also influenced by the religiopolitical extremism of a minority of Islamists. From the time of the rise and spread of Islam, the forces of which over many centuries conquered or threatened Christian-ruled territories in Iberia, Sicily/Italy, and Eastern Europe, most Christians who wrote about Islam have portrayed it as a threatening, false religion with a false prophet and doctrines to be combated. This long-standing fear and Christian-centered view of Islam continue to influence ideas today.

To this has been added the hostility arising from the numerous wars between Christian Europeans and Muslims, including the early Arab and later Ottoman conquests of European territory, European conquests in medieval Spain and Sicily, the various Crusades, and anti-Ottoman wars up through the successful nineteenth- and twentieth-century nationalist movements in the Balkans and beyond. In the eighteenth and nineteenth centuries, Western powers increasingly took control in Muslim lands, the majority of which either became colonies and protectorates or remained formally independent but subject to Western economic and political controls. Increasing numbers of Muslims saw Zionism and Israel as dispossession by a Western people. While in the earlier periods power swung back and forth between the two sides, from the eighteenth century on, the Christian West increasingly gained ground on its Muslim rivals, and this imperial expansionism was accompanied by efforts at indoctrinating colonized populations with convictions of Western superiority.

Eighteenth-century Western Enlightenment thinkers were divided in their views of Islam and of race. While several advocated a tolerant universalism, others pioneered in changing the already widespread and often religiously informed racism of earlier periods into doctrines of so-called scientific racism, which later became especially pervasive in the age of imperial conquest and rule, roughly 1830–1950. In these doctrines, Muslim Arabs were not at the bottom of the totem pole—darker-skinned peoples were—but they were considered far inferior to northern Europeans.

Bolstering these prejudices was a view of Muslim women as horribly oppressed, sexually enslaved, miserable or degenerate, and either overworked or totally idle, depending on their class and status. Westerners reified a negatively conceived Islam and overstressed its importance in determining the condition of women. While imperial powers almost never took measures that could help women, and while imperialist and capitalist economic relations actually worsened the position of many women, numerous Western travelers, missionaries, writers, and scholars presented a picture of Middle Eastern women that was almost totally negative and looked exclusively to Western solutions, such as Protestantism, Western education, or other forms of wholesale imitation of the West, for women's oppression. Many Middle Eastern reformers, finding no indigenous model for changing women's status to one more suited to modern realities, similarly argued for such wholesale imitation, although they sometimes constructed an indigenous pedigree for it.

In the late nineteenth and early twentieth centuries Muslim reformers, who were often tied to the wealthier classes and their social, political, and economic relations with Westerners, tended to favor reforms that were in fact, if not always in name, of Western origin. Recent decades have seen a revived assertion of the virtues of Islam and tradition, mainly among classes hurt by Western influence and imperialism. In this charged political atmosphere in which Middle Eastern secularism, both leftist and nationalist, has failed to fulfill its promises and is losing out to Islamic revivalism while at the same time women everywhere are increasingly claiming rights, women's studies scholars of the region have generally emphasized the positive possibilities within Islamic societies, past and present, and played down negative realities.[2] Much good scholarship has emerged showing that women had and have more varied and independent lives than would be supposed from a reading of male travelers and writers or Islamic law books. Several recent scholars have avoided the most sensitive or negative subjects, such as honor killings, slavery, and physical abuse. They have also tended to cite Western observers as authoritative only when such scholars have positive views of women in the Middle East, and to reject most critical evaluations or observations.[3]

The work done in Middle Eastern women's studies in recent decades is enormously important and valuable, but much of it is still characterized by an unacknowledged reactive stance. While the reluctance to discuss women that prevailed among scholars until the 1970s has been overcome, and our knowledge of the Middle Eastern past and present has enormously increased as a result, there are still great sensitivities about trying to discuss the subject comprehensively. This is especially true with respect to nonapologetic treatments of the role of Islam, with all its variations in practice, in women's lives. With the spread in the Muslim world of ideologies that see Islam as the solution to all human problems, Western scholars sympathetic to the people of the area are often loath to risk unpopularity by studying topics that many of their contemporaries might view as overly negative.[4] While this reluctance is not as extreme in women's studies as it is in the study of another sensitive subject, slavery and slave trading by Muslims, it shows some similar features. Ehud Toledano, in his recent book on slavery and abolition in the Ottoman Empire, discusses this self-imposed censorship, which "has severely restricted the scholarly discussion of topics that are somehow viewed as potentially unflattering to the image of Muslims, especially those living in the Middle East."[5] In the case of women's studies, such self-censorship has not prevented many important and well-researched books and articles from being written without reactive distortions. These works should be read by students and scholars outside the field of Middle Eastern studies, many of whom still seem to hold overwhelmingly negative stereotypes of Middle Eastern women.

In discussing some of these positive scholarly contributions, this essay will focus on a number of English-language works of significance to women's history. There is not space to cover all such works or the significant work done in journal articles, including the extensive article production by theoretically oriented sociologists such as Deniz Kandiyoti and anthropologists such as Mary Hegland and Suad Joseph, nor the recent historical monographs relevant in part to women, such as those of Janet Afary, Julia Clancy-Smith, and Donald Quataert.[6] I include within the text and in the notes books in the social sciences of particular interest to historians, but I have had to leave out historical works on literature and the arts, the adequate treatment of which would require a separate article. I do not attempt to cover areas mostly outside the Ottoman and Iranian spheres, but some important work has been done on North Africa, Afghanistan, Pakistan, central Asia, and the Arabian Peninsula, especially Yemen, where researchers, mostly anthropologists, have been active in recent decades.[7] Following this survey, I will raise some of the interpretive problems in Middle Eastern women's studies.

ACHIEVEMENTS IN MIDDLE EASTERN WOMEN'S HISTORY: 1970–2000

The creation and development of many fields of Middle Eastern women's studies, including the history of women, gender, and the family, have been startling and impressive in the past thirty years. Before the rise of the women's movement and women's studies scholarship in the late sixties and the seventies, I can remember that studying women in the Middle East as a scholarly topic was not only very rare, but also considered second-class and of little interest. Even women anthropologists and sociologists, who did not have to depend only on male-oriented documents but could have moved among women in conducting fieldwork, rarely did so, except sometimes in preparation of a subtopic within a larger work whose main protagonists were male.

An important but abortive start in women's history is represented by the three significant works on the early period, Gertrude Stern, *Marriage in Early Islam* (1939), and Nabia Abbott, *Aishah, the Beloved of Muhammed* and *Two Queens of Baghdad* (originally 1940s), as well as by a short monograph by Ilse Lichtenstadter, *Women in the Aiyam al-'Arab: A Study of Female Life during Warfare in Preislamic Arabia* (1935), all of which should be read by everyone in the field. (Although some scholars say nothing can be reliably known about the pre-Islamic or early Islamic periods, as the documents we have were written down later, I give credence to most of the social practices shown in texts attributed to these early periods, which contrasted in historically convincing ways with those of the era in which they were recorded.) Remarkably, these works had no significant book-length monographic successors before the mid-1980s— a gap of over forty years. Taken together, Stern, Lichtenstadter, and Abbott, all Orientalists (in the only sense of the term that I use outside of the arts—a scholar of Asia/North Africa with a primarily philological linguistic training), used new methods to paint a convincing picture of Arab women's lives before Islam and soon after its rise. They strongly suggest what later scholarship has often confirmed—a higher position for women in both the pre-Islamic and early Islamic periods than that of later periods. When state institutions were formed, class and gender divisions became sharper, and practices such as upper-class veiling, seclusion, court harems, and slavery were imported from Near Eastern societies that already had such state, class, and gender divisions, including the conquered Persians and the partly conquered Byzantine Near East. Also, patriarchal tribal practices that were altered in the Quran were later reasserted. With the recent increase in Muslim apologetic writings focusing on early Islam, some scholars have forgotten or ignored important points made by Stern, Lichtenstadter, and Abbott. All three sometimes express themselves in ways we would not today, but their basic points remain convincing.[8]

There has been a tendency in recent decades to see the active early participation of women in the public sphere as a result of the Quran's teachings (which were indeed reformist in some matters, notably in forbidding infanticide, making women's property rights part of Islam, and giving the dower directly to the bride), while what we know of pre-Islamic Arabia makes it clear that such participation antedated the Quran and decreased later. Fatima Mernissi, for instance, in *Beyond the Veil: Male-Female Dynamics in Modern Muslim Society* (1975), rev. ed. (Bloomington: Indiana University Press, 1987), argues that pre-Islamic society was more gender-egalitarian than Islamic society. Although Mernissi here attributes the decline of such gender-egalitarianism to the birth of Islam and to the Quran, she indicates in her later work that this decline should instead be traced to changes in state and society after the rise of Islam.[9] Two excellent recent books have also documented the decline in women's role in society due to non-Islamic or post-Quranic influences subsequent to the rise of Islam: Barbara Freyer Stowasser's *Women in the Qur'an, Traditions, and Interpretation* (Oxford: Oxford University Press, 1994), and Denise Spellberg's *Politics, Gender, and the Islamic Past: The Legacy of A'isha bint Abi Bakr* (New York: Columbia University Press, 1994).

There are a few books dating to the decades before the recent revival in the subject that have remained important for women's history. One, which dealt with both women's history and contemporary themes, is Germaine Tillion's *The Republic of Cousins: Women's Oppression in Mediterranean Society* (London: Al-Saqi Books, 1983; French original *Le Harem et les cousins*, 1966). A tour de force and a pioneering if flawed theory explaining Islamic customs as part of a Pan-Mediterranean pattern, the book is today little read, and its stress on women's oppression is unpopular with multiculturalists. The outstanding study of the medieval Middle Eastern Jewish community in the multivolume work by S. D. Goitein includes a more extensive, documented, and intimate presentation of women's lives than is available for Muslim women, but it is very relevant to their study.[10] Another important and underused work from the period before the recent flowering of Middle Eastern women's history is Gregory Massell's *The Surrogate Proletariat: Moslem Women and Revolutionary Strategies in Soviet Central Asia, 1919–1929* (Princeton: Princeton University Press, 1974), which discusses the strong backlash following the Soviet Union's attempts forcibly to unveil and otherwise radically change the status of women. Massell failed to note, however, the importance of these reforms' having been imposed by a foreign colonial power, the key difference between central Asia and a country like Turkey, where such changes were implemented from within. However, his discussion of reaction to reforms imposed suddenly from above remains relevant.

A number of important monographic articles were written in the 1970s, some of them for the edited Lois Beck and Nikki R. Keddie collection, *Women in the Muslim World* (Cambridge, MA: Harvard University Press, 1978), and others in various journals. The first important, single-authored scholarly books in the field of women's history did not appear until the 1980s. Publication in women's history began some years later than that in several other fields of women's studies, primarily because in other fields it was easier to find or create sources: literary works about and by women were easily available, and social scientists could design studies involving participant observation or interviews with women. The sources for women's history, however, were more difficult to locate.

Several of the pioneers in using new sources, including legal records, were men, who used them in articles and parts of books—Ronald Jennings, Abraham Marcus, and Haim Gerber were among the first to use Ottoman sources for women's history in Anatolia and in Ottoman Arab lands.[11] Basim Musallam's *Sex and Society in Islam: Birth Control before the Nineteenth Century* (Cambridge: Cambridge University Press, 1983) had implications for women's history, documenting the practice of various birth control methods and the tolerance of it by Islamic thinkers, issues first raised in a French book by G.-H. Bousquet.[12] While few scholars were convinced by Musallam's effort to show that pre-nineteenth-century population decreases in certain areas of the Middle East were influenced by hypothesized increases in the practice of birth control, his work on medieval Islamic tolerance of the practice continues to be important. This tolerance is in contrast to a number of contemporary attitudes. Leila Ahmed has, however, noted that the tolerance may not have been a woman-friendly attitude so much as a way to limit the children of slave-wives, children who, despite the legal status of their mothers, were born free under Islamic law and might share or contest the inheritance of children born to free women.[13]

The scholarly books published in the eighties relevant to women's history addressed a variety of topics, but most concentrated on the nineteenth and twentieth centuries and dealt in different ways with relations with the West and with imperialism. Eliz Sanasarian's *The Women's Rights Movement in Iran: Mutiny, Appeasement, and Repression from 1900 to Khomeini* (New York: Praeger, 1982) was the first book written on a Middle Eastern women's rights movement, a topic later researched by several authors, especially for Iran and Egypt.[14] More comprehensive was Judith E. Tucker's *Women in Nineteenth-Century Egypt* (Cambridge: Cambridge University Press, 1985). Though some criticisms have been made of this book, as of most others, it pointed the way to integrating women's history and socioeconomic history, to addressing the history of urban and rural popular classes, and to locating useful sources. It raised points that are still relevant and debated about the dialectical positive-negative role of Western interactions and of imperialism. A notable edited collection from the eighties is Asghar Fathi, ed., *Women and the Family in Iran* (Leiden: E. J. Brill, 1985), which was pioneering in including several articles about the family as well as historical articles.

A brilliant and disturbing anthropological work that should be read by all historians is Willy Jansen, *Women without Men: Gender and Marginality in an Algerian Town* (Leiden: E. J. Brill, 1987). It is a close study of marginal and poor women, both with and without men, and brings into sharp relief difficulties in women's lives that many scholars ignore or gloss over. As historical documentation is more available for the upper classes than for the popular classes, historians often ignore the phenomena of severe abuse and honor killings that rarely enter the court records and seem more prevalent among the popular classes. Another historically relevant anthropological study is Shahla Haeri's *Law of Desire: Temporary Marriage in Shi'i Iran* (Syracuse: Syracuse University Press, 1989), an extensive study of the Shi'i institution of temporary marriage. These and other works suggest the need for caution in generalizing about the whole region: Iranian and Shi'i practices differ from others, and scholars who know different areas often make observations orally about comparative practices that they would rarely commit to writing. I have heard such scholars say, for example, that conditions for popular-class women are worse in Algeria than Tunisia and worse in Pakistan than Iran. The comparative experiences of women on the ground are often different from those generally stressed by Western scholarship, which tends to concentrate on such things as the prevalence or necessity of veiling. Differences within countries across time periods, regions, ethnicities, modes of production, and classes can also be significant.

The vast majority of books on Middle Eastern women's history date from the 1990s, and only a few can be mentioned here. These include several useful overviews by Leila Ahmed, Guity Nashat, and Judith E. Tucker, as well as Nikki R. Keddie's introduction to *Women in Middle Eastern History* [reprinted as Part 1, above].[15] The decade also saw a number of useful article collections on the subject, including those by Lila Abu-Lughod, Deniz Kandiyoti, Nikki R. Keddie and Beth Baron, Margaret L. Meriwether and Judith E. Tucker, Amira Sonbol, and Madeline Zilfi.[16] One should especially note that Gavin R. G. Hambly, ed., *Women in the Medieval Islamic World: Power, Patronage, and Piety* (New York: St. Martin's Press, 1998), goes beyond its title to include several very useful articles on the Ottomans and Safavids, as well as on pre-Islamic subjects.

A few points deserve special note regarding the books published in the 1990s. One is the abandonment by nonapologetic historians of speculative statements about the early Islamic period in favor of an extensive reading and analysis of actual texts. When early Islamic times are discussed in scholarly monographs, as by Barbara Stowasser in her *Women in the Qur'an, Traditions, and Interpretation* and by Denise Spellberg in her *Politics, Gender, and the Islamic Past: The Legacy of A'isha bint Abi Bakr* (New York: Columbia University Press, 1994), it is with close attention to documents and their biases. These books also turn away from stressing, as did Stern, Abbott, and Lichtenstadter, the reconstruction from texts of what society was like. Rather, they show through a close study of texts of different periods how attitudes toward women changed in the course of Islamic history in response to changing historical circumstances and practices. These new works may, however, be seen as reinforcing in their textual analyses the earlier authors' argument that changes unfavorable to women occurred after the death of the Prophet and the earliest Islamic period.

The second general point seen in many recent works is a growing recognition of variations in women's status and roles by period, region, class, and the prevalence of different modes of production. These variations appear in the work of anthropologists who have conducted research in different areas or in the same area over time. Notable is Erika Friedl's brilliant article in Keddie and Baron, *Women in Middle Eastern History*, which shows the growing exclusion of women from the public sphere as modernization grew in a tribal village she visited for thirty years.[17] Works on the Mamluks and on regions of the Ottoman Empire, such as those by Margaret L. Meriwether, Judith E. Tucker, and Afaf Marsot discussed below, show variations in women's position over space and time. Modern theoretical developments in defining separate spheres and ideals of domesticity are explored in various works, notably in Beth Baron's book discussed below and in Afsaneh Najmabadi's chapter in Lila Abu Lughod's *Remaking Women: Feminism and Modernity in the Middle East* (Princeton: Princeton University Press, 1998). Variations in women's status over a longer time span can be found in Leila Ahmed's discussion of negative changes instigated by the Abbasids and also in a growing recognition by historians that women among the Turks, Mongols, and Mamluks enjoyed high status and political power, especially within the ruling classes. This phenomenon was reflected in the history and politics of Mamluk Egypt, the Ottoman Empire, and Safavid Iran, although women's public role in these states decreased over time.[18]

There are by now enough studies of women in nomadic tribal settings and in the early stages of tribally ruled states to warrant hope for future general works dealing with the important impact of lineage-based family structures and customary law on the social history of the Middle East. Notable is the more open and important public role of women in many tribes until today, while at the same time tribal areas are often those with the most "honor killings." The latter may be related both to the importance given to the purity of the lineage in many tribes and to the scant attention paid to Islamic law in many tribal and rural areas, where customary means of maintaining social order often take precedence.

In the past decade, women's historians have concentrated on areas with good documentation, meaning more emphasis on later rather than earlier periods, with the Mamluks and Ottomans, including Ottoman Arab lands and also the last two centuries especially favored. For the Ottoman Empire, legal documents are most important and revealing, and are extensively used, although scholars now recognize that they pose such problems as incompleteness, bias, and a potential theory-practice disjuncture.[19] Such methodological challenges, especially the framing of court cases in the source material in terms that conform to legal theory more than reflect practical reality, are successfully negotiated and insightfully analyzed in books dealing with contemporary legal processes, such as Ziba Mir-Hosseini's *Marriage on Trial: A Study of Islamic Family Law, Iran and Morocco Compared* (London: I. B. Tauris, 1993).

The decade of the 1990s also ushered in important studies of the family and of the household. Households comprised, among the upper classes, more than extended families, functioning as basic social units made up of several generations, servants, slaves, and clients, and often playing a major political role. The largest and most extended household was that of the Ottoman sultan, brilliantly and extensively studied by Leslie Peirce in her *The Imperial Harem: Women and Sovereignty in the Ottoman Empire* (New York: Oxford University Press, 1993), which, like the works based on legal documents, gives some voice to pre-nineteenth-century women. Recent books concerning the family include Judith E. Tucker's *In the House of the Law: Gender and Islamic Law in Ottoman Syria and Palestine* (Berkeley and Los Angeles: University of California Press, 1998) and Margaret L. Meriwether's *The Kin Who Count: Family and Society in Ottoman Aleppo, 1770–1840* (Austin: University of Texas Press, 1999), which succinctly summarizes the state of research.[20] Tucker notes a limit to the potential of legal cases, which rarely dealt with sexual transgressions, for women's history. Such transgressions, she says, were, despite the contrary admonitions of Muslim jurists, most often judged and penalized within the family circle (sometimes resulting in the murder of the accused women). Property is another important topic dealt with in legal documents related to the family and is stressed in Afaf Marsot's important *Women and Men in Late Eighteenth-Century Egypt* (Austin: University of Texas Press, 1995).

The flowering of documentary research on Ottoman topics has given rise to contradictory interpretations, partly based on different realities and partly on different views of them.[21] On the one hand, the legal documents from the Ottoman period importantly indicate a more equitable treatment of women, who could and did fight for their rights in court, than either foreign or domestic commentators have supposed. On the other hand, these documents tell us little about large areas of women's lives, especially those of tribal and rural women. For pre-nineteenth-century periods, less documentation has been unearthed on women and the family, especially comprehensive documentation pertaining to all classes, than for Europe, China, or Japan, and historians have come to these topics only recently. Nonetheless, there has been an important start, and ample sources exist for much further monographic study of many areas and periods.

In a class by itself is Alan Duben and Cem Behar's *Istanbul Households: Marriage, Family and Fertility 1880–1940* (Cambridge: Cambridge University Press, 1991), which applies contemporary methods of demographic history and a study of censuses with primary texts and interviews to reconstruct family history in Istanbul. It shows that the average family size before the late nineteenth century in Istanbul was small, marriage late, family planning frequent, and the end of women's childbearing early, despite the prevalence in both the West and in Istanbul itself of opposite assumptions. This means that such elements of demographic transition occurred as early in Istanbul as in many parts of Europe. The authors also contrast Istanbul to the countryside and to most of the Middle East, in which such phenomena occurred later—if at all. This book is one of several works showing the importance of demographic methods for historians and the novelty of the conclusions that may be drawn from combining demography with texts and interviews. Among works dealing with demography in the Middle East for more recent periods, notable is Carla Makhlouf Obermeyer, ed., *Family, Gender, and Population in the Middle East: Policies in Context* (Cairo: American University in Cairo Press, 1995).

The decade also saw extensive treatment of modern topics—women's movements, women's writing and the press, and women's relations to politics and the state. Among the works especially worthy of mention are the important books by Beth Baron, *The Women's Awakening in Egypt: Culture, Society, and the Press* (New Haven: Yale University Press, 1994);

Parvin Paidar, *Women and the Political Process in Twentieth-Century Iran* (Cambridge: Cambridge University Press, 1995); Margot Badran, *Feminists, Islam, and Nation: Gender and the Making of Modern Egypt* (Princeton: Princeton University Press, 1995); and Deniz Kandiyoti, ed., *Women, Islam, and the State* (Philadelphia: Temple University Press, 1991). Baron was the first to pay extensive attention to, and to analyze, the importance of what may be called scientific domesticity as a new topic in the women's press and education of the late nineteenth and early twentieth centuries, a topic elaborated on more recently by others, including Afsaneh Najmabadi and Jasamin Rostam-Kolayi.[22] Badran sees this as an overwhelmingly conservative trend and concentrates on women activists, but the other works show the reality to be more complex. Paidar's is probably the best comprehensive work on women in Iran, including women's movements, in the twentieth century.

For Turkey there are still relatively few works on women's movements in the nineteenth and early twentieth centuries, perhaps because many Turkish scholars interested in women's studies, several of whom pioneered such studies, are sociologists who do not conduct research in the Ottoman language, while those who do are often more interested in earlier periods.[23] Much interesting and relevant material is, however, found in Duben and Behar, *Istanbul Households*, and in Fanny Davis's *The Ottoman Lady: A Social History from 1718 to 1918* (New York: Greenwood Press, 1986), which, like *Istanbul Households*, is of much broader interest to the entire Middle Eastern field than its title implies. Less attention has been paid to modern Arab women outside Egypt, with Palestine and Yemen partial exceptions. A brilliant exception is Elizabeth Thompson's *Colonial Citizens: Republican Rights, Paternal Privilege, and Gender in French Syria and Lebanon* (New York: Columbia University Press, 2000), which treats gender in the changing context of colonial and local rulers and elites, and of the oppositional Communist/labor, nationalist, and Islamist movements.

This essay has space to mention only some of the important books in English in the field of Middle Eastern women's studies. [More of those dealing with the modern period are mentioned and analyzed in an article reprinted as Part 3 of this volume.[24]]

CONTEMPORARY ATTITUDES TOWARD MIDDLE EASTERN WOMEN
AND WOMEN'S STUDIES: RELATIVISM AND UNIVERSALISM

The study of women carried out both inside and outside the Muslim world has been affected by two contradictory intellectual trends in the past thirty years. The first is the trend increasingly to emphasize women's studies in all countries and disciplines. The second, partially contradictory trend has been the rise of Islamic politics in the Muslim world, especially in the Middle East and Pakistan. This development has numerous causes, among them the failures of all governments, including secular ones, to meet people's needs and the persistent struggles against Western powers and Israel, which is seen as a colonial implantation in the area. Though Islamic politics involve many tendencies, from right to left, they are similar in seeing human salvation as coming from a restoration of early Islamic beliefs and practices, including a state-enforced shari'a, or holy law. Though this law was never unified or codified before modern times, and historians have shown its past flexibility, it is now often seen as requiring state-enforced literal application, especially with regard to crimes and punishments contained in the Quran. The Quran is predominantly read as endorsing polygamy, male control (both within and beyond marriage), veiling, and punishment for adultery. Of these, a Quranic basis for the endorsement of veiling is the most doubtful, but it is part of early Islamic legal developments and Tradition.

With the spread of Islamic ideologies it is understandable that many (though not all) defenders of women's rights in the Muslim world should turn to reinterpretations of the Quran and to the example of the early Islamic period, and that many who may privately be secularists should resort to Islamic arguments. We may question whether scholars not subject to these immediate pressures should accept such historically problematic arguments. A second question is whether women's rights advocates can hope in the foreseeable future to change widespread views on male superiority and dominance by appealing to a reinterpretation of the Quran and the early Islamic period, at a time when male-supremacist interpretations are both more in line with the literal text and more dominant in the religious establishment as well as in lay circles. To anticipate my conclusion, I would say that the advances made by women since the early legislation of the Islamic Republic of Iran (IRI) are relevant to the questions faced by Muslim women elsewhere. These advances, however, are less due to Islamic feminist reinterpretations of the Quran and the early Islamic period than to their effective emphasis on the needs of modern society for educated, working women and for lower birthrates. When Khomeini himself wanted to legitimize novel legislation in 1988, he did not appeal to the Quran or to the early Islamic period, but said that the interests of the Islamic state allowed the abrogation even of their central rulings on prayer and pilgrimage. Similar appeal to public interest or welfare is today quite characteristic of scholarship from and about Iran.

Because the story of women in Iran has lessons for women elsewhere, and as it embodies many of the wider problems regarding women's issues, I will make it a case study. Much of the story of the role and position of

women immediately before and since the 1979 revolution has been widely
and ably told. The active participation in the 1978–79 revolution by
women from left to right, with the hope of most women, including leftists
and liberals, that conditions would improve, and the subsequent shock
to many of the annulment of the Family Protection Law of 1967/75, the
imposition of "Islamic dress," and the removal of women from many
spheres of life and work have been covered. So has been the more recent
gradual and incomplete regaining of some rights and roles. Recent scholarly and journalistic work has discussed the emergence of an "Islamic
feminist" trend that fights for women's rights in Islamic terms and reinter-
prets Islam in more woman-friendly and egalitarian ways, and also the
resistance, both vocal and everyday, of many women to reversals of rights,
which has helped bring change. Women's role in the Khatami election and
in other liberalizing electoral and political trends has been highlighted.[25] A
few authors, notably Parvin Paidar and Afsaneh Najmabadi, have written
outstanding analytical accounts of the changing status of and ideological
trends regarding women in twentieth-century Iran—accounts that should
be widely read by all interested in contemporary Iran or in gender.[26]

Among the issues needing further discussion are the often-debated, sensitive, and related questions of whether Islam can become egalitarian for
women; whether societies that call themselves Islamic can recognize and
implement women's rights; and whether, specifically, the IRI can be gender-egalitarian. These questions continue to be contested, rather than re-
solved, not only because they are highly political and involve current strategy and tactics, but also because they all relate to what can be expected
or hoped for in the future and hence are intrinsically not fully resolvable.
All we can use is our understanding of the past and present of both Islamic
and non-Islamic regions and our own convictions regarding appropriate
tactics, which are closely related to that understanding.

The first framing of the question, whether Islam can be gender-egalitarian, is no longer commonly stressed among scholars outside Muslim countries who tend to see global general statements about Islam as an unwarranted reification of a phenomenon that has varied by time or place.
Elements of this question emerged in the contrasting chapters by Nahid
Yeganeh (Parvin Paidar) and Azar Tabari (Afsaneh Najmabadi), in their
pioneering work, *In the Shadow of Islam* (London: Zed, 1981). At that
time Najmabadi thought Islam was a strong barrier to women's equality,
but she has since openly changed her views and formulations. A similar
controversy, also in the eighties, was found in the *New Left Review.*[27]
Today it is mostly nonspecialists who say that Islam is and will continue
to be a barrier to equality. Even specialists highly critical of Islamic regimes' de facto record on human and women's rights, such as Ann Mayer,
suggest that not Islam but those who use its name limit the rights of

women.[28] Despite the current scholarly avoidance of global statements about Islam, it is important to note points rarely found today in scholarship on the Islamic Middle East—for example, that Islamic countries stand lower than economically equivalent non-Muslim countries in the usual indexes of women's welfare compiled by international agencies, and that this is likely to be connected with widespread and long-standing religious-ideological beliefs and practices. Also, although all revealed religions have male-supremacist content, appeals to inegalitarian revealed texts are more common in Islamic areas today than elsewhere.

Today controversy tends rather to center on different but related questions, especially whether it is a good practice for both activists and scholars to encourage, participate in, or ally with the growing movements for bettering the position of women who proclaim themselves Islamic. On the whole, most scholars and other involved persons accept such ties on the part of secularists as the most practical way to promote women's rights in many countries. There are, however, those who decry the intellectual compromises that secularists often make to accept or promote such alliances. Among them is Reza Afshari in a critical article and many of those who write from the point of view of the international movement that centers its appeal on universal human rights.[29] They may point out that no government that calls itself Islamic or upholds Islam as the state religion has been gender-egalitarian, and that these governments, such as those of Iran, Pakistan, and Sudan, have lessened the legal and real status of women as compared to prior governments that did not thus stress Islam. They may also object to women who are not believers pretending to be so and using apologetic rather than factually supportable arguments and scholarship to try to show Islam as basically gender-egalitarian.

Perhaps ironically, the record of twenty years of the IRI seems to provide ammunition both for those who believe in allying themselves with groups working within an Islamic framework, sometimes called Islamic feminists, and for those who believe that such alliances may backfire in the end, strengthening Islamists' ideological and political control and legitimacy. On pragmatic grounds nobody in Iran, male or female, who, especially between 1981 and 1996, questioned the bases of the IRI or Khomeini's rulings and statements, could hope to win a public platform. This reality encouraged activists to work within the framework of the IRI's rules, by, among other things, framing women's demands within the parameters of the IRI and its laws and ideological prescriptions. Therefore, while women's demands, voiced in the press, parliament, and elsewhere, often highlighted such issues as suffering or fairness, overall these demands did not question an Islamic framework.

Resistance to the limits placed on women's rights and status since 1979 contributed greatly to the partial restoration of such rights and status, as did political and economic realities, such as the Iran-Iraq War and the need for women in the labor force.[30] On the other hand, it could be argued that as long as such resistance occurs within an Islamic framework, it reinforces acceptance of an ideological and legal tradition that has overwhelmingly seen women as inferior to men, as subject to male control, as not deserving equal rights in marriage, divorce, child custody, legal status, and inheritance, and so forth. Critics of ideological acceptance of Islam may say that there is no reasonable way to interpret the Quran, hadiths, or shari'a as egalitarian in intent or practice. (Islamist feminists counter by citing Quranic nonlegal verses stressing the equality of all believers, male and female, and say that these, rather than the legal rulings, are the true message of Islam.)

This controversy is part of a wider contestation centering on the question of whether a universalism stressing human rights is the best approach to women's issues for either scholars or activists, or whether it is better to deal with cultural contexts and refrain from strong criticism of countries whose human rights limitations are, or appear to be, largely based on widely believed cultural concepts. This conflict may be more acute for the Islamic Middle East than for most other parts of the Global South for two main reasons: (1) the Quran and Traditions (hadiths), despite revisionist interpretations, contain inegalitarian elements, and a greater proportion of Muslims than of Christians and Jews practice considerable literalism regarding the legal prescriptions of their revealed texts and the laws derived from them. Also, strict observance of Quranic and shari'a rules on personal status and on practices of veiling and seclusion has been more characteristic of the Middle East than of areas that were converted later and not by conquest, such as Southeast Asia, where Quranic strictness is less prevalent; and (2) the long record of Western hostility to Islam, going back many centuries, and of more recent imperialism in the Middle East resulted in a stronger counterreaction to modern Western ideas than in non-Muslim areas. Such factors, along with the failures of many Westernizing nationalist governments, encouraged the rise in Islamism among both men and women, though these were not the only reasons for this rise. In this context, it is possible for some scholars to see the emphasis on universal human rights, or any special publicity given to bad treatment of women in Muslim countries, as primarily a new version of the "civilizing mission" of the imperialists. This is especially true as many imperialist-minded Westerners did stress and often exaggerated the bad position of women in Islamic countries, as many do to this day. Some variety of cultural relativism, which could today also be called multiculturalism or Third-Worldism, is thus prevalent among contemporary liberal and leftist scholars, even though, ironically, it also has great appeal for those who are concerned with defending traditional or government-imposed Islamic practices on the grounds of defending cultural autonomy or difference.[31]

The strength of the counterreaction to Western ways became evident in ideological trends before, during, and immediately after Iran's 1978–79 revolution. The ideological and cultural reaction to attacks on what were considered Islamic practices regarding women and to the wholesale acceptance of Western norms regarding women emerged strongly in Iran during these years. Islamists were able to take advantage of the "two cultures" gap that existed in many countries in the Global South and was very strong in Iran—those in urban popular and bazaar classes tended to follow modified traditions, including veiling and other limits on women, while the new middle and upper classes, with Western-oriented educations and jobs, accepted modern or Western models for women's rights and status. I would argue that the great majority of these models were not exclusively or intrinsically Western, but were rather the result both of socioeconomic changes and of the struggles of women and men that happened to take place first in the West but then appeared elsewhere in varying but related forms. This was not how they were perceived by many involved in what is often called the traditional or Islamic culture, however, who constituted most of the popular classes, especially in urban areas, and also much of the bazaar bourgeoisie.

The Islamists also gained support among some Westernized students, intellectuals, and others because of the association of the autocratic Pahlavis, who increasingly lost support for a variety of reasons, with wholesale Westernization, so that Islamism came, in the 1970s especially, to be seen as the best (or most politically potent) counterideology, rejecting both Pahlavi dictatorship, and Pahlavi Westernism and imperialism. Even secularist liberal and leftist groups and parties were willing to ally with Islamists and greatly underestimated the possibility of their political ascendancy once the old government was overthrown. Some adopted the veil as a form of protest, and even after the revolution some saw positive aspects to hijab, such as reducing class differences in female display, reducing sexual harassment, and ending sexual distraction at work.[32] Similar trends can be seen down to today in several Middle Eastern countries.

Haideh Moghissi has argued in an important book that secular leftists did not seriously promote or defend women's rights. Although she is right in this, it is hard to see that women's rights could have been effectively promoted in the early years of the IRI no matter what leftist groups had done.[33] The total appeal of the anti-Pahlavi movement relied overwhelmingly on the ideology of Khomeini, along with his clerical supporters—an ideology that took a widely believed religion and interpreted it in a politically effective way. His interpretation included antimonarchism, strong resistance to the dominance of foreign powers, especially the

United States, in Iran, and a return to Islamic practices and laws, emphatically including ending modern reforms in the position of women. Khomeini's ideas were far from traditional in many respects, including a new rejection of monarchy, a new claim justifying political dominance by a top cleric, and, regarding women, an endorsement of women's public activism and even a change from opposition to advocacy of women's voting. Nonetheless, returning to and rigidifying what could be called Islamic, traditional, or popular-class standards regarding women was an inseparable part of the ideology of Khomeinism, as of other Islamist ideologies. Just as the position of women had been considered a central question by early oppositional nationalists, so, with a new and powerful rationale, it was now seen as a central aspect of resistance to imperialism and the restoration of morality. The veiling and seclusion of women came to be a major symbolic element in identifying the new Iran as Islamic. Indeed, today it is perhaps the only widely visible thing, in an environment of Western popular culture and expensive consumer goods and advertisements, that proclaims Iran to be Islamic.[34]

I will conclude this section with some personal views on its issues, which can be a subject of discussion. First, secular scholars in the field of Islamic studies, while recognizing the sensibilities and contributions of those who follow or appeal to Islamic models, need not appear as defensive and apologetic about Islam and about current practices in Islamic societies as they often do. This apologetic stance, which often includes a refusal to say anything negative about Islam, while they would do so about other religions, and an unwillingness to expose antiwoman practices that are prevalent in many Islamic societies, sometimes puts such scholars in a position of failing to support publicly women in Islamic societies who are battling such practices. There seems to be an idea that openly opposing widespread policies in some countries (worse in Afghanistan, Pakistan, and Saudi Arabia than in Iran) will hurt scholars' credibility among potential Islamist allies and give comfort to those prejudiced against Islam and the Muslim world. Hence even many progressive activists limit their activity largely to letters and protests that do not get publicity, rather than joining open letters or the like that may be supported by nonspecialists. Though there are some good reasons for this, it may have the unintended effect of isolating rather than helping local people who work for women's rights, such as the Muslim women in Jordan and Pakistan who in 2001 supported and contributed to television documentaries about honor killings in those countries. Recently, there has been a welcome trend among specialists, perhaps especially notable in the Association for Middle East Women's Studies, toward more open criticism of violence against women, deprivation of rights in family law, and other unequal treatment of women. There is, however, a continued defensiveness among specialists and a trend of strong criticism of journalistic books and articles that document actual practices in the Muslim world, such as Jan Goodwin's *Price of Honor: Muslim Women Lift the Veil of Silence on the Islamic World* (New York: Little Brown, 1994). Such books, like past travelers' accounts, should be recognized for presenting facts about women's oppression even as they may be criticized for prejudice or imbalance.

I cannot, however, agree with an opposite tendency, voiced by Azar Nafisi in the *New Republic* and by some others, that sees the IRI's clerical regime, including Khatami as part of it, as incapable of reform.[35] Only time will tell whether reformist clerics like Khatami can carry out their program. On the basis of experience to date, however, it seems to be worth the risk and effort to continue to work for basic reforms by pushing the envelope within a system that, for all its faults, has allowed some opposition via speaking out, election campaigns, publication, and other means. Even the closing of newspapers and arrests of oppositionists in 2001 do not demonstrate that effective opposition is impossible.

CONCLUSION

Perhaps there can be some rapprochement, however incomplete, between those scholars who do not want to attack phenomena that are perceived as Islamic and those who take a more universalist view of reform that does not stress the special features of any region. One route to this is to write and speak in a way that is both more historically contextual and more dialectical than many views that are now voiced. Such an approach would recognize the historical origins of Islamic and Islamist trends, be critical of some past and present impositions of purely Western models, and encourage cooperation with Islamic feminists. At the same time, it would stimulate informed international resistance to discrimination against women in the Muslim world as elsewhere and would not make apologetic statements about Islam that are not really believed even by some of those who now endorse or voice them. Finally, it would not be apologetic or defensive regarding criticisms of current realities in the Muslim Middle East made by noninsiders or nonspecialists, but would treat them for what they are worth. Overreaction to such criticisms hurts the credibility of many scholars of Islam not only in the scholarly community, but also among many local women who are battling retrograde practices in their own countries.

To paraphrase my recent article dealing with such issues worldwide:[36] Too often neither side in the debate between multiculturalist or Third-Worldist feminists and universalist feminists grants significant truth or weight to the other side. A more nuanced perspective would see that women's roles and status at any stage of historical development reflect historical, social, and cultural circumstances, including class and gender systems that favor and are favored by those with wealth and power. Some authors have succeeded in writing in ways that show the advantages for many women at a given stage of societal development of existing conditions, such as the protection family and kinship communities have offered, without implying that old customs are the best ones in modern circumstances. More such scholarship, with more explicit statements of such views, could help overcome the current split between feminists who attack practices in Third World countries and those who spend so much time presenting them in context and opposing Western interference that they are sometimes seen as apologists for traditional and religiously sanctioned forms of gender inequality.

Even in an age that favors some degree of intellectual relativism, past and present phenomena are too often seen as good or bad, rather than as dialectical, involving contradictions and intermixtures of good and bad from the viewpoint of human happiness and fulfillment, at every stage. The history of veiling is an example of the dialectical nature of historical change, as is the rise of fundamentalism, partly in reaction to state capitalism and state-sponsored secularism, which were often associated with the disliked policies of states that did little for large numbers of the population. A dialectical approach is necessary if we are to understand a factor that many nonfundamentalists may find baffling: Why are so many women attracted to, and often active in, fundamentalist movements?

Another example of a topic needing dialectical treatment is the modern development of new ideas of marriage, motherhood, and domesticity. Until recently, feminists treated this as mostly positive, while now its negative features are often stressed, such as the breakdown of women's transclass social groups, paralleling the breakup of larger household units in the modern period. This view risks idealization of past conditions—for instance, a failure to recognize that interclass contacts were heavily based on slavery or servant systems inappropriate to the modern world. Women and men are also sometimes criticized for aping Western practices in the family, as elsewhere, without scholarly recognition that this was not just blind imitation but involved the conscious adoption of practices suitable to new socioeconomic conditions, first experienced by the urban middle and upper classes, but later spreading to others. Needed are clearer statements of the relationship of former gender and family structures to a society's modes of production and governance and the necessary change to this relationship, involving both gains and losses, with the development of dependent capitalism and new types of states and state policies.

The tendency of even some secular scholars to idealize past conditions, whether those in the earliest Islamic period or those that preceded imperialism, while criticizing modern developments, risks inadvertently playing into the hands of the Islamists, who also idealize the past. One may say that relativism is useful insofar as it means situating practices and ideas in their specific past or present context, socioeconomic and political, as well as ideological.[37] On the other hand, understanding the complex reasons why certain ideas and practices, including nonegalitarian ones, became prevalent should not at all preclude scholarly criticism of such practices that takes into account egalitarian and universalist views that are widely seen as appropriate to more modern societies and conditions.[38]

NOTES

Thanks to Azita Karimkhany for checking bibliographical references. I speak of Muslim women in the Middle East rather than Middle Eastern women more generally both because this is where research has been concentrated, rather than on non-Muslim minorities, and because the problems I discuss relate to the treatment of Islam by scholars.

1. For example, the scholarly neglect of women and gender in fundamentalist movements, including Islamic ones, is discussed in Nikki R. Keddie, "The New Religious Politics and Women Worldwide: A Comparative Study," *Journal of Women's History* 10, no. 4 (Winter 1999): 11–34.

2. The influential Moroccan feminist writer Fatima Mernissi is a special case, and analyzing her shifting emphases would require a separate article. In the 1987 revised edition of her 1975 book, *Beyond the Veil: Male-Female Dynamics in Modern Muslim Society* (Bloomington: Indiana University Press, 1987), she lets stand the following: "Sexual equality violates Islam's premises, actualized in its laws, that heterosexual love is dangerous to Allah's order. Muslim marriage is based on male dominance. The desegregation of the sexes violates Islam's ideology on women's position in the social order; that women should be under the authority of fathers, brothers, or husbands. Since women are considered by Allah to be a destructive element, they are to be spatially confined and excluded from matters other than those of the family. Female access to non-domestic space is put under the control of males" (19). In more recent writings she stresses feminist reinterpretations of early Islam.

3. See the remarks of Asghar Fathi in the introduction to his edited *Women and the Family in Iran* (Leiden: E. J. Brill, 1985), 3n6, regarding the widely cited words of Morgan Shuster on women's heroic role in the 1905–11 revolution and the frequent references to Lady Mary Montagu's favorable comparison of Ottoman to Western women.

4. This and related problems of self-censorship are even more acute in anthropology, which deals with living people. See the first two chapters of Sondra Hale,

Gender Politics in Sudan: Islamism, Socialism, and the State (Boulder, CO: Westview, 1996), beginning on 8.

5. Ehud Toledano, *Slavery and Abolition in the Ottoman Middle East* (Seattle: University of Washington Press, 1998).

6. See Janet Afary, *The Iranian Constitutional Revolution, 1906–1911: Grassroots Democracy, Social Democracy, and the Origins of Feminism* (New York: Columbia University Press, 1996); Julia Clancy-Smith, *Rebel and Saint: Muslim Notables, Populist Protest, Colonial Encounters—Algeria and Tunisia, 1800–1904* (Berkeley and Los Angeles: University of California Press, 1994); and Donald Quataert, *Ottoman Manufacturing in the Age of the Industrial Revolution* (Cambridge: Cambridge University Press, 1993). These and other scholars have also published articles about women. An important chapter on upper-status women in tribally based Turkic dynasties can be found in Ann K. S. Lambton, *Continuity and Change in Medieval Persia: Aspects of Administrative, Economic, and Social History, 11th–14th Century* (Albany: State University of New York Press, 1988).

7. Among the anthropological books on areas not discussed that merit mention are Susan Dorsky, *Women of 'Amran: A Middle Eastern Ethnographic Study* (Salt Lake City: University of Utah Press, 1986); Martha Mundy, *Domestic Government: Kinship, Community and Polity in North Yemen* (London: I. B. Tauris, 1995); and Vanessa Maher, *Women and Property in Morocco: Their Changing Relation to the Process of Social Stratification in the Middle Atlas* (Cambridge: Cambridge University Press, 1974).

8. For a discussion and presentation of these authors, see Ruth Roded, ed., *Women in Islam and the Middle East: A Reader* (New York: I. B. Tauris, 1999).

9. See n3. Also for examples of Mernissi's later work, see Fatima Mernissi, *The Veil and the Male Elite: A Feminist Interpretation of Women's Rights in Islam* (Reading, UK: Addison-Wesley, 1991); and *Women and Islam: An Historical and Theological Enquiry* (Oxford: Blackwell, 1991).

10. See especially S. D. Goitein, *A Mediterranean Society: The Jewish Communities of the Arab World as Portrayed in the Documents of the Cairo Geniza*, vol. 3, *The Family* (Berkeley and Los Angeles: University of California Press, 1978).

11. Ronald Jennings, "Women in Early Seventeenth-Century Ottoman Judicial Records—the Shari'a Court of Anatolian Kayseri," *Journal of the Economic and Social History of the Orient* 18 (1975): 53–114; Haim Gerber, "Social and Economic Position of Women in an Ottoman City, Bursa, 1600–1700," *International Journal of Middle East Studies* 12 (1980): 231–44: Abraham Marcus, "Men, Women, and Property: Dealers in Real Estate in Eighteenth-Century Aleppo," *Journal of the Economic and Social History of the Orient* 26 (1984): 138–63.

12. G.-H. Bousquet, *L'Ethique sexuelle de l'Islam*, rev. ed. (Paris: G.-P. Maisonneuve, 1966), chap. 9. Bousquet also notes that despite permission of birth control by several medieval scholars, the ulama and populations of his time opposed it. He concludes, "theory and reality should not be confused, and it is impossible to understand the actual functioning of a social institution by only studying doctrinal texts" (184).

13. "[I]n contrast to the laws regulating marriage, those governing contraception and abortion appear remarkably liberal in the measure of control they allow

women in preventing and terminating pregnancy. . . . In fact . . . these laws may also be seen as entirely in harmony with an androcentric perspective. The legal system that permitted polygamy and concubinage also stipulated . . . that males were economically responsible for their offspring and that if a man's concubine bore him a child, the concubine could not thereafter be sold; she became legally free on the man's death, her child becoming the man's legal heir along with children born to his wives . . . it was evidently economically to men's advantage that wives not bear many children and that concubines . . . not bear any children . . . a wife who did not give birth would present no hardship for the man, because he had the options of divorcing her, taking another wife . . . or taking a concubine." Leila Ahmed, *Women and Gender in Islam: Historical Roots of a Modern Debate* (New Haven: Yale University Press, 1992), 92. G.-H. Bousquet's book, cited in n12 above, cites texts giving more support to practices limiting births of concubines than of wives.

14. Parvin Paidar, *Women and the Political Process in Twentieth-Century Iran* (Cambridge: Cambridge University Press, 1995); Baron, *The Women's Awakening in Egypt*; Margot Badran, *Feminists, Islam, and Nation: Gender and the Making of Modern Egypt* (Princeton: Princeton University Press, 1995). Cynthia Nelson, *Doria Shafik, Egyptian Feminist* (Gainesville: University Press of Florida, 1996).

15. Ahmed, *Women and Gender in Islam*; Guity Nashat and Judith E. Tucker, *Women in the Middle East and North Africa: Restoring Women to History* (Bloomington: Indiana University Press, 1999); *Women in Middle Eastern History: Shifting Boundaries in Sex and Gender*, ed. Nikki R. Keddie and Beth Baron (New Haven: Yale University Press, 1991).

16. Lila Abu-Lughod, *Remaking Women: Feminism and Modernity in the Middle East* (Princeton: Princeton University Press, 1998); *Women, Islam, and the State*, ed. Deniz Kandiyoti (Philadelphia: Temple University Press, 1991); Keddie and Baron, *Women in Middle Eastern History*; *A Social History of Women and Gender in the Modern Middle East*, ed. Margaret L. Meriwether and Judith E. Tucker (Boulder, CO: Westview, 1999); *Women, Family, and Divorce Laws in Islamic History*, ed. Amira E. Sonbol (Syracuse: Syracuse University Press, 1996); *Women in the Ottoman Empire: Middle Eastern Women in the Early Modern Era*, ed. Madeline C. Zilfi (Leiden: E. J. Brill, 1997).

17. Erika Friedl, "The Dynamics of Women's Spheres of Action in Rural Iran," in Keddie and Baron, *Women in Middle Eastern History*.

18. Several chapters in Hambly, *Women in the Medieval Islamic World* (New York: St. Martin's Press, 1998), deal with the higher position of women among Turkic ruling groups.

19. For an up-to-date summary of scholarship on women's history and law, see Annelies Moors, "Debating Islamic Family Law: Legal Texts and Social Practices," in Meriwether and Tucker, *Social History of Women and Gender in the Modern Middle East*. Regarding problems, she writes: "The relation between the information provided by written sources and the reality of social practice always must be questioned. . . . With respect to court actions, authors have pointed out that women may turn to the court to ask one thing . . . in order to get something

else . . . women's turning to the court in itself may have divergent meanings. While such an activity indicates their ability to act in a legal capacity, it may also point to the lack of any other viable options . . . women's access to property does not necessarily imply gendered power; women may claim their share of an inheritance because they find themselves in a highly problematic situation rather than as an expression of strength. A major challenge is then to understand how specific genres of legal writing interact with social relations" (167).

20. Margaret L. Meriwether, *The Kin Who Count: Family and Society in Ottoman Aleppo, 1770–1840* (Austin: University of Texas Press, 1999). Among other important points, Meriwether writes: "Within the household, age hierarchies were as important, if not more important, than gender hierarchies. Older women exercised great influence . . . over both males and females. Young men were often as vulnerable and powerless as young women. With maturity, women, as well as men, acquired positions of greater authority and responsibility. Moreover, short life spans and male mortality sometimes made women de facto heads of households" (211). Other authors note high male mortality as a reason for women's power among the Mamluks.

21. For example, Meriwether writes: "Hatem argues that the weakening of the Ottoman state led to larger kinship structures giving way to a family type in which the power of the patriarch over the extended household was greatly expanded. . . . Linda Schilcher sees a similar connection in Syria between weakening Ottoman control and changes in the family. She argues that the patriarchal extended family emerged there in the late seventeenth century. . . . Two other historians of Egypt take a different view. . . . They . . . do not believe that it [the loosening of Ottoman authority] led to a more patriarchal family. Instead, these changes gave women more room to negotiate with husbands and fathers, greater autonomy within the family, and increased opportunities to amass wealth that in turn provided them more leverage. . . . These advantages were lost with state centralization and modernization in the nineteenth century" (ibid., 6–7). The two historians of Egypt to whom she refers are Afaf Marsot and Nelly Hanna.

22. Afsaneh Najmabadi, "Crafting an Educated Housewife in Iran," in Abu-Lughod, *Remaking Women*; Jasamin Rostam-Kolayi, "The Women's Press, Modern Education, and the State in Early Twentieth-Century Iran, 1900–1930s" (Ph.D. diss., UCLA, 2000).

23. For treatment of late Ottoman topics, see Fanny Davis, *The Ottoman Lady: A Social History (1718–1918)* (London: Greenwood Press, 1986); Geoffrey Goodwill, *The Private World of Ottoman Women* (London: Saqi Books, 1997); and other articles. Among the useful books by sociologists is Nilüfer Göle, *The Forbidden Modern: Civilization and Veiling* (Ann Arbor: University of Michigan Press, 1996).

24. Nikki R. Keddie, "Women in the Limelight: Some Recent Books on Middle Eastern Women's History since 1800," *International Journal of Middle East Studies* 34 (2002): 553–73 [reprinted as Book Two, Part 3 of this volume].

25. These changes have been widely discussed both in well-informed journalistic accounts, notably those of Elaine Sciolino, *Persian Mirrors: The Elusive Face of Iran* (New York: Free Press, 2000), and Robin Wright, *The Last Great Revolu-*

tion: Turmoil and Transformation in Iran (New York: Knopf, 2000), and in the scholarly writings of such writers as Nayereh Tohidi, Haleh Esfandiari, Val Moghadam, Mahnaz Afkhami, and numerous others. See Nikki R. Keddie, "Women in Iran since 1979," *Social Research* 67, no. 2 (Summer 2000): 405–38.

26. Paidar, *Women and the Political Process in Twentieth-Century Iran*; Afsaneh Najmabadi, "Hazards of Modernity and Morality: Women, State and Ideology in Contemporary Iran" in Kandiyoti, *Women, Islam, and the State.*

27. See Reza Hammami and Martina Reiker, "Feminist Orientalism and Orientalist Marxism," *New Left Review* 170 (1988): 93–106.

28. "Although officials of the Islamic Republic have often claimed to be committed to following an Islamic scheme of human rights, it is an oversimplification to say that the post-revolutionary setbacks in human rights are ascribable to Islamic law. There have been progressive ways of interpreting Islamic law that would harmonize its requirements with human rights, as the examples of Mehdi Bazargan and others have shown. It was owing to the predilections of Iran's ruling clerics that Islam was interpreted as requiring extensive curbs on rights and freedoms" (Ann Elizabeth Mayer, "Islamic Rights or Human Rights: An Iranian Dilemma," *Iranian Studies* 29, nos. 3–4 [Summer–Fall 1996]: 269).

29. Reza Afshari, "Egalitarian Islam and Misogynist Islamic Traditions: A Critique of the Feminist Reinterpretation of Islamic History and Heritage," *Critique* 4 (Spring 1994): 13–33.

30. Gender-inegalitarian arguments and effective resistance to them are covered in Haleh Afshar, *Islam and Feminisms: An Iranian Case Study* (London: Macmillan, 1998). In the conclusion of the chapter "The Family and Motherhood," a typical chapter conclusion in this work, Afshar writes: "Thus although the discourse of marriage and women's family duties has been framed in an oppressive context and many of the Islamic Republic laws were formulated to confine women to the sphere of domesticity, over the years there has been a systematic resistance to these retrograde views. Elite Islamist women have linked up with secularist women and, helped by a group reinterpreting Islamist scholars, have set about dismantling all the fundamental assumptions made by the traditionalists. Using Islamic teaching and Koranic texts, they have had a rigorous scholarly and political engagement which is creating some space and freedom for those who are able and willing to insist on and regain their rights" (167).

31. According to Douglas Lee Donoho: "Relativism clearly has a tremendous capacity to serve as the rhetorical justification for repressive practices by ruling elites. The fact that relativism is most often supported by repressive regimes . . . is ample grounds for a healthy skepticism regarding vague claims of cultural or ideological necessity for deviations from specific requirements of human rights norms" (*Stanford Law Review* 27 [1991]: 380, quoted in Mayer, "Islamic Rights or Human Rights"). Others would argue that demands for rapid and total implementation of such norms can be counterproductive.

32. For quotations from working women on these points, see Maryam Poya, *Women, Work and Islamism: Ideology and Resistance in Iran* (London: Zed, 1999). These quotations form an interesting counterpoint to Haleh Esfandiari's quotations from elite women in her revealing work, *Reconstructed Lives: Women*

and Iran's Islamic Revolution (Washington, DC: Woodrow Wilson Center Press, 1997). Some women's acceptance of hijab as a means to avoid sexual harassment should not, however, obviate working for changes in male socialization that would change many men's vision of unveiled women as sexual prey.

33. Haideh Moghissi, *Populism and Feminism in Iran: Women's Struggle in a Male-Defined Revolutionary Movement* (New York: St. Martin's Press, 1994).

34. As dramatically put by Sciolino, "*hejab* . . . is the most visible symbol of the Islamic Republic's power, and so it will be the last to go. I sometimes think that Iran will have some sort of relationship with Israel before it allows its women to go bareheaded" (*Persian Mirrors*, 132).

35. According to Azar Nafisi, "Khatami does not represent the opposition in Iran—and he cannot . . . he had to be, and clearly is, committed to upholding the very ideology his constituents so vehemently oppose" (*New Republic*, February 22, 1999, 24). This article provides a good overall summary of the active role of women in challenging IRI policies. [By 2005 many reformers had given up on Khatami and the Islamic Republic and some came to share Nafisi's view.]

36. Keddie, "The New Religious Politics and Women Worldwide," 26.

37. Regarding Lila Abu Lughod's seminal and rather relativist work *Veiled Sentiments: Honor and Poetry in a Bedouin Society* (Berkeley and Los Angeles: University of California Press, 1986), Sondra Hale writes: "[I]n her work and in that of most experimental ethnographers there is no analysis of the West's and capitalism's impact on the Bedouins. . . . Not dealing with world capitalism's effect on a former pastoral, nomadic people runs the risk of our seeing them as isolated outside of history and culture, and, ultimately romantic" (*Gender Politics in Sudan*, 45). Similar things could be said of some recent presentations of the past and, especially, of the earliest Islamic period.

38. In writing the above, I realize that scholars' tendencies and the pressures on them differ significantly in different parts of the Middle East: In most of the Arab world except Tunisia many scholars accept, or must adjust to, a positive view of the relationship between Islam (as they interpret it) and women; this is true also in Iran, but probably more Iranian than Arab scholars in the West write as secularists, not concerned with defending Islam; and in Turkey women's scholarship has been and is primarily secularist, and those seen as too friendly to current Islam are sometimes criticized by their colleagues.

PART 3

Women in the Limelight: Recent Books on Middle Eastern Women's History since 1800
2002

THE STUDY OF WOMEN in the Middle East was almost dormant for the quarter century after 1945. Since then, it has flowered, especially in the United States but also elsewhere, and it seems useful to take stock via a review of some of the main English-language scholarly books of the past decade that are of special interest to historians, including brief mention of some relevant works in the social sciences. To keep this to a reasonable length, this review concentrates on books relevant to women's history since 1800 on Iran, Egypt, greater Syria, Turkey, and North Africa, and omits journalistic and biographical books, and the important work done in literature and the arts, and also in the books primarily about other subjects. It also omits articles that were published in books not primarily about Middle Eastern women, gender, or the family. It does not claim to include or analyze every significant book, as significance is partly a question of individual judgment and scholarly interests. The article is limited to books published since 1990.

There have been several areas of concentration of recent books on Middle Eastern women's history: (1) books emphasizing the early period of Islam, including changes in certain ideas, laws, and practices from the time of Muhammad until the Abbasids, some of them carrying their issues down to modern times; (2) books on the role of women and the family in the Ottoman Empire, especially its Arab and Turkish provinces, and relatedly, books that include chapters on women in other Turkish or Turko-Mongol-ruled areas, including Safavid Iran, and on Mamluk women; and (3) books on women in modern times. These make use of the greater documentation and participant observation available for this period, and include cultural, biographical, and socioeconomic books as well as works concentrating on women in politics and women's movements. I here limit myself to some of the important works about the modern period, having discussed some works in the other categories elsewhere.[1]

Recent Books on Nineteenth- and Twentieth-Century Middle Eastern Women

Many works on the two past centuries have particular foci important to this period. Among them is what is often called colonialism: however, as the Middle East includes countries that were never colonies but were nevertheless heavily affected by Western economic and political controls—Iran, Turkey, Afghanistan, and most of the Arabian Peninsula— the phenomenon might more broadly be called Western hegemony with colonialism as a subcategory. The impact on women of the increasing ties of the Middle East to the world market has been discussed mainly in articles and in books primarily about other subjects. This impact includes, for popular-class women, loss of land, property, and traditional employment, which decreased in several fields, while jobs in the new economy and in exported handicrafts increased. It also includes urbanization and the coming of more outsiders to villages, both of which uprooted women and changed their lives, often bringing increased veiling and segregation as a reaction to the greater presence of strangers or a sign of emulation of "respectable" town mores.

Growing Western domination also led more middle- and upper-class men and women to have ties to the West and to adopt many Western ways partly as a means to build up national, family, and personal power. There grew up an increasing cultural divide, despite many overlaps and permeable borders, between Westernized and "traditional" classes, which comprised mainly the popular classes and those tied to the old economy. This meant a growing differentiation in gender norms in these classes, with the second group increasingly associated with "traditional" mores, often identified as "Islam," and the first increasingly adopting ways associated with the West.[2] In recent years the movement toward reveiling by some women in the previously Westernized classes has complicated this picture.

The early twentieth century saw the first women's and feminist groups and struggles in several countries, and most of the books discussed that cover these movements recognize the class differences that meant that early feminists were predominantly educated Westernizers who came from the upper and upper-middle classes, and that they met resistance not only from male conservatives and ulama but also from some women. Variants of this phenomenon have existed, and been written about, down to today.

Some scholars on various subjects have emphasized colonial attitudes and practices, including those regarding women. These are often subsumed under the heading "Orientalism," from Edward Said's seminal book, but this seems inadequate as an explanatory term. The West's special hostility to Islam goes back to religious and military confrontations, including early Arab and later Ottoman military advances in Europe and the European conquests of Islamic territory from the Crusades onward. This hostility was more to Islam than to the Orient, with Muslims seen as a dangerous group of unbelievers. In the nineteenth and twentieth centuries, so-called scientific racism arose, which stressed concepts of race more than religion. This was often characterized by a synthesis (or confusion) of language families and race, with Ernest Renan leading in the distinction between two language groups—Indo-European ("Aryan") and Semitic—with the former superior in everything but religion. In the dominant racial scheme, Middle Easterners stood higher than darker peoples; thus these powerful racial attitudes cannot meaningfully be called Orientalism. Specific negative attitudes toward Islam, and especially toward Arabs, that combined religious, racial, and colonial attitudes were widespread in the West, but so were specific negative attitudes toward most peoples of color. Professional Orientalists other than the unusually famous Renan did not play the main role in spreading these attitudes among the public; they were spread more by politicians, missionaries, journalists, and artists and writers—unsurprisingly in a period of Western economic and military advances and growing Western domination of Muslim lands. The erotic exoticization of Middle Eastern women was far more prevalent among artists and writers of fiction and travel accounts than it was among scholars of the Orient. It is in part a linguistic coincidence that both these groups were called Orientalists, as their roles were quite different, even though both are open to many of the criticisms made by Said and others. Some professional Orientalists may be faulted for giving respectability to ideas that were already widespread, including the reification of Islam as the essential independent variable that largely determined the behavior and practices of Muslims. The development and change over time of some of these attitudes—specifically those of Western women toward women in the Islamic Middle East—has been well analyzed and put in changing historical context in Billie Melman's *Women's Orients*.[3] It might be better to speak of anti-Islamic or anti-Arab prejudice when that is what is intended, and of Eurocentrism when that is what is meant, as the term "Orientalism" is today used for such a wide variety of attitudes regarding the Global South that important distinctions are often lost and the word often becomes a substitute for clear thought.

The role of women in Islamic societies was frequently stressed by Westerners sure of their own superiority, and Muslim women were widely seen as little better than slaves, either totally repressed or erotic objects, and as needing Western control or tutelage to gain any rights. Many Westerners saw women's bad conditions as stemming directly from Islam. Such attitudes were expressed and felt most forcefully in colonized countries, and, probably coincidentally, the only countries in the Middle East that were colonized were countries in which Arabic was the main language. This may have contributed to the invidious Aryan-Semitic construction, as the Arabs were the main Middle Eastern speakers of a Semitic language, and it meant a different modern history—of gender, as of other matters—in countries on different sides of the colonized-noncolonized divide, which was also largely the Arab–non-Arab divide. As Margot Badran notes, the timing of colonialism in different Arab countries also had an impact on women's movements, as Egypt, with much internal independence from colonial rule after 1922, was able to become a pioneer in women's organization, while the Arab East (Syria, Lebanon, Iraq, Jordan) did not get independence until later, and their politics concentrated more heavily on nationalist goals, while separate feminist organizations were discouraged.[4]

Another important category comprises two primarily Arabic-speaking countries that were not only colonized but heavily settled by European settlers: Algeria and Palestine. The latter, like other countries from Ireland to South Africa where settler presence was strong, saw far more colonial and settler appropriation of land and domination of the economy, affecting women in specific ways, than did nonsettled colonies. Settler areas worldwide have also seen more prolonged armed struggles, in which women play an important role, as settlers refuse to give up their privileges. They have also seen more denial of their identity by colonizers, many of whom insisted that Algeria was part of France and that Palestinians did not exist. In such areas it is not surprising that activist women long identified overwhelmingly with nationalist struggles, and that for a long time they did not insist on working for women's rights. Connections between gender and colonization have been examined in important books on different Arab countries, notably those by Julia Clancy-Smith and Elizabeth Thompson.[5]

A variable that has entered the social science literature, though not to the degree it merits in the literature on modern women's history, is the great importance in the Middle East of family and lineage ties and power, sometimes connected to tribal organization, even in areas where conjugal families are now predominant. This point is stressed for Lebanon by Suad Joseph and for the Maghreb by Mounira Charrad, who notes the importance for women's rights of overcoming the power of lineages, as has been done by the Tunisian state, but not by the Moroccan, Algerian, or Lebanese states.[6] This is part of a point that is underemphasized in most recent works on Middle Eastern history: the great role of tribes and lineages in the political, socioeconomic, and gender history of the region. It also relates to another understudied category: the effective resistance of various groups to gender reforms, including many religious leaders and their followers, persons tied to lineage and tribal organization, and popular-class people who associate problems brought by imperialism and Westernization with emulating Western ways.

In recent books about the history of women in the past two centuries, there is a geographic concentration of works on Egypt and Iran, with a few significant works on Palestine, greater Syria, North Africa, and Turkey; other areas have been covered mostly in social science works and in articles. The areas discussed here are primarily those that have had books on the history of women and the family. The fine general work on women's history in the Middle East, Leila Ahmed's *Women and Gender in Islam*, explicitly takes Egypt as the only example meaningfully covered in the modern period, as only for Egypt did the author find a substantial body of secondary work to serve as the basis for a narrative.[7] This was more true when the book went to press at the opening of the 1990s than it is today. A more comprehensive view of women in the modern period is found in the sixty-page chapter by Judith Tucker in the useful and up-to-date general *Women in the Middle East and North Africa*, edited by Guity Nashat and Judith E. Tucker and covering all of the major countries of the Middle East.[8]

Turkey

One near-omission from the historical-book literature on women in Western languages deserves comment: women in the late Ottoman Empire and in the pre-1945 period in Turkey. Although more recent Turkey has seen important works by a number of pioneering anthropologists and sociologists—several of them Turkish women—who have written and continue to write important works on contemporary conditions, these scholars have rarely worked in Ottoman sources. Indeed, the widespread lack of knowledge of Ottoman Turkish among both Western and Turkish scholars interested in modern subjects has produced a gap in women's history scholarship for this period that is only beginning to be filled, in part by recent works in Turkish. Too often, for example, it has been said that there were no significant women's organizations or programs until Atatürk imposed "state feminism." This is turning out to be untrue. Women's newspapers and magazines have now been gathered in one Turkish library, and they are beginning to be used in historical study—especially, thus far, in Turkish. Some of the work done in Turkish is indicated in two chapters of Zehra F. Arat's *Reconstructing Images of "The Turkish Woman"* summarizing such work in a collection with several historical chapters.[9] Among this book's historical chapters are those by Palmira

Brummett on the Ottoman satirical press in 1908–11; by Aynur Demir-direk on the Ottoman women's movement; by K. Pelin Başci on American missionary texts on women; by K. E. Fleming on Zia Gökalp and women's reform; and by Zehra F. Arat on educating the daughters of the republic. The most historical chapter in *Women in Modern Turkish Society*, edited by Sirin Tekeli, is by Nora Şeni, on women's fashions in Istanbul's satirical press.[10]

A major exception to the lack of unified books on Turkey relevant to modern women's history is Alan Duben and Cem Behar's *Istanbul Households: Marriage, Family and Fertility, 1880–1940*, which applies contemporary methods of demographic history with primary texts and interviews to reconstruct family history in Istanbul.[11] It shows that the average family size even before the late nineteenth century in Istanbul was small; that marriage was late; that family planning was frequent; and that the end of women's childbearing came early, despite the prevalence in the West and in Istanbul itself of opposite assumptions. Hence the demographic transition came as early in Istanbul as it did in many parts of Europe. Istanbul is contrasted to the countryside and to most of the Middle East, in which such phenomena occurred later, if at all. This book shows the importance of demography for historians and the new conclusions that can be drawn from combining demography with texts and interviews. It also goes beyond its title in using primary literary sources, as does a useful book written before 1990, Fanny Davis's *The Ottoman Lady: A Social History from 1718 to 1918*.[12]

The 1990s saw a continued flowering of important social science studies about Turkey, several of which have significance for historians. Among them are Carol Delaney's *The Seed and the Soil* and Jenny B. White's *Money Makes Us Relatives*.[13] Both books have wide implications for periods and areas beyond contemporary Turkey. White's book suggests a major rethinking of the usual separation between family or household labor and capitalist production. She shows that the family organization of labor and small enterprises is often at least partly fictive; that wage labor, exploitation, and capitalist relations are central to this type of enterprise; and that the indigenous denial that women in such enterprises are working allows for greater exploitation at the same time that it provides certain familial protections for women. White shows an economic basis for many customary gender practices and presents a realistic and often disturbing picture of attitudes and behavior toward working-class women that can, on the basis of what we know of other Middle Eastern areas, be usefully applied to other countries and earlier periods. Among the useful works by Turkish social scientists is Nilüfer Göle's provocative and original *The Forbidden Modern*, which discusses veiling and Islamism among contemporary Turkish women.[14]

Iran

The most comprehensive work on women in any country in the twentieth century is Parvin Paidar's *Women and the Political Process in Twentieth-Century Iran.*[15] As a historical sociologist, Paidar hesitates less in making large generalizations based on secondary works than some historians would, and her boldness serves the field well. Paidar provides a good account of the roles women have played in the twentieth-century political process, despite some errors regarding the early decades of the century, with which she is less familiar than she is with the later ones. Her book is part of a trend showing that women had more important and varied political roles than might be imagined from the prevalence of veiling and seclusion. In addition, like a number of authors dealing with the Middle East, she shows how politically crucial questions regarding women's roles have been for more than a century. These debates and the state acts relating to them are central to her book.

Paidar shows the diversity by class, region, language, and religion in the premodern condition of women—an approach found in several other works. Iran was different from the Arab world in the picture of the past constructed by its educated nationalists, male and female. Whereas Arab nationalists, both religious and secular, predominantly held a positive view of early Islam and its Prophet, Iranian (like Turkish) nationalists often did not. Rather, they stressed the pre-Islamic virtues of their ethnic group. Since the late nineteenth century, Iranian intellectual and middle-class nationalists have constructed an idealized pre-Islamic Iran, with all the modern virtues they want, including a more equal position for women. Paidar recounts this process well. In Iran, not only Westerners but also local nationalists often traced the bad position of women to Islam and to the Arab Islamic conquest, though a few spoke instead about misinterpretations of true Islam.

In Iran, as elsewhere, it was often wealthy, well-educated women and men more tied to Western ways and interests who became pro-feminist in their writings and activities, while poor men and women, as well as those of the bazaar classes, tended to defend older mores. Paidar finds this split already in the 1906–11 revolution, and it was dramatic in the 1978–79 revolution and its immediate aftermath, with advocates of forced veiling mainly in the urban popular and bazaar classes and opponents mainly bourgeois.

Paidar describes the partial achievements for women under the two Pahlavi shahs, especially the Family Protection Law of 1967 and 1975 that embodied new rights for women in marriage, divorce, and child custody. Although this law and others favoring women were reversed in the early years of the Islamic Republic, a combination of secular and religious women has been able over the years to reinstate some of the provisions of these laws and end several discriminatory measures. The importance of advances in girls' education, birth control, and women's health under the Islamic Republic are perhaps not adequately stressed, as Paidar follows a trend in feminist writings of emphasizing legal advances and changes brought by women's struggles, more than changes favorable to women brought by government social policies. She gives a good summary of the women's movement and the women's press, building on the pioneering work by Eliz Sanasarian, *The Women's Rights Movement in Iran.*[16]

Paidar is nuanced: nationalists and socialists were not as gender-egalitarian as a first reading of their ideas would suggest, nor were Islamists as uniformly antiwoman as their enemies claimed. Throughout the twentieth century, in Iran (as elsewhere) opposition groups, whether nationalist, liberal, socialist, or communist, postponed work for women's rights until after the future victory, and nearly all had subordinate women's auxiliaries who were told to work for the group's main goal. Women's demands, however, have not been as restricted as these groups would wish, and in these groups and in women's organizations and writings women pushed successfully for several reforms throughout the century.

A number of other books have added importantly to the picture of Iranian women summarized by Paidar. A few works give a more extensive picture of women and gender in the 1906–11 revolution, notably Janet Afary's extensive and detailed treatment of women's activities in her *The Iranian Constitutional Revolution, 1906–1911*, which usefully expands on work on this subject pioneered by Mangol Bayat.[17] A monograph detailing male discourse and ultimate inaction regarding one group of women in this period is Afsaneh Najmabadi's *The Story of the Daughters of Quchan.*[18] Since Sanasarian's book there are no others that concentrate on the Pahlavi period, though there is some good work in articles, collected works, and dissertations, among which Houchang Chehabi's article on unveiling under Reza Shah, which disproves many commonly accepted "facts," deserves special mention.[19] An important book by Camron Amin covers the late Qajar and early Pahlavi periods.[20]

Most recent works cover Iran since 1979, with some of them also discussing the late Pahlavi period. Notable are works that discuss particular classes of women on the basis of on-site study and interviews. The lives and often surprising thoughts of educated women are beautifully caught in the edited interviews presented in Haleh Esfandiari's *Reconstructed Lives: Women and Islamic Revolution.*[21] Equally original is Maryam Poya's book, based on extensive work and interviewing in the Islamic Republic, *Women, Work and Islamism.*[22] Among other things, Poya shows that far more women work for wages than is suggested by the official figures of the Islamic Republic. Not only is women's unwaged work not counted, but even urban women wage workers are very often not listed to the government, mainly in order to escape government taxes and workplace regulations. (Much of this was also true under the Pahlavis and in many Middle Eastern statistics.) Another important work on popular-class women is Homa Hoodfar's short work based on observation of female volunteer health workers, which documents the government's program to enlist local women to deal with women's health and birth control in their neighborhoods. It also shows that many of these women become local social activists.[23]

Other significant books on women in the Islamic Republic include the collection, edited by Mahnaz Afkhami and Erika Friedl, *In the Eye of the Storm: Women in Post-Revolutionary Iran*, whose authors include Patricia Higgins, Fatemeh Moghadam, Hamid Naficy, and the two editors.[24] Two books by Haideh Moghissi use primary and sometimes participant research to support important if sometimes controversial views. Her *Populism and Feminism in Iran: Women's Struggle in a Male-Defined Revolutionary Movement* argues that movements in opposition to the Pahlavi dictatorship, however leftist or gender-egalitarian in theory, in practice did very little for women and (like such movements elsewhere) told women to wait until the movement's main goals were achieved before putting forth gender-egalitarian demands.[25] Moghissi's *Feminism and Islamic Fundamentalism: The Limits of Postmodern Analysis* is polemical but well worth reading even by those who may not accept everything she argues.[26] This analysis criticizes cultural relativists who have increasingly emphasized the positive in traditional or Islamic beliefs and practices, and, in particular, criticizes feminists who have put aside parts of their programs or analyses in order to join forces with Islamist women who may agree with them on some issues but not on many important ones. Some readers may accept much of her analysis but still defend the alliances she decries as the only way to achieve any important women's goals in a country such as Iran.

A more favorable view of cooperation by feminists with Islamist reformers is presented or implied in books by Haleh Afshar and Ziba Mir-Hosseini cited later and in various articles by Afsaneh Najmabadi and Nayereh Tohidi. The Iranian women mentioned here as writing about Iran since 1979 were nearly all active in the 1970s. Mahnaz Afkhami, minister of women's affairs in the 1970s, and Haleh Esfandiari were leaders in the government-sanctioned but often effective women's organization. They have not adopted the hostility to every act of the Islamic Republic espoused by one group of exiles. Most of the other scholars emerged from leftist movements in opposition to the Pahlavi regime, and their ideas have evolved in different ways, ranging from the leftist, Marxist-influenced feminism of some to the postmodernist feminism of Najmabadi, expressed in a number of articles and in *Women with Mustaches and Men without Beards: Gender and Sexual Anxieties of Iranian Modernity*, which deals with the modern history of gender and sexuality in an original way. A different line of ideological division is between the majority who accept alliances with Islamist reformers, and working within the current political structure, and those who are pessimistic about this tactic. Haleh Afshar's *Islam and Feminisms* is a survey of its topic in Iran from the viewpoint of one who believes in cooperation with gender-oriented reformers among the believers.[27]

The anthropologist Ziba Mir-Hosseini's first book, *Marriage on Trial. A Study of Islamic Family Law: Iran and Morocco Compared*, is based largely on participant observation of the two legal systems and underlines how differently Islamic law can operate in two very different contexts.[28] It also shows how different the real picture of marital and divorce questions may be from what is presented in court. (In the United States before some states adopted no-fault divorce laws, many of the causes given in court for divorce were, are are, in other states, similarly fictional.) This book, along with others on current operation of Islamic courts, provides a warning against taking past court records too literally as a reflection of reality. Mir-Hosseini's second book, *Islam and Gender: The Religious Debate in Contemporary Iran*, recounts her discussions with ulama, especially in the city of Qom, with emphasis on a very few reformist figures.[29] The discussions are interesting, but it is worth noting that reform in women's status under the Islamic Republic thus far is more due to struggles and to contemporary realities than it is to advocacy by reformist clerics or to new interpretations of Islam. Another anthropologist, Shahla Haeri, also combines legal knowledge with participant observation, in *Law of Desire: Temporary Marriage in Shi'i Iran*, a book that shows how the distinctively Shi'i institution of temporary marriage affects its female practitioners, and demonstrates that it has several uses beyond the obvious and primarily sexually oriented ones.[30]

With the continued journalistic and scholarly interest in the evolution of the Islamic Republic, especially since the series of reformist-majority elections for president and Parliament since 1997 and the clampdown on the press and arrests of reformists in 2000–2001, more studies of Iran can be expected. Although it is understandable that most such studies focus on the struggles of male and female reformers, it would be worth looking more deeply into the causes, problems, and results of the major advances made in this period in such areas as women's health and education, including the very successful birth control program in which, as Hoodfar has shown, popular-class female health workers have played an important part and have sometimes become leaders in local advocacy groups.

Egypt and the Arab World

Egypt rivals Iran for the number of significant books about women. The history of women's rights in the two countries provides significant contrasts and questions that so far have not been dealt with comparatively at any length, but deserve comparative consideration, as do comparisons with other countries, including Turkey and Tunisia. Egypt has had the strongest, longest, and most varied women's movement of all the countries of the Middle East, and there has been significant social change in fields such as health, education, family structure and practices, and women's employment in paid positions. Yet in terms of changing the laws affecting women, Egypt has done less than Tunisia, Turkey, or Iran under the Pahlavis. This should lead scholars to try to weigh the relative importance of social change as compared with legal change, and of women's movements and struggles as compared with state action that may have been only slightly influenced by such movements and may have other causes. As a preliminary generalization, it is notable that the greatest changes in women's *legal* status have come in countries with strong secular nationalist rulers (Turkey, Iran, Tunisia) or Soviet-style rule (South Yemen, the Muslim Soviet republics), and not necessarily in the countries with the longest and strongest women's movements or the strongest elected parliaments. And although legal rights are far from being absolute indicators of women's status, the inability of Iran's clerical rulers to make their total reversal of such rights stick is one indication that legal changes are not insignificant.

Despite the relatively small results of Egypt's women's movements and writings in the legal sphere, they were important in other spheres, including women's education, both formal and informal; job training; changing the image of women; and expanding public roles and employment for women, including the achievement of woman suffrage and eligibility for election in 1956. A major book on what was locally called the women's awakening is Beth Baron's *The Women's Awakening in Egypt: Culture, Society, and the Press*.[31] Baron shows that, although men had been considered the important early figures introducing women's rights, a large number of female writers expressed themselves on these rights and other issues, particularly in the new women's press that began and flowered in the late nineteenth and early twentieth centuries. Baron's book pioneered the study of the women's press, a topic now being researched for other countries, including Iran and Turkey. After giving biographical studies of important female journalists between 1890 and 1920, Baron discusses different positions taken in the women's press regarding the rights of women and the campaign for women's education. Very original is her discussion of women and the family, in which she deals with new forms of family life and structure and with the campaign for what many call scientific domesticity.

From the viewpoint of the twenty-first-century West, a stress on domesticity by female writers might seem old-fashioned and not at all liberating. However, just as in the West, the nineteenth-century movement for domesticity was a necessary stage in the Middle East's development of modern women's roles in such areas as hygiene, rationality in household management, and child rearing: it also involved women's education. Although some writers today stress the virtues of premodern times, when women from different classes mixed with one another more than they do today, this mixing was intertwined with systems involving large households, harems, and slaves and servants, while the new domesticity was congruent with the decline or end of these conditions and the creation of more autonomous nuclear families. Women of classes that formerly looked down on manual work and had few ideas about hygiene became educated, and educated others, on how to manage a household of a new type. As usual, gains in one area involved losses in others, and in some ways scientific domesticity in both East and West was a straitjacket, binding women to unnecessarily long hours of cleaning, cooking, and child rearing, and placing important new limits on their behavior and language. The frequent tendency to see scientific domesticity and other ideas proposed by educated women as blind copying of the West, however, leaves out both the strong indigenous elements intertwined in all modernization and the local socioeconomic changes that made certain ideas appropriate to capitalism or partial capitalism (even dependent capitalism) everywhere. Baron's book was the first to introduce the domesticity debate as being of major importance for recent women's history, which cannot be limited to a study of women's movements and struggles. Baron recognizes the dialectical, contradictory nature of the domesticity project, a point developed further by Afsaneh Najmabadi and others in *Remaking Women*, edited by Lila Abu-Lughod.[32] Chapters in that book also carry further another point noted by Baron's book and articles: that the growing role of the conjugal as compared to the natal family could be both constraining and liberating for women.

In addition, Baron analyzes a number of influential female intellectuals who took advantage of the spread of literacy and cheap printing to diffuse a variety of new ideas regarding the roles and capabilities of women. She, like Leila Ahmed, breaks with the tendency to cite only men as significant writers on women's and other issues and presents a wide range of influential and intelligent women who for the first time published their very varied views on an even wider range of issues.

Margot Badran's *Feminists, Islam, and Nation: Gender and the Making of Modern Egypt* presents a comprehensive survey of women's activism in Egypt in the twentieth century until the suppression of independent women's organizations and their merger into state-controlled organizations after 1956. Egypt has had the most dynamic and varied women's movement of any Middle Eastern country, not only because of its early exposure to the West and to capitalist forces, but also because it had the longest modern period of any Middle Eastern country when independent feminist organization was possible—from before World War I until 1956. Iran and Turkey, just when independent feminist organizations were flourishing in Egypt, came under strongman regimes that disallowed such organizations. (In the 1930s, the government-supported women's organization in Turkey was disbanded after women got the vote, and in Iran, women's groups were increasingly brought under a single government-controlled umbrella organization and some women's publications were ended at the same time that unveiling was introduced.) Syria and Iraq had only a few years between colonial regimes and local autocracies, and autocracy with a tribal flavor characterized the Arabian Peninsula.

Egypt, as described by Badran, was hence unique in having a feminist organization of international importance and affiliations, the Egyptian Feminist Union (EFU), headed for decades by the outstanding pioneer of Egyptian feminism, Huda Sha'rawi. Badran gives particularly detailed coverage to Sha'rawi, including her multifaceted activities, writings, and partially unpublished memoirs, to which Badran had access. The campaigns of Sha'rawi and the EFU on a range of issues, including political and legal rights, as well as their social service and educational and training activities, are well covered, as are some of the difficulties faced by this movement in a male-dominant culture. The final chapter tells of the role of Egyptian feminists in Pan-Arab feminism and of the end of independent women's organizations in the Arab world.

Because she had so much more to discuss about Egypt than one would in a history of feminism in any other Middle Eastern country, Badran perhaps lacked the time and space to cover the surrounding social, economic, and political circumstances to the degree that Parvin Paidar and Elizabeth Thompson do in their books. There may also be some overemphasis on Sha'rawi as compared with feminists with a different outlook, such as Doria Shafik and the leftist Inji Aflatun, who do, however, get some coverage. The actual and potential conflict with Islamist women, which began in the period Badran covers, also gets rather brief treatment. Badran's book, however, is important and pioneering in being the only work to give a coherent narrative and show the importance of a movement that has been quite consistently underestimated in more general histories of Egypt.

Cynthia Nelson's *Doria Shafik, Egyptian Feminist: A Woman Apart* is an extensive, well-written, and readable biography of one of the main figures in Egypt's women's movement, based partly on her unpublished memoirs and including intelligent discussion of the surrounding Egyptian situation.[33] Shafik, who achieved several educational firsts for an Egyptian woman, including a *doctorat d'État* from the Sorbonne, was the founder of the second important Egyptian feminist organization, the Bint al-Nil Union; editor of its various publications; and a prolific writer and poet. She was also an increasingly controversial figure, who had tense relations with several other women's leaders and was often regarded as too French, too Western, too upper bourgeois, and not identified enough with ordinary Egyptians, despite her strong nationalist record. After she launched a hunger strike in 1957, protesting primarily Gamal Abdel Nasser's incomplete granting of full citizenship rights to women, she was confined to house arrest for three years, spent the rest of her life in partly self-imposed isolation, and committed suicide in 1975. Her life story suggests some of the conflicts, felt by others less dramatically, between those liberal feminists who took many of their models from the West and Middle Eastern believers in various ideologies in which women's issues either played a secondary role or were interpreted in nonfeminist ways, whether these ideologies were conservative, nationalist, socialist, or Islamist. Such contradictions were found not only in Egypt but also in the other countries of the Middle East, in all of which feminists often had to make tactical decisions about how strongly to push demands for gender equality.

Leila Ahmed's *Women and Gender in Islam* devotes its longest section to the twentieth century and takes Egypt as its model for discussion, an approach that allows a deep and enlightening consideration of Egypt but does not deal with the important differences between Egypt and other countries. A briefer general work, which incorporates the results of others' research to analyze a major topic in three twentieth-century periods, is Selma Botman's *Engendering Citizenship in Egypt*.[34]

Syria and Lebanon

An outstanding work that shows the very distinct pattern of women in twentieth-century Syria and Lebanon is Elizabeth Thompson's *Colonial Citizens: Republican Rights, Paternal Privilege, and Gender in French Syria and Lebanon*.[35] Thompson's is one of the very few works to deal extensively not only with women but also with the local and colonial power structures and with all the major opposition movements—nationalist, communist and trade unionist, and populist Islamic. The study of women and gender here takes its rightful place as a central issue in politics and society, which both affects and is affected by a number of other major groups and issues.

Although it is difficult to summarize all the important points in this complex work, some of which do not center on women and gender, points that do emerge strongly and are relevant to other countries include the following: (1) the women's movement in Syria and Lebanon, although it had many strengths, was never strong enough seriously to challenge dominant colonial and local patriarchal structures and forces, among them a growing hostile populist Islamic movement; (2) the movement for women's rights (as in many other countries) was mainly a movement of elite, educated women, while many popular-class women showed no signs of being concerned with it or its programs; (3) at several crucial points, other actors made implicit or explicit alliances with one another at the expense of women or women's demands; this included nationalists' giving in to Islamist demands and many other cases; (4) the (now often ignored) major role of the communist parties of Syria and Lebanon and of trade-union activities included effective support of the growing body of female workers, even though the communists, like the nationalists, backed down on their earlier espousal of women's political demands; and (5) as elsewhere, many women participated courageously in nationalist struggles for independence, but when independence came, the nationalist elite did very little for women—less overall than the colonial welfare state had done in the last years of colonial rule.

Thompson usefully suggests the need for comparative studies and notes that colonized countries such as Syria and Lebanon—where the main struggle was against foreign rule, and where nationalists wanted to distinguish themselves from Europeans—had a harder time enforcing a ("Western-style") approach to women than did noncolonial Iran and Turkey.[36] But (as she suggests), particular situations are contradictory and complex: colonized Tunisia behaved like some noncolonized countries, while noncolonized Iran saw an anti-Westernizing backlash at the same time that Syria moved toward secularist government and away from governmental compromise with Islamists. Another difference in categories Thompson notes is between republican France, which supported republican institutions in the Levant, and monarchist Britain, which supported monarchies, affecting local politics. Thompson's coverage of the importance of leftist political and trade-union groups in women's history could usefully be emulated by historians of other Middle Eastern countries, where the emphasis has been on the deficiencies of the Left regarding women rather than on significant positive contributions.

Although most recent books try to put women into a broader historical context, Thompson's book is probably the historical work that comes the closest to the aims stated in Diane Singerman and Homa Hoodfar's fine collection on contemporary questions, *Development, Change, and Gender in Cairo: A View from the Household*:

Though the early profusion of research on women expanded the breadth of our knowledge available on women and gender relations, it also made it clear that focusing on women and theoretically and methodologically isolating them as a meaningful social category is as partial as a male-centric point of view. It perpetuates an inaccurate and incomplete view of society. Moreover, this approach could marginalize women, hence defeat the very purpose it set out to achieve. The paramount goal must be to integrate the study of women into the study of society. . . . Even in the most segregated societies . . . men and women are in constant interaction and therefore any research should take account of this context.[37]

Palestine

An important work is Annelies Moors's *Women, Property and Islam: Palestinian Experiences, 1920–1990*.[38] Moors combines extensive anthropological participant observation and interviewing with the use of archival sources to produce a highly complex picture of her subject, with its many variations by time, place, and class. She has chosen a particularly complicated historical subject as her area of research: Palestine (in and around Nablus). This area has seen an unusual number of wrenching historical changes in the period covered, with three separate wars leading from Ottoman rule to British Mandate, Jordanian annexation, Israeli occupation, and the intifada and after. Moors traces the impact of these events on gender and recounts many women's individual stories, giving general conclusions. She shows how legal and judicial protections for women, many of them emphasized in recent historical works based on Ottoman judicial records, predominantly benefit certain classes of women, and how court judgments are often not enforced. She is also convincingly critical of Jack Goody's treatment of Islamic dower payments (which, I might add, is based mostly on a few cases that their authors did not claim represented all of the Islamic Middle East).

Moors shows how modern developments have affected different classes of women, with middle- and upper-class women as well as some from the popular classes able to benefit from new educational opportunities to get professional jobs that give them some economic independence. Rural women, however, have largely seen their importance in agriculture decline, which often makes them more dependent on men and less in control of property than before. A trend found in all classes is toward greater importance for the conjugal family and less for the natal family, which has led to more pooling than formerly of conjugal property and more individual choice of marriage partners. (This trend toward increased centrality of the often nuclear conjugal family is also noted in other works, such as the Hoodfar and Singerman and Abu-Lughod collections cited earlier and in articles by Baron.)

Among the issues Moors discusses are inheritance and direct and delayed dower in terms of different classes and changing circumstances. She gives greater subtlety to the generally correct notion that urban more than rural women tend to inherit according to Islamic law, noting that the type of property (land is rarely inherited by women) and women's agreement not to impoverish poor brothers further are involved. Moors also gives details on relations with the Israeli occupiers, with many women used as cheap labor in textile factories, and others affected by the jailing of male relatives and by refusing to work in Israel—or, in some cases, for Israelis in Palestine. The Palestinian women's situation is in some ways unique, owing to the Israeli occupation, but Moors makes many points that are applicable to women outside Palestine. The combination of anthropological and archival sources and methods, including an appreciation of change over time, is especially to be commended.

An important and comprehensive anthropological work that covers twentieth-century history and theoretical questions, although it does not use many primary written sources, is Julie M. Peteet's *Gender in Crisis: Women and the Palestinian Resistance Movement*.[39] Soon to appear is a comprehensive historical study of the Palestinian women's movement in 1920–48 by Ellen L. Fleischmann, *The Nation and Its "New" Women*.[40]

North Africa

The most varied, often brilliant, discussions of women in North Africa since 1800 are the two books by Julia Clancy-Smith mentioned earlier: the prize-winning *Rebel and Saint* and the coedited *Domesticating the Empire*. Some of her articles in collections about Middle Eastern women are also noted in the section on collections,[41] and she has published other major articles. Clancy-Smith has written about many subjects, including education, crafts, religion, politics, and the relations of French men and women involved in the colonies with different North African women and men.

The contrasting twentieth-century gender history of Algeria, Morocco, and Tunisia is well analyzed in a book by Mounira Charrad.[42] In all three areas, tribal groups were historically very powerful, and governments were limited in their control of tribes, especially those far from governmental centers. Charrad analyzes the main historical features of Islamic family law, not with the common stress on individual women's rights, but as reflecting the interests of the extended male family line as far more important and permanent than those of the conjugal family. She thus interprets wives' property's being kept separate from husbands' and women's carrying second names coming from their fathers, not their husbands, as signs of the superior role of the agnatic family. This is also reflected in North Africa in the relative ease of divorce and the return to the agnatic family by divorced or widowed women. Much of this analysis is applicable in the rest of the Middle East, as is the discussion of tribal law and custom, which, for all its variations, was and is predominantly even more favorable to the agnatic patriarchal family than is Islamic law. Charrad shows that only a state such as Tunisia that could put down the power of the tribes and effectively centralize rule could get rid of most of the patriarchal features of law. Charrad's emphasis on tribal power could be applied to much of the Middle East and could be supplemented by a stress on religious forces, comprising both those involved in traditional religious institutions and those attracted to newer Islamic politics. Another work on North Africa with some points about women's history is Marnia Lazreg's *The Eloquence of Silence: Algerian Women in Question*.[43]

WORKS ON CONTEMPORARY SOCIAL SCIENCE

Several works of social science significant for historians were discussed in the earlier sections on Turkey and Iran. The Arab world, and especially Egypt, has been the particular focus of several important anthropological, sociological, and political science works of importance to historians, and I do not have the space to discuss them individually here. Historians should read social science works for many reasons, among which are the controls they give regarding the reliability and probable direction of bias in the documents on which historians must rely. Among the many points relevant to women's history that arise from such contemporary scholarly literature are these: (1) the great variability by time, place, class, and ethnic group in women's positions; (2) the degree to which Islamic law regarding women is and is not observed in practice—for example, women rarely inherit land (and some other property) according to law, but may be (partially?) compensated in other ways by their natal families; (3) the degree to which courts' documents and conclusions may deviate from the real situation and that court decisions may not be carried out; (4) the huge underestimation of women's work in official statistics and the real nature of women's agricultural and "family" labor; and (5) the importance of the attitude and biases of researchers, some of whom tend to make women's situations look relatively good, while others stress male dominance and widespread female oppression and suffering.

Several social science works center on women and the family in contemporary Cairo, including Evelyn Early's *Baladi Women of Cairo*; Homa

Hoodfar's *Between Marriage and the Market: Intimate Politics and Survival in Cairo*; Arlene Elowe Macleod's *Accommodating Protest: Working Women, the New Veiling, and Change in Cairo*; Diane Singerman's *Avenues of Participation: Family, Politics, and Networks in Urban Quarters of Cairo*; Unni Wikan's *Tomorrow, God Willing: Self-Made Destinies in Cairo*; and Sherifa Zuhur's *Revealing Reveiling: Islamist Gender Ideology in Contemporary Egypt.*[44] These are primarily well-researched anthropological or sociological works that provide in-depth studies of the lives and ideas of popular-class and lower-middle-class women. They afford new pictures and analyses of women and gender in Cairo that are not matched for any other Middle Eastern area, and they provide material for future comparative and historical studies that could go beyond the Middle East. The books by Macleod and Zuhur shed important light on the phenomenon, widespread in the contemporary Muslim world, of reveiling of previously unveiled women, showing that there are many reasons for it beyond the Islamist or religious ones. One may wonder, however, whether Macleod's subjects' rejection of fundamentalism did not apply to extremist groups rather than to nonviolent Islamists.

Another work on contemporary Egypt, Nadje Al-Ali's *Secularism, Gender and the State in the Middle East: The Egyptian Women's Movement*, discusses contemporary secularist women, who in works on women's recent ideas have been somewhat neglected in favor of Islamist women. Although it is full of important ideas and insights, the book suffers from overcomplexity in its language and theorizing.[45]

In a class by itself is Laurie A. Brand's outstanding *Women, the State, and Political Liberalization*, which discusses these topics in depth in the period of liberalization in Morocco, Jordan, and Tunisia against a convincing theoretical background with comparisons to Eastern Europe and Latin America.[46] A work that covers the whole region from Turkey and the Arab world through Iran and Afghanistan and includes several points of interest to historians is Valentine M. Moghadam's *Modernizing Women.*[47]

Several of the most useful anthropological works about the Arabian Peninsula were published in the 1980s and hence will not be mentioned here. Of the anthropological works about Yemen relevant to women's history published in the 1990s, Martha Mundy's *Domestic Government: Kinship, Community and Policy in North Yemen* is an important theoretical contribution.[48] Going beyond my self-imposed geographic boundaries is Sondra Hale's pioneering and comprehensive *Gender Politics in Sudan.*[49]

Although these works have been divided by country rather than topic, it should be noted that an important theme is the recent rise in Islamism, which is discussed in a number of the works mentioned here and in Jenny White's *Islamist Mobilization in Turkey*, which compares and contrasts men's and women's expectations of Islamism.[50]

COLLECTIONS WITH A MODERN FOCUS

The 1990s saw the publication of many collections of articles, some more useful and focused than others. Several have a modern emphasis, although they may go back earlier in time and beyond the Middle East in geography. One of the most notable is *Women, Islam and the State*, edited by Deniz Kandiyoti, which intelligently analyzes the intersection of the three title items in Turkey, Iran, Pakistan, Bangladesh, India, Iraq, Lebanon, Egypt, and Yemen.[51] Also highly focused and including several articles on non–Middle Eastern areas is the collection edited by Valentine M. Moghadam, *Identity Politics and Women*.[52] Comprehensive in its geographic coverage is *Women in Muslim Societies*, edited by Herbert L. Bodman and Nayereh Tohidi.[53] A collection that is both scholarly and activist-oriented is *Muslim Women and the Politics of Participation: Implementing the Beijing Platform*, edited by Mahnaz Afkhami and Erika Friedl.[54]

There are a few collections with fine articles on modern history. One with several authors but more unity than most collections is *A Social History of Women and Gender in the Modern Middle East*, edited by Margaret L. Meriwether and Judith E. Tucker.[55] It includes chapters on work and handicrafts in North Africa by Julia Clancy-Smith; on the state and family by Mervat Hatem; on women's movements by Ellen Fleischmann; on law and social practices by Annelies Moors; and on religion by Mary Hegland. Another well-researched historical collection is *Women, the Family and Divorce Laws in Islamic History*, edited by Amira El Azhary Sonbol.[56] On the modern period (mostly pre–World War I) are original articles by Sonbol on violence against women and by Dalenda Largueche on the disciplining of "disobedient" wives; on French North Africa by Clancy-Smith; on Ottoman Iraq by Dina Rizk Khoury; on Damascus by Najwa al-Qattan; and on Aleppo by Meriwether. Nikki R. Keddie and Beth Baron's *Women in Middle Eastern History* also comprises several articles on modern history, with relevant articles on Turkey by Donald Quataert and Nermin Abadan-Unat; on Iran by Erika Friedl and Mary Hegland; and on the Arab world by Tucker, Clancy-Smith, Baron, Virginia Danielson, and Nelson.[57]

A pioneering work on various topics, many of them historical, is *Remaking Women: Feminism and Modernity in the Middle East*, edited by Lila Abu-Lughod, in which Afsaneh Najmabadi's chapter, "Crafting an Educated Housewife in Iran," is of special interest.[58] It, like other articles in the book, shows the two-sided nature of scientific domesticity, which both presented strong arguments for women's education, which ultimately led to roles outside the home, and limited the contacts among women of different classes and the language that women were free to use. Also of importance to historians in this collection is Khaled Fahmy's chapter, "Women, Medicine, and Power in Nineteenth-Century Egypt," a convincing and well-documented revisionist work showing that Muhammad 'Ali's famous school for midwives (or female doctors), like most of his programs, was undertaken with the needs of the new army in mind, and that, although the women educated in that school held a position that was higher than it would have been otherwise, they were lower in status than the lowest men in the medical system.

In a similar vein is the collection *Reconstructing Gender in the Middle East: Tradition, Identity, and Power*, edited by Fatma Müge Göçek and Shiva Balaghi.[59] Other well-researched collections on particular areas include *Arab Women: Old Boundaries, New Frontiers*, edited by Judith E. Tucker, and *Women in Modern Turkish Society*, edited by Sirin Tekeli.[60] Further useful articles, the contents of which are suggested by the book titles, can be found in *Feminism and Islam: Legal and Literary Perspectives*, edited by Mai Yamani, and *Arab Women: Between Defiance and Restraint*, edited by Suha Sabbagh.[61]

Several important original articles on modern women's history can be found in *Iran and Beyond: Essays in Middle Eastern History in Honor of Nikki R. Keddie*, edited by Rudi Matthee and Beth Baron. These include chapters on Iran by Houri Berberian and Houchang Chehabi; on women's education in North Africa by Julia Clancy-Smith; and on Egypt by Sherifa Zuhur and Beth Baron.[62] Various other collections contain articles on modern history. There are also collections and individually written books that focus on anthropology and social science in areas that are not yet well served by works on women's history including Lebanon and the Arabian Peninsula, especially Yemen, and hence have not been extensively discussed here.

CONCLUSION

The works discussed in this article build on pioneering studies published between 1965 and 1990, such as Lois Beck and Nikki Keddie's edited book *Women in the Muslim World*; Judith E. Tucker's *Women in Nineteenth Century Egypt*; Fatima Mernissi's *Beyond the Veil: Male-Female Dynamics in a Modern Muslim Society*; Lila Abu-Lughod's *Veiled Sentiments: Honor and Poetry in a Bedouin Society*; and several books by Elizabeth Warnock Fernea.[63] Probably the most developed area of subsequent studies concerns women and politics, including women's writings and organizations; feminism; women and the state, including state actions regarding women's political rights, personal status and other laws; and political and religious-political ideologies concerning women and gender. Some scholars have studied the family and domestic sphere, including the rise of conjugal nuclear families, changes in domesticity and child rearing, and the growth in domestic advice literature. Other topics receiving some coverage are ideologies regarding women, including Islamist, conservative, liberal, and leftist ones, and women and nationalism, which crosses these categories. Relatively little coverage in recent historical works has been given to women and work; to especially oppressive aspects of some women's treatment; to sexuality, including different practices and lifestyles; to demography; to ethnic and religious minorities; to rural and tribal areas; to the impact of slavery and its abolition on women and the family; and to evolving ideas of maleness. Surprisingly little coverage has been given to recent legal changes, and there is great need for a book or article that compares, with context, the legal situation and changes in at least the most populous countries of the Middle East or the Islamic world.[64] Some of these areas (though not the legal one) are hard to document, and some are probably avoided because of their sensitivity. In view of the breadth of coverage already achieved in Middle Eastern women's studies, however, scholars should be encouraged to tackle even sensitive topics. These include questions about why most Middle Eastern societies have been more patriarchal, more autocratic, and less economically dynamic than many others in recent times; the relationship of such points to women's status; the reasons for continued or revived conservatism regarding gender-related laws and practices; and the roles of both traditional Islamic forces and Islamist movements in gender relations and ideologies. There has been a tendency, in reaction to common exaggerated criticisms of Middle Eastern societies, to respond apologetically and not to grant that women have faced special problems in the modern and contemporary Middle East, or that economic stagnation in the contemporary Middle East is importantly related to women's status, including low levels of education, health, personal autonomy, and labor-force participation. In my experience, arguments that sound apologetic are simply rejected by most of those who are skeptical or hostile regarding the position of Middle Eastern women. Some skeptics can be convinced by careful presentation of historical background and context, and the actual effects of imperialism and Western hegemony in the Middle East in partially undermining ideas and practices regarding women that are associated with the West, if these are accompanied by analyses of local and regional forces and not by blaming relations with the West for every major problem. Scholars, including those who now understate the importance of women and gender, should also be encouraged to deal with women's history as part of integrated human history, going beyond both gender and geographic boundaries in order to achieve a more holistic and comparative picture than is yet available.[65]

NOTES

Thanks are due to Azita Karimkhany for checking the bibliographical entries.

1. See Nikki R. Keddie, "The Study of Muslim Women in the Middle East: Achievements and Remaining Problems," *Harvard Middle Eastern and Islamic Review* 6 (2000–2001): 26–52, and my "Women in the Middle East since the Rise of Islam," in *Women's History in Global Perspective*, ed. Bonnie E. Smith (Urbana: University of Illinois Press, 2005).

2. See Deniz Kandiyoti, "Islam and Patriarchy: A Comparative Perspective," in *Women in Middle Eastern History: Shifting Boundaries in Sex and Gender*, ed. Nikki R. Keddie and Beth Baron (New Haven: Yale University Press, 1991).

3. Billie Melman, *Women's Orients: English Women and the Middle East, 1718–1918: Sexuality, Religion and Work*, 2nd ed. (Ann Arbor: University of Michigan Press, 1995).

4. Margot Badran, *Feminists, Islam, and Nation: Gender and the Making of Modern Egypt* (Princeton: Princeton University Press, 1995), chap. 12.

5. Elizabeth Thompson, *Colonial Citizens: Republican Rights, Paternal Privilege, and Gender in French Syria and Lebanon* (New York: Columbia University Press, 2000); Julia Clancy-Smith, *Rebel and Saint: Muslim Notables, Populist Protest, Colonial Encounters—Algeria and Tunisia, 1800–1904* (Berkeley and Los Angeles: University of California Press, 1994). See also Julia Clancy-Smith and Frances Gouda, eds., *Domesticating the Empire: Race, Gender, and Family Life in French and Dutch Colonialism* (Charlottesville: University Press of Virginia, 1998), esp. Clancy-Smith's excellent "Islam, Gender, and Identities in the Making of French Algeria, 1830–1962."

6. See the chapters and bibliographical items by Suad Joseph and Mounira Charrad in *Gender and Citizenship in the Middle East*, ed. Suad Joseph (Syracuse: Syracuse University Press, 2000), and Mounira Charrad, *States and Women's Rights: The Making of Postcolonial Tunisia, Algeria, and Morocco* (Berkeley and Los Angeles: University of California Press, 2001).

7. Leila Ahmed, *Women and Gender in Islam: Historical Roots of a Modern Debate* (New Haven: Yale University Press, 1992).

8. Guity Nashat and Judith E. Tucker, *Women in the Middle East and North Africa: Restoring Women to History* (Bloomington: Indiana University Press, 1999).

9. Zehra F. Arat, ed., *Reconstructing Images of "The Turkish Woman"* (New York: St. Martin's Press, 1999).

10. Sirin Tekeli, ed., *Women in Modern Turkish Society* (London: Zed Books, 1995).

11. Alan Duben and Cem Behar, *Istanbul Households: Marriage, Family and Fertility, 1880–1940* (Cambridge: Cambridge University Press, 1991).

12. Fanny Davis, *The Ottoman Lady: A Social History from 1718 to 1918* (New York: Greenwood Press, 1986).

13. Carol Delaney, *The Seed and the Soil: Gender and Cosmology in Turkish Village Society* (Berkeley and Los Angeles: University of California Press, 1991); Jenny B. White, *Money Makes Us Relatives: Women's Labor in Urban Turkey* (Austin: University of Texas Press, 1994).

14. Nilüfer Göle, *The Forbidden Modern: Civilization and Veiling* (Ann Arbor: University of Michigan Press, 1996).

15. Parvin Paidar, *Women and the Political Process in Twentieth-Century Iran* (Cambridge: Cambridge University Press, 1995).

16. Eliz Sanasarian, *The Women's Rights Movement in Iran: Mutiny, Appeasement, and Repression from 1900 to Khomeini* (New York: Praeger, 1982).

17. Janet Afary, *The Iranian Constitutional Revolution, 1906–1911: Grassroots Democracy, Social Democracy, and the Origins of Feminism* (New York: Columbia University Press, 1996); Mangol Bayat-Philipp, "Women and Revolution in Iran, 1905–1911," in *Women in the Muslim World*, ed. Lois Beck and Nikki Keddie (Cambridge, MA: Harvard University Press, 1978).

18. Afsaneh Najmabadi, *The Story of the Daughters of Quchan: Gender and National Memory in Iranian History* (Syracuse: Syracuse University Press, 1998).

19. H. E. Chehabi, "The Banning of the Veil and Its Consequences," in *The Making of Modern Iran: State and Society under Riza Shah, 1921–1941*, ed. Stephanie Cronin (London: RoutledgeCurzon, 2003), which also contains articles on women by Jasamin Rostam-Kolayi and Shirin Mahdavi.

20. Camron Michael Amin, *The Making of the Modern Iranian Woman: Gender, State Policy, and Popular Culture, 1865–1946* (Gainesville: University of Florida Press, 2002).

21. Haleh Esfandiari, *Reconstructed Lives: Women and Iran's Islamic Revolution* (Washington, DC: Woodrow Wilson Center Press, 1997).

22. Maryam Poya, *Women, Work and Islamism: Ideology and Resistance in Iran* (London: Zed Books, 1999).

23. Homa Hoodfar, *Volunteer Health Workers in Iran as Social Activists: Can "Governmental Non-governmental Organisations" Be Agents of Democratisation?* Women Living under Muslim Laws Occasional Paper no. 10 (n.p., 1998).

24. Mahnaz Afkhami and Erika Friedl, eds., *In the Eye of the Storm: Women in Post-Revolutionary Iran* (Syracuse: Syracuse University Press, 1994).

25. Haideh Moghissi, *Population and Feminism in Iran: Women's Struggle in a Male-Defined Revolutionary Movement* (New York: St. Martin's Press, 1994).

26. Idem, *Feminism and Islamic Fundamentalism: The Limits of Postmodern Analysis* (London: Zed Books, 1999).

27. Haleh Afshar, *Islam and Feminisms: An Iranian Case Study* (New York: St. Martin's Press, 1998).

28. Ziba Mir-Hosseini, *Marriage on Trial. A Study of Islamic Family Law: Iran and Morocco Compared* (London: I. B. Tauris, 1993).

29. Idem, *Islam and Gender: The Religious Debate in Contemporary Iran* (Princeton: Princeton University Press, 1999).

30. Shahla Haeri, *Law of Desire: Temporary Marriage in Shi'i Iran* (London: I. B. Tauris, 1993).

31. Beth Baron, *The Women's Awakening in Egypt: Culture, Society, and the Press* (New Haven: Yale University Press, 1994).

32. Lila Abu-Lughod, ed., *Remaking Women: Feminism and Modernity in the Middle East* (Princeton: Princeton University Press, 1998).

33. Cynthia Nelson, *Doria Shafik, Egyptian Feminist: A Women Apart* (Gainesville: University Press of Florida, 1996).

34. Selma Botman, *Engendering Citizenship in Egypt* (New York: Columbia University Press, 1999).

35. Thompson, *Colonial Citizens.*

36. On differences between colonial and noncolonial countries, see Nikki R. Keddie, "Western Rule versus Western Values," *Diogenes* 26 (1959): 71–96.

37. Diane Singerman and Homa Hoodfar, eds., *Development, Change, and Gender in Cairo: A View from the Household* (Bloomington: Indiana University Press, 1996).

38. Annelies Moors, *Women, Property and Islam: Palestinian Experiences, 1920–1990* (Cambridge: Cambridge University Press, 1995).

39. Julie M. Peteet, *Gender in Crisis: Women and the Palestinian Resistance Movement* (New York: Columbia University Press, 1992).

40. Ellen L. Fleischmann, *The Nation and Its "New" Women: Feminism, Nationalism, Colonialism, and the Palestinian Women's Movement, 1920–1948* (Berkeley and Los Angeles: University of California Press, 2002).

41. See the items by Julia Clancy-Smith in n5. Some of her articles are found in the collections referenced in nn53, 54, 55, and 60.

42. Charrad, *States and Women's Rights.*

43. Marnia Lazreg, *The Eloquence of Silence: Algerian Women in Question* (New York: Routledge, 1994).

44. Evelyn Early, *Baladi Women of Cairo: Playing with an Egg and a Stone* (Boulder, CO: Lynne Rienner, 1993); Homa Hoodfar, *Between Marriage and the Market: Intimate Politics and Survival in Cairo* (Berkeley and Los Angeles: University of California Press, 1997); Arlene Elowe Macleod, *Accommodating Protest: Working Women, the New Veiling, and Change in Cairo* (New York: Columbia University Press, 1991); Diane Singerman, *Avenues of Participation: Family, Politics, and Networks in Urban Quarters of Cairo* (Princeton: Princeton University Press, 1995); Unni Wikan, *Tomorrow, God Willing: Self-Made Destinies in Cairo* (Chicago: University of Chicago Press, 1996); and Sherifa Zuhur, *Revealing Reveiling: Islamist Gender Ideology in Contemporary Egypt* (Albany: State University of New York Press, 1992).

45. Nadje Al-Ali, *Secularism, Gender and the State in the Middle East: The Egyptian Women's Movement* (Cambridge: Cambridge University Press, 2000).

46. Laurie A. Brand, *Women, the State, and Political Liberalization: Middle Eastern and North African Experiences* (New York: Columbia University Press, 1998).

47. Valentine M. Moghadam, *Modernizing Women: Gender and Social Change in the Middle East* (Boulder, CO: Lynne Rienner, 1993).

48. Martha Mundy, *Domestic Government: Kinship, Community and Policy in North Yemen* (London: I. B. Tauris, 1995).

49. Sondra Hale, *Gender Politics in Sudan: Islamism, Socialism, and the State* (Boulder, CO: Westview Press, 1997).

50. Jenny B. White, *Islamist Mobilization in Turkey: A Study in Vernacular Politics* (Seattle: University of Washington Press, 2002).

51. Deniz Kandiyoti, ed., *Women, Islam and the State* (Philadelphia: Temple University Press, 1991).

52. Valentine M. Moghadam, ed., *Identity Politics and Women: Cultural Reassertions and Feminisms in International Perspective* (Boulder, CO: Westview Press, 1994).

53. Herbert L. Bodman and Nayereh Tohidi, eds., *Women in Muslim Societies: Diversity within Unity* (Boulder, CO: Lynne Rienner, 1998).

54. Mahnaz Afkhami and Erika Friedl, eds., *Muslim Women and the Politics of Participation: Implementing the Beijing Platform* (Syracuse: Syracuse University Press, 1997).

55. Margaret L. Meriwether and Judith E. Tucker, eds., *A Social History of Women and Gender in the Modern Middle East* (Boulder, CO: Westview Press, 1999).

56. Amira El Azhary Sonbol, ed., *Women, the Family and Divorce Laws in Islamic History* (Syracuse: Syracuse University Press, 1996).

57. Keddie and Baron, *Women in Middle Eastern History.*

58. Abu-Lughod, *Remaking Women.*

59. Fatma Müge Göçek and Shiva Balaghi, eds., *Reconstructing Gender in the Middle East: Tradition, Identity, and Power* (New York: Columbia University Press, 1994).

60. Judith E. Tucker, ed., *Arab Women: Old Boundaries, New Frontiers* (Bloomington: Indiana University Press, 1993); Tekeli, *Women in Modern Turkish Society.*

61. Mai Yamani, ed., *Feminism and Islam: Legal and Literary Perspectives* (New York: New York University Press, 1996); Suha Sabbagh, ed., *Arab Women: Between Defiance and Restraint* (Brooklyn, NY: Olive Branch Press, 1996).

62. Rudi Matthee and Beth Baron, eds., *Iran and Beyond: Essays in Middle Eastern History in Honor of Nikki R. Keddie* (Costa Mesa, CA: Mazda, 2000).

63. Beck and Keddie, *Women in the Muslim World*; Fatima Mernissi, *Beyond the Veil: Male-Female Dynamics in a Modern Muslim Society*, rev. ed. (Bloomington: Indiana University Press, 1987); Judith E. Tucker, *Women in Nineteenth Century Egypt* (Cambridge: Cambridge University Press, 1985); Lila Abu-Lughod, *Veiled Sentiments: Honor and Poetry in a Bedouin Society* (Berkeley and Los Angeles: University of California Press, 1986); and several works by Elizabeth Warnock Fernea, including *Guests of the Sheik* (New York: Doubleday, 1965), and Elizabeth Warnock Fernea, ed., *Women and the Family in the Middle East: New Voices of Change* (Austin: University of Texas Press, 1985).

64. Existing books and articles, including *Women in Muslim Family Law*, ed. John L. Esposito with Natana J. DeLong-Bas, 2nd ed. (Syracuse: Syracuse University Press, 2001), give only partial coverage of this topic, which should be re-

searched for a needed comparative work. A still largely valid comparative summary of women's legal situation and position in the workforce until 1987, which could be updated, is found in Nadia Hijab, *Womanpower: The Arab Debate on Women at Work* (Cambridge: Cambridge University Press, 1988).

65. Several well-known general books on Islamic or Middle Eastern history and anthropology provide background and context for such questions. An important and underutilized work, which has an original separate chapter on women and discusses differences between Turkish and Arab kinship patterns, is Charles Lindholm, *The Islamic Middle East: An Historical Anthropology* (Oxford: Blackwell, 1996). Deniz Kandiyoti wrote to me in January 2002 that some Turkic groups' kinship and marital patterns differ from Arab patterns in ways noted by Lindholm, but her research with many Turkic groups shows that today they have a variety of kinship systems and marital preferences.

PART 4

Problems in the Study of
Middle Eastern Women
1979

Women's History

The study of Middle Eastern women, past and present, poses a number of methodological problems, some common to Third World studies and others peculiar to the Middle East. Recent research and editorial experience lead me to some conclusions regarding research on Middle Eastern women, both historical and contemporary. The most obvious problem is that, as compared either with many other areas of Middle Eastern history or with numerous geographical areas of women's history, almost no serious scholarly historical work has been done. A few pioneering works by N. Abbott on prominent women in the early Islamic period, some articles and a book chapter by Nada Tomiche, the article by Ronald Jennings, and the recent monograph on Mamluk women written by 'Abd ar-Rāziq in French and published in Cairo are among the few serious works on pre-twentieth-century women in the Muslim Middle East published before 1977.[1] Middle Eastern history has long been a "backward area" in many ways—the training of its historians in historical and social theory and methods, and interest in past social and economic developments, are almost exclusively post–World War II phenomena—and the field as a whole lacks the theoretical and methodological sophistication of European or East Asian history. It is therefore not surprising that historians of the Middle East should come late to an interest in women's history, and that results thus far have been quantitatively small.

A few words on the importance of historical studies to contemporary issues are relevant. Clearly, every social ideology uses historical arguments to buttress its position. In the Middle East and elsewhere ideologies stressing the eternal differences or inferiority of women, along with their possible lust, demonic powers, and deceitfulness, are illustrated by supposed historical examples and arguments to bolster practices of women's seclusion, men's domination, and a sexual double standard. Imperialists use historical arguments to try to show that women's position in the Middle East was dreadful until these areas came under Western tutelage, while nationalists may counter that women were well off until another nation lowered their position. In regard to women's position as on other matters, frequently the Iranians blame the Turks, and the Turks blame Arab and

Persian influences. Such ideological arguments may provide positive models in the national past for improving women's position in the present, but they fall far short of giving a practical guide as to how to improve this position and increase the pace and quality of development for both women and men. While the past can never be a mechanical guide to the present and future, processes of change can be strengthened through an understanding of how changes, particularly those that have benefited the people, have occurred in the past.

An accurate picture of the past must take into account all classes and groups in society in their different roles, and this is far more difficult for the historian than for the scholar who works with contemporary material. The latter generally has, or can have, direct or indirect access to nearly all classes and groups, whereas the historian has access only to what his or her documents reveal. This accounts for much of the urban upper- and middle-class male bias of historical works on the Middle East. Nevertheless, there are means, most of them scarcely tried, for beginning to meet this problem.

1. Historians of both women and men could and should make much more use of the findings of contemporary anthropology, and they could figure out a methodology for doing so. For example, if it is found that in nomadic tribes over a large geographical region certain features are almost universal among the women, such as carrying out particular pastoral, agricultural, and handicraft work, being unveiled, rarely inheriting (as they should by Muslim law), and if in addition some historical evidence can be found for such conditions in the past, it may be argued as at least highly probable that these conditions are congruent with the pastoral nomadic mode of production, and were probably as widespread in the past as in modern times. This type of argument is best made when there exist a wide geographic spread, a large number of examples, some understanding of why certain conditions for women should be functional with a given socioeconomic organization, and a knowledge of which features of the societies studied almost surely predated modern socioeconomic changes. Given these caveats, however, there seems every reason to ask historians to make careful and guarded use of anthropological findings, and particularly to try to master the best social and economic theory of contemporary anthropology; otherwise historians will all too often be left in the situation of omitting the rural population and the urban poor and of taking a very few class groups as representative of the whole. The best studies of contemporary women, particularly when taken together, demonstrate that women's lives and status vary greatly according to class and productive unit: nomadic women, village women, and the different classes of urban women have quite different life structures—more so today than in the past, perhaps, but differences in the past were also great.

2. Archaeology for historical periods, a discipline mostly neglected by historians, should be encouraged as a specialization not only for the history of ordinary women but also for that of ordinary men. 'Abd ar-Rāziq's book lists some of the women's objects found in digs near old Cairo, and the very structure of old towns, tools, utensils, and homes can tell the trained archaeologist a great deal about the mode of life of both men and women.

3. Some remarks are to be found in traditional sources, as well as in more recently exploited ones, about nonelite women; these sources include chronicles, geographies, travelers' accounts, legal and theological writings, wills, and legal cases.

4. There is much to be learned from prose, poetry, and the arts, and historians should know how to deal with this material, just as they should study the historical use of folktales and oral tradition pioneered by Africanists.

5. Some, but not enough, use has been made of written records about slave girls in upper-class harems. Although they were perhaps not the "typical" lower-class urban women, they did form part of that group, and unused written sources on their lives are relatively abundant.

Many of the above sources have not, of course, been nearly adequately exploited even for middle- and upper-class women, much less for lower-class ones—'Abd ar-Rāziq suggests what can be done for the former from chronicles, geographies, books by Eastern and Western travelers, archaeology, and *The Thousand and One Nights*. His book, for all its wealth of material, does not, however, seriously confront the problem of the lower class-woman, urban or rural.

Another and related problem hindering the profound study of women's history in the Middle East has been a philosophically idealist bias—represented in this field by an assumption that the Quran, the Traditions of the Prophet, and the writings of theologians and jurists were the main determinants of women's position. Thus perhaps the best-known Western survey of the history of Islamic women gives the great majority of its space to women in poetry and in law, without an extended serious discussion—which could draw on considerable modern evidence—regarding the extent to which this "ideal" evidence is to be taken literally or what other sources or contemporary knowledge might lead us to modify it, and in what directions.[2] Another recent book has two parts that are both, one assumes, meant in some way to represent reality, but the premodern section is entirely ideal, covering the Quran, Muhammad, the theologian al-Ghazali, and a modern opponent of al-Ghazali's views on sexuality (this opponent is even "replaced" by the more logically thinking Freud), while the modern section is largely based on contemporary realities.[3] Such idealism has its roots in the training of both Western Orientalists and Muslims.

For years Orientalists tended to begin their studies with theology, language, and literature, and those scholars were inclined to give inordinate emphasis to religious and judicial books and traditions, taking them to represent reality. Islam, like Christianity, Judaism, and other religious traditions, similarly tended to overemphasize the power of the ideal and of the word. Yet all societies provide numerous examples of the deviation of the followers of religions from their religious books and leaders, and also of deviation from the law. This has been underlined by recent anthropological studies showing, for example, that many, and probably most, nomadic and village women do not inherit real property or flocks, but, at most, inherit movables far below the value of what the Quran (which believers take to be the literal word of God) says they should inherit.[4] So widespread a phenomenon, found from Morocco to Iran, also existed in the past, we may assume, especially as its causes were as operative then as now. Dividing up a flock or fields may weaken or destroy the economic viability of the family unit, but its impact is less drastic on the city middle or upper classes, or even on wage workers, especially as intermarriage among related families means that a family that loses something to a daughter may get something back before long from a woman who marries into the family. In rural areas, however, the gap in time between these two events may not be supportable. (Germaine Tillion has found in years of study in North Africa that, ironically, until recently it was veiled women [i.e., urban middle and upper classes] who usually inherited, and unveiled women [rural and lower classes] who did not.)[5] Hence the veiled woman was advantaged not only in social status but also in personal property rights.

"Ideal" sources—the Quran and the traditional sayings of Muhammad, jurists, and theologians are, of course, the easiest to find and to put into a coherent picture, which helps to account for their popularity. Nonetheless, other sources exist, and many of the remarks made above regarding nonelite women apply—chronicles, geographies, travelers' accounts, biographical dictionaries (which include prominent women), oral tradition, as well as contemporary anthropology, sociology, and economics can help overcome an idealist bias. Very important sources, just beginning to be used on women as on other matters, are actual legal cases—especially decisions handed down by courts—as opposed to legal texts. These include adjudications of wills and other legal documents that cast light on women's inheritance and property holdings, recently studied for the Ottoman Empire by Ronald Jennings and others.[6] This type of material exists in addition for considerably earlier, pre-Ottoman, periods, and could be a gold mine regarding not only women but also other aspects of social and economic history. (It could also be digitized for use by various scholars with different purposes.) One word of caution about case law: although it comes closer to true social history than do the lawbooks, it, too, has been found to be a somewhat "idealized" source. One anthropologist who tested court decisions against what actually followed found that the two often did not coincide. Whereas the judge felt constrained to make his decision as "Islamic" as possible, those regarding whom the judgment was made often found ways to get around it, with the stronger of the affected parties winning out. Although the historian may not be able to get closer to reality than the court decision, he or she should keep this anthropological finding in mind before assuming, say, that women overwhelmingly had real and effective control over the inheritance that a judge might award them according to Islamic law. We are dealing here with three levels of reality—the law, the court decision, and what happened. Historians should keep a sharp eye out for any material that goes beyond the second level—a level that they have just recently begun to reach—and that indicates to what degree court decisions were carried out.

The utility of "ideal" sources is undeniable, but they, like all sources, must be used with caution, and hard work must be done to piece together less accessible but more historically revealing sources in addition. The utility, as well as the possible pitfalls, of ideal sources is suggested in the very important work being done by Basim Musallam. By demonstrating that the most important medieval Muslim jurists and theologians did not forbid birth control (chiefly coitus interruptus), but either approved it or at most considered it reprehensible but legal, he has shed new light on an aspect of Islamic history with important implications for women. Particularly interesting are those jurists and theologians who made women's consent a precondition for birth control on the grounds that women had a right to have children and also to sexual satisfaction.[7] Musallam and others have noted the concern and understanding of a major theologian, al-Ghazali, regarding the sexual satisfaction of women in marriage, and he was not unique in these attitudes. It is only when Musallam speculates that birth control was practiced by significant numbers of people, and may account for late medieval declines in population in Egypt, that some scholars part company with him, since there is as yet no way of knowing whether the masses either knew or followed elite statements on birth control. Population decline seems better explained by such factors as the endemic nature of the plague in hot climates, where the bacteria do not perish in the cold, than by presumed birth-control practices,[8] although even this should not be made a monocausal explanation of a population decline that went along with a general socioeconomic decline. Musallam's study suggests there is still more to be learned from ideal sources, but that they should be used, as he nearly always uses them, in a detailed and systematic way.

There is little or no evidence that the vast majority of rural or lower-class urban Middle Easterners went to court for decisions, or read or heard of the ideas of jurists and theologians, except as they might be filtered down and perhaps changed by popular preachers. Nevertheless, we are not completely without recourse regarding sources that might tell us something about their lives, although there has scarcely been a hunt for them. Travelers from one part of the Middle East to another were often struck by special local customs, many concerning the nonelite; Western travelers began reporting as early as the thirteenth century, and their works have hardly been touched for women's history. Nobody has even hazarded an explanation of the fifteenth-century Italian travelers to Iran who reported that the women of that country exposed their bodies shamelessly—surely not our usual concept, but one that finds some confirmation in later periods.[9] Some foreigners left drawings, and later photographs, that have scarcely been used as sources for the history of women. Scanty past references should also be tied more often to practices known from more detailed recent studies.

If women's history for the Middle East has been almost nonexistent, concentrated insofar as it exists on urban upper classes, and has relied too much on ideal sources, it has also, ironically, not even given adequate treatment to upper-class women. In numerous periods a few women were extremely powerful politically—one may mention parts of the Abbasid, Mamluk, Ottoman, and Qajar periods, where queen mothers, in particular, might virtually rule the empire, or at least have a strong influence over rulers. Historians usually report this negatively, and "harem rule" is almost a synonym for decadence and decline. Surely it is time to look again at some of these powerful women and see what they actually accomplished and what the circumstances were that might have impeded them. In a related sphere, preconceptions are beginning to be overturned as the supposedly faceless, idle, voluptuous harem is now seen by a few scholars as an organized social unit that included many who worked hard, and produced women of managerial and artistic abilities.[10]

Remarks thus far deal mainly with the history of women before the period of Western impact and incursions. After 1798, and for much of the Ottoman Empire even before, sources, especially Westerners' accounts, are much more numerous, and the possibility of reconstructing the lives of women in some areas becomes much greater; yet even for this period little has been done. In addition to a growing number of travelers' accounts and continued sources of the type mentioned above, there is now relevant material in Western diplomatic and consular reports; a great increase in serious Western treatises on Middle Eastern countries by persons who lived there a long time; and more local treatises by and about women. For Iran there is a famous treatise, of which an English translation exists, that states it is written by five women. Although some have considered it to be a satire, written by a male, the newer view is that it *is* the work of women. It recommends various means of flirting with men on the street, "accidentally" removing the veil, deceiving one's husband, and so forth.[11] The French-language Orientalist Chodzko wrote that it represented a genuine school of thought and behavior among Iranian upper-class women.[12] Even if it is a satire, to be effective as satire it must exaggerate an actual trend, which implies that some Persian upper-class women were more daring in their relations with men than we might have supposed. Another Persian treatise by a man is written to make wives good housekeepers, docile, unquarrelsome, and obedient to their husbands—again the treatise would hardly have been necessary if these qualities were so ingrained in childhood as not to need stress. There are other treatises on and by women in Iran in the nineteenth century, and similar things must exist for other Middle Eastern countries. We also get Western reports of peasant and nomadic ways from the nineteenth century often included in general or travel books and often having observations on women.

The late nineteenth century saw the first suggestions of feminist ideas, especially in Egypt. In the twentieth century in some countries these grew into defined movements, and in others there were individual struggles, either specifically feminist or in combination with male-led nationalist and social movements. Despite the interest in such movements all over the world their history, too, has scarcely been studied for the Middle East, although there is a relative abundance of sources.[13]

MODERN PROBLEMS: IDEOLOGY VERSUS ANALYSIS

Most of what little there is of historical work that has been done about Middle Eastern women in Islamic times has been characterized either by the empiricism that dominated nineteenth-century Western historiography, with its faith that a search for the best documents and a summary of their salient points would lead to a reconstruction of history "as it really was," and/or by various national and cultural biases. In the embryonic state of women's history in the Middle East, empirical studies based on unearthing new documents are frequently enlightening, but they could be far more so if they took into account some of the nonempirical ideas and considerations discussed above, as well as more profound theoretical ideas. 'Abd ar-Rāziq's book on Mamluk women is perhaps the most thorough and useful of the existing empirical books, but it suffers from a lack of consideration of how one might bring in the "undocumented" women, from a failure to consider the negative aspects of the "respect" in which he finds women were held (Western medieval and Victorian ladies were similarly "respected"), and from nationalism. He clearly aims to show us that women in Egypt were much better off before the Ottoman conquest, and he ends his book with a mid-nineteenth-century quotation suggesting that Egyptian women had far fuller lives than the stupid creatures who inhabited Ottoman harems.[14] Turkish historians have similarly idealized their pre-Ottoman and pre-Islamic past, and Iranians claim a high position for their pre-Islamic women—in all three cases the point is, in line with modern nationalist feeling, to prove that some other nation and culture were responsible for deterioration in this, as in other, spheres.

To write good history one must go beyond empiricism, however useful some of its methods are, and beyond national and cultural biases, whether in favor of or against the people being studied. Needed for the best history are both a comparative perspective and theoretical underpinnings, which are really two sides of the same coin, since comprehensive theories must rest in large part on profound studies, done by many persons, of a wide variety of societies and of how they change and function.

For Middle Eastern women's history it is important to recognize that whereas in preclass societies the most important division of labor was that between men and women, in class-divided, city-dominated societies this division becomes crosscut by important divisions among city, village, and nomadic tribe, as well as by stratification and class divisions within each of these areas, which are particularly marked in towns and cities. In the Islamic case, women in different classes and productive units lived quite different lives. Statements, still made by serious Islamic scholars, such as "women inherited and controlled their own property," or "most women were veiled," or "polygamy was widespread" relate to a part of the urban middle and upper classes, about whom we have the most documentation. While we continue to need more documentation of the lives of these groups, our knowledge of other societies and of the contemporary Middle East should keep us from confusing them with women as a whole.

With a considerable deepening of theory and an extension of historical understanding, scholars should have some historical background for understanding such contemporary phenomena as the Middle East's being characterized by the world's highest population growth rates, among the lowest rates of female education and labor-force participation, the relative conservatism in Muslim family and personal status laws in most countries, the spread of veiling in small towns and rural areas as it declines in the cities, as well as more optimistic trends, such as the rise in professional education and employment, legal reform, and women's participation in political and feminist activities. (Some of the theoretical and factual background for understanding these and other developments is suggested in the introduction and essays in the book of original articles edited by Lois

Beck and myself, *Women in the Muslim World* [Cambridge, MA: Harvard University Press, 1978].) The special features still found in the status of most Middle Eastern women are tied to their historical past, although not in the simplistic ways that often are still suggested.

The transition to a modern and Western-influenced life structure has not been a simple progressive one for Middle Eastern women. Too many scholars use "modernization" as a simple equivalent to the more obviously ethnocentric "Westernization," retaining the implication that modernization is essentially a straight-line progressive process, which either immediately or very soon improves everyone's way of life. For male workers and peasants this is often untrue, and for women of several classes it is equally so; scholars should study their evolution more profoundly than they have thus far. It should not be expected that there will necessarily be a single answer to the question of whether the Western impact, or modernization, made things better or worse even for a single class or group. Regarding women, even in Western Europe we find the rise of capitalism in the seventeenth century removing women from many productive tasks and sources of income that had been theirs since the Middle Ages, but the same century saw the voicing and advancing of the first feminist ideas as another side of the rise of capitalism.[15] The influence of Western and indigenous capitalism in the Middle East was similarly two-sided, although different in some ways from capitalism's influence in the West. Female peasants, nomads, and city craft workers have increasingly lost their productive role as the goods they made came to be purchased from distant producers, although a very few women's products, like hand-woven carpets, found greatly increased markets. Even with these products, however, women's conditions were not necessarily improved as they often had to work hard for long hours in dark, damp, and unhealthy surroundings. Many male workers also faced difficult conditions, often exacerbated by the Western impact. While working urban, rural, and tribal women probably lost in productive role and status with the growth of a market economy, the position of the top urban groups generally improved. As upper- and upper-middle-class men were often tied to Western businessmen and politicians (especially when their countries were directly or indirectly ruled by the West), they began to acquire Western or Western-style educations, and to qualify as modern professionals, businessmen, and bureaucrats. Traveling to Europe and moving largely in Western and Westernized circles, such men were the first to respond to, or even encourage, women's demands for liberation—for modern education, for unveiling, and for professional lives. There came to be an exacerbation of differences in lifestyles between the urban upper- and middle-class women, who increasingly adopted Western or "modern" ways, and lower-class women, whose families found the old ways still functional, and whose men have tended to see dangers rather than advantages in the abandonment of customs sanctioned by tradition, law, and religious leaders. The extremely skewed income distribution of nearly all Middle Eastern countries adds to the "two cultures" phenomenon noted above.

The discussion thus far has suggested the importance of constant attention to differences in *class*, which involve both the tripartite (if simplified) division among village, nomadic tribe, and urban areas, and numerous differences between classes and strata within each of these, particularly the complex urban area. In discussing ideologies regarding women, as in other issues, a consideration of class is vital—not necessarily the class origin of an individual who puts forth specific ideas, but rather what class groups he or she appeals to and represents. This has scarcely been discussed in relation to ideologies regarding women, and yet if these are studied attentively the class appeal of the holders of different views is usually clear. In Egypt both the earliest advocates of the liberation of women, like Muhammad Abduh and Qasim Amin, and their more thoroughgoing pre–World War II male and female followers tended to belong, or at least to appeal, to an upper- or upper-middle-class group with ties to the British, who were moderate in their politics both toward the British and on local issues. Egypt's more radical anti-imperialists, beginning with Mustafa Kamil and continuing through the Muslim Brotherhood, were both more petty bourgeois and popular in their appeal and more defensive of traditional ways, including traditional law and status regarding women. The same contrast can be found elsewhere, as with the upper-middle-class moderate politics, strongly Western-influenced, of Bourguba and his followers, as contrasted with the petty bourgeois and popular appeal of Algerian leaders, who have been conservative regarding women. Really radical stands regarding women's equality have come from those who have mobilized popular struggles and also carried out mobilization, education, and organization of and about women, as in Marxist-led South Yemen, neighboring revolutionary Dhofar (part of Oman), and parts of the Palestinian and Sudanese movements. So we get a complex picture whereby upper- and upper-middle-class groups closely tied to the West materially and ideologically have taken important steps to improve the status of women (Turkey, Kuwait, and Iran could be added to the relevant countries here), whereas less well off anti-imperialist groups, whose material and cultural interests are often hurt by Western incursions, may become defensive about traditional ways, and seek security in a return to tradition and preservation of male domination. It is the radical Marxists (and very rarely the "Islamic" or "Arab" socialists) in some countries who try to mobilize the popular masses and to improve the position of women not only by action from the top, the method favored with partial success by the upper-class group, but also through the mobilization of women and their participation in organized struggles.[16]

The application of class analysis of ideologies and movements on more than a crude simplistic level is rare for the Middle East and virtually non-existent in the study of attitudes toward women and of women's activities. In fact, there are few studies of women's movements and women's partici-pation in politics on anything above a journalistic or oversimplified level that disregards the need to verify facts or demonstrate theories. If conser-vative scholarship is often characterized by an inability to utilize modern theory and to cut through the biases of sources, radical scholarship some-times makes sweeping unsupported statements; overestimates the size and significance of many radical and pseudoradical movements; and ignores uncomfortable facts, such as the relative progressiveness regarding wom-en's rights of the nonradical, Western-oriented regimes noted above. The theoretical understanding of society presumably desired by such radicals is surely not obtained through the distortion of facts: If Iran has done better than Algeria in improving the status of women, radicals gain noth-ing from denying or ignoring this fact; the point is to explain and under-stand it. "You will learn the truth and the truth will make you free," is surely a motto for all who wish to better the human condition.

THE STUDY OF CONTEMPORARY MIDDLE EASTERN WOMEN

The preceding discussion of historical theory has led us from the past into the present in one of the many areas in which past and present are intertwined—the class basis of attitudes and actions regarding the posi-tion of women. This question is clearly an important one in the study and planning of economic development; other areas of past experience that relate to realities of today and tomorrow could also be found. The high birthrates, low labor-force participation rates, and low education rates of Muslim women in Middle Eastern countries are clearly obstacles to economic growth in their societies as a whole, as well as to women's own development. Studies of historical reasons for these phenomena and of those areas and programs in the Middle East that have best overcome these obstacles could provide guidelines for future action. Good ideas, however, will not suffice: many governments do not want to move rapidly to improve women's conditions, either because of conservatism, male un-employment, a desire to retain petty bourgeois support and not to encour-age possibly disruptive changes, or for other reasons. Blueprints alone will not solve problems; political action, often involving large numbers of people, is usually needed if real change is to occur with any rapidity. Nonetheless, as scholars, few of us can be directly involved in political action in the Third World; on the political level, the most we can hope for is that some of our scholarship and ideas may help especially our own compatriots and sometimes others to understand what is occurring in a given country and, possibly, what might be done either here or there to better the lives of most people.

Some of the suggestions made for historians also apply, in whole or in part, to scholars of contemporary subjects. Such scholars should also differentiate among various classes of women and should not confuse laws and pronouncements with reality. Just as historians should study the works of contemporary anthropologists and sociologists and examine other societies for comparative purposes (much that is called "Islamic" in fact existed in a variety of other societies), so should contemporary scholars study scholarship on other societies and on the past of their own. The number of significant works in women's studies is small enough to make this recommendation fairly easy to comply with, as regards works on women, and still leave time for other works of theoretical importance. The importance of a theoretical background that includes both comparative and socioeconomic bases is as true for contemporary studies as for history.

Some methodological problems weigh more heavily on those doing contemporary work than on historians. One, faced to a lesser degree by historians, is statistics, most often local census data or the like. Although almost every scholar knows that statistics and censuses of the Middle East are even more inaccurate than those of the West, the usual approach is to make a disclaimer somewhere in one's book or article, to add that nothing better is available, and to go right on to use these poor statistics. A better approach is possible, both in terms of existing material and, one may hope, of convincing Middle Eastern governments to adopt more accurate census policies. Regarding existing material, for a lengthy or serious work, at least one trip to the area should be made. With such a trip, and sometimes even without it (through letters, contacting nationals at the UN or World Bank, etc.), one should be able to determine possible biases in the data from discussion with governmental or other knowledgeable sources. Of importance are what definitions were used for such concepts as "labor force," "employed," and "unemployed" (some scholars seem unaware that these are not immutable categories but are defined differently in different countries), and also how data were, in theory, collected (i.e., in a village did the census taker talk only to the headman, or to every "household head"? were the women consulted? or was another method used?). Ideally this information should be included in every census volume and in every official publication using census statistics, but this is now far from the case. Still, it is worth checking to see whether the information can be found in any such publication. On the scene, one can try to talk to the people who headed a census-gathering group, or actually collected figures, to find out how it was done. Finally, it is worth finding out whether anyone has done careful sample studies for any area, and if so to compare these results with the census results. It would be even better to become involved as a sociologist or an observer in such a sample study, which should, in part, replicate census questions.

In Iran I did not attempt all these steps, but they should have been possible had it been necessary for my research on handicrafts and carpets. William Bartsch's London dissertation on unemployment in Iran contains the information that Iran's census defines the "unemployed" in the same way that the United States does—as persons not employed who have sought work in the past week.[17] This definition is poor enough in the United States where unemployment insurance laws in theory require that work be sought if insurance is to be collected. It is ludicrous in Iran, where labor exchanges scarcely exist, and where the majority of the rural population knows very well when employment may or may not be available, so that the situation of the rural unemployed seeking work rarely arises. Sample studies done by Iran's former Ministry of Cooperatives and Rural Affairs show that women's employment, labor-force participation rate, and unemployment (the latter defined more sensibly than in the census as those wanting and able to work but unable to find it) were all far higher than reported in the census. Similar conclusions can be found in an article in an international journal.[18] Even without fieldwork, it was easy to conclude, as Bartsch's work demonstrated in detail, that unemployment (a few years ago, at least) was much higher than the official figures show (he gives an alternative estimate), and also that women's rural unemployment was far above official figures. Moreover, women's employment in the countryside, in agriculture, handicrafts, and carpets, was far above that reported in the census. The reasons for the discrepancies, which would apply to much of the Middle East, are not hard to guess. If a village headman or a husband is approached with a question like "How many women in this household (or village) work for money?," the answers will show a total much lower than the reality, because it is often considered demeaning for a woman to work, and for other reasons. The woman herself might answer the same question in the negative. Nonetheless, the Iranian sample survey came up with figures that appear plausible, based on my village observations. The most recent Turkish census also arrives at a figure for employed rural women that is several times higher than that of most Middle Eastern countries. It seems highly unlikely that the real Turkish figures are significantly higher than Iran's (especially as the Turkish figures reflect mostly agricultural work, and Turkey does not have Iran's huge village female employment in carpet weaving). Thus it would be very important for anyone who might influence census designers anywhere in the Middle East to study the methods of the Turkish census takers who arrive at what must, on the face of it, be the most accurate figures for female rural employment in the Middle East.

The designers of the last Iranian census were aware of some of the problems listed above, but said in conversation that only sample surveys can give accurate results. This may in fact be true for countries at a certain stage of development, which are characterized by traditional responses to certain questions. Scholars should probably make more efforts to acquire sample surveys, often unpublished, and rely less on census data. They should certainly specify the direction in and degree to which such data are likely to be skewed. Iranians involved in the latest census have also said that they wanted it to be comparable to earlier censuses, and that if they counted all men, women, and children working in agriculture, the result would be a serious overcount, since the work of the whole family in agriculture is seasonal and does not exceed that of one full-time year-round worker. These are serious decisions made by intelligent, experienced, and well-educated persons. Yet it is difficult not to think that international attention should be given to the revamping of census categories in most of the Middle East, and perhaps the entire Third World. This is not only important for accuracy in the work of scholars, but even more important for planning for development. For the Middle East, inaccuracies are significantly greater in regard to women than to men, so that this becomes a women's issue, although not exclusively so.

It should be recognized that "labor force," "employed," and "unemployed" are artificial categories that come somewhere near reflecting the realities of advanced, urbanized societies where most workers keep regular schedules and receive wages, but that are far murkier for predominantly rural societies. Instead of considering a rural family as one man because it does the work of one full-time worker—as the Iranians propose—it would seem much more sensible to adopt categories appropriate to the work cycles in the rural areas being studied. It surely should not be impossible to find out the approximate number of days a year husband, wife, and children work. This would give a far more accurate picture of male and female underemployment than we now possess—an important statistic not only for scholars but for those planning rural by-employment for Middle Eastern countries. Other categories and forms of questioning could similarly be rethought; if one goes to a rural home, it is easy to determine whether the woman makes carpets, and even approximately how much time she spends doing so. The construction of more accurate censuses is scarcely a radical reform, and is in the self-interest of even conservative governments that wish to devise development programs. It is an area where concerned scholars may be able to contribute some ideas. At a minimum they should make more efforts than hitherto to find the direction of bias in their figures. For women, especially in the countryside, the data nearly always underestimate both employment and unemployment, and hence labor-force participation.

Another area presenting methodological problems for contemporary scholars—particularly for anthropologists who should have the closest access to it—is that of studying sex. I raised this point at a Middle East Studies Association meeting in November 1975, and the same issue was discussed at the American Anthropological Association meeting in December of the same year. There the anthropologists were accused of virtually ignoring the sexual habits of the people they were studying, and avoiding questions about sex, while often giving time to more obscure and less important topics. One participant was quoted as saying that if she asked people about their sexual habits, they would ask her about hers. This seems to be the crux of the problem of not asking about sex—a Western belief, which has persisted despite the "sexual revolution," that sex habits are intimate affairs not to be discussed except with very close friends. Many Western women never discuss their own sex lives with anyone and therefore are embarrassed to ask anyone else about hers.

Discussion of this point at Middle East Studies Association meetings indicated that there is probably a barrier for an anthropologist who is an unmarried Muslim woman in discussing sexual matters, of which she would be presumed to have no direct experience or knowledge. One Western man said Muslim men were also hesitant to discuss their relations with their wives. Such was not the experience, however, of the French sociologist, Paul Vieille, who headed a team of men and women who questioned members of their own sex about their sexual habits and beliefs, and came up with extremely revealing and important findings.[19] Other researchers have recently made further findings by questioning people about their sex lives.[20] Western and Muslim women have come up with important information about women's sex lives when they have questioned women about just sex or even participated in such discussions, as, for example, in Nancy Tapper's London master's thesis and Elizabeth W. Fernea's *Guests of the Sheik*.[21] These few works are exceptional, however, and several anthropologists I talked to clearly hesitated to broach such a subject, alleging lack of the right vocabulary, of sufficient acquaintance with the women, and so on. Yet it is clear both that information can usually be quite easily obtained by those who try, and that the reticent one is usually the Western or Westernized anthropologist. The worst that can happen to a researcher is to have to draw back temporarily or permanently from a line of discussion, without harm's being done. Sexual information is not a matter of titillation; it is extremely important from several viewpoints. First, the way men and women relate sexually is often a microcosm—and in any case, an important part—of the male-female relationship. Nothing could be more false than to assume that sex is about the same in all societies and in all groups and classes within a society. Second, sexual relations and male-female discussions (or lack of discussions) about them relate closely to birthrates and to attitudes toward birth control. The suggestion has been plausibly made that many husbands and wives discuss sex so seldom that practicing birth control is especially difficult.[22] If marital sex has scarcely been investigated, even less have such obvious problem areas as sexual ignorance and repression, frigidity, impotence, prostitution, rape, child marriage, clitoridectomy (which continues in a few areas, including parts of Egypt despite its outlawing there in 1959), and pederasty. Homosexuality and extramarital sex have also scarcely been studied. The external aspects of sexual relationships have begun to be discussed adequately in recent studies. But the directly sexual aspects, which should form an inseparable whole with the externals, remain largely and unnecessarily a matter of opinion and speculation. Some scholars note that evidence on sex must of necessity be indirect and verbal, but this is true of many other matters that are investigated by scholars. Methodologically the problems involved are not peculiarly difficult, and may involve nothing more than learning the right terminology for simple questioning and discussions. The problem lies with the hesitations of researchers and a training that does not accustom them to deal with such matters.[23]

For students of both past and present, attention to a wider variety of sources, to all major social classes and groups, to comparative studies and a variety of disciplines, to gaps in methodology and sources, and to theories that take into account social and economic structures will advance the embryonic field of Middle Eastern women's studies.

Addendum

Since writing the above I have read the excellent and relevant essay by Judith Gran, "Impact of the World Market on Egyptian Women," *MERIP Reports* 58 (June, 1977): 36, which suggests important new avenues for research on Muslim women.

Notes

An earlier draft of this essay was presented to the conference on Women and Development, Wellesley, MA, 1976.

1. See Ahmad 'Abd ar-Rāziq, *La femme au temps des Mamlouks en Egypte* (Cairo: Institut français d'archéologie orientale du Caire, 1973); Ronald C. Jennings, "Women in Early 17th Century Ottoman Judicial Records," *Journal of the*

Economic and Social History of the Orient 18 (January 1975): 53–114; Nada Tomiche, "The Situation of Egyptian Women in the First Half of the Nineteenth Century," in *Beginnings of Modernization in the Middle East*, ed. W. R. Polk and R. L. Chambers (Chicago: University of Chicago Press, 1968), 171–84, and idem, "La femme en Islam," in *Histoire mondiale de la femme*, ed. Pierre Grimal, vol. 3 (Paris: Nouvelle Librairie de France, 1967), chap. 3. Since 1977 the most notable further work may be found in the relevant parts of E. W. Fernea and B. Q. Bezirgan, eds., *Middle Eastern Muslim Women Speak* (Austin: University of Texas Press, 1977), and in the historical chapters by Ülkü Bates, Mangol Bayat-Philipp, Ian Dengler, Afaf L. Marsot, and Thomas Philipp, in *Women in the Muslim World*, ed. Lois Beck and Nikki Keddie (Cambridge, MA: Harvard University Press, 1978) (hereafter cited as Beck and Keddie).

2. Tomiche, "La femme en Islam."

3. F. Mernissi, *Beyond the Veil* (New York: Schenkman, 1975).

4. See the several relevant studies on rural and tribal women in Beck and Keddie.

5. Germaine Tillion, *Le harem et les cousins* (Paris: Editions du Seuil, 1966), chap. 9, "Les femmes et le voile."

6. See Jennings, "Women in Early 17th Century Ottoman Judicial Records," and Ian C. Dengler, "Turkish Women in the Ottoman Empire: The Classical Age," in Beck and Keddie, which cites a German-language study using such materials.

7. Basim F. Musallam, "The Islamic Sanction of Contraception," in *Population and Its Problems* (Oxford: Oxford University Press, 1974); and idem, "Birth Control and Middle Eastern History," in *The Islamic Middle East, 700–1900: Studies in Economic and Social History*, ed. A. L. Udovitch (Princeton: Darwin Press, 1981).

8. M. W. Dols, *The Black Death in the Middle East* (Princeton: Princeton University Press, 1977), chap. 5; and "The General Mortality of the Black Death in the Mamluk Empire," in Udovitch, *The Islamic Middle East.*

9. Numerous Western travelers and observers have noted that Middle Eastern women, while careful to cover their hair and some part of their face, were often more casual than Western women about exposing their legs and their breasts. This may account for the shock of fifteenth-century Italian observers.

10. Perhaps the best of the discussions of this question is Afaf L. Marsot, "The Revolutionary Gentlewomen in Egypt," in Beck and Keddie.

11. *Customs and Manners of the Women of Persia*, trans. James Atkinson (1832; reprint, New York: Burt Franklin, 1971).

12. A. Chodzko, "Code de la femme chez les persans" (unidentified nineteenth-century offprint seen at the Institut Nationale des Langues Orientales Vivantes, Paris).

13. Some serious scholarly studies on women in feminist and political movements appear in Beck and Keddie: Mangol Bayat-Philipp, "Women and Revolution in Iran"; Juliette Minces, "Women in Algeria"; and Thomas Philipp, "Feminism and Nationalist Politics in Egypt."

14. 'Abd ar-Rāziq, *La femme au temps*, esp. the last page of his text.

15. Alice Clark, *Working Life of Women in the Seventeenth Century* (reprint, London: Frank Cass, 1968); Eileen Power, *Medieval Women*, ed. M. M. Postan

(Cambridge: Cambridge University Press, 1975), chap. 3, "The Working Woman in Town and Country."

16. The contrasting and complex role of the representatives of different classes noted here was in part suggested to me by unpublished papers by Hollis Granoff and Judith Gran. It is to be hoped that they and others will continue this important line of scholarship.

17. For a short version of W. Bartsch's University of London dissertation, see his *Employment and Incomes Policies for Iran* (Geneva: International Labour Office, 1973).

18. Sunil Guha, "The Contribution of Non-Farm Activities to Rural Employment Promotion: Experience in Iran, India and Syria," *International Labour Review* 109, no. 3 (March 1974): 235–50. Far more extensive information is to be found in the (ex-) Ministry of Cooperatives and Rural Affairs's sample surveys, mimeographed and sometimes available. It would be a mistake simply to reject official statistics if they contain the best available data, as they often indicate important trends. See the excellent comparative work done from such statistics in Nadia Haggag Youssef, *Women and Work in Developing Societies* (Berkeley: Institute for International Studies, 1974), and in papers by Youssef and by Elizabeth White in Beck and Keddie.

19. See Paul Vieille, "Iranian Women in Family Alliance and Sexual Politics," in Beck and Keddie, and his brilliant *La féodalité et l'état en Iran* (Paris: Anthropos, 1975), esp. chap. 2, "Naissance, mort, sexe, dans la société et la culture populaires."

20. M. Kotobi in particular is continuing to work on sexual attitudes and practices in Iran. See especially the relevant tables in his "Attitudes et problèmes des étudiants entrant à l'université en pays en voie de developpement" (unpublished Doctorat d'Etat thesis, University of Paris, 1973). See also the articles on contemporary Egypt in Beck and Keddie.

21. Elizabeth Warnock Fernea, *Guests of the Sheik* (Garden City, NY: Doubleday, 1969); Nancy S. S. Tapper, "The Role of Women in Selected Pastoral Islamic Societies" (unpublished M. Phil. thesis, University of London, 1968).

22. See especially the two works by Vieille, cited in n19.

23. A Society for Iranian Studies panel, "Sex and Society in Iran," was held in conjunction with the MESA convention, New York, November 1977. Participants included Donald Stilo, Michael Hillman, Kaveh Safa-Isfahani, Marvin Zonis, and myself. The panel discussed some of the questions raised above, including survey research and other forms of questioning of individuals; homosexuality; and women's theater games as an indicator of unsuspected sexual attitudes. Other useful works on sex in the Muslim world (although not based on questioning) include Abdelwahab Bouhdiba, *La sexualité en islam* (Paris: Presses Universitaires de France, 1975), and G.-H. Bousquet, *La morale de l'Islam et son éthique sexuelle* (Paris: A. Maisonneuve, 1953).

PART 5

Sexuality and Shi'i Social Protest in Iran
Coauthored with Parvin Paidar (Nahid Yeganeh)
1986

I

Introduction
by Nahid Yeganeh

Twelver Imami Shi'ism has been the official religion in Iran since 1501. Students of its role and place within Iranian society have often described Shi'ism as a religion of protest. Various elements specific to Shi'ism, such as the theory of *imamat* (succession of the twelve Shi'i imams) and the practice of *ijtihad* (exertion of opinion on social and religious matters by religious leaders), have been taken as indicating an inherent oppositional tendency of Shi'ism (as opposed to other branches of Islam) to worldly governments.[1]

This view, however, has recently been challenged. It has been pointed out that at various stages of its development, Shi'ism has represented quietism and/or cooperation with central governments, as well as opposition and protest. Social and political contexts have been emphasized as important in determining the stand of Shi'ism toward governments.[2]

The aim of this essay is to extend the above challenge to encompass Shi'i protest on sexuality. Is Shi'ism inherently oppositional on questions of sexuality? To be oppositional, Shi'ism needs to contain its own specific concept of sexuality. It is important to ask, then, whether it is possible to talk about a *Shi'i concept of sexuality* as such.

It will be argued here that, as with politics, sociopolitical context is important in determining the place of sexuality in Shi'i social protest. Shi'ism is neither a mere reflection of Iranian social relations nor its sole determinant. Shi'ism, rather, is intricately interwoven with Iranian social relations. Its specific role and effect, however, must be seen within particular contexts. While Shi'ism has historically attained a specific concept of sexuality, often it is the dominant social relations that specify the Shi'i concept of sexuality. The relationship between the Shi'i and non-Shi'i concepts of sexuality can be determined only within a particular context.

We will discuss these questions in the context of the history of Shi'ism in Iran as well as Iran in the 1970s. Part I will assess the attempts within the literature to attribute an essential concept of female sexuality to Islam in general and to Shi'ism in particular. Part II will discuss the historical aspect of Shi'i social protest on the question of women, particularly in comparison with Sunnism, the mainstream branch of Islam. Part III will concentrate on the context of Iran in the 1970s and discuss a variety of contemporary Shi'i social protests on the question of sexuality, particularly in comparison with concepts of sexuality in secular writings.

The General Theory of Sexuality in Islam

The presence of a homogeneous concept of sexuality in Islam has been stressed by Fatima Mernissi and, with regard to Shi'ism, by Farah Azari.[3] Since views like theirs are widely accepted, they merit consideration.

The practices of veiling, seclusion, and polygamy in Muslim societies, Mernissi argues, are due to the Muslim concept of female sexuality.[4] Mernissi takes the views of Freud and al-Ghazali as representative of their cultures and compares them. She then presents an interesting and well-informed analysis of the dynamics of the male-female relationship in modern Moroccan society.

Regarding the assumptions behind Mernissi's theory, problems arise from assigning a single conception of female sexuality to a complex of relations within a society, especially one as extended temporally and spatially as either Muslim or Western society. Mernissi's dichotomies of active female sexuality in Muslim society and passive female sexuality in Western society do not necessarily hold when dealing with different concrete situations. Also, taking a single thinker to represent each of two huge and changing cultures is a procedure of doubtful validity.

In practice, cultures are much more varied and complex than Mernissi's methodology allows. They contain contradictory elements and inconsistent conceptions. There are a variety of women's positions within every society, the determinants of which are related to various differences, such as ethnicity and class.

Mernissi herself acknowledges the presence of both passive and active conceptions of female sexuality among Muslims. Her choice of al-Ghazali, then, as the representative of a "Muslim" conception of female sexuality seems arbitrary. What is wrong is the assumption that women's present condition is the expression of an unchanging view of a passive or active female sexuality. Women's oppression is not seen as occurring within immediate practices and institutions but as functioning outside them. In the case of societies where the essential concept of female sexuality is called Islamic, the result is a confused conceptualization of the relationship between Islam and the prevailing social relations.

It remains unclear why al-Ghazali's "identity between male and female sexuality" should in some passages be praised as compared to Freud's differentiation of male and female sexuality, while at the same time, according to Mernissi, the former leads to female seclusion and the latter to lack of coercion and surveillance of women. Nor is it clear why al-Ghazali's concept is "Islamic." His belief in female ejaculation, which she stresses, was also widespread in Europe and is still part of common non-Muslim folk beliefs.[5] These criticisms, however, do not apply to the second part of Mernissi's book, which deals with concrete Moroccan situations.

Following Mernissi's approach, Farah Azari has tried to demonstrate the social mechanism through which the suppression of female sexuality is maintained within Iranian society. In "Sexuality and Women's Oppression in Iran" (1983), Azari looks at various present-day practices and institutions within Iranian society, such as the ritual of mourning for the martyrdom of the third Shi'i Imam Husain in Karbala, the institution of the family, hijab (modesty/Islamic dress), prostitution, and virginity.[6] She uses the psychoanalytical insights of Wilhelm Reich to show the ways in which social institutions in Iran operate to oppress women sexually and socially. Azari presents interesting and fresh points and opens up a new space for exploration in relation to women's position in Iran. Her efforts, however, are hampered by her application of a mixture of the two general theories of Mernissi and Reich to the case of Iran. Having relied so heavily on these general theories, Azari's analysis necessarily shares their inadequacies in accounting for the specificity of practices and institutions.

Following Wilhelm Reich's attempts to wed psychoanalysis to Marxism, Azari takes Shi'i practices, such as rituals of mourning, as a space through which "release from the 'inner tension' is sought not just in individual terms, but also in a religious ritual organized on a mass basis."[7]

Such practices, then, are spaces for the expression of a fixed and presocial biological "inner tension." There is no difference between the nature of the institutions and practices across various societies: they all produce the same effect. Indeed, in such an analysis, one can replace "Germany" with "Iran," and "Nazism" with "Shi'ism" without affecting the outcome of the analysis.

The specificity of various institutions and practices in constructing sexuality and sexual differences is hampered in Azari's work by her adoption of Mernissi's essentialized conception of what constitutes the social in a Muslim society. Azari finds the "sexual norms and attitudes of Iranian society" rooted in Shi'ism:

> With Ali's teachings forming the most important sources of Shi'ite ideology (after the Koran, of course), it is easy to see why in Iran—a predominantly Shi'ite society—Ali's attitudes to women and sexuality were established socially. These attitudes are reflected in the social institutions that affect male-female relationships, such as matrimonial affairs and in the sexual affairs of most men here.[8]

Institutions and practices in contemporary Iran are seen as passive recipients of a point of origin of women's oppression, Ali's sayings. The present is seen as a mere reflection of the distant past, and history is denied any relevance to the present, since it is seen not as a process but as a reified point of origin.

In contemporary Iran, popular religious practices, such as the rituals of mourning, *rauzeh* ceremonies (religious recitals) and *sofreh* (religious feasts), Friday prayers, progovernment demonstrations, and chanting of slogans provide their own definitions of sexuality and express certain patterns of male-female relationships at the expense of others. Formal religion, too, depending on the context and its role and place within society, reproduces certain concepts and represses others. So do various other social and political institutions. These practices and institutions give rise to a variety of conceptions of male-female relationships that are heterogeneous and often contradictory. As long as they are seen as mere expressions of an essential "unconscious" or "Shi'ism," one cannot take into account the complexity and variety of discourses in one's analysis. One has to suppress many attributes of various societies in order to make them fit into a single general theory.

The problems involved in attributing a single universal concept of sexuality to Islam, or the West, indicate the need to look into the differentiations and varieties of concepts of sexuality within various cultures and the need for studying such concepts contextually.

II

Variations in Past Ideology and Practice
by Nikki R. Keddie

To an outsider, or even an insider acculturated to new ways, the whole of a foreign culture (or foreign-seeming domestic culture) often appears similar. The visual aspects of this are well known, as in the frequent observation that to white Westerners all Chinese or all blacks may look similar, whereas differences among one's own ethnic group are easily noticed. So too, sweeping generalizations about traditional Islam, Hinduism, or whatever are based not wholly on bad faith but also on the tendency to lump together a set of unfamiliar beliefs and practices that indeed have many elements in common, but whose inner differences often pass unnoticed. Having criticized views that tend to see both Islamic and Western approaches to women and sexuality as internally identical over long periods of time and great distances, we should note concretely some of the evidence of differences in Muslim, and more specifically Shi'i, views and practices regarding women that precede the theories of the 1970s on which the final section of this essay concentrates.

Even within the Quran there are some passages suggesting near equality for women and others speaking of women's subordination to men. Men are told that, unless they fear they cannot treat them equally, they may marry up to four wives; but later in the same sura men are told that no matter how hard they try, they will not be able to treat their wives equally—exactly the same Arabic verb for "equal treatment" is used both times. This sura, along with others, has been the source of quarrels between liberal modernists and conservatives, in this case over whether the Quran intended to encourage, permit, discourage, or disallow polygamy. Traditionally the propolygamy view was dominant, but not exclusive, whereas in the last century antipolygamy views have grown, not because of textual changes, but because of social ones.[9]

Questions of veiling and seclusion are others in which there has been a far wider variation in theory and practice even in the area of early Muslim conquest than most people realize. Contrary to widely held opinion, veiling is nowhere enjoined in the Quran, which has just two passages that discuss women's dress. One calls on Muslim women to draw their cloaks (*jalabiya*) tightly around them when they go abroad so that they may be recognized and not annoyed; the other tells believing women to cover their bosoms and hide their ornaments (*zina*).[10] The latter was later often interpreted, usually on the basis of supposed Traditions from the Prophet, to mean covering all but the hands, feet, and perhaps the face, though some interpreters said this, too, should be covered. This interpretation, which became widespread, is improbable; if the Quran had wanted this much covered, why would it have referred specifically to the bosom, which would automatically have been included in later formulas? Also, the widespread interpretation of zina to cover hair, neck, forearms, and so on is linguistically far-fetched.

Nonetheless, strict veiling and seclusion became the ideal, although they could in fact be practiced by only a small minority of Muslim women—those who did not have to work in the fields or elsewhere in public—and they were a sign of class status. More important, they were a sign of male control over a wife whose fidelity was guarded even more by household seclusion than by veiling. Veiling and seclusion also made it difficult for many women really to control their property or to be entrepreneurs.

Veiling originated not with Muslim Arabs, but in the pre-Islamic Near East, many centuries before Muhammad. We have an early Palmyran bas-relief of veiled women and know the practice existed among elite Sassanian and Byzantine women.[11] Veiling and seclusion in various forms and at various times was also practiced in European Mediterranean cultures,

Hindu India, and elsewhere. It has been more tenacious in many Islamic countries than elsewhere partly because of its presumed sanction by the Quran, believed to be the word of God, and partly as a reaction against the culture of Western imperialism. Largely because the Western impact began earlier in the Middle East than elsewhere, and because of Europe's proximity geographically and associations with the state of Israel, it has brought a stronger cultural counterreaction in Muslim countries than elsewhere in the Third World.

Veiling, however, was never a universal phenomenon in Islam, among either Sunnis or Shi'is. Nomadic and peasant women have evidently rarely veiled unless they were forced to, or they or their husbands wished to emulate the traditional bourgeoisie of the towns. We know that many dynasties of nomadic origin spread the custom of nonveiling among part of the elite and even beyond. This was true of Turko-Mongol rulers who ruled Iran for many centuries.[12] The miniatures of this period showing women in diaphanous head coverings similar to those worn by many modern nomads are surely depicting dress realistically, and we know that Italian travelers spoke of being shocked at the dress of Iranian women in early Safavid times![13]

As to the position of women, there are also significant differences in theory, and far more in practice, regarding their traditional rights to property and inheritance. The Quran lists legal heirs and says that daughters inherit half as much as sons, which Muslims rightly note was more than women inherited and held in most traditions. Without entering the controversy over the position of Arab women before Islam—which seems to have been better in some tribes and in some respects and worse in others than after Muhammad—one may agree with Coulson and others who have shown that, very soon after the appearance of the Quran, representatives of the patriarchal tribes quickly whittled away at women's Quranic rights, including property rights. Thus the Sunni schools of law added to the Quranic heirs a series of agnates, or relatives on the male side, who had rights to inherit, whereas relatives on the female side had no such rights. The Shi'is, however, developed a significantly different inheritance law, based in part on their desire to legitimize succession in the female line (Muhammad had no adult sons, and the Shi'i imams descended from his daughter Fatima) and in part on Shi'i belief that Muhammad and the Quran had intended to end the old tribal system of inheritance in favor of a more equitable one. The Shi'is, therefore, gave rights to female-line relatives to inherit and did not recognize the prior rights of distant male relatives, so, for example, in Sunni law, a single surviving daughter was limited to a maximum of half of the inheritance, no matter how distant the next eligible male-line relative was, but in Shi'i law the same daughter got the whole Quranic inheritance.[14]

Another Sunni-Shi'i difference was less favorable to women. This was *mut'a* (temporary marriage, or more literally, marriage for pleasure), a pre-Islamic custom, never renounced in the Quran, by which a man paid a sum of money for sexual rights to a girl or woman for a specified period of time. It differed from prostitution and it and its offspring were legitimate. Among the Sunnis it was forbidden by Caliph Umar, who was not recognized by the Shi'is, and the Shi'is have insisted on mut'a's legitimacy under Muhammad and since. Like many institutions mut'a developed a variety of uses according to context, from filling up the harems of the powerful to allowing two people who might have no sexual relations to mix freely in a common home. In the twentieth century, however, many Shi'is saw it as an abuse, especially as poor families might "sell" or "rent" their daughters at ages as young as nine.

In the Islamic Republic, however, it has again come into its own with some new justifying arguments. It is now said that since teenagers have sexual urges but are not ready for permanent marriage, mut'a is a way for them to fulfill these urges or, more often, to have a kind of trial marriage before taking the big step of permanent marriage. Some Shi'i writers note that since boys and girls cannot get to know each other in view of sexual segregation, it is recommended that they undertake temporary marriages, while at the same time vowing not to have sexual relations, as a means of getting acquainted.[15] Here we have a mixture of an age-old institution with a "modern" usage designed precisely to overcome some of the barriers imposed by the "traditionalist" Islam that these writers on temporary marriage support.

Variation according to time, place, and class in Muslim institutions has existed in veiling and seclusion, as has been shown primarily by certain anthropologists and sociologists. It also existed regarding women's holding and controlling of property, whatever the law might say. Very early there were legal attempts to get around the requirement of female inheritance, and, as noted by Schacht, this was one of the main motives behind the early creation of the family *waqf*, an endowment in favor of descendants that kept property from being divided and allowed the endower (it might be said, against the intent of the Quran) to name his own heirs instead of having to respect the Quranic heirs.[16] Claude Cahen argues persuasively on the basis of early sources that these family waqfs developed first among Arabs and preceded the pious waqfs that receive more attention. Further, he writes regarding waqf:

We are certain that from the best-known early times until today the institution was in fact used to undermine as far as possible the rulings of Muslim succession law in favor of daughters. . . . the great majority of planned endowments excluded, if not the daughters of the founder, at least their descendants, reserving the benefits for the descendants of sons. . . . There seems to be no doubt that the waqf was utilized right away to reinforce the patriarchal family, beyond, or contrary to, Quranic law.[17]

In this matter, despite their relatively profemale position on Quranic inheritance, the Shi'is have not been shown to have behaved differently from the Sunnis, although further research may indicate a difference. A minority of waqfs gave women larger inheritances than they would otherwise have had, and some women were waqf trustees, again indicating significant variations.

Other forms of absolute or relative deprivation of females of Quranically due inheritance have been noted, especially by anthropologists and especially among tribal and rural groups, and it is reasonable to suppose that further research in legal documents and elsewhere will underline that this is not solely a modern phenomenon. Naturally, some women did inherit as they were supposed to, and, especially in times of prosperity or of relatively greater freedom for women, some might even use their money and property entrepreneurially or for planning their own pious donations.[18] Also, even poorer women who might not inherit might find other means to exercise significant control or influence over the use of family income. Thus although there has been great similarity in mainstream legal views, there has always been much variation over time, place, and class in the actual property rights and control exercised by women.

When one turns away from the main legal schools to other Islamic groups and movements, one finds even greater variation in both theory and practice regarding the position of women. Movements labeled heterodox by the main legal schools, which were mostly proto-Shi'i or Shi'i rebellious movements, frequently preached and practiced a more egalitarian treatment of women. Scholars have shown that the charge of "communism of women" often lodged against such frequently rebellious movements was almost surely based on their opposition to the concentration of women in the harems of the rich and powerful, which left some ordinary men without wives and lowered the overall position of women. Some Shi'i movements held special reverence for Muhammad's daughter. Fatima, putting her at the same level as her descendants, the imams, or occasionally higher. Eyewitness reports tell us of the higher role of women among the Shi'i Fatimids and especially the radical Shi'i Qarmatians, both of whom came to be rulers.[19] They were associated with Isma'ili, or Sevener Shi'ism, which at least through the thirteenth century was the most radical of the three major branches of Shi'ism in both sexual and nonsexual matters.

Although Twelver Shi'ism does not have the same radical record on women (or, until modern times, on other questions), it does show some significant differences from mainstream Sunnism. For example, there have been "heresies" within Twelver Shi'ism, especially among Turks, Iranians, and Kurds, that have promoted a higher position for women. One of these is the Ahl-e Haqq, often called Ali Ilahis, concentrated among Iranian Kurds, who allow women a freer and higher position in ritual and daily life than do their orthodox Shi'i neighbors. More dramatic is the Babi movement that began in Iran in the 1840s, and most of whose adherents converted to the new Baha'i revelation in the 1860s. In both Babism and Baha'ism women were given a higher position and polygamy was limited or discouraged. The early Babi woman poet and preacher Qorrat al-'Ain apparently preached unveiled.[20]

Among both Sunnis and Shi'is, many mystic or Sufi teachers and writings also promoted greater equality for women, and some prominent teachers and poets were women. It must be added that, although these "heterodox" movements were convinced that *they* represented true Islam and the spirit of the Quran, the association of greater women's equality with what the legists considered heterodoxy probably hurt the cause of greater gender equality among the legists.

There is also a social class question to be noted. Whereas since the nineteenth century it has been, on the whole, the upper classes and those with better posts in the modern economy who have adopted Western ways, including greater equality for women, in earlier times the heterodox movements that often favored greater equality arose more from nonelite urban tradespeople, peasants, and nomads. (When nomads with more egalitarian gender relations, whether heterodox or not, took over a dynasty, some of them became part of the elite but might still retain many of their egalitarian customs regarding women, as in Iran.) In recent times it has often been the popular classes, rather than the elite, who have clung to gender inequalities. The reasons for this change need study, but one of them surely is that "modernizing" the position of women brought far more advantages for those benefiting from the modern economy and world system than it did for the popular classes, who might be hurt by it. Running a modern economy requires mothers well enough educated to facilitate their children's education and at least some women specifically educated for such jobs as nurses, teachers, secretaries, and so on. Also, mixing with international society is far easier if women are not secluded. Peasant, nomadic, and working women, however, were not generally perceived as deriving any tangible benefit from education, and greater equality for them might end the one sphere in which popular-class men could exercise dominance; elite men had other spheres for this. In earlier times, by contrast, extreme female seclusion and the arbitrary placing of significant numbers of women into large harems, along with the widespread use of slave girls in court for entertainment and sex, were all elitist privileges that at times aroused the anger of the popular classes, especially when they knew that the strict sexual rules that seclusion was supposed to protect were not in fact followed by most of the elite.

If mainstream Twelver Shi'ism, which has its own juristic orthodoxy based on its own school of law, did not enter heavily into revolts including a profemale element, it did have some features that might be considered favorable to women. The relative favoring of women in its inheritance law has been noted. In addition in Twelver Shi'ism, at least in its main centers, Iran and Iraq, and possibly elsewhere, orthodox women religious leaders have held a position closer to that of male religious leaders than in most Sunni countries. These leaders, among Shi'is called mullas like their male counterparts, preside over frequent women's religious ceremonies. In Iran, these are especially women's rauzehs, where stories of the imams, and especially the martyred Imam Husain, are recounted, and women's sufrehs, ceremonial meals involving vows at which women mullas read from the Quran and explicate it.

In addition, some Iranian women have, in the centuries Iran has been Shi'i, received enough higher religious education and certification of education to be capable of ijtihad, or independent judgment on legal and other questions. There is disagreement among authorities as to whether these women are properly to be called *mujtahids*, as many say that being male is a prerequisite to being a mujtahid and to giving rulings binding on a group of followers. In any case, such women have often given their opinions orally or in writing, and have had an important influence.[21]

Playing a different role were those Iranian women who, from the early nineteenth century on, wrote treatises advising women how to get around their husbands, carry on flirtations, and otherwise subvert strict "Islamic" rules. There seem to have been groups of women, probably mostly elite, who consciously followed such advice, while many in all classes no doubt did similar things without having to read about them. This was not a specifically Shi'i phenomenon. Also not exclusive to Shi'ism was the great influence in Iran as elsewhere of many royal family women on government policy, which scholars have begun to reevaluate as a more positive phenomenon than had been thought.[22]

Iranian women also entered heavily into many riots, revolts, and revolutions, whose aims were not specifically profeminist. In bread riots, frequent in the nineteenth century, women were often the leading element, partly because popular-class women shoppers experienced directly the price of bread, and partly, it seems, because men preferred to have *chador*-clad anonymous and theoretically inviolate women do the dangerous work. Women participated in the 1891–92 tobacco movement, and especially in the constitutional revolution of 1905–11, when there were a few women's societies and newspapers and more than one dramatic demonstration by women.[23] Women's rights became an important issue in the twentieth century, but was promoted mostly by the educated and modernized elite and even Muhammad Reza Shah's government, neither of which popular-class women could relate to.

The heavy and multiclass women's participation in the revolution of 1978–79 involved a minority of modernized women, whose agenda included some feminist demands, and a great majority of popular-class women. The latter, like their male relatives, were more likely to identify the wealthier classes, even if antishah, with being favorable to Western economic and cultural domination than they were to join their elite sisters in such things as abandoning chadors. The Iranian revolutionary ulama were successful both before and after the revolution in emphasizing discontent with Western ways. Such ways were associated with Western domination, with attacks on the bazaar economy, on the nomads, and on many peasants in the name of modernization, and with cultural changes such as Western dress and sexual mores. Even more than in most Muslim countries, an idealized Islam became an increasingly popular alternative for those who associated their ills and those of their country with the West and Westernization. In this process, at least in its current fundamentalist stage, women seem almost bound to lose out, as Pahlavi-period reforms in family law, seclusion, and so on are seen by fundamentalists as being against the Quran—even if what is really involved is the especially patriarchal interpretation of the Quran that evolved in later centuries. Among important Iranian groups only the *Mojahedin-e Khalq* attempted a reinterpretation of the spirit of Islam and the Quran in twentieth-century terms that included substantial equality for women as well as a form of socialism.

The popularity of the Mojahedin, despite brutal repression, is the most recent example we will give of the variability of Islamic theory and practice according to time, place, social class, and other factors. There is no doubt that the much-needed documented studies of the history of women, for which there are good sources in legal, waqf, and other documents, biographical dictionaries, art, poetry, folklore, and material culture, will reveal and explain far more variations and complexities in the history of Muslim women than have been suggested above. This history, in addition to the existence of current Islamically oriented organizations and thinkers who take a variety of positions on women, should show that if Islam, like most religions, has until now mostly reinforced patriarchy, other developments are possible within it, despite cultural difficulties.

As to the question of whether Shi'ism contains elements that might particularly encourage social protest among women, this too appears to be a matter of context. The tradition of the martyrdom of Husain and his followers, who included brave women, has been used in both Iranian twentieth-century revolutions to justify revolt against tyranny. And yet, as Mary Hegland has shown, in nonrevolutionary periods the role of Husain as intercessor for the individual believer is stressed, not his role as a rebel against unjust tyranny.[24] Shi'ism contains elements that in some periods are interpreted as denying the legitimacy of any temporal government, but this has not always been presented as a cause for revolt. On the contrary, some religious thinkers have stressed solidarity between ulama and government. As a matter of fact rather than theory, it may be noted that Shi'i Iran has had an extraordinary number of rebellions and revolutions since the mid-nineteenth century. To a degree, though not exclusively, this was because of the growing ideological and material split between the government and frequently dissenting ulama. The ideological part of this estrangement stressed the illegitimacy of temporal rulers, and some preachers even, during both twentieth-century revolutions, compared the shahs to the tyrant Yazid who ordered Husain's death. There were thus elements in Shi'ism that were developed in a rebellious direction, although in earlier centuries many of the same basic doctrines had been interpreted in favor of clerical-state cooperation. Some ulama continued to cooperate with the state, and political neutrality was preached by many nonroyalist clerics. It was only with Khomeini that the argument that Islam is intrinsically antimonarchical became popular.

There seems little in Shi'ism, as compared to Sunnism, that would lead women in particular to protest, and so Shi'ism is probably not a major cause of women's participation in revolts. But the very development of many crises and rebellions in Iran that involved great numbers of people in antigovernment actions did encourage women's political action. As long as this action was not directed toward feminist goals, it was on the whole encouraged by revolutionary ulama. The constitutional revolution of 1905–11 was accompanied by modernist measures, including the beginnings of feminist literature and women's organizations and newspapers, whereas the 1978–79 revolution has resulted in antifeminist measures. In neither case was an "essence of Shi'ism" important but rather a changed socioeconomic and cultural context.

III

Sexuality in Contemporary Shi'i Texts
by Nahid Yeganeh

The period between the late 1960s and early 1980s was a fertile time for the production of various Shi'i texts on the position of women. Basically, the 1970s were a period within which a degree of plurality of social thought existed alongside the shah's strong and dictatorial central government. Although the state set limits on the expression of thought, censorship focused mostly on party political opposition and to a lesser extent on social opposition. While a severe crackdown on Marxist-Leninist and other guerrilla movements was going on, Marxist academic thought was finding some expression through publications, university lectures, and public debates. In the realm of Islam, too, although the Fida'iyan-i Islam (a small Iranian analogue of the Muslim Brothers) had been suppressed and the antishah political movement led by Ayatollah Khomeini in 1963 was crushed, various Shi'i texts were taking up the issue of the position of women in Islam. The clergy's position in this period was that of a diverse social category, simultaneously in dialogue with and in opposition to the Pahlavi state.

The question of change was a social issue, and the question of women a subject for public debate. Various trends of thought expressed ideas on sexuality and different aspects of women's position. The official state ideology, and its associated women's organization, Shi'i texts of various kinds, Marxist pamphlets, fiction, and poetry all reflected conceptions of female sexuality in explicit or implicit terms. Looking at some of this literature, one finds that although the prescribed legal and social position of women in each text is often very different from the others, they all share many of the same ideas about female sexuality. Moreover, one often finds it difficult to differentiate, within this literature, which conception of sexuality is Shi'i and which secular.

The complex of social relations ensured that, whether in Shi'i or non-Shi'i texts, certain definitions of sexuality were reproduced widely while others could find only minimum expression.

One of the views that had little space for expression was the idea of sexual equality between men and women. Some Marxist writings, the poetry of the outstanding woman poet Furugh Farrukhzad, and the lifestyle of a small section of Iranian intellectuals and artists, who risked social stigma, implied sexual freedom for women. Another socially disfavored view, at the opposite end of the scale, was advocacy of polygamy and mut'a (temporary pleasure marriage). The most accepted view of sexuality favored legitimate monogamous marriage. This view was represented across a whole series of ideologies, including state ideology and its associated feminism, Shi'ism, nationalism, and Marxism. In many ways, there was nothing specifically Shi'i about Iranian social thought of the time. Indeed, various views, from those presented in Shi'i texts to the idea of sexual liberation of women, found their parallels in Western social thought and fed intellectually on it. Iranian social relations defined what views on sexuality were to be taken as Shi'i and what as secular.

The shah's secular conception of female sexuality expressed the following doubt about women's emancipation:

Just what constitutes the emancipation of a woman? To hear some so-called feminists talk, you would think it means freedom not to marry, freedom not to have children, freedom not to devote themselves to their children's welfare. . . . The women of Persia can enjoy all those freedoms if they want to—there is nothing in either law or binding custom which prevents it—but our enlightened women reject them all. They know that women possess certain unique endowments, and that with those go unique responsibilities.[25]

As we will see, the shah left it to the Shi'i theorists to formulate what women's "unique endowments" and their corresponding "unique responsibilities" were.

The Pahlavi regime, however, was associated with the idea of women's emancipation and legal reforms in the position of women. Such associations encouraged oppositional groups, both Shi'i and Marxist, to reject feminism as a bourgeois preoccupation.

Marxist-Leninist pamphlets (mainly distributed outside Iran) occasionally specified their conception of women's relationship to the institution of family. One pamphlet argued:

It has recently become fashionable amongst the educated and progressive women to complain about women's housework and childrearing duties. . . . Those who are concerned with their own individual liberation are no more than bourgeois and daydreaming intellectuals. . . . Anyone demanding women to give up domestic responsibilities, or perform them partially and share them with men should know that this will not lead to mobilisation of the masses. The masses know very well that under present conditions housework, and reproduction and rearing of children are a necessity to ensure the continuance of the struggle of the masses.[26]

In the realm of fiction, too, certain concepts of sexuality found widespread expression. During the 1970s it became popular in fiction and poetry to object to the conception of women's emancipation advocated by the official state ideology. Furugh Farrukhzad objected to the hypocrisy involved in the official conception of female emancipation, and some other writers complained about the disturbance of old ways and the uprooting of women's traditional role.

During this decade, quite a range of Shi'i texts were available on the question of women. To cover the range reasonably, we can look at texts by Ayatollah Khomeini, Ayatollah Motahhari, Ali Shariati, the organization of Mojahedin-e Khalq, and Zahra Rahnavard.

Ayatollah Khomeini's main text discussing women was a *Tauzih al-Masa'il* (book of religious instructions). Tauzih al-Masa'ils were the volumes within which various major Shi'i *marja'-i taqlid*s (sources of imitation) provided instructions on bodily, religious, and social functions for their followers. Sexual functions usually constituted an important section of these books, and other sections also referred to sex-related taboos and pollutions. In these texts, instructions on sexual intercourse had a degree of frankness and detail that went well beyond the soft-porn fiction that was becoming increasingly popular (though denounced by the clergy). In this, Tauzih al-Masa'ils enjoyed the kind of status accorded to medical books on these matters. Yet, in a sexually repressed social atmosphere, they also functioned as pornography. Ayatollah Khomeini's text was quite similar to other Tauzih al-Masa'ils.[27] In his text, the definition of male and female sexuality and the institutions built around them is one that favors a maximum rate of reproduction. Incest is defined narrowly,[28] marriage age is the lowest possible,[29] and polygamy and temporary marriages are allowed.[30] Sex and reproduction are separated to a considerable extent in male but not female sexuality. Male sexuality is active; female sexuality is passive. Women, as had been true since early Islamic times, have the religious duty to submit to their husband's sexual wishes. Sexual intercourse is equated with penetration. Marriages can be dissolved and inheritance annulled if penetration does not take place.[31] Pregnant women are treated with favor in Khomeini's text, and a whole series of regulations are built around breast-feeding.[32] All this creates the broadest conditions for legitimate reproduction. Khomeini's opposition to women's enfranchisement and to the new family protection laws introduced by the shah in the 1960s and 1970s expressed a fear of damage to the reproductive capacity of the "Muslim community."

Yet this does not necessarily dictate a corresponding political position for Khomeini under all circumstances. Khomeini's conceptions of sexuality, like anybody else's, mean different things in different contexts. The "Muslim community" he tried so hard to preserve and multiply in his Tauzih al-Masa'il was asked to offer its youth for martyrdom for the Islamic Republic.[33] In the same context, women's enfranchisement, which Khomeini had previously found "disturbing to the peace of mind of the religious leaders,"[34] after the revolution brought him peace of mind.

Ayatollah Motahhari was a reformist Shi'i clergyman and professor of theology at Tehran University. After February 1979, he became a member of the Revolutionary Council and was assassinated by a fundamentalist group in May of that year. His major text on women's position is a collection of his articles published in a women's magazine (*Zan-e Ruz*, Today's Woman) as a debate with Westernized Iranian women.

Ayatollah Motahhari's text concerns biological differences between men and women.[35] For him biology includes both physical and psychological attributes, and sexuality is strictly biological. Reproductive sexuality is the only "natural" form, nonproductive sexuality being against nature. The family, the only legitimate site for sexual intercourse, is therefore in the realm of "nature."[36] This view of the physical and psychological attributes of humans creates a fertile ground for Motahhari's production of stereotypes of "femininity" and "masculinity": man is rational, woman emotional; nature has invested in man the need to love and seek, and in woman the need to be loved and sought; man is strong, woman weak; man seeks beauty in woman, while woman wants strength in man; man is a slave to passion, woman a prisoner of love and affection; man is zealous, woman jealous.[37] Sexual intercourse is defined as a moment of total unity and possession. The only "natural" form of marriage for Motahhari is monogamy, with polygamy and temporary marriage reserved for times of crisis when men and women must sacrifice for the sake of society. Men and women are both monogamous by nature. Men's tendency to seek variety in sex has social reasons and can be changed.[38] Sexual instinct is active, strong, and deep in both men and women. The difference between them lies in woman's greater ability to bring her sex drive under control.[39]

Motahhari is aware of modern debates and tries to choose allies within them. He allocates a chapter to the question "Is the idea of biological differences between men and women a medieval one?"[40] His answer is negative, and the Western intellectuals he mentions regarding this position range from French biologists to English philosophers and Alfred Hitchcock.[41] Yet Motahhari wants to think independent of these trends in the West that, in his words, despite the outcries of Western natural scientists and philosophers, argue for sexual liberation. These include Freud, the women's movement, the Declaration of Human Rights, prostitution, pornography, alcohol, drugs, and so on. These are all seen as "inherently" Western, and if we see them in Iranian society, it is because of the power of the West to export them and Iranians' intellectual dependency, which leads Iranians to accept them. The effect of these Western trends for Motahhari is to dilute the boundaries of the family and social spheres. In Motahhari's writings, once sexuality is defined in biological terms and situated in the realm of nature, other human activities gain a nonsexual character. All sexual functions are to take place within the sphere of the family. The sphere of the social is for thinking and working, and sexual difference does not belong here.[42] This separation is to be achieved through Islamic devices such as modest dress and behavior in public.

Motahhari's concept of nature was a cultural construction that went well with the then-dominant image of woman as part-time mother and part-time worker. The social atmosphere of the time encouraged a partial release of women from home to take up social and political responsibilities.

Ali Shariati was a lay Shi'i reformer who opposed the shah in much more radical terms than did Motahhari and was imprisoned for it. Shariati studied at the University of Paris. In the 1970s his ideas gained enormous support among Iranian youth and formed the cornerstone of a new Shi'i opposition to the West and its manifestations within Iranian society. He died in 1977 in exile. Shariati produced a number of texts on the Shi'i model of revolutionary women, within which he rejected the Tauzih al-Masa'il approach toward women.

In one text Shariati praised Motahhari's model of the natural family:

Although Islam is strongly against "prejudices" against women, it does not support "equality" for them. Islam tries to find the "natural place" of men and women within society. . . . Nature has created man and woman as complementary beings in life and society. This is why unlike Western civilisation, Islam offers men and women their "natural rights" and not "similar rights." This is the most profound word to be said on the matter and its depth and value should be clear to those conscious readers who would dare to think and see without Europe's permission.[43]

But Shariati's alliance with Motahhari on women's "natural position" and "natural rights" ends here. Shariati must have had a different definition of nature to conceptualize his ideal woman as an asexual one. Shariati's text revolves around a criticism of a conception of woman as a sex object. In his attempt to deobjectify woman, Shariati desexualizes her. There is no place for sexual instinct in his discourse. Woman is an object of desire, but the desire should be for her love, not her body. The main fault with the capitalist system is that it has replaced love with sex. In the hands of capitalism, woman, who was the main source of inspiration throughout history, has become a sexual image aiding the transformation of the values of a traditional spiritual society into an absurd consumer society.[44]

For Shariati sex is not only opposed to love but also opposed to work, intellect, leisure, political struggle, and spiritual inspiration. Freud's "sexual liberation" is a Western conspiracy against all innovative activities by Muslims.[45] Shariati's ideal woman, Fatima, is simple and pure. She has a heart full of love for Islam. She challenges social and political injustice and respects just authority.[46] She reproduces and provides service to her family. But she has no sexual desire and is not sexually desired by any man, including her husband, Ali. Fatima's shyness and chasteness are counted by Shariati as among her virtues.[47]

Her father, the Prophet, however, is allowed to desire women and be desired by them. Shariati goes out of his way to describe the Prophet's love for one of his wives, A'isha, and her emotions toward him[48] and his romance with Zainab (the wife of the Prophet's adopted son).[49] The nature of the Prophet's desire, however, is portrayed to be beyond the comprehension of ordinary mortals. His love is not the sexual, biological, and impure desire portrayed by the Christian clergy and Western Orientalists.[50] His love and desire are divine. It is a silent, patient, humble, and painful love that inspires him to do good and brings him close to God. For Shariati, it cannot be otherwise. Love is a "reality" like anger, hatred, and fear. Therefore, Muhammad (as a prophet) is bound to feel love, and feel it in a pure and divine sense.[51] This is the ideal type of love toward which Muslims should aspire.

For Shariati, "pure desire" should replace "sexual passion" in the minds of the new generation of Muslims. This conception of sexuality in his view matches the new militant role of Shi'i women. A woman who is militant and responsible for her society is a source of inspiration for the Muslim man. She is an object of man's desire but does not have an independent desire of her own for men. Shariati, then, attempts to purify and cleanse Khomeini's and Motahhari's biological essentialist conception of sexuality, by replacing "sex instinct" with "love instinct." This is in accord with a popular interest in romance and pure love among the young generation of the early 1970s. Motahhari's regulation of sexuality released women's labor power by making the sphere of the social nonsexual, and Shariati's political ideology gave the nonsexual militant woman an important role to play on the political scene. Both of these were part of general trends within Iranian society. The role of woman as mother/worker/politician was propagated by the formal state ideology as well.

Shariati's conception of women is mainly a result of the problematic of his discourse. The discourses of Khomeini, Motahhari, and Shariati are not concerned with the same problem. The distinctive and traditional function of Tauzih al-Masa'il within Iranian religious culture determines its problematic. The relationship between marja'-i taqlid and followers within the context of the prevailing definition of authority made Tauzih al-Masa'ils religious guidebooks that gave instructions on sex and reproduction without a need for rationalizing them.

Motahhari was not a marja'-i taqlid and his book was not a Tauzih al-Masa'il. As a reformer who saw Islam as an ideology opposed to Western infiltration of Iranian society. Motahhari tried to construct a rationalized Shi'i system of the male-female relationship, centered on an ideal Shi'i family.

Shariati's discourse centered on concerns different from those of either Khomeini or Motahhari. He was neither in a position to issue religious instructions on sex and reproduction, nor was he interested in rationalizing and regulating these matters. His mission was to create an ideal model for Muslim women to follow, and his concern was primarily political. He tried to provide the ideological basis for creating a new generation of Iranian women who, by relying on their "Shi'i" tradition, would resist and fight "cultural imperialism." Shariati allowed nothing to stand in the way of the militant Shi'i woman: neither her role as mother nor her legal position. His ideal woman, Fatima, was a wife and mother and was subject to all the Quranic injunctions on the position of women. Shariati's Shi'i woman could not exist without Marxist theories of dependency, existentialism, the Algerian resistance to French rule, Arab Islamic reformism, Iran's subordination to the superpowers, and a concrete anti-imperialist movement in Iran.[52] A combination of such elements, with which Shariati was acquainted, formed the condition of existence for Shariati's concept of sexuality.

As is true of Khomeini, Motahhari, and Shariati, the discourse of Mojahedin-e Khalq on women can also not be reduced to a historical concept of sexuality. The context within which Mojahedin's series of articles appeared in their paper was that of revolutionary fervor and freedom of expression. The Iranian Revolution of 1979 had just succeeded, and various ideologies were struggling for a place within the future social and political order.

The Mojahedin-e Khalq organization was an anti-imperialist group that engaged in armed struggle against the shah's regime. By 1979, most of its members were killed by security forces, executed, or in prison. The imprisoned members of the Mojahedin were released during the revolution and led the organization into a popular Shi'i movement. The Mojahedin supported the leadership of Ayatollah Khomeini during the revolution but were alienated from power by the postrevolutionary Islamic state. Today the Mojahedin constitute the major Shi'i force in armed struggle with the regime of Ayatollah Khomeini.

The Mojahedin's text on women's position presented a challenge to a tendency among some members of the 1979 assembly of Islamic experts to give "priority to the element of sexuality before that of humanity"; for making "absolute the motherhood role of women to such extent that it confines them to the house and deprives them of any social and political activities"; and for regarding "women as delicate and in need of support."[53] For the Mojahedin, the attempt by this tendency to portray "the social reality of discrimination between men and women" as "a natural and necessary phenomenon, and even try, by means of various justifications to present it as scientific or even divine law"[54] had to be challenged. This was mainly because it encouraged many Muslim women to accept their second-class position as the natural order of things.[55] The Mojahedin's alternative was a *tauhidi* (nonantagonistic) society that was "against any class, racial, national and sexual discrimination" and could not, therefore, "accept the discrimination between women and men as a holy matter and approve it."[56]

The Mojahedin replaced the appeal to nature with an appeal to reality, which was their primary reference point in exploring the position of women. Iranian social reality for the Mojahedin was the discriminatory class and sexual structure of that society. This reality was rooted in history and could be changed only in the future. Any attempt to change the position of women here and now faced disapproval from the Mojahedin. The liberation of women, they argued, means a "total destruction of the historically determined relations within the society that oppresses women," and not "just minor changes and superficial reforms."[57] This view, placed in the context of anti-imperialist sentiments preceding the revolution, determined the Mojahedin's position on the question of women's rights. Addressing women's demonstrations in March 1979 against the intention of Ayatollah Khomeini to make the hijab compulsory for women, the Mojahedin invited women to abandon their protest "because the heavy burden of the imperialist culture cannot be eliminated all at once and other than through a long term and gradual process."[58]

However, the Mojahedin's realism and ideology of nonantagonism contained a conception of equality of rights for men and women in all spheres, including the family, excluding the hijab. They rejected the argument of "equal but not similar." The exact translation of their conception of equality into legal rights, however, would depend on the political context—as is true of any ideology. The Mojahedin's position on the male-female relationship was no different from the general Marxist-Leninist trend of the time. Neither included sexual liberation as part of women's liberation. Sex outside marriage was considered a "bourgeois perversion" for both sexes. Yet the social atmosphere ensured that female members received tougher treatment than male members if they committed the sin. Sex and reproduction were firmly placed within the family, and in this sphere, mutual and two-sided relationships, including sharing of domestic responsibilities, were encouraged.[59]

What separated the Mojahedin from purely Marxist-Leninist groups was the woman's hijab. This was the link they insisted on preserving with popular religion within Iranian society, which also ensured the ideological identity and uniformity of their followers. What constituted the Mojahedin's Shi'iness was the hijab; they kept the institution without believing in all that went with it in Motahhari's system. Hijab is defined in their educational text as "the boundary of dressing for men and women" set by "the culture of revolutionary Islam." But why has this culture asked women but not men to cover their hair? There is no justification apart from a reference to "tradition" and the personal choice of "Iranian militant Muslim women."[60]

One can find much that is "moral" in the Mojahedin's views on women, but little that is "Shi'i" as such. In that sense, the Mojahedin's religiosity is to be found in the expression rather than the content of their ideology. This can be said about the texts on women written by other Shi'is, nationalists, Marxists, feminists, royalists, and so on at the time. The immediate indigenous and international relations set the terms for various discourses and debates on the male-female relationship in Iranian society.

The revolutionary and postrevolutionary context provided a fertile ground for the birth of another Shi'i protest on women's position. Tens of thousands of Iranian women took part in the revolution of 1979, and many Iranian women turned to Shi'ism for their liberation. During the revolution, a heterogeneous body of Shi'i women's movements began to take shape, and soon after the revolution various Shi'i women's groups began to educate the masses of women about their Islamic rights and attempted to mobilize them. The Shi'i women's movement was not an oppositional movement. An ideologically significant section of it, however, soon came face to face with the practices and policies of the postrevolutionary Islamic state. The works of a few individual women assumed particular significance for the direction of this movement. One of the major ideologues of the Shi'i women's movement was Zahra Rahnavard.[61]

Zahra Rahnavard studied in the United States and was an active supporter of the Islamic revolution. After the revolution she became editor of the women's magazine *Ittila'at-i Banuvan* (Women's Information) and changed its name to *Rah-i Zainab* (Zainab's Way). In the summer of 1980, the magazine was shut down by the board of directors of the *Ittila'at* newspaper on the grounds of economizing. In November 1981, Rahnavard's husband, Mir-Husain Musavi, became the prime minister of Iran. Some members of the Islamic Parliament objected to his premiership because of Rahnavard's feminist ideas. This, no doubt, further contributed to her silence since the closing of her magazine.

Rahnavard's major text is an expression of a Shi'i feminist protest.[62] She begins the book by pointing to a change of mind on her part about the importance of the question of women:

> To be honest, earlier on when the question of women was raised, both in Iran and abroad, I used to think it was a passing and momentary matter. I used to believe that the materialists talk about it in order to make women weary of Islam, and the ruling system made it an issue in order to implement its conspiracies against women. But with further contemplation, I perceived the one-dimensional nature of my thought. I realised that the woman question is a historical one and it is a social and political necessity to find a solution for it.[63]

No doubt the availability of writings on Shi'i woman, her oppression and her rights, made an important contribution to the transformation of Rahnavard's (and many other women's) thought regarding the question of women.

Rahnavard adopts Shariati's protest against the Western infiltration of Iranian society. She complains about the imperialist conspiracy to rob Iran of its economic resources and cultural heritage by winning the hearts of women (through makeup and fashion), and turning men's attention away from poverty and oppression by preoccupying them with sex. Following Shariati's protest against the exploitation of Iranian women through superstitious Shi'ism and corrupt Western culture, Rahnavard condemns both women's imprisonment in the house and her liberation as a sex object.[64]

Having established the fact of women's oppression in Iran and having discussed the reasons behind it, Rahnavard turns to Motahhari to explain women's Islamic rights. Following Motahhari, she argues that in the Quran the question of *value* is treated as separate from the question of *right*. Therefore, the existence of division of labor in the economy, which is based on the physical and psychological differences between men and women, should not give rise to social superiority of one sex. She believes it is "natural, very beautiful, both fair and reasonable" for men to offer financial support to women.[65]

It would be wrong, however, to see Rahnavard's text as a mere repetition of Shariati and Motahhari. Rahnavard was involved in a concrete feminist politics within a concrete political situation. As an ideologue of a Shi'i women's movement, she relied on the ideological tenets provided by male theorists and presented her own special articulation of what women's Islamic rights consist of. Rahnavard defined the objective of a Shi'i women's movement as equality of opportunity for men and women to develop their talents and capacities. She argued for participation of women in every sphere and field. Yet she emphasized women's participation in politics as the most significant step in liberating them.[66] For Rahnavard, Western feminism has gone wrong in assuming men to be the main enemy, and communism has failed to liberate women because of its emphasis on the importance of women's participation in production. Both, she argues, have resulted in recklessness, chaos, and prostitution, and only the systems have benefited from it, women themselves being left helpless and unhappy.[67]

In her search to find a system that would make women "happy," Rahnavard discovers "the true Islam": "Muslim woman is a perfect woman, a multidimensional being."[68] The true Islam, she argues, allows woman to realize both her motherhood instinct and her need to participate in the liberation of her country. Communism violates the latter by leaving the care of the infant to the nursery, and capitalism violates the former by turning woman into a sex object. Islam, by advocating monogamous family with the man as the breadwinner, makes this possible. In the monogamous family, woman has the opportunity to free herself from productive activities in order to give birth and look after her infant. Her need for physical and psychological support is also fulfilled within the monogamous family. With the attainment of political consciousness, and with progress of technology to allow her to control and limit her housework duties, Muslim woman, Rahnavard argues, can be on her way to liberate her country and herself.[69]

Rahnavard's Shi'i feminism presented yet another conception of women's emancipation to be added to those of the prerevolutionary official women's movement and the poetry of Furugh Farrukhzad. All three conceptions were protests against Ayatollah Khomeini's taken-for-granted conception of women's place in Iranian society. Motahhari, Shariati, and the Mojahedin, too, rejected lawful and unlawful pleasure and polygamous sexuality, although in different degrees and for different reasons. Motahhari emphasized "fulfillment of sexual needs of the partners" in the setting of the "ideal family." Shariati prescribed pure love and romance between the partners. The Mojahedin added to the variety of Shi'i conceptions of women's position by protesting against the "dissimilarity of rights" among men and women.

CONCLUSION

It has been argued in this essay that the attribution of a universal concept of sexuality to Islam is untenable. The study of Shi'i history in Iran and the contemporary Shi'i movements demonstrate that sociopolitical context is important in determining the form and content of Shi'i social protest on sexuality.

We saw that, historically, Shi'i ideology on women's position has varied contextually and that Shi'i protest at one time and place became the status quo in another time and place. The history of Shi'ism in Iran does not suggest intrinsic elements in Shi'ism to activate social protest on women's position regardless of contextual factors.

In contemporary Iran, too, there is no substantial evidence of intrinsic Shi'i concepts of female sexuality. Social and political relations in this period were important in specifying what concepts of sexuality were counted as Shi'i and what constituted a Shi'i protest on sexuality. In this period, the available Shi'i concepts of sexuality were drawn into the context of immediate social and political issues, and there emerged new formulations of relevance to present conditions. The Shi'i texts of the 1970s presented a variety of views. Each of these texts had different functions and was written for different purposes. Although certain concepts of female sexuality were often reproduced, nevertheless, these discourses were far from repetitions of an essential Shi'i concept of sexuality. Immediate indigenous and international relations were major factors in setting the terms for various Shi'i discourses and debates on male-female relationships in Iran of the 1970s.

NOTES

The authors thank Sami Zubaida, Juan Cole, and Ali Zarbafi for reading and commenting on this essay.

1. As an example, see Hamid Algar, "The Oppositional Role of the Ulama in Twentieth Century Iran," in *Scholars, Saints and Sufis*, ed. Nikki R. Keddie (Berkeley and Los Angeles: University of California Press, 1972).

2. Sami Zubaida and Abbas Vali, "Religion and the Intelligentsia in the 1979 Iranian Revolution" (unpublished paper, 1979), 3; Nikki Keddie, "Religion, Society, and Revolution in Modern Iran," in *Continuity and Change in Modern Iran*, ed. Michael E. Bonine and Nikki Keddie (Albany: State University of New York Press, 1981), 20.

3. Fatima Mernissi, *Beyond the Veil: Male-Female Dynamics in a Modern Muslim Society* (Cambridge, MA: Schenkman, 1975); Farah Azari, ed., *Women of Iran: The Conflict with Fundamentalist Islam* (London: Ithaca Press, 1983).

4. Mernissi, *Beyond the Veil*, 6.

5. Mernissi's objections to Freud's theory of female sexuality are in many ways similar to these presented by the influential radical feminist movement in Western Europe and North America. I would like to draw the reader's attention to a different reading of Freud as presented in Juliet Mitchell, *Psychoanalysis and Feminism* (Harmondsworth, UK: Penguin, 1974), and Juliet Mitchell and Jacqueline Rose, *Feminine Sexuality* (London: Macmillan Press, 1982).

6. In Azari, *Women of Iran*, 90–156.

7. Ibid., 142.

8. Ibid., 104.

9. For a convenient translation of verses of the Quran relevant to women, see Elizabeth Warnock Fernea and Basima Qattan Bezirgan, eds., *Middle Eastern Muslim Women Speak* (Austin: University of Texas Press, 1977), 7–26. The verses I discuss I have read in the Arabic original. The traditional and modern literature giving varying interpretations of the meaning of many of these verses is vast.

10. Ibid.,, 20, 25; Quran, 24:31; 33:59. Frequently these and other verses are translated so as to imply the meaning preferred by the translator; hence some English-speakers, for example, may get the impression from translations as well as from interpretations that veiling is enjoined by the Quran.

11. Nikki Keddie and Lois Beck, introduction to *Women in the Muslim World* (Cambridge, MA: Harvard University Press, 1978), 25; and, especially on Sassanian veiling and seclusion, Guity Nashat, "Women in Pre-Revolutionary Iran: A Historical Overview," in *Women and Revolution in Iran*, ed. Guity Nashat (Boulder, CO: Westview Press, 1982), 5–35.

12. Ibid.

13. Nikki R. Keddie, *Roots of Revolution* (New Haven: Yale University Press, 1981), 14, and the original sources cited therein.

14. Noel J. Coulson, *Conflicts and Tensions in Islamic Jurisprudence* (Chicago: University of Chicago Press, 1969), 31–33.

15. Shahla Haeri is continuing the most complete study of mut'a. See especially her "The Institution of Mut'a Marriage in Iran: A Formal and Historical Perspective," in Nashat, *Women and Revolution in Iran*, 231–51.

16. Joseph Schacht, in relation to waqf, enumerates its roots, among which "a fourth, which expanded enormously, particularly in Iraq, in the first half of the third/ninth century, and which was, perhaps, most decisive in shaping the final doctrine of Islamic law concerning *waqf*, arose from the desire of the Muslim middle classes to exclude daughters and, even more so, the descendants of daughters from the benefits of the Qur'anic law of succession; in other words, to strengthen the old Arab patriarchal family system" (J. Schacht, "Law and Justice," in *Cambridge History of Islam*, ed. P. M. Holt, Ann K. S. Lambton, and Bernard Lewis [Cambridge: Cambridge University Press, 1970], 2:561).

17. C. Cahen, "Réflexions sur le Waqf ancien," *Studia Islamica* 14 (1961). 37–56; the quotation is on 54–55.

18. See Ian C. Dengler, "Turkish Women in the Ottoman Empire: The Classical Age," and Ülkü U. Bates, "Women as Patrons of Architecture in Turkey," in Beck and Keddie, *Women in the Muslim World*, 220–24 and 245–60.

19. The best brief discussion of this is in a manuscript in progress by Leila Ahmed on the history of Middle Eastern Muslim women [published in 1992 by Yale University Press as *Women and Gender in Islam: Historical Roots of a Modern Debate*].

20. Discussion of the Babis and Baha'is, including their position on women, is found in numerous works: see Mangol Bayat, *Mysticism and Dissent: Socioreligious Thought in Qajar Iran* (Syracuse: Syracuse University Press, 1982), chap. 4; and Keddie, *Roots of Revolution*, 49–52.

21. This discussion is based largely on my own interviews and observations, including women's religious ceremonies led by women mullas, in Iran. The first writer to draw attention to women mullas in Shi'i Iraq was Elizabeth Warnock Fernea, *Guests of the Sheik* (New York: Doubleday, 1965), and, with Robert A. Fernea, "Variations in Religious Observance among Islamic Women," in Keddie, *Scholars, Saints and Sufis*. Disagreement over mujtahid status comes from several oral and written sources.

22. See especially Nashat, "Women in Pre-Revolutionary Iran."

23. See especially Mangol Bayat-Philipp, "Women and Revolution in Iran, 1905–1911," in Beck and Keddie, *Women in the Muslim World*, 295–308.

24. Mary Hegland, "Two Images of Husain: Accommodation and Revolution in an Iranian Village," in *Religion and Politics in Iran*, ed. Nikki R. Keddie (New Haven: Yale University Press, 1983), 218–35.

25. Muhammad Reza Shah, *Mission for My Country* (London: Hutchinson, 1960), 235.

26. International Confederation of Iranian Students, *Roshana-i*, no. 3 (n.d.): 6.

27. Ruhullah al-Musavi al-Khomeini, *Risalih-i Tauzih al-Masa'il* (Qum, n.d.); Adele K. and Amir H. Ferdows, "Women in Shi'i Fiqh: Images through the Hadith," in Nashat, *Women and Revolution in Iran*, 56, say Khomeini's rulings on women are almost identical to those of the late Safavid theologian Muhammad Baqir Majlisi (whose own works draw on earlier Shi'i treatises).

28. Khomeini, *Risalih*, Instructions: 238–2411.

29. Ibid., 2410, 2379.

30. Ibid., 2412–32.

31. Ibid., 2775, 2381.

32. Ibid., 2464–97.

33. Ibid., 312–14.

34. Khomeini's telegram to the shah in October 1962; quoted in Haleh Afshar, "Khomeini's Teachings and Their Implications for Iranian Women," in *In the Shadow of Islam: Women's Movement in Iran*, ed. Azar Tabari and Nahid Yeganeh (London: Zed Press, 1982). See also 98–103 of this book for Khomeini's changing position toward women's status during and after the revolution of 1979 in Iran.

35. Murtaza Motahhari, *Nizam-i Huquq-i Zan dar Islam* (The System of Women's Rights in Islam) (Qum, 1979).

36. Ibid., chap. 6.

37. Ibid., 172–75.

38. Ibid., 332, 389, 391.

39. Murtaza Motahhari, *Mas'alih-i Hijab* (The Question of Modesty) (Tehran: Arjuman-i Islami-i Pizishkan, 1969), 69, 71, 96–106.

40. Motahhari, *Nizam*, 167.

41. Motahhari, *Hijab*, 51–57.

42. Motahhari, *Nizam*, 150–53.

43. Ali Shariati, *Zan dar Chishm va Dil-i Muhammad* (Women in the Eye and Heart of Muhammad) (n.p.: 1979), 5.

44. Ali Shariati, *Fatima Is Fatima*, trans. Laleh Bakhtiar (Tehran: Shariati Foundation, 1980), 100–105.

45. Ali Shariati, *Intizar-i Asr-i Hazir az Zan-i Musalman* (The Expectation of Present Era from Muslim Woman) (n.p., n. d.), 27.

46. Ibid., 20, 32.

47. Shariati, *Zan*, 6.

48. Ibid., 8.

49. Ibid., 13.

50. Ibid., 13–15.

51. Ibid., 16.

52. On Shariati and Khomeini, see Sami Zubaida, "The Ideological Conditions for Khomeini's Doctrine of Government," *Economy and Society* 11, no. 2 (May 1982): 138–72.

53. The Organization of Mojahedin-e Khalq of Iran, *Zan dar Masir-i Rahai* (Woman in the Path of Liberation) (Tehran, 1981). All my references to this text are to its English translation in Tabari and Yeganeh, *In the Shadow of Islam*, 115.

54. Ibid., 113.

55. Ibid.

56. Ibid.

57. Ibid., 114.

58. Ibid., 127.

59. Ibid., 113.

60. Ibid., 121.

61. For a more detailed discussion of the Shi'i women's movement and its role within the postrevolutionary society, see Tabari and Yeganeh, *In the Shadow of Islam*, 26–74. For exposition of the works of other ideologues of the Shi'i women's movement, see 171–200 in the same book.

62. Zahra Rahnavard, *Tulu'i Zan-i Musalman* (The Dawn of Muslim Woman) (Nashr-i Mahbubih: n.p., n.d.). The book became available in Iran after the revolution of 1979.

63. Ibid., 6.

64. Ibid., 10–12.

65. Ibid., 81. See also 77–82 and 100–103.

66. Ibid., 22–23, 103–18.

67. Ibid., 32–37.

68. Ibid., 91.

69. Ibid., 99.

BOOK THREE

Autobiographical Recollections

PART 1

Autobiographical Interview

NIKKI KEDDIE, born in Brooklyn in 1930, specializes in the history of modern Iran. She studied history and literature at Radcliffe College, Harvard University, and received her Master of Arts Degree at Stanford University and her doctorate at the University of California, Berkeley. She taught European history at the University of Arizona, Tucson, Western civilization at Scripps College in Claremont, and modern Middle Eastern history at the University of California, Los Angeles, where she is professor of history. She has received a Rockefeller Foundation Fellowship and a John Simon Guggenheim Fellowship; she has been president of the Middle East Studies Association and a guest scholar at the Woodrow Wilson Center for International Scholars. She currently lives in Santa Monica, California.

Interviewed at her home in Santa Monica on January 7, 1990, by Farzaneh Milani and on April 22, 1990, by Nancy Gallagher.

FM: *Can you tell us about your early years?*

NIKKI KEDDIE: My parents named me Anita [Ragozin], but I grew up being called Nikki. When I was three, my family—I have a brother two years older than I—moved to a small town in upstate New York where my father was the manager of a textile plant. We stayed there until I was six, when we moved back to Brooklyn where I went to public school and then a private school, City and Country School. I now learn that it is the oldest remaining private, progressive school. It had its seventy-fifth anniversary this year. It was a very good school; it had the idea of learning by doing. We did all sorts of projects: there was a theme each year such as the Middle Ages with manuscript production, or the Renaissance with printing. It was the best school I've ever attended, and a lot of people who went there ended up having fairly important positions. I guess the most important is a friend in the Chinese foreign service, now ambassador to Great Britain. When I was about ten we moved to Manhattan. Before that I used to commute on the subway from Brooklyn to this school. I went to a very good high school. Horace Mann-Lincoln, also quite a well-known progressive school. It belonged to Teachers' College of Columbia University, which closed it down a couple of years after I was there. I was interested in history even then.

My parents were very interested in intellectual things although they were not professionally intellectuals. My mother had wanted to be an engineer. When she was twenty, she came to the United States from Russia. She had had to stay home in Bessarabia (Moldava) during World War I, although her family had gone ahead, because they didn't have enough money to guarantee her immigration. She went to the University of Wisconsin and wanted to become an engineer, but they told her that women couldn't be engineers in the U.S. (although they could even in prerevolutionary Russia), so she majored in mathematics, although she did not do it professionally. From time to time she worked, mainly as a translator from Russian into English. She translated the first edition of Vasiliev's important history of the Byzantine Empire. My father read a lot. We always had books at home, and we saw a lot of theater when I was a child. My parents were very permissive. I remember mainly eating hot fudge sundaes, reading comic books, and listening to the radio a lot. My parents really didn't bother me about it which maybe is an indication that you really don't have to push your kids if you have a general environment that encourages education.

I didn't start reading fiction and poetry until I was a junior in high school, and then I got very interested in Russian literature. But already when I was eleven I said that I wanted to do a report about some other part of the world, not Europe, so I did one on the Mongols, which I remember as being taken from one book, because the school's sources were limited. But I did get interested in the idea of looking beyond the West. We made up and put on plays at City and Country—I don't for the life of me know how it was done, because there was no script. It was some sort of cooperative project. These plays were usually historical, and often quite distant in time or place. There was one on the fourteenth-century English peasants' revolt in which I was King Richard II—on the wrong side. My brother was in one on India in which he was Nehru. This was before Indian independence. My class did one on China in World War II, so whoever was guiding us was guiding us not only toward history and politics, but also to areas other than Europe.

In 1947, I went to Radcliffe. At that time all the classes were coeducational, except for sections of elementary classes, but Radcliffe still had a separate identity [from Harvard] and gave separate degrees. I majored in history and literature, which was a combined honors major. You picked either a period or a country and the major would cover anything cultural in that period, including art and philosophy. It was a very good major. I picked nineteenth-century European history and literature. Their nineteenth century went from 1789 to 1939—a very long century. At that time I was interested in Italian history and did my B.A. thesis on the Italian socialist party.

Even before Radcliffe, I was very involved in left-wing politics. I grew up in the far Left. I was influenced by my parents, who were leftists, especially my mother, so I wasn't rebelling. If grade school was ice cream sundaes and radio programs, then college was definitely political activity. It is interesting that people in the far Left were pioneering in subjects that did not become part of the national agenda until the 1960s. We worked for special efforts to admit more blacks to universities and to get them better jobs, and we fought for women's rights. Most people stress all the negative things about the far Left, its very naive acceptance of things that were going on elsewhere, but what we actually did wasn't, in the great majority of cases, to support the Soviet Union, but rather to work for peace and for issues like civil rights and women's rights. We helped set up the first NAACP chapter at Harvard and Radcliffe. I was involved in a temporarily unsuccessful but ultimately successful struggle to open the undergraduate library at Harvard, the Lamont Library, to women.

They had done an incredible thing. They built a new Harvard library, and although the old library, the big Widner Library, was then open to women, the new undergraduate library, where they put practically all the books that were of interest to undergraduates, was not open to women. This was particularly hard because at Radcliffe at that time we lived further away from campus than the Harvard people did, but most of our classes were on the Harvard campus and you had to walk over there. You might have an hour between classes, and exactly what you wanted to do was to go to the library and read books for your courses in that hour. There was only one little crummy place where you could go with your own books. It was a really discriminatory thing. And when we approached them, they said the exclusion of women was in Thomas Lamont's will. It actually wasn't in Thomas Lamont's will; he didn't say to bar women. All he said was that it was to be a library for the use of Harvard undergraduates. If they were going to bar Radcliffe people, they should have barred Harvard graduate students or faculty members and anyone who was not a Harvard undergraduate. And they said, "Women and men in the stacks together make noise or they do terrible things." They judged that partly on the basis of summer school when women were allowed. They said it had been noisier then, but that was because the Lamont Library was the only air-conditioned place on campus so people came there to cool off. We didn't succeed when I was there, but within a few years the policy changed.

I might add that while I was at Radcliffe a couple of Harvard friends who had decided to go on to graduate school changed from the European field to the Far East, and that may have given me some of the idea to study non-Western history. Already by the time I left, I thought I might want to switch to what we might now call (or what we would have called a few years ago) the Third World. I had the feeling that the Third World was less studied and hence a more interesting area.

Then I came to Stanford, where I got my M.A. in one year. I went there because my husband had a job at Stanford as an instructor of Western civilization. I had got married when I was nineteen. I was an undergraduate in history and literature, and he was a graduate student in history. We were in the same kinds of political activities. At Stanford I did an M.A. thesis titled "The Philosophy of History of Giambattista Vico." I really didn't like Stanford very much then. It is much better academically now. At that time the historians and the fellowship office treated me as second-class, as some kind of beginner who couldn't take graduate seminars yet, and they said they couldn't give me a fellowship or even tuition because my husband was teaching there (at $3,200 a year!). So I switched to Berkeley. It was the only other possibility because my husband was teaching Western civilization at Stanford, and I couldn't leave the area.

Berkeley is a good school, and I loved going there, even though they didn't have anyone who taught Middle Eastern history. The only places that had Middle East programs were Princeton and Michigan, and Princeton didn't admit women at that time.

FM: *So you commuted to Berkeley?*

KEDDIE: For two hours each way because I didn't want to drive. I took a car from home to the train, then a bus, and finally a trolley. My former husband had only a three-year contract at a time when jobs were very hard to get, and I think that it was a lot of strain on him, especially when he approached the end of his contract. He had favored my going to Berkeley and not Stanford, but it was a strain. The first year I commuted two hours each way three days a week. The second year I wanted to take seminars, which were in the late afternoon or evening, so I stayed in Berkeley three days a week, and I think that made it more strained. I think there were other causes that helped break up the marriage.

Then I moved up to Berkeley and became involved almost immediately with the person who became my second husband. That was a rebound thing. You often lose judgment when you are young. I know practically nobody who confirms the view of youth as being the greatest time in your life. I think the younger years are years in which you often feel yourself kind of pushed around by emotions and hormones and things you cannot control.

FM: *How long did you stay in Berkeley?*

KEDDIE: I stayed in Berkeley until 1957. I got my degree very young, when I was twenty-four, in 1955. I wouldn't take that date too utterly seriously because I had had only a year of Persian and two of Arabic at that point, and didn't really know Persian yet. I did a thesis that didn't involve Persian language material. If I had waited until I had learned Persian better, it would have taken me longer. However, they scarcely taught Persian at Berkeley then, so I had to wait until I could take it elsewhere.

FM: *So at Berkeley you decided to study Iran?*

KEDDIE: Yes. I didn't have any ties to Iran, which everybody seems to think is very peculiar. At the time, Iran was in the Mossadeq period, which was especially interesting. Iran also appealed to me as a country with a very long cultural tradition, like Italy. It had an ancient history with a lot of artistic and literary achievements and was politically interesting. So I chose it.

FM: *Were you working with someone at that time?*

KEDDIE: There wasn't anybody at Berkeley. That was also peculiar because most people seem to think they have to work with somebody who knows something about their field. I worked mostly with the late Joseph R. Levenson in Chinese history. He was a very brilliant and fascinating historian. He did critical intellectual history. He was a real genius. Most unfortunately, he died at the age of forty-eight.

I knew people mostly in Japanese and Chinese history, but I had the feeling that because there were so many good smart people in Japanese and Chinese history, it would have been harder to get a job in those fields, especially as a woman. Also, I wasn't convinced I could master Chinese: it is hard to remember characters and also to look up things in the dictionary when there is no alphabet.

FM: *How did you choose your dissertation topic?*

KEDDIE: I didn't have the possibility of doing a monograph, partly because even if I had known enough Persian at that time, there was extremely little Persian language material in this country. R. K. Ramazani remembers that I wrote him a letter asking to borrow his copy of Kasravi's classic history of the Iranian constitutional revolution, *Tarikh-i mashruteh-ye Iran* (History of the Constitution of Iran).[1] I couldn't go abroad, because, for political reasons, I couldn't get a passport. So I chose a very general topic, the impact of the West on modern Iranian social history. I am sure it would embarrass me if I reread it, but some people still comment on it. I kind of knew that it wouldn't work as a general book, although interestingly enough, in the back of my mind I had the idea that twenty-five years later I could use a lot of the material in a general book, and indeed I did. That is one reason I was able to get *Roots of Revolution* out so quickly.[2] That is a completely different book, but on the earlier period the dissertation research was helpful.

FM: *You had started learning Persian?*

KEDDIE: Yes, they had Professor Walter Fischel at Berkeley who mainly taught Arabic, but who knew some Persian. I had taken Arabic, two years, especially with William Brinner, who was a fine teacher, and I took more later. Actually I think by now I've had more Arabic than any other language, which doesn't mean I know it terribly well. In addition to what Persian I took at Berkeley, I also worked with a tutor. I took an intensive summer course at Harvard, and later I worked on it with a tutor when I went to Iran in 1960.

FM: *After you graduated from Berkeley, what happened?*

KEDDIE: I didn't have a teaching job right away. I had a one-year research job in Berkeley concerning India and Pakistan. My second husband had a job in Oakland, and we thought we might stay in Berkeley, so I got a secondary credential. Actually, I never got the credential because I never wrote away for it, but I could have. I did all the coursework, and did my practice teaching in high school, in world history and world literature. I was even a secretary in a real estate office for a month. We were also cook-managers one summer in a Yosemite high camp. I used to be a very good cook. Then my husband's situation changed. He had a job that involved physical labor, and he injured his back so he couldn't continue. At that point he was willing to leave Berkeley. For a few months we went to Tucson, Arizona, so he could help his father with a vitamin business. I thought I could spend most of my time doing research. When we arrived in Tucson, his father said he could pay him only two hundred dollars a month, which wasn't as bad as it sounds now, but you couldn't live on it so I had to get a job. As there was nothing appropriate, I took a half-time job as secretary to the dean of the Graduate Division of the University of Arizona.

My academic teaching career started when a professor in the history department there died from a heart attack, and they needed somebody to take over his courses immediately—in European history, twelve hours a week. He didn't have to teach twelve hours a week, but they gave me twelve. So I took over all these courses in history and political science. That was a great break for me because I was writing around for jobs, and I certainly improved my chances after I started teaching. I ended up with four job possibilities. This was a period before jobs were advertised, and you were not supposed to write around. Your professor was supposed to recommend you for jobs he had heard about. I wasn't on particularly good terms with the professor who chaired my dissertation committee, and he wasn't in my field anyway. So I wrote about seventy-five letters to places in general. As three out of the four jobs that came through were from people I knew, I am still not sure it was useful to write around broadside to people I did not know. I got an offer from Scripps College in Claremont to teach what was essentially the third year of Western civilization, though it had a Third World component. My then husband wanted to go back for his Ph.D. in economics, which he could get in Claremont, so we went there in the fall of 1957. Then there was another chance—I am sure lots of people have chancy histories, but women probably more—because in my fourth year at Scripps, Professor Gustave von Grunebaum came out and gave a talk there. I talked to him and later gave papers at a couple of conferences in the Los Angeles area—one at UCLA, which he attended. He was also an editor of *Comparative Studies for Society and History* and had read an article I had submitted to the journal and that was published there.[3] He was a remarkable man in many ways and, unlike most of his peers, didn't care what credentials you had. I would have had a very hard time getting a job at most major universities in the Middle East field, because I didn't have people in the field to recommend me, but he didn't care about things like that. He was very good at spotting people and didn't worry about the proper lineages. He also didn't discriminate on the basis of color, nationality, or gender.

I was at Scripps for four years, one of which I spent in Iran. The first two I was teaching in a Western civilization program, and then I did Asian history. We had two historians: the other did America and I did the rest of the world. I began publishing. I wrote one article based on my research job in Berkeley called "Labor Problems in Pakistan," published in 1957, and not very relevant to anything anymore. I have another article, which I don't think anybody reads, but it is really one of my best articles. It was published in 1959 in *Diogenes*, the international journal of UNESCO, and is a general analysis of Asian intellectual history. It discusses and compares major intellectual trends in different Asian countries, based especially on their different relationships to imperialism.[4]

Meanwhile, it had become possible to get passports because there was a Supreme Court ruling in 1958 which said that the government couldn't deny passports. So my husband and I decided to try to go to Iran. He was willing to do his economics thesis on Iran. So we applied for grants and went to Iran for 1959–60. During that year we found no other American scholars doing research in Iran, though there might have been some archaeologists. It is really amazing to remember when one thinks of the 1970s, when American scholars seemed to be everywhere in Iran.

My topic was the Constitutional Revolution of 1905–11. A number of people who have subsequently decided on this topic have come to the same conclusion as I did, that it is a topic which has a huge amount of material in Persian and English, and you really can't master it all unless you are willing to devote very many years to it. But at the time nobody knew that, so I ended up going to Iran with this topic in mind. Indeed I have a lot of research notes on it, concentrating on the prerevolutionary period, especially the Tobacco Movement of 1890–91, which started out as an article and then became a book. As of 1990 no Western scholar had covered the Constitutional Revolution. (More recently Vanessa Martin, Mangol Bayat, my former student, and Janet Afary have done more general works on this revolution.)[5]

It was very interesting to be in Iran, and quite adventurous at that time. We were part of a small group that somebody had dubbed "AWOPs" or

334 • Book Three: Recollections

"American without privileges." Practically every American in Iran had either duty-free entry of goods—groceries were sent in from Europe—and/or commissary privileges, which even Fulbright fellows got. We had very little money, and it was hard to live with American habits on the Persian market. In 1960 there were very few Iranian canned or processed foods, and meat was not always safe, even when cooked.

I wouldn't say it was harder being a young American woman in Iran than it was in America. It was hard to be taken seriously in both places. When I had my business cards made in Iran, I said I was an assistant professor, and they made it sound like I was an assistant to a professor, which was the European system. I should have just put *ustadh* (university teacher), but I didn't, and people kept asking me what professor I was assistant to. It took me months and months to get the late Sayyid Hasan Taqizadeh to see me, but when he did, I got a lot of good interviews. It was he who first told me that many intellectuals who pretended to be religious Muslims really were not, and gave details regarding men he had known during the Constitutional Revolution.

It was kind of rough, but in America it wasn't much better. Often only the really big people—not only von Grunebaum at UCLA and H.A.R. Gibb at Harvard but also Vladimir Minorsky, Maxime Rodinson, Claude Cahen, Albert Hourani, and Bernard Lewis with whom I began friendships between 1959 and 1963—took me seriously.[6] Those who didn't tended to be those just a couple of years older than I was, or older academics insecure about their own scholarship.

In Iran there were a number of people, such as Taqizadeh, who at first didn't take me seriously, but in the end I was able to get through to many of them. I certainly didn't have a bad time with anybody, except one old man who told me I was dressed wrong. It was very hard to adjust to the fact that there were very different mores among different Iranians. When we came to Tehran in September of 1959, there were all these women walking around with skirts above their knees, which wasn't what I expected. In fact, it was the first time I had ever seen it. I thought it was some kind of a local thing, but it turned out that a major Paris designer had just come out with skirts above the knee. He was the most famous designer, and people used to say, "He comes out with something in Paris and the next week it is in Iran," even though it wasn't yet accepted in Europe. You had women with beehive hairdos, wearing miniskirts and very high-heeled shoes with very pointed toes. Taqizadeh had given me a whole list of people to try to talk to, but somehow it hadn't registered that there was some kind of religious connection for the man who objected to my sleeveless dress, which was common summer attire in Tehran. It was quite interesting in retrospect: I went in a dress with a full skirt well below the knees, and he went on and on about how I should not dress like that, it excited men too much.

I started out not liking Iran much, but I ended up really liking it, partly because it was strange and hence interesting to me.

Then I had one more year at Claremont during which there was an academic crisis in my life. Luckily it turned out fine. I had just learned I was to be terminated at Scripps (partly because the other historian found me uppity), and the next morning the phone rang. It was von Grunebaum offering me a year's position at UCLA. This kind of juxtaposition doesn't happen very often, but you sometimes make up for your bad luck with good luck.

There had been a woman, Marie Boas Hall, before me in the UCLA history department, but there were some real antiwoman people in the department, some very openly and others not openly. There was a group called the History Guild, which I hadn't known anything about. It is made up of historians of all the different schools of southern California. Women were not allowed to become members until Marie Boas applied, and, after arguments, it changed its membership policy and admitted her. I was still at Claremont when I began receiving invitations to the Guild. I attended a meeting that was held at Claremont. A member of the UCLA history department, when I said I was coming to UCLA, commented, "You know what I think about women and academia . . ." I said, "No, I don't." And he said, "I don't think they belong there, but it's all right for them to come to parties." He added, "I quit this organization when they let in their first woman, and I'm just now coming back." I hadn't realized he had quit over the admission of his own colleague.

When there aren't a lot of women at a school, it is rather isolating. On the other hand, I knew quite a few historians, mainly because I go to international conferences. People noticed me more because I was a woman.

When I was at Scripps, I was divorced from my second husband. That marriage had been a mistake from the beginning.

NEG: *As you mentioned, research carried out on your first trip to Iran resulted in the book entitled* Religion and Rebellion in Iran: The Tobacco Protest of 1891–1892.[7] *Would you consider the book to be a narrative history?*

KEDDIE: I think the tobacco book is pretty much narrative history though I try to bring in social, economic, and religious trends. The first book on Jamal al-Din al-Afghani is mostly an intellectual analysis, rather than a narrative.[8] The second book on Afghani, the long biography, is mostly narrative, but I don't think of myself as a narrative historian.[9] My articles are not narratives, and in many ways I have always been most interested in the kinds of problems and analyses I stress in my articles.

I also wrote some early analytical articles: "Western Rule vs Western Values," "Religion and Irreligion in Early Iranian Nationalism," and "Symbol and Sincerity in Islam."[10] The books are also concerned with answering problems, but you often have to have more narrative in a history book. In the articles, I was dealing with new approaches to intellectual history problems and with the relations between Islam and politics. I was, strangely enough, one of the first to ask, "Why did the Iranian religious class, the ulama, uniquely in world history put themselves on the side that was opposed to the rulers, to the shahs (I am not talking about the current situation, but rather the pre-1914 era) and actively participate in an antigovernment revolution"? It was a unique phenomenon. In "The Roots of the Ulama's Power in Modern Iran," I suggested reasons for the unique position of the Iranian ulama.[11]

In trying to explain a figure like Jamal al-Din al-Afghani, a topic that I got into from these questions about the Iranian religious classes, I discovered that a whole series of people considered to be Islamic religious figures involved in these radical movements were not very religious at all. Afghani is not the only one. A couple of participants in the radical wing of the Babi movement probably were freethinkers identifying themselves with the religious opposition. Afghani himself is a very complicated figure. He was certainly not in a traditional religious mold at all. If anything, he was something like an Islamic deist. Aristotelian-based or Platonic-Aristotelian-based philosophy was important in Iran much later than in other parts of the Middle East. Afghani had grown up in this tradition and in the tradition of some of the radical religious movements of Iran. These movements would come out with a new synthesis that tied religion to more rationalist ideas as well as to a political activism of a new kind. I would say that Afghani and that kind of person whom we see again in a new guise today, such as Ali Shariati, come out of this tradition. At the same time I tried not to get away from economic and social forces working on these people, and on political events, although that was not my main focus. My approach to Afghani was earlier suggested in Albert Hourani's *Arabic Thought in the Liberal Age* and Elie Kedourie's and Homa Pakdaman's work, but mine was more extensive and had some new ideas.[12]

I try not to simply summarize what various intellectuals have said nor to analyze the influence of some past people on the person I was studying. I have tried rather to put the person in the political context in which he was living. At the time, this approach to intellectual history was reasonably new in Western and Chinese intellectual history. It is not so special now. If you want to reduce it to a single sentence, it is bringing these newer methods of social and intellectual history into Iranian history and breaking with older philological or simply straight narrative traditions.

But it is also important to know what questions are important, like the ones about the relations of the Iranian ulama to politics.

I worked on the Afghani book for a long time, from 1963 to 1971. It was published in 1972. After that I worked for a time on articles and edited books.[13] I think editing books is important, by the way. From early 1971 there were a few years when I was in a really deep depression and didn't do much of anything. I had the idea of doing a general book on modern Iran, but I thought I would wait until the shah fell or died. In this period I wrote an article called "Is There a Middle East?" in which I tried to say that the concept of the Middle East shouldn't be reified.[14] In some ways, it is part of the Muslim world, in some ways part of the Mediterranean world. I said that the term does make sense as a kind of a series of concentric circles. The areas closest to the Mediterranean that have more trade and agriculture tended to develop more than the semiarid and the very arid areas. The three areas have interdependent economies. The very arid areas form a kind of border, not only in Africa, but Arabia and Afghanistan, delimiting the Middle Eastern cultures, so in some sense there is a Middle East as a cultural unit. The presence of, and frequent conquest by, nomadic tribes from the more arid areas is also an important characteristic of the Middle East.

My next project was *Roots of Revolution*, which came out in 1981.[15] I called the book an "interpretive history," though today the word "interpretive" like the word "discourse" has been ruined by people who mean something postmodern and relativistic. I meant that I was trying to get at history in a way that brings in interpretations and not just narrative history. It is deliberately doing something that people tend to do anyhow, which may be part of the reason it has been successful: it emphasized those factors that looked important in the 1980s, such as religion and politics. I was conscious of doing that. It is possible that they won't look as important in the 1990s.

NEG: *Has the current interest in social history and the Annales school influenced you?*

KEDDIE: I suppose that the people who do social history have influenced me to try to look at what identifiable groups of people do, instead of looking entirely at individual intellectuals, or individual powerful people. To me social history is the kind of history that deals with such groups as workers, peasants, nomads, ulama, women, or ethnic groups, and I think I have done that in my writing to a considerable degree. I have studied the nomadic way of life and the interaction of nomads with other groups. I think it is one of the distinctive things about Middle Eastern history that many historians now don't like to write about because they don't like to make Middle Eastern history look somehow inferior to or different from Western history. So they don't talk much about nomads. I think, to the contrary, that the heavy presence of nomadic tribes since particularly the eleventh century with the Turkish invasions was of major historical importance. I think there was even before the eleventh century a decline in productivity in the soil with erosion, desiccation, and salination. This is one reason why settled agriculture declined and the area was open to conquerors and dynasties of nomadic origin.

I don't think that the big questions of why there wasn't economic development and why there was economic regression can be discussed without attention to the nomads and the underlying geographical and ecological phenomena such as the declining fertility of the soil. I have written an article suggesting that geography and technology are neglected fields of Middle East history.[16] I think that for the world in general, but particularly for the Middle East, historians tend to deal with the kinds of things they are familiar with in their own lives, like intellectuals and politics. People have gone into new areas recently, but these are partly based on interest groups such as ethnic groups or women. Technology really hasn't been stressed. Yet I think technology, ecology, and geography and their interaction with human beings are extremely important. They help explain why the Middle East was the earliest developing area. The Mesopotamian and Egyptian civilizations developed because of the great river valleys and the relative ease of irrigated agriculture. At a later stage when the northern Europeans mastered the heavy plow and knocked down the forests with iron tools, those areas became much more productive. I am greatly oversimplifying the argument, but you can read a thousand history books without learning about the influence of geography and technology. I think it is terribly important, even though it is not an area of primary research for me, and I want to encourage people to work on it.

I am interested in economic history, though not so much of a quantitative type. I go to a lot of international economic history conferences, so I have some idea of what economic historians are doing, and I guess it is the less quantitative, more social history–oriented kind of economic history that I appreciate more. I am not conscious of having been influenced by the Annales intellectuals. I have read some Braudel and Marc Bloch. I think the Annales work is very good. It gets into new areas of history, but in general I would say that Marxism has had a much greater influence on me than has the Annales school.

NEG: *Could you assess how Marxist thinking has influenced your writings?*

KEDDIE: Marxism, which of course is interpreted differently by different people, provides an analysis that combines both structural and historical features and emphasizes explanations for change—all matters of interest to historians. It is also, in principle, universal and not racist or sexist, even though Marx himself and many of his followers were often both. In principle, however, it stresses the importance of circumstances, and not innate superiorities and inferiorities, in determining the lives of people and peoples, and says that some nations advanced more quickly basically for economic reasons, and not because their people were superior. This approach long made it attractive to Third World intellectuals also. Marxists in fact tend to underrate the differences among societies and cultures, and this is one reason many intellectuals turned to more nuanced and culturally oriented views. Others were disillusioned by the political failures or even the crimes of self-styled Marxist regimes, especially after they took power. But the basic idea, based on fundamental interactions of groups of people with their environment and with developing and changing technologies and ideologies, remains important for understanding history.

Part of my own formation comes from the fact that I have learned a great deal from living in other countries. In addition to a total of three years in Iran and many months in other Muslim countries (mostly for my work on Afghani and for current work on Islam and politics), I have spent a great deal of time in Europe. I spend most summers there, primarily in London, which I find an excellent place to work. Also as a result of an invitation from Claude Cahen, professor of Islamic history, and Gilbert Lazard, professor of Persian, I was visiting professor for two years (1976–78) at the Sorbonne, at the University of Paris III, which has a Middle East program. Luckily I had an excellent French teacher in high school who was French and who insisted we speak only French in class—a radical idea at the time. I have also attended a number of international conferences. Hence I am in touch with the excellent group of French social scientists who work on Iran: Bernard Hourcade, Yann Richard, Jean-Pierre Digard, Paul Vieille, and others. I also know many scholars who concentrate on the Arab world in France, England, and Italy, as well as many persons from the Middle East and Pakistan. However, I identify more as a historian, influenced by anthropology and sociology, than as an area specialist. In fact, the majority of my friends are non–Middle East specialists, particularly historians and social scientists.

I have found it useful and interesting to spend time abroad. In Pakistan, for example, I met many brilliant, courageous, and strong women, including Asma Jahangir, a leader of the Women's Action Forum and of human rights groups, and Abida Husain, now Pakistan's ambassador to the United States. Many of the friends I made in Iran are now in the U.S., so I think of them now as American friends.

Among my activities have been photography, sometimes professionally, and videotaping interviews. I have taped interviews with activist women and with a number of interesting Muslim personalities worldwide. I have even given courses on photography, audiotaping, and videotaping for historians, because I think these are increasingly important, especially in fields like women's history, where written documentation is limited.

NEG: *How would you assess current trends in historical writing?*

KEDDIE: Economic history has been strong for a number of years and continues to be. I think it is important to grasp that economic history can shed light on social structures. In Europe the congresses of economic historians are always interesting. Their participants continue to break new ground, as in ecological history and world economic history. The main current trend, which I think is trendier in the United States than in Europe, is deconstructionist discourse. I'm mildly sympathetic to some of the elements of deconstruction. To take a thing apart, to see how it sits within society, and to identify the forces that lead people to state certain things intellectually is valuable. The trouble is that so many of the people going into it get carried away until that is all they talk about and they seem not to believe in reality any more. They believe in texts and in deconstructing texts. Even though a lot of the people who do it are on the left, I think it is essentially reactionary, noncommunicative, and elitist. It gets some intellectuals into a little elite group who communicate only with each other. It gets them away from thinking that the world and its problems are real. I think Michel Foucault's work is better because it is more rooted in reality. It suggests new ways to understand prisoners or mad people, for example. But much of his history is empirically wrong. What deconstructionists do often seems an intellectual game, though I imagine they don't see it that way.

NEG: *When did you become interested in women's history?*

KEDDIE: In 1969 or 1970 when I was compiling articles for *Scholars, Saints, and Sufis*,[17] it suddenly occurred to me that I had done the whole book without having an article on women. I immediately approached E. W. Fernea, who agreed, with Bob Fernea, to write an article for the book. This interest in women was part of the general atmosphere of the times. I had read Robert Briffault's *The Mothers*, about matriarchies, which almost nobody reads any more and is probably mostly inaccurate.[18] I had also read Simone de Beauvoir's book *The Second Sex*, when it first came out.[19] I had read Betty Friedan's book *The Feminine Mystique* when it first came out. I went out and bought a copy and thought it was great.[20] So I'd read some things on women, but I can't say that I brought them into my own work much until other people also became interested in working on women. Before that, like a number of other women, I would have felt that a woman writing about women would be considered second-class. One of the professors I knew at Berkeley assumed that I would be writing about women for my dissertation, and I was quite indignant. I don't think I was entirely wrong. I think writing about women was regarded as a second-class thing to be handled only by second-class people. In a conference I once brought up something about women and some man said, "Oh, I can see why *you* brought it up." Many people avoided the topic until there was a group that was willing to push against the barriers, to say, "Women are important." And there were not that many women historians around.

In the early 1970s I began to think women were something to pay attention to. When I saw how many interesting papers on women were being given at places like the Middle East Studies Association, I thought that the time had come to put together a volume on women in the Muslim world. Lois Beck also had this in mind. We were corresponding about something else, and it came up so we decided to edit the book together.[21] I got into the topic of Middle Eastern women early, but I have not done heavy primary research. As with a number of other subjects, I have had general ideas that have proved useful to other people. By the way, my true métier is as an editor. I do that better than anything else. I have recently coedited, with Beth Baron, a new book entitled *Women in Middle Eastern History.*[22]

NEG: Has the rise of the Islamist movements affected your work?

KEDDIE: In my early article "The Roots of the Ulama's Power in Modern Iran," I predicted that the power of the ulama is going to decline.[23] I wasn't alone in that. I have been writing about religion and politics since almost my first publication, so I had the background to analyze how social, political, and psychological factors have contributed to the new Islamic movements.

NEG: *Could you assess the Orientalist debate as of 1990?*

KEDDIE: I think that Edward Said's book *Orientalism* was an important work around which to center a debate and to make people think of the problems in Western approaches to the Middle East. I think that it is important to point out that Western scholars, coming in large numbers from colonialist countries, tended to have prejudiced attitudes toward Orientals, as well as toward a lot of other people. The book is very well written. I think that has had some unfortunate consequences. I think that there has been a tendency in the Middle East field to adopt the word "Orientalism" as a generalized swear-word essentially referring to people who take the "wrong" position on the Arab-Israeli dispute or to people who are judged too "conservative." It has nothing to do with whether they are good or not good in their disciplines. So "Orientalism" for many people is a word that substitutes for thought and enables people to dismiss certain scholars and their works. I think that is too bad. It may not have been what Edward Said meant at all, but the term has become a kind of slogan.

Then there is the interesting critique that some Arab leftists such as Sadik Jalal al-'Azm and others have brought forth, saying that Said has created a kind of monolithic Western Orientalism, an essentialist entity, from which there was almost no deviation.[24] Al-'Azm stresses what could be called the "essentialism" of Said. He points out that Said talks about Orientalism as if it were the same thing from the Greeks to the present, and that he makes an entity of Orientalism although he objects to people making an entity of the Orient. I think that is an important critique. While Said's book is important and in many ways positive and informative, it may also be used in a dangerous way because it can encourage people to say, "You Westerners, you can't do our history right, you can't study it right, you really shouldn't be studying it, we are the only ones who can study our own history properly."[25] This is a trend among Middle Eastern intellectuals. It is not founded exclusively on Said's book, but it does make use of it, even though Said himself does not take this position.

Said's book seems to have had more of an impact in other Asian fields than in the Middle East field. The problematic seems to be somehow more exciting to them, maybe in part because it doesn't get quite as directly involved in problems such as the Arab-Israeli dispute that polarize the Middle East field. Having said that, let me add that I think that the general ideas that people hold about Orientalism would have been fairly similar even if the book had not existed. I don't believe that someone writes a book and then everybody changes their views. I am glad the book was written, and it has contributed to very important international and interdisciplinary debates, but it should be read along with its critics.

NEG: *Could you assess the role of Gustave von Grunebaum?*

KEDDIE: I think one of the really unfortunate things in our field—and maybe it is this way in all fields—is that the giants of the recent past tend to be largely forgotten as soon as they are dead, if not before, especially if what they have written isn't what is now considered fashionable or central. There is also an optical illusion, in the sense that much of what these people have contributed is not recognized because it has entered so much into the field that people do not realize how novel a contribution it was. They are criticized when they are in error, but their achievements are forgotten. So Middle Eastern history has become a field without its own history. It is too bad. In my field, who talks about Minorsky, a true giant? Who in the younger generation talks about Gibb? These people are much more important than most of the people who have criticized them. It is the same for von Grunebaum. Few people talk about him, though he was such a remarkable person. I don't mean only his intellectual work, although *Medieval Islam* is a truly great book, a kind of integrated cultural history.[26] He was somebody who could administer a major center, building it up from nothing at UCLA, and at the same time carry on his scholarly work. Abdullah Laroui, a Moroccan historian, carried on a discourse critical of von Grunebaum, but he was very well aware that he was a great man and scholar. And von Grunebaum could appreciate and help scholars who criticized his work, and tried hard to get Laroui to stay at UCLA. Now there is no mention of von Grunebaum or the other scholars who have died in the past two or three decades, nor even of the true early giant Ignaz Goldziher, the Hungarian-Jewish Arabist and Islamist. I think that is really mistaken.

NEG: *Could you comment on Marshall Hodgson's work?*

KEDDIE: I read his book when it was in the form of a manual for Chicago students. But the thing that got me really interested in Hodgson was his brilliant article on conceptualizing world history. He thought that it was best perhaps to divide world history into four major civilizational areas: the East Asian, the South Asian, the Middle Eastern, and the Western or European. Then he said if you wanted to take two of these four that would go together most closely in terms of their influences and culture, it would be the Middle Eastern and European. And I think that is absolutely true. Middle Eastern and European civilizations were both influenced by Greek logic and by monotheism. We are used to thinking of these two civilizations as enemies, but their cultural backgrounds have more similarities than do South Asian or East Asian civilizations.

NEG: *Is the political activism of your early years reflected in your work?*

KEDDIE: Clearly I am concerned about greater egalitarian justice for all groups in society, and that probably shows in my work. Even when I write about intellectual history, I don't just talk about the self-development of the ideas of elite intellectuals. Somebody like Afghani is interesting because his ideas caught on with large groups of people, not so much in his own time but afterwards. Some elements in his thoughts are very important today.

I suppose my political point of view is now confused and skeptical. I think that is true for a lot of people. But I can be clear about what I want to fight against: war, prejudice, poverty, ignorance, disease, inequality, and unequal treatment.

NEG: *What is your current project?*

KEDDIE: I am currently working on a comparative historical study of Islamic militant movements, and for this I've traveled all the way from Senegal to Sumatra over a number of years. I have studied Islamic movements from the eighteenth century to the present. I am also putting together an article called "Why Has Iran Been Revolutionary?" And I am editing a new journal, called *Contention*. It addresses itself to debates in all fields of academic endeavor. It is written in comprehensible language, as people write for the *New York Review* or magazines like *Natural History* or *Science*, for people who are interested in knowing about the central issues in other disciplines or between disciplines. People are interested in scholarly debates. For example, in the *American Historical Review*, the section that my colleagues will read and talk about is the Forum, where people write letters back and forth debating issues. I am getting a lot of enthusiastic interest, and prominent scholars like Eric Hobsbawm, Ernest Gellner, Paul Ehrlich, and David Landes are writing for us.

NEG: *Could you comment on the current development of Iranian studies?*

KEDDIE: On the one hand it is a rapidly growing field, which is very encouraging; on the other hand, I see hardly any American students in it any more. This is not surprising, because they feel that they have to go to Iran in order to study the field and that is more difficult now. It is the fashion of our times to think one must travel to an area, though for historians this could be delayed until after the Ph.D., as it was for me. And look at many of the great nineteenth-century scholars who never went anywhere, yet they learned languages much better than we do. Someone has said in relation to southern California that Iranian studies has become a kind of ethnic studies program like a other ethnic studies programs. I think a mix of students is better. But there is a positive side to this Iranian majority because we have a large number of students who are doing very good work. They can combine what they know from their own culture with recent Western scholarship. Some of the Iranian scholars who were originally going into science or engineering have been traumatized by the revolution and have decided instead that they have to understand their own society. So they are Iran-oriented rather than Middle East-oriented. Ten years ago most Iranian students had difficulty with English, but now they have graduated from places like Beverly Hills High School and write better than 90 percent of the American students. I also have had a few Japanese students, a Dutch student, and a few American and Israeli students. The students today are outstanding in the sense that many of them turn out publishable and published work even before their Ph.D. comprehensive examinations.

NEG: *Do you have some advice for students who are only beginning to consider specializing in Middle Eastern history?*

KEDDIE: I think they should go in two, apparently contrary, directions: on the one hand they should stress their language training much more than most of them do, in both the Middle Eastern languages and the European languages, and on the other hand they should keep up with main currents in European history because it is more developed. Then they can concentrate on the history of the Middle East. There is a kind of dichotomy among the younger historians, between their general theoretical outlook and the limited nature of the work they do. We are not seeing many big synthetic works. Maybe it is harder to do now, but we don't see the von Grunebaums, the Hodgsons, people coming up with new ideas for a real synthesis. Of course you can't encourage everybody to do that because not everybody can. I would like to see students concentrate more on material, technological, geographical, and ecological questions. Hardly any primary work has been done on them. Certainly political, socioeconomic, and women's history are important, but many people are working in these areas. Almost no one is doing the kind of work pioneered by Richard Bulliet's *The Camel and the Wheel* and by Andrew M. Watson's *Agricultural Innovation in the Early Islamic World*, and we cannot really understand the rise and decline of Middle Eastern states without more such work.[27] Finally, in a period when the supply of Iranian history students is exceeding demand, they should get training in subjects such as Pakistan, Central Asia, Russian and the Turkic languages, comparative women's history, religious studies, and other fields. This may lengthen their training, but it will increase their chance for employment.

NOTES

1. Ahmad Kasravi, *Tarikh-e mashruteh-ye Iran* (History of the Constitution of Iran) (Tehran: Amir Kabir Publications, 1951).

2. Nikki R. Keddie, *Roots of Revolution: An Interpretive History of Modern Iran* (New Haven: Yale University Press, 1981).

3. Idem, "Religion and Irreligion in Early Iranian Nationalism," *Comparative Studies in Society and History* 6, no. 3 (1962): 265–95.

4. Idem, "Western Rule vs Western Values: Suggestions for a Comparative Study of Asian Intellectual History," *Diogenes* 26 (1959): 71–96.

5. Vanessa Martin, *Islam and Revolution: The Iranian Revolution of 1906* (Syracuse: Syracuse University Press, 1989); Mangol Bayat, *Iran's First Revolution: Shi'ism and the Constitutional Revolution of 1905–1909* (New York: Oxford University Press, 1991); Janet Afary, *The Iranian Constitutional Revolution, 1906–11: Grassroots Democracy, Social Democracy, and the Origins of Feminism* (New York: Columbia University Press, 1996).

6. Vladimir Minorsky, *Medieval Iran and Its Neighbours* (London: Variorum Reprints, 1982).

7. Nikki R. Keddie, *Religion and Rebellion in Iran: The Tobacco Protest of 1891–1892* (London: Frank Cass, 1966).

8. Idem, *An Islamic Response to Imperialism: Political and Religious Writings of Sayyid Jamal ad-Din "al-Afghani"* (Berkeley and Los Angeles: University of California Press, 1968).

9. Idem, *Sayyid Jamal ad-Din "al-Afghani": A Political Biography* (Berkeley and Los Angeles: University of California Press, 1972).

10. "Religion and Irreligion in Early Iranian Nationalism," and "Symbol and Sincerity in Islam," *Studia Islamica* 19 (1963): 27–63.

11. Idem, "The Roots of the Ulama's Power in Modern Iran," *Studia Islamica* 29 (1969): 31–53.

12. See Albert Hourani, *Arabic Thought in the Liberal Age, 1798–1939* (New York: Oxford University Press, 1962); Elie Kedourie, *Afghani and 'Abduh: An Essay on Religious Unbelief and Political Activism in Modern Islam* (New York: Humanities Press, 1966); Homa Pakdaman, *Djamal-el-Din Assad Abadi, dit Afghani* (Paris: G.-P. Maisonneuve et Larose, 1969).

13. The books I edited in the 1970s are *Scholars, Saints, and Sufis: Muslim Religious Institutions since 1500* (Berkeley and Los Angeles: University of California Press, 1972), and *Women in the Muslim World*, coedited with Lois Beck (Cambridge, MA: Harvard University Press, 1978).

14. Nikki R. Keddie, "Is There a Middle East?" *International Journal of Middle Eastern Studies* 4, no. 3 (1973): 255–71.

15. Idem, *Roots of Revolution*.

16. Idem, "Material Culture, Technology, and Geography: Toward a Holistic Comparative Study of the Middle East," in *Comparing Muslim Societies: Knowledge and the State in a World Civilization*, ed. Juan Cole (Ann Arbor: University of Michigan Press, 1992), 31–62, first published in *Comparative Studies in Society and History* 26 (October 1984): 709–35.

17. Idem, ed., *Scholars, Saints, and Sufis*.

18. Robert Briffault, *The Mothers: A Study of the Origins of Sentiments and Institutions* (New York: Macmillan Co., 1927).

19. Simone de Beauvoir, *The Second Sex* (New York: Knopf, 1953).

20. Betty Friedan, *The Feminine Mystique* (New York: Norton, 1963).

21. Lois Beck and Nikki Keddie, eds., *Women in the Muslim World* (New Haven: Yale University Press, 1978).

22. Nikki R. Keddie and Beth Baron, *Women in Middle Eastern History* (New Haven: Yale University Press, 1991).

23. "Roots of the Ulama's Power."

24. Sadik Jalal al-'Azm, "Orientalism and Orientalism in Reverse," *Khamsin* 8 (1981): 5–25.

25. Nikki Keddie, "The History of the Muslim Middle East," in *The Past before Us: Contemporary Historical Writing in the United States*, ed. for the American Historical Association by Michael Kammen (Ithaca: Cornell University Press, 1980), 131–56.

26. Gustave von Grunebaum, *Medieval Islam: A Study in Cultural Orientation* (Chicago: Chicago University Press, 1946).

27. Richard Bulliet, *The Camel and the Wheel* (Cambridge, MA: Harvard University Press, 1975); Andrew M. Watson, *Agricultural Innovation in the Early Islamic World: The Diffusion of Crops and Farming Techniques, 700–1100* (New York: Cambridge University Press, 1983).

PART 2

Supplement to the Interview

WRITING IN 2005, I can add something regarding a few events in the past fifteen years, and also include some experiences that I found too delicate or painful to talk about in 1990. First I will give a brief chronology of my academic life, which may help to situate the events discussed above and below. I attended Radcliffe College, taking classes at Harvard University, from 1947 through 1950, finishing in an accelerated three-year program, and getting my degree in 1951. I was at Stanford for the year 1950–51, when I got my M.A., and at Berkeley 1951–55, when I got my Ph.D. After a year's research job I taught at the University of Arizona in the spring of 1957 and at Scripps College, Claremont, California, 1957–61. I have been at UCLA since 1961, taking advantage of an early, phased, retirement program in 1993. I have had several fellowships, from the American Association of University Women, the Social Science Research Council, and the Guggenheim Foundation, some of which enabled me to go to Iran in 1959–60, 1973–74, and a few summers, and I went to Europe and to various Muslim countries in Asia and Africa over several summers. In the fall 1970 I was visiting associate professor at the University of Rochester, and 1976–78 I was visiting professor at the University of Paris III. In the early 1980s I spent several months in Washington, DC, on a Rockefeller Foundation fellowship, and on another I went to Bellagio, Italy, for a month in 1992. I have received several lifetime awards and honors for my research and mentoring, most recently the international Balzan Prize in 2004, which has enabled me to create fellowships for scholars of women and gender in the Muslim world. The fellows for 2005–6 are A. Holly Shissler and Nayereh Tohidi.

In 1993 the University of California proposed the third and most favorable round of an early retirement program, which saved them money from their general funds and was also favorable to eligible faculty. I along with most history colleagues in their sixties accepted this program, which allowed us to teach for several additional years and to keep supervising graduate students. I have had truly outstanding and interesting graduate students, the most recent of whom got his Ph.D. in 2005, while the last candidate has now returned to finishing her dissertation. Nearly all my Ph.D.'s have published significant books and have good jobs. This has been a source of great satisfaction.

I have continued research, writing, and participation in conferences (of which I have planned four over the years—all published after editing).[1] In the 1990s I also took a few drawing and painting classes, going back to something I did when very young. In this period I published several books and articles, and those published since 1995 are listed in the following bibliography. Two of my Ph.D.'s, Rudi Matthee and Beth Baron, published a book in my honor with chapters by my Ph.D.'s and friends, all of very high quality.[2]

I have also decided to include some words about areas that I touched only lightly in my 1990 interviews—political and sexual harassment and health problems. These certainly produced much stress and distress and made my scholarly and teaching life more difficult over the years, though they may also have added to my resolve to keep up my efforts and not give in to obstacles.

As I discussed in the interviews, I was for several years involved in left-wing politics. In my years at Radcliffe, 1947–50, this was as a member of the Communist Party, which I, like many others, then saw mainly as a promoter of a more just and egalitarian socialist society. When I left Cambridge for Stanford, party membership was supposed to be transferred by the mechanism of tearing a dollar bill in half, keeping one half and having the other half go through whatever hands were needed to get it to someone empowered to reestablish contact with me in California. For unknown reasons this transfer did not go through as planned; I did not try to rejoin the party, and over the years I developed major principled differences with it.

When I went to U.C. Berkeley, I applied too late to get a fellowship, but the next year, 1952–53, I had my undergraduate adviser, H. Stuart Hughes, with whom I had been on very good terms, write a letter for me for a fellowship, which I got, and I was told this was the best letter they had ever seen for an undergraduate. The next year I applied again and used Hughes again as a reference. In the meantime Hughes had been denied tenure at Harvard and had come to teach at Stanford; there was a job opening in his field in Berkeley, where at that time conservative professors were powerful in European history. I had very little contact with Hughes at Stanford, and my only political contact was my request that he sign a petition against the death penalty for the Rosenbergs—a request he denied. Hughes now wrote a letter with the same academic enthusiasm as before, but ending, according to what a friendly Berkeley faculty member told me, "My only objections are political. She was known at Radcliffe as a leader in Communist-based organizations. I have seen no evidence since coming to Stanford that she has changed her views." (No political comments were requested or were normally included on such letters.) At U.C. Berkeley in the early 1950s, soon after their big loyalty oath fight, and in a department with several conservatives, this letter caused me a lot of trouble with some members of the faculty, especially my dissertation adviser, whom I never used for recommendations. I later learned that some professors who had been supporting Hughes as a future colleague now stopped supporting him. I also saw it as a huge personal betrayal, seemingly done in the hope of possible personal advantage.

In the early 1950s, when I was living in Berkeley, two men from the FBI came to my door. The policy recommendation on the left was then not to talk with the FBI in these circumstances, as one risked inadvertently giving away harmful information about oneself or one's friends. I had not yet heard of the idea of saying, "I will be glad to talk with you as soon as we can make an appointment with my attorney present," which those who used it said never resulted in further questioning. I therefore said I did not want to talk, and one of them said they had wanted to talk to me about the internment camps formerly used for Japanese-Americans that were now being prepared for occupation (this was true), and which camp I wanted to go to! This was very upsetting at the time, when many of us seriously thought we might end up in jail or in camps based on our past or present activities.

I was constantly worried about possible political discrimination in getting and retaining academic jobs, and I did run into major problems, some of them coming well after the heyday of McCarthyism and the House Un-American Activities Committee. As was clear from points raised in my encounters with the government, part of the reason I continued to be targeted later than most other academics was that my mother had worked many years for the Soviet-American trade organization Amtorg.

In the spring of 1959, when I was teaching at Scripps, a man came to my door with a subpoena to appear before the Un-American Activities Committee on a future date, at what would have been one of its last big public sessions and was in fact later cancelled, so that I became probably the only person in this wave of subpoenas who actually had to deal with the committee. My ex-husband and I were planning to go to Europe, then Iran for a year. I phoned Jerry Pacht, an attorney whom I knew from my activities in the grassroots California Democratic Council; he said I should tell my college president right away, and recommended Fred Okrand, an ACLU lawyer. My Scripps college president was somewhat shaken, but said it would be all right if I could say I was not then a Communist and some other things, which though true I was not sure I could say without giving up my Fifth Amendment rights. In these years nearly everyone called before the committee had to take the Fifth Amendment barring self-incrimination, given that if one took the preferred First Amendment guaranteeing freedom of speech and assembly, one was likely to end up in jail, like my friend Chandler Davis. If one took the Fifth

Amendment, however, one was not free to answer those questions one chose, as this risked waiving one's Fifth Amendment rights.

My further problem was that I and my then husband were planning to be in Iran at the time the committee met. We were soon going to New York on our way abroad, and my father recommended hiring Leonard Boudin to represent me there. He arranged to have the committee counsel depose me in New York in place of the whole committee. Boudin said it would probably not be bad, and recommended that I could answer that I was not a Communist and not a spy without waiving Fifth Amendment rights, and meeting my college president's request. This turned out to be possibly worse than if I refused to answer anything, as the counsel immediately asked whether I had quit the party, and quit spying, after getting the subpoena, and Boudin said not to answer, so it looked as if the answer might be yes. Boudin said when we emerged, "That was rough," which I thought he should have expected and prepared for better. However, as the hearings were then cancelled, they did not make my testimony public, though I did not know for months that this would not be done. It was in the year after my return that I learned that Scripps was not going to extend my contract, and though there was a conflict with an older historian at Scripps involved, it was probably also connected with this political history.

Another behind-the-scenes crisis occurred beginning in the spring of 1963, in my second year at UCLA. I had been brought to UCLA as a visitor in the fall of 1961, and the appointment was supposed to be made into a tenure-track one the next year. This was delayed for reasons unknown to me, but probably because I had an enemy in the department who was leaving after the 1961–62 academic year. My political problems became intertwined with issues of salary and rank unfairness, which may have had a gender discrimination component. There was (and is) a step salary system at U.C., and I argued successfully that as I had been brought in very low, at step one assistant professor, I should at least go to step two for my second visiting year. When my appointment was made into a tenure-track one, however, it was, to my great surprise, put back to step one, though the History Department chair agreed to put through a change to step two when I complained. This had to be approved by the administration, but it should have been automatic, as I had had my Ph.D. for eight years, had published several articles and was working on a book, and had taught successfully at university level since 1957. Step two was itself lower than most people with a similar record had. I was less concerned with salary than with proximity to tenure.

Soon after I received notice of my Guggenheim Fellowship in spring 1963, I got a request from Chancellor Franklin Murphy's office that I make an appointment to see the chancellor, with no indication as to what it was about. I made the appointment, and Chancellor Murphy was there with Vice-Chancellor Foster Sherwood. Chancellor Murphy began with a short speech saying he was an educator, but the Regents, based on university policy, had asked him to ask me one question only, and if my answer was all right I would have no further trouble. He then asked me if I was a member of the Communist Party, and I said no. He asked Vice-Chancellor Sherwood whether he had anything else to ask, Sherwood said no, and Murphy reiterated that would be the end of it. I soon went on to Harvard and Europe on my Guggenheim Fellowship, not totally reassured. I did not know until several years later, when the case of Angela Davis's appointment at UCLA established the point, that it was illegal even to ask a faculty member or proposed appointee this question. At that time the practice of asking the question, and also the faculty Academic Senate rule against appointing Communists, were ended. In my case, however, the question was asked and answered.

Meanwhile, the supposed routine administrative agreement to correct my step salary from step one to step two did not go through, and Professor Gustave von Grunebaum, the prestigious director of UCLA's Near East Center, on a trip to Europe told me that Vice-chancellor Sherwood had not been satisfied, and I would be asked some more questions on my return. I was extremely upset during my months abroad. When I returned to UCLA in the fall of 1964, I learned that the FBI had come to the chancellor with several charges against me, and that despite the chancellor's promise, Vice-chancellor Sherwood had used this to deny my step increase and intended to keep doing so in the hope I would leave. The social science dean was delegated by Sherwood to quiz me about the charges, which he said were in the following categories, with my comment summarized.

1. My mother had been a Communist and had worked for a Soviet organization. (True, and the latter was open and legal.)
2. I had been a Communist at Harvard and initiated a transfer membership to California. (The transfer was not accomplished.)
3. My Italian then boyfriend was a Communist. (He had been very briefly some years before but had quit.)
4. I had dated Soviet embassy couriers while in Iran 1959–60. (A total invention; I was married, not dating anyone. Possibly originated with a "man in Havana" delegated to spy on me who found I was only doing research about the early twentieth century.)

The dean said he was satisfied with my answers and all would then go well; I noted that it was not even charged that I was a Communist or had been one recently. A routine step increase, now to step three, was again denied by the vice-chancellor, and I was told by my department chair that Sherwood was still was trying to get me to leave. I decided to look for a job offer with tenure (by then it was 1965, and I had a book in press and many articles published). I got two tenure offers, from the University of Washington and the University of Colorado. The UCLA History Department voted to advance me to tenured associate professor with only one dissenting vote. This time the all-UCLA faculty committee said it was too big a jump to go from a low step to tenure, and offered me the top step, step four assistant professor, without tenure. I was about, unwillingly, to go to the University of Washington, but also made an appointment with Chancellor Murphy to see whether anything could be done.

Chancellor Murphy insisted he had not known what the vice-chancellor was doing, but defended Sherwood's acts as having been motivated by the good intention to defend him, Murphy. He said that when I made the appointment with him, he had consulted with Prof. von Grunebaum, who had spoken strongly in my favor, and if I was all right with Prof. von Grunebaum I was all right with him. (I had tried unsuccessfully to get von Grunebaum to talk to Murphy about my case, and Murphy's interview with von Grunebaum was not about me but about an offer von Grunebaum had from Harvard; Murphy brought my name up because I had made the appointment to see him.) I pointed out that the charges against me did not say that I had been a Communist since undergraduate times, or that I had violated any university policy. He replied using the analogy of homosexuals who, he said, one would not want teaching at the university. When I asked why not, he said because they could wrongly influence impressionable young undergraduates. If one heard that someone had been frequenting a homosexual bar and otherwise behaving like a homosexual, one could with reason question that person. (I later heard from a knowledgeable faculty member that there was apparently at that time an unofficial and unwritten university policy, which went beyond the UCLA campus, that if there were complaints that a faculty member was homosexual, that person would be interviewed and, if judged to be homosexual, encouraged to leave on pain of disclosure.) Murphy then said that he, with Sherwood's concurrence, had agreed I would go to step four the next year and tenured associate professor the following year, automatically and without further review, and I accepted this.

When Murphy was satisfied regarding politics, he moved over to the couch next to me and began touching me, making various physical and verbal advances, and invited himself to my apartment for a drink. I rejected all this and found it deeply upsetting on top of all my job uncertainties. In the wake of Anita Hill's testimony against Clarence Thomas, sexual advances by a man, especially one with power, to a female employee have come to be widely known and sometimes addressed as sexual harassment, but neither the term nor any redress was generally available before that. The promotion did go through, and most of my subsequent academic problems have been due to one or two people's antipathy to me, which may not have been based on politics.

The other area that has, since age forty, caused me traumas and difficulties has been my health, which has social and political aspects, as most of my major health problems have apparently been the result of medical and dental treatments. I had mood problems, including a long depression, after treatment of an eye ailment with cortisone in 1970, although my depression fortunately ended with better treatment after a few years and has not since recurred. More recently I needed a major back operation in 1994, which reduced but did not end my back pain. Soon after that, a persistent burning mouth and other pains were diagnosed after tests by a complementary medicine M.D. as being due to very high levels of mercury, which in my case I find impossible to bring out of my system without suffering weeks of debilitating symptoms. The most plausible cause, as I had no other special exposure to mercury, was so-called silver dental fillings, which many people and dentists can handle without trouble, but others cannot. In the course of seeking relief for my symptoms, I noticed and also read that various unexplained painful syndromes and symptoms with probable environmental causes—which especially affect women, children, those exposed to modern wars and weaponry, and poor and nonwhite people and nations—have not attracted much medical research compared with that given to developing profitable drugs for groups that have money to pay for them. This is part of a general relative neglect of environmental causes of illness and insufficient attention to the negative effects of powerful drugs like cortisone. Only now are the bad effects of some recent drugs beginning to get significant attention, but few seem interested in the well-documented negative effects of older drugs like cortisone or of treatments like mercury-laden amalgam fillings. My ailments have cut down my travel, though I have been able to continue research and writing.

Since the largely successful struggles for women's rights that began in the sixties and became stronger afterwards, I have rarely felt discriminated against as a woman, although rank and salary studies at universities including my own show that discrimination continues in those areas. My own rank and salary, having started far too low, probably never caught up with what faculty members with similar records received. It is an ironic paradox of recent decades in America that while discrimination against women, Jews, African Americans, and homosexuals has decreased, largely owing to struggles by these groups, other areas of American life have gotten worse—notably the income gap, the availability of good jobs, and the brutalities committed in the name of the "War on Drugs" and now the "War on Terror." My activities on such questions are now mostly limited to public talks, signatures, and donations.

On the political front we are also seeing a revival of targeting unpopular groups, dubious trials and prison sentences, attacking liberals as unpatriotic or treasonous, and guilt by association, not to mention the holding of persons without charges, lawyers, or trials. This new McCarthyism is tied to what appears to be an endless "War on Terror" rather than the Cold War, but its effects on civil liberties are similar. Regarding women, some women's rights in the United States are now under attack, and it appears that in occupied Afghanistan and Iraq women's rights are losing out to U.S. expediency and to Islamist and tribal forces, for all our words about democracy.

For all its difficulties, my life has been one of major satisfactions, and I am often mindful that my current physical sufferings are far less intense than those of many people throughout the world. I have the satisfaction of my friends and relatives, and of my works' influence on many people in Iran and in the West regarding Iranian and Middle Eastern history and women's studies. Naturally not everyone agrees with my scholarly views, but out of criticism and dialogue comes a better understanding of humanity.

NOTES

1. The conferences published after editing changes are *The Iranian Revolution and the Islamic Republic*, ed. Nikki R. Keddie and Eric Hooglund (Syracuse: Syracuse University Press, 1986); *Neither East nor West: Iran, the Soviet Union, and the United States*, ed. Nikki R. Keddie and Mark J. Gasiorowski (New Haven: Yale University Press, 1990); *Iran and the Surrounding World: Interactions in Culture and Cultural Politics* (Seattle: University of Washington Press, 2002); and several papers on comparative fundamentalism published in *Contention*, nos. 11–12 (Winter and Spring 1995). Most of my edited and coedited books, including the two on women cited in notes 13 and 21 to Book Three, Part 1, were not based on conferences.

2. *Iran and Beyond: Essays in Middle Eastern History in Honor of Nikki R. Keddie* (Costa Mesa, CA: Mazda, 2000).

Bibliography of Works
by Nikki R. Keddie since 1995

For prior works, see bibliography in first item below, *Iran and the Muslim World*. Titles preceded by an asterisk appear in the current volume.

BOOKS AND SPECIAL ISSUE OF JOURNALS

Iran and the Muslim World: Resistance and Revolution. London: MacMillan, 1995.

Ed. *Debating Revolutions*. New York: New York University Press, 1995.

Ed. *Debating Gender, Debating Sexuality*. New York: New York University Press, 1996.

Qajar Iran and the Rise of Reza Khan: 1796–1925. Costa Mesa, CA: Mazda, 1999.

Coed. with Jasamin Rostam-Kolayi. "Women in Twentieth Century Religious Politics." Special issue of *Journal of Women's History* 10, no. 4. (Winter 1999).

Coed. with Rudi Matthee. *Iran and the Surrounding World: Interactions in Culture and Cultural Politics*. Seattle: University of Washington Press, 2002.

Modern Iran: Roots and Results of Revolution. New Haven: Yale University Press, 2003. New ed., 2006.

ARTICLES AND CHAPTERS (EXCLUDING ENCYCLOPEDIA ARTICLES AND BOOK REVIEWS)

"Secularism and the State: Towards Clarity and Global Comparison." *New Left Review* 226 (November/December 1997): 21–40.

"The New Religious Politics: Where, When, and Why Do 'Fundamentalisms' Appear?" *Comparative Studies in Society and History* 40, no. 4 (October 1998): 696–723.

"The New Religious Politics and Women Worldwide: A Comparative Study." *Journal of Women's History* 10, no. 4 (Winter 1999): 11–34.

"Women and Religious Politics in the Contemporary World." *ISIM Newsletter*, no. 3/99 (July 1999).

"Women in Iran since 1979." *Social Research* 67, no. 2 (Summer 2000) [special issue: "Iran: Since the Revolution"]: 405–38.

* "The Study of Muslim Women in the Middle East: Achievements and Problems." *Harvard Middle Eastern and Islamic Review* 6 (2000–2001): 26–52.

"Shi'ism and Change: Secularism and Myth." In *Shi'ite Heritage: Essays on Classical and Modern Traditions*, ed. L. Clarke, 389–406. Binghamton, NY: Global Publications, 2001.

Coed. with Azita Karimkhany. "Women in Iran: An Online Discussion." *Middle East Policy* 8, no. 4 (December 2001): 128–43.

* "Women in the Limelight: Some Recent Books on Middle Eastern Women's History since 1800." *International Journal of Middle East Studies* 34, no. 3 (August 2002): 555–73.

"Secularism and Its Discontents." *Daedalus* 132 (Summer 2003): 14–30.

"L'Iran evolverà ma da solo." *Aspenia: No. 22. America Black and White* (Aspen Institute,, Rome) (October 2003): 185–92. English version, "Iran: Change Will Come from Within." *Aspenia International. No. 21/22. Economy & Security* (Aspen Institute, Rome) (December 2003): 150–57.

"A Woman's Place: Democratization in the Middle East." *Current History* 103, no. 669 (January 2004): 25–30.

"Trajectories of Secularism in the West and the Middle East." *Global Dialogue* 6, nos. 1–2 (Winter–Spring 2004): 23–33.

"Women in the Middle East since the Rise of Islam." In *Women's History in Global Perspective*, ed. Bonnie G. Smith, 68–110. Urbana: University of Illinois Press, 2005.

"My Life and Ideas: A Brief Overview." In *Premi Balzan 2004: Laudationes, discorsi, saggi*, 109–25. Milan: Libri Scheiwiller, 2005.

"Secularization and Secularism." In *New Dictionary of the History of Ideas*, ed. Maryanne Cline Horowitz, 5:2194–97. New York: Charles Scribner's Sons, 2005.

"Revolutionary Iran: National Culture and Transnational Impact." In *The New Cambridge History of Islam*, ed. Robert W. Hefner. Vol. 6, *Muslims and Modernity: Society and Culture since 1800*. In press.

Opinion Pieces

"Divine Inspiration." *New York Times*. December 16, 2001, Op-ed.

"Why Reward Iran's Zealots?" *Los Angeles Times* February 17, 2002, Sunday Opinion, sec. M.

"War without End Brings Endless Dangers." History News Service syndication to several newspapers and online services. Published online by History News Network (February 2002), as "Endless Enemies," and by the Gulf/2000 Project: http://gulf2000.columbia.edu.

Index